Peter Farb has served as Consultant to the Smithsonian Institution in Washington D.C., as Curator of American Indian Cultures at the Riverside Museum in New York City and as Visiting Lecturer at Yale University, where he is a Fellow of Calhoun College. His books include *Face of North America*, *Man's Rise to Civilization as Shown by the Indians of North America* and *Word Play: What Happens When People Talk*.

Peter Farb

# HUMANKIND

TRIAD PALADIN

Published in 1978 by Triad/Panther Books
Frogmore, St Albans, Herts AL2 2NF

ISBN 0 586 04159 8

Triad Paperbacks Ltd is an imprint of
Chatto, Bodley Head & Jonathan Cape Ltd and
Granada Publishing Ltd

First published in Great Britain by
Jonathan Cape Ltd 1978
Copyright © Peter Farb 1977

Made and printed in Great Britain by
Richard Clay (The Chaucer Press) Ltd
Bungay, Suffolk
Set in Monotype Baskerville

*To my mother and father*

Wonders are many, and none is more wonderful than man; the power that crosses the white sea, driven by the stormy south-wind, making a path under surges that threaten to engulf him; and Earth, the eldest of the gods, the immortal, the unwearied, doth he wear, turning the soil with the offspring of horses, as the ploughs go to and fro from year to year.

And the light-hearted race of birds, and the tribes of savage beasts, and the sea-brood of the deep, he snares in the meshes of his woven toils, he leads captive, man excellent in wit. And he masters by his arts the beast whose lair is in the wilds, who roams the hills; he tames the horses of shaggy mane, he puts the yoke upon its neck, he tames the tireless mountain bull.

And speech, and wind-swift thought, and all the moods that mould a state, hath he taught himself; and how to flee the arrows of the frost, when 'tis hard lodging under the clear sky, and the arrows of the rushing rain; yea, he hath resource for all . . .

– SOPHOCLES, *Antigone*

# Contents

# Illustrations

## Drawings

## Diagrams and charts

## Maps

# I: The Ascent of Humankind

# I

# Ape or Angel?

Human beings have long regarded one another with awe, perplexity, pride, and fear, for they have not known what to make of themselves. 'What is man?' asked the Psalmist – and replied, 'a little lower than the angels', crowned 'with glory and honour'. Others, looking upon a human history filled with nauseating acts of violence and bestiality, have regarded our species as being at the opposite pole: only a little higher than the animals. The question behind these extreme views of humankind's essential nature was posed in the Victorian age by Benjamin Disraeli: 'Is man an ape or an angel?'* The picture we hold of ourselves has indeed often alternated between one or the other of these extremes.

What does make humankind different from all other living things? Human beings in all societies have always attempted to discover the source of their own uniqueness. Of course, every species of life on the

---

* This footnote is the only one in the book. Hereafter, all references, documentation, and amplifications of statements made in these pages will be found in the Notes and Sources section that begins on page 456. The reader will be alerted to them by the appearance of the symbol ♂♀. Pronunciations of unfamiliar words are not given in the body of the text but rather are to be found in the Index.

In this quotation from Disraeli, ♂♀ the word 'man' is used to refer to the entire human species, male and female. Such usage has been traditional because 'man' is a direct translation from the Latin of the scientific word *homo* used to describe our species today and those closely related species that existed in the past. The usage, though, is unjust to the more than half of the world population that is female. 'Human', on the other hand, is derived from the Latin *humanus*, which is the word for human being of either sex. I cannot avoid the use of 'man' to refer to our species when I am quoting directly, as I do in this line from Disraeli. In my own sentences, though, I have avoided it in favour of such words as 'humankind', 'human beings', and 'people'. I have also avoided the grammatical use of masculine pronouns (unless, of course, the male sex is specifically referred to), sex-linked nouns (such as 'poetess'), and sex-role stereotypes (such as the assumption that 'secretary' is of the female gender). To some readers, my concern may appear exaggerated – but it is valid. This book attempts to get at our essential humanity. It cannot do so if my perspective is distorted and sustained by a male-oriented vocabulary.

planet is unique, or else it would not be regarded as a separate species, and so a list of distinguishing traits could be drawn up for any of them. In this book, though, I am interested only in the distinguishing traits of the human species. Some of the earliest attempts to define human uniqueness were made on the basis of the possession of a soul. Because a soul's reactions could not be observed, the definition was later changed to mean a rational mind; and indeed in the age of rationalism our species was given the scientific name *Homo sapiens*, 'wise man'. This definition, though, has not withstood scientific scrutiny because animals much lower on the evolutionary tree than humans display behaviours that appear to be rational.

Other definitions of human uniqueness have subsequently been proposed. One, dating back to Benjamin Franklin, stated that humans were the only tool-using animals. But numerous kinds of animals employ tools, among them the California sea otter, which carries a stone under water with which to pound molluscs loose from rocks. So the definition was revised once again, this time to identify humans as the only tool-*making* animals. That one lasted for decades, until chimpanzees living under natural conditions were observed to make tools. Most recently, language has been fastened upon as the single, uniquely diagnostic trait for humankind. For the time at least, it appears to be a valid distinction, even though in recent years several chimpanzees have been trained in laboratories to communicate by the use of American Sign Language, by arranging plastic discs, and by pushing buttons on a computerized control board.

In any event, the search for such a single unique trait is futile. Scientists now know that the chasm separating humans from animals is not so wide as it once appeared. Some animal species have evolved a rich communication system, while others make and use tools, solve difficult problems, educate their young, live in complex social organizations, and apparently possess an aesthetic sense. On the other hand, no other species even approaches the human one in the scope and intensity of these behaviours. Humans obviously make and use tools in ways that far transcend the capacities of any other species. Humans give a prominence to learning throughout the life-span that is found in no other living thing, and with this learning humans have developed societies and cultures that are unthinkable for any other species. Human language is so much more complex, can express so many more things rapidly and efficiently, than the signs used by trained chimpanzees that the two systems simply cannot be equated.

So any definition of human uniqueness obviously would have to be based on differences in degree. Humans exhibit more of certain behaviours than other animals. In addition, although behaviours that appear similar to those of humans are exhibited by various animal species, no other species shows the full spectrum of human behaviours.

The preoccupation of humankind with its own essential nature is, so far as can be determined, a distinctively human trait. No other animal is known to fret about itself the way humans do. This concern is demonstrated by the prevalence in many societies of stories of 'wolf children' who were supposedly abandoned in the wild as infants and reared there by female wolves. The prototype for such legends is, of course, the story of Romulus and Remus, the twin founders of Rome, who were supposedly suckled by a wolf that found them on the banks of the Tiber. Such children have always excited interest because they seemingly provide a base line for determining the minimal requirements for being human. Deprived of the layers of civilization, such children appear to stand socially naked, revealing the true nature of our species. The existence of feral children poses an important question: Does an individual become a human being simply by being born into the species *Homo sapiens*, or is something more needed to achieve humanity?

In France during the bitter winter of 1799, the 'Wild Boy of Aveyron', a feral child about twelve years of age who had eluded capture for a year, emerged from a forest in search of warmth and food. He immediately became an object of speculation and wonderment. For some, he testified to the extraordinary physical resilience of Rousseau's 'noble savage', who had survived naked in a rigorous climate, enjoyed robust health, and was not subject to the numerous vices of society. For others, he represented an object lesson in how low the human being might fall without social constraints. Still others saw in him, to their horror, the personification of their own darker and untamed natures. To the romantics, he evoked a picture of a glorious past in which humans were one with all Nature. And finally, for the clergy, he was testimony to the beneficence of that Creator who looked after His children, even when they had been cast out by parents and society. The object of all these speculations turned out to be a disgustingly filthy child, who swayed back and forth like a monkey in a zoo, his body shaken by spasmodic movements, who bit and scratched and showed no affection for those who fed him. The philosophers eventually joined most of the doctors of medicine in concluding that the boy had been left in the woods because he was an idiot. Dr Jean-Marc-Gaspard Itard thought otherwise. For him, the boy acted like an idiot because he had been abandoned in the woods. Itard named the boy Victor and set out to humanize him.

Itard had no precedents for his attempt, so he had to depend upon trial and error, experimentation, and pioneering scientific procedures. Within a few years, he taught Victor to dress and behave in a reasonably acceptable manner. Victor also learned to understand French, although not to speak it. Hearing other humans speak during early childhood is apparently crucial for learning language. Itard finally concluded that Victor was by no means retarded, but that the effects of social isolation had been disastrous and were irreversible:

Cast upon this globe without physical strength or innate ideas, incapable by himself of following the fundamental laws of his nature which call him to the first rank of the animal kingdom, it is only in the heart of society that man can attain the pre-eminent position that nature has reserved for him. Without civilization he would be one of the feeblest and least intelligent of animals. ♂♀

Considerably more scientific knowledge exists today about feral children who have been kept isolated by deranged or cruel relatives. These children are rarely mental defectives. Their unusual behaviour does not result from isolation in itself but from lack of opportunity to learn from other humans. We inherit our basic shape and our proportions and the life-sustaining systems of our bodies, but something more is needed to become a fully functioning human being: contact with other members of our species. Children isolated from other children are not behaviourally human but only potentially so. Aside from such reflexes as grasping and sucking, children are born with very few specific inherited patterns of behaviour. They cannot survive without those patterns obtained simply by being a member of a particular human society. The infant and the child need other human beings to satisfy their physical needs – and also to give them love and attention, as was demonstrated by a cruel experiment reportedly ordered by Frederick II, the thirteenth-century ruler of Sicily. A gifted poet, artist, and naturalist, Frederick also

... wanted to find out what kind of speech and what manner of speech children would have when they grew up, if they spoke to no one beforehand. So he bade foster mothers and nurses to suckle the children, to bathe and wash them, but in no way to prattle with them or to speak to them, for he wanted to learn whether they would speak the Hebrew language, which was the oldest, or Greek, or Latin, or Arabic, or perhaps the language of their parents, of whom they had been born. But he laboured in vain, because the children all died. For they could not live without the petting and the joyful faces and loving words of their foster mothers. ♂♀

These lamentable findings have been confirmed in more recent times. In 1915 a doctor at the Johns Hopkins Hospital noted that an astounding 90 per cent of the infants admitted to orphanages and foundling homes in Baltimore, Maryland, died within a year – even though they received adequate care. And about three decades ago, a psychoanalytic researcher concluded that an absence of maternal care, stimulation and love lead to physical and emotional retardation and also to a high mortality rate. In fact, thirty-four of the ninety-one foundling-home infants that he studied in the eastern United States and Canada died 'in spite of good food and meticulous medical care'. ♂♀ Numerous other studies have also concluded that the skills and qualities of personality that are distinctively human emerge only as a result of association with other humans, particularly in the very early years of life. This involvement with human society, in turn, gives rise to a whole series of further needs, and these to still others, with the result that the fully developed human being is a complicated amalgam of drives, motivations, skills, and emotions.

*

Those qualities that make us human are only several million years old out of the many hundreds of millions of years of animal evolution. But underlying these are our basic physical structures, almost all of which have been inherited from ancient forms of life. Human beings are, for example, bilaterally symmetrical – that is, they have easily distinguishable right sides and left sides, backs and bellies, with most organs and appendages arranged in pairs. This development in the procession of life occurred first in sea-dwelling animals more than half a billion years ago. Our central nervous system lies along the dorsal (back) side of our bodies, a characteristic that evolved with the primitive fishes of more than 400 million years ago. The first animals to walk on two legs were certain reptiles dating back about 225 million years. Sweat glands, which have enabled humans to regulate their body temperature regardless of the temperature of the environment, arose in mammals possibly 200 million years ago. Even our stereoscopic vision, which enables us to perceive depth, dates back at least fifty million years.

To appreciate just how ancient our evolutionary heritage is, suppose that the procession of life, after the development of single-celled organisms, were compressed into a single year. Thus we would date the world of single-celled organisms already existing 750 million years ago as 1 January. Multicelled organisms would not, on such a time-scale, evolve until the end of April, and the first vertebrates (the earliest fishes) would appear by the end of May. Amphibians would crawl on to dry land in August and reptiles would make their appearance about the middle of September. Dinosaurs would dominate October and November. The first primitive mammals would appear in November, and the ancestors of monkeys and apes in December. Not until about midday on 31 December would the precursors of human beings evolve on the grasslands of Africa. With only about an hour remaining in the year, the earliest humans would begin to chip stone tools. A mere fifteen minutes before the year ended, they would develop a primitive agriculture. Only a minute or so of the year would be left as complex civilizations began to arise in the Near East, in China and Southeast Asia, in Mexico and Peru. On this compressed scale, in other words, humans have been in existence for the equivalent of no more than about twelve hours of an entire year – and most of the technological and intellectual accomplishments of which they boast are crammed into the final seconds.

Bearing in mind both the antiquity and the novelty of human beings, any definition of humankind must take into account half a dozen crucial characteristics:

Humankind is an animal species. Human beings send spaceships to the moon and planets, invent a diversity of complex social and political codes, establish institutions, worship deities, and speak learnedly on an infinitude of subjects. Nevertheless, none of these accomplishments prevents humans from being classified as animals – which is not to say that humans are nothing but animals. Indeed, they constitute a very special kind of animal (as does every other kind, from amoeba to elephant). The boxes on the following pages delineate the zoological categories into which human beings fit. Each box excludes more kinds of animals than the preceding one, until eventually modern humans alone remain, sharing their particular set of characteristics and evolutionary history with no other living thing on earth. Note that the human being is not simply a 'naked ape', as has sometimes been asserted. Humans belong to a different species, genus, and family from any of the apes.

Humankind is a generalized animal. Humans do not see as far as the eagle, detect odours as well as the dog, run as fast as the antelope, swim as well as the dolphin, or possess the strength of the lion. Such physical abilities, though, represent specializations for very narrow ways of life. Humans cannot equal the peculiar abilities of these specialists – but humans are well equipped to see, smell, run, and swim, and they have a high degree of physical strength. In short, humans excel in very few particular attributes but nevertheless succeed in doing many things because they are generalized in their capacities. Humankind has avoided committing its survival irrevocably to a particular way of life, as have the elephant, the giraffe, and other highly specialized mammals. This is not to say that humans lack any specializations. They do, of course, possess a very large and complex brain, upright posture, and the ability to walk on two legs. But, paradoxically, our paramount adaptation has been our lack of specialized behaviour. We have been specialists in non-commitment. In other words, humankind can originate novel adaptations to changing conditions and then capitalize upon them.

Humankind has departed little from the ancestral pattern of physical structure but greatly from the ancestral pattern of behaviour. Structural differences between humans and apes are mostly of degree rather than of kind. Fossil evidence reveals that the basic pattern of the human hand scarcely differs from that of many species of monkeys that lived twenty-five million years ago, except for such minor structural refinements as the merging of a few of the wrist bones and a shift in the muscles of the thumb. Although humans are unmistakably primates in their structure, they have departed notably from the other primates in their behaviour. The key to the different evolutionary directions taken by structure and by behaviour lies in the nature of the human brain. This brain is able not only to receive sensory impulses, but also to analyse, store as memory, and then synthesize them – after which those impulses are converted into a wide repertory of behaviours. This repertory has been possible only because the human body remained generalized. Such behaviour would be out of the question for, let us say, a dog, even if a human brain could somehow be transplanted into a dog's body. The transplanted brain would issue complex instructions, but the specializations of the dog's sense of smell, four-footed gait, and teeth would prevent the animal from executing them.

Species for species, humankind is the most numerous and the most widespread mammal on earth. Humans are exceeded in size by certain kinds of whales, sharks, hippopotamuses, giraffes, elephants, crocodiles, snakes, and numerous other animals. Yet more than 99 per cent of all animal species are smaller than humans. Among the approximately 200 primate species now living, only the gorilla is larger. The total weight of all humans on the planet, estimated at upwards of 400 billion pounds, far exceeds the total weight of all members of any other mammalian species. And no other species – except for dogs, rodents, body lice, and the internal parasites that depend on humans for their sustenance – inhabits so many environments. Human beings range from below sea level to mountain villages 16,000 feet above it; they inhabit both the tropical rain forests and the frozen Arctic; they have even developed ways to take their environment with them deep under the sea and into outer space.

Humankind has developed culture. Although social scientists disagree about the exact definition of culture (one descriptive inventory totalled 164 items♂♀), they do agree about its general character. Culture is human-made; it includes ideas, values, and codes known to all members of the group; it is a learned system of behaviour based upon symbols; it is transmitted from generation to generation. A culture does not exist until it is shared with other human beings. It influences the way in which a person behaves towards others in the group and also the way that person expects others to behave. Culture represents a new stage in evolution: the ability to acquire, store, and exchange information and then to pass it on to the next generation so that it will not have to be relearned from scratch. An individual human thereby accumulates vastly more information than could ever be acquired by experience alone.

Humankind uses symbols. The development of culture is intimately related to the human ability to employ symbols, primarily those of spoken and written language but also those used in painting, music, attire, body ornamentation, and gestures. The fascinating thing about a symbol is that it uses one facet of a person's experience to evoke emotions, actions, beliefs, and awareness with respect to other facets of experience. Symboling thus assigns meanings to things and events that extend beyond the mere sensory awareness of them.

Symboling reaches its highest expression in human language. Nothing in the arbitrary sounds of the word *home* denotes the rich symbolism it can evoke for speakers of English: family, children's voices, ancestors, holiday feasts, privacy ('an Englishman's home is his castle'), a place of return ('home is the sailor, home from the sea'), and simplicity ('be it ever so humble, there's no place like home'). The ability to symbol, particularly through language, has led to certain behaviours that exist in all human societies but are never found in other animal species – among them, food taboos, funeral rites, inheritance rules, the assignment of kinship terms, mythology, property rights, propitiation of supernatural beings, and restrictions on sexual conduct.

*

Humankind today rides the crest of the evolutionary wave. So far as is known, it is the only species with the capacity to project present hopes, fears, and imaginings into future actions. Above all, humans are assuredly the only animals who try to discover just what sort of animal they are. Aristotle began his *Metaphysics* with the statement: 'All men by nature desire to know.' The human species is the only one that has been a perpetual source of wonder and speculation – to itself. Such a self-centred view of the world is known technically as 'anthropocentrism' (from the Greek *anthropos*, 'human'). Throughout much of recorded history, humankind has assumed that the living world was created for its own exclusive benefit. The modern ecological crisis has dramatized the dangers of anthropocentrism, yet it is a valid stance to take in this book simply because anthropocentrism is a hallmark of our species. To look upon the world anthropocentrically means to recognize that human beings value themselves more highly than they do other forms of life. It is as proper for humans to think this way as it would be for any other kind of animal, given the ability, to do so. Were an individual belonging to the Coleoptera (those insects commonly known as beetles and weevils) able to produce a portrait of its own species, its point of view undoubtedly would be Coleopteracentric. In a beetle's presentation, *Homo sapiens* would be scarcely noticeable as a single species among the million or so on the planet – and assuredly insignificant when compared to the astronomical populations represented by some 250,000 different species of beetles. The perspective of this book, therefore, will be – without apologies – anthropocentric. ♂♀

The entire animal world can be arranged in an hierarchy of increasing specificity – until eventually each species occupies its own category with its own set of distinctive characteristics. This process might be visualized as a series of boxes within boxes, as shown in the drawing on the next page. The outermost box represents the animal kingdom (distinct from the plant kingdom and the protist kingdom composed of bacteria and other micro-organisms not clearly plant or animal). Inside this box is another representing the phylum Chordata, which has certain defining characteristics, such as an internal backbone, a nerve cord ending in a brain, and gill slits at some stage in the lifecycle. These characteristics are found also in the next innermost category, the class Mammalia – but mammals have their own distinctive characteristics which include hair, milk-secreting glands, and the maintenance of a constant body temperature regardless of the temperature of the environment. This description would apply equally to all mammals (including the primitive mammals known as marsupials, such as kangaroos and opossums, which nourish the embryo in an external pouch). A smaller box is therefore placed inside that of the Mammalia, for those mammals that belong to the infraclass Eutheria and are principally distinguished by a placenta, which nourishes the developing embryo inside the mother's body.

Placental mammals include a wide diversity of forms – cats, dogs, bats, whales, elephants, and rodents, among others, as well as humans. So the next enclosed box represents the array of characteristics adapted to an arboreal environment that distinguish the order Primates: a large brain, stereoscopic vision, and manual dexterity. The next category distinguishes those primates known as Anthropoidea (monkeys, apes, and humans) from others known as Prosimii (tree shrews, lemurs, tarsiers, lorises). The category of superfamily Hominoidea includes only those anthropoids (apes and humanlike forms) that lack tails and that also have developed two modes of locomotion: brachiation (swinging by the arms) and bipedalism (walking on the two hind legs). The Hominoidea have also lost the rhinarium, a strip of moist skin that connects the upper lip with the nose and is an organ of smell, such as can be seen in the wet snout of most mammals. In humans the two vertical ridges between the nose and upper lip are all that remain of the rhinarium.

The family Hominidae is narrower still. It includes only those humanlike primates that developed erect posture and bipedal locomotion. The genus Homo consists of both early and modern forms of the Hominidae that possess large brains, make tools, and communicate by abstract symbols. The smallest and final box at the very centre represents the lone species Homo sapiens, which includes Neanderthals, Cro-Magnons, and all contemporary humans.

In summary, as animals we have been chordates for some 400 million years, placental mammals for about 125 million, primates for 70 million, anthropoids for at least 40 million, and hominids for perhaps 5 million. Only within the past several million years did our ancestors become terrestrial foragers – and only within the past 100,000 years or so did recognizably modern forms arise. Not until about 12,000 years ago did a few groups of modern humans build permanent settlements, increase in population, practise agriculture, and develop the wondrous diversity of human life known today.

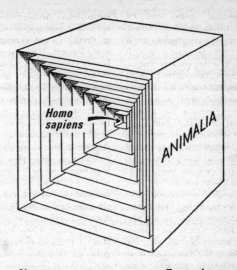

| Category | Name | Examples |
| --- | --- | --- |
| Kingdom | Animalia | All living things that are not plants or protists. Generally, animals possess the power of directed movement but lack the capacity to manufacture their food by photosynthesis. |
| Phylum | Chordata | Fishes, amphibians, reptiles, birds, mammals |
| Class | Mammalia | All groups of mammals : kangaroos, rodents, cats, dogs, elephants, monkeys, apes, humans, and so on |
| Infraclass | Eutheria | Placental mammals |
| Order | Primates | Tarsiers, lemurs, monkeys, apes, humans |
| Suborder | Anthropoidea | Monkeys, apes, humans |
| Superfamily | Hominoidea | Orangutans, gibbons, gorillas, chimpanzees, humans |
| Family | Hominidae | Extinct forms with humanlike characteristics plus modern humans |
| Genus | *Homo* | Extinct forms of early hominids, Neanderthals, modern humans |
| Species | *Homo sapiens* | Neanderthals, modern humans |

The ability to act to our advantage in the future demands an understanding of our species today: the way we evolved to reach our present state, the roots of our behaviour, the potentials and the limitations of our capacities. Humankind is apparently the first species on the planet that has so propagated itself in huge numbers and so fouled its nest that it threatens its own survival. Humans have used their unprecedented dominion over the world's environments to transmute flora and fauna into ever more human beings. This alchemy has produced a population that already exceeds four billion people and is expected to double in another thirty-five years.

This book represents an attempt to solve some of the mystifying unknowns in the human equation, to examine the axioms and postulates about our biology and behaviour, and from these variables to deduce at least some understanding of our past for our future. With this aim in mind, the book has been divided into five major sections, concluding with an epilogue that assesses the variables in the human equation today. To show the core of our biological inheritance, those developments that still influence us today must be traced. Accordingly, the first section deals with those capacities, both ancient and more recent, that have been passed along in the course of human evolution. The next section summarizes the major adaptations we have made: hunting–gathering, food production, peasantry, urbanization, and modernization. The third section analyses the remarkable diversity, both biological and behavioural, of human beings today. The fourth section examines our unusual abilities to perceive and to understand the world we inhabit. The final section places the individuals who compose humankind in the intricate social networks they have created.

An effort has been made to chart a course between attempting to tell everything about humankind and telling too little – the same problem faced by the scholars who, reports Anatole France in his *Opinions of Jerome Coignard*, were ordered by the Persian prince Zémire to write the history of our species so that his rule would be enlightened by past experience. Twenty years later the scholars appeared before Zémire, now king, with a caravan of twelve camels, each of which carried five hundred volumes. The king demanded a shorter version and, after they returned with three camel loads, the king ordered them to condense still more. Ten years later, the scholars brought a single load and, again rejected by the king, finally came with one giant volume carried by a donkey. The king was on his deathbed and he lamented, 'I shall die without knowing the history of humankind.' The one surviving scholar replied: 'Sire, I will summarize it for you in three sentences. They were born. They suffered. They died.'

Before anything else, though, it is essential to be aware of one crucial aspect of humankind: our primate heritage.

# The Importance of Being a Primate

Beginning late in the fifteenth century, European explorers encountered the great apes: first the chimpanzee of West Africa, later the orangutan of Sumatra and Borneo, and finally the gorilla of Central Africa. After that, the Europeans' view of the human species could never again be the same. The apes were disturbingly human-like in size and facial expressions, occasionally ran on their two hind legs, and in their intelligent behaviour seemed uncannily like ourselves. Europeans were particularly enthusiastic about the human-like qualities of the orangutan (whose name is derived from Malaysian words meaning 'wild man'). The president of the Berlin Academy of Sciences even declared in 1768 that 'voyagers assure us they have seen wild men [that is, orangutans], hairy men with tails: a species intermediate between the monkey and us. I would rather one hour of conversation with them than with the finest mind in Europe.'♂♀ At that very time, the finest minds in Europe were dissecting and studying ape specimens to determine the extent of their humanity. Some even suggested that much might be learned by mating an orangutan with a prostitute.

The status of the ape specimens brought back to Europe was debated endlessly. Were they simply unusual kinds of beasts, or possibly a 'missing link' between humans and the lower animals, or even some primitive form of human being? In 1699 a noted English physician, Edward Tyson, published the inconclusive results of his painstaking anatomical study of a chimpanzee. He listed forty-eight characteristics that allied the chimpanzee with humans, but added another thirty-four that connected it more closely to the lower animals. The skeleton of Tyson's specimen survives to this day in a display case at the British Museum of Natural History in London. It is mounted in a standing position, in accordance with Tyson's final belief that the chimpanzee represented a pygmy form of human life.

Tyson's anatomical study was daring for its time because it proposed a direct linkage between humans and the rest of the animal world. Humans had previously been accorded a place in the hierarchy of life that had set them apart from the rest of creation and only slightly below the angels. Tyson established the human affinity to the great apes 172 years before Charles Darwin published *The Descent of Man*, and more than 250 years before biochemical proofs of a close relationship between humans and apes. Nowadays, of course, no reputable scientist would deny that humans are primates, or that much of human biology and behaviour can be explained as direct outgrowths of our species' evolution within that biological order. To acknowledge the existence of a close relationship, however, is not to say that modern humans are descended from chimpanzees, gorillas, baboons, or any other primate species now living. In fact, to say that humans are descended from the apes, as was erroneously done by those who misinterpreted Darwin, is as mistaken as it would be to state that two first cousins are descended from each other because they share one pair of grandparents. The truth is, rather, that just as cousins share grandparents, so various primates have had common ancestors at earlier stages of their evolution.

Some seventy million years ago the earliest primates, the prosimians (literally, 'previous to monkeys and apes'), appeared among the mammals as a branch of the insectivores ('insect-eaters'), which includes shrews, moles, and hedgehogs. The prosimians expanded both in number of species and in geographical range. They populated much of the warmer part of the globe and reached a position of dominance on the planet that was not again equalled by any primate until the evolution of modern humans. Unlike other arboreal mammals such as squirrels and opossums, which climb trees by digging their claws into the bark, prosimians climb by grasping. Inconsequential as this difference may seem, it offered prosimians a new way to move about in their environment and to find the insects and small animals that most of their present-day descendants still hunt for food. During tens of millions of years, their fingers and toes gradually lengthened and the tips developed into fleshy pads protected on the back by nails. A better grasp and greater sensitivity of touch were achieved by ridges and lines on these pads, the precursors of the human fingerprint.

Such seemingly minor structural changes opened new ecological niches for the prosimians, which could now travel efficiently from branch to branch and thus take advantage of the forest up to the highest treetops. Their deft hands could grasp prey quickly, in contrast to most insectivores' relatively inefficient method of sniffing out prey and then catching it in the mouth. The new emphasis on vision meant larger eyes that face forward, thereby giving partial stereoscopic vision through the overlapping of two images. Nevertheless, the prosimians belong to the most primitive branch of the primate order. Beginning with the prosimians – and continuing through the monkey, ape, and hominid branches – each stage of the primates' evolution has left its mark on modern humans.

The reign of the prosimians was short, as measured in evolutionary time. Their adaptation to the trees had been incomplete. The fields of vision of the eyes of most prosimians overlap only partially, depriving them of the true stereoscopic vision that is essential for animals that hunt by sight or that must leap accurately from limb to limb. They retain the long snout, the sensory whiskers around the mouth, and the wet muzzle of most mammals – all clear indications that smell and touch are still very important to them. Some of their descendants evolved into monkeys, with their far superior adaptations for arboreal life, and the prosimians declined both in number of species and in geographical range. Nowadays they survive competition from monkeys in parts of Africa and Southeast Asia by having become nocturnal and by having developed specialized adaptations for feeding.

Monkeys first appeared about fifty million years ago. So rapidly did they fill the niches formerly occupied by prosimians that within only about ten million years every major monkey group had evolved. Furthermore, by about thirty-five million years ago, a separation had already taken place between the Old World monkeys, which are ancestral to apes and humans, and the New World monkeys, which are not. A structural hallmark of the monkeys is the tail; it is absent in only a few species, whereas all apes and humans are tailless. The vestiges of a tail do, though, appear in the human embryo during a portion of its development in the womb. The tail of an Old World monkey serves as an excellent balancing organ because it is usually longer than the combined length of its head and body. Only the New World monkeys possess a prehensile (grasping) tail that functions as a fifth limb. Some New World species, such as the nimble spider monkey that ranges through forests from Mexico to Bolivia, possess a prehensile tail strong enough to hang by yet sensitive enough at the tip to pick up a berry. The presence of a tail in almost all monkey

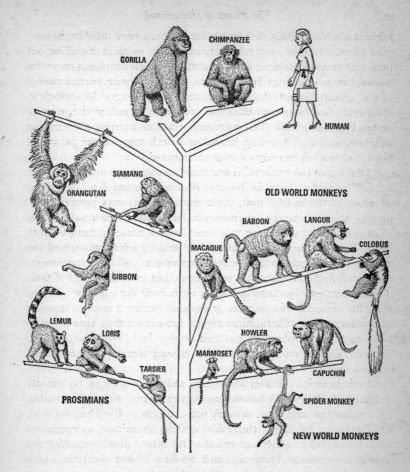

THE PRIMATE FAMILY TREE

This chart outlines the evolutionary stages (prosimians, New and Old World monkeys, and apes) that eventually led to humankind. All the species depicted here are contemporary ones, and so none could possibly be the ancestor of modern humans, any more than one cousin could possibly be the ancestor of another cousin. Primatologists consider the gibbons of Asia to be sufficiently distinct from the great apes (chimpanzee, gorilla, and orangutan) to place them in a family of their own. Many primatologists further subdivide this family into gibbons and the siamang.

species, and its absence in apes and humans, indicates contrasting modes of locomotion. Since monkeys walk on all fours, the tail is needed as a counterweight to the body, and as an airbrake and rudder as well. Neither apes, which hang by their arms, nor humans, which walk upright, have any need for a tail.

For the anthropocentric observer interested solely in the emergence of humankind, monkeys surely represent a major advance over the prosimians. The eyes of all monkeys point straight ahead, affording full stereoscopic vision. Sight is further enhanced by the ability to discern colours, something absent in prosimians and in almost all other mammals except apes and humans. Fruit is a major food source in the trees and colour vision allows it to be detected at a great distance. Monkeys use their hands much more skillfully than do prosimians as they carefully pluck fruit from a branch, gently remove the skin, and delicately break off a morsel at a time. One other development in monkeys was later crucial for humans. Most mammals bear several young at a time, but even twins are a rarity for monkeys, and for apes and humans as well. As between monkeys and apes, and then between apes and humans, infants are born increasingly helpless and dependent upon the mother. One at a time is all she can handle.

Beginning about thirty-five million years ago, some of the Old World monkeys gave rise to an unmistakably different way of life, that of the apes. This evolutionary change refined certain trends already present in the monkeys – better vision, superior eye-hand co-ordination, and most notably an increase in the size and complexity of the brain. A basic change in locomotion led to a remodelling of virtually the entire monkey skeleton. Almost all monkeys walk on four legs. Apes, on the other hand, have the potential to brachiate – that is, to hang suspended by one or both arms from a branch, allowing them to move efficiently through the forest. This became possible because the ape's wrist and elbow joints evolved in the direction of greater strength, and the shoulder became completely transformed so that the arm rotated a full one hundred and eighty degrees. The same thing is true of the human shoulder and arm – which is the reason that the overhead straps on buses and subways were invented.

The ape adaptation was, for a time, extremely successful. About fifteen million years ago, more different kinds of apes than monkeys existed, and their total population was considerably greater. But several million years later the ape supremacy ended, and monkeys once again became much more abundant. Today only four kinds of apes survive: the chimpanzee and gorilla in Africa, and the orangutan and gibbons in Southeast Asia. The geographical ranges of all the apes have dwindled to small pockets, and their numbers continue to decline. Indeed, both the gorilla and the orangutan are threatened with extinction unless their habitats can be preserved and predation by humans be prevented. No one knows for certain why the apes went into so precipitous a decline some ten million years ago, but one obvious answer is competition from the more humanlike forms that were then evolving.

\*

An anthropocentric look backward, over seventy million years of primate evolution, makes clear that certain biological features have become increasingly important. The primates show progressive changes from the four-footed gait of prosimians and monkeys to the upright, arm-swinging brachiation of apes, and finally to the two-legged walk of humans which liberated the hands for tool-making. The primacy of sight also was crucial. Life in the trees demanded precise judgment about the distance between tree branches; an error of only a few inches might mean a disastrous fall to the forest floor. Such judgments cannot be made accurately without stereoscopic vision, and also the colour discrimination that helps to distinguish between a rotted tree branch and a sound one. The emphasis on vision over smell led to several behavioural modifications in monkeys, in apes, and ultimately in humans. The loss of the mammalian wet snout, for example, gave a new mobility of the lips that made possible a wide repertory of facial expressions for communicating emotions. A cat can only grin, but a visitor to the zoo can witness a great number of facial expressions in monkeys and apes.

Superior eye–hand co-ordination demanded a more complex brain. The primate brain is large in relation to body size, as well as internally complex, equipped as it is to receive, analyse, and synthesize incoming sensory impulses and convert them into appropriate behaviour. Beginning with the prosimians, the size of the primate brain increases steadily. The weight of the simplest monkey brain (which belongs to the marmoset, a tiny South American monkey) is nevertheless three times the weight of the brain of the galago, a prosimian of about the same size. The increase in size and weight is partly due to the tremendous expansion from stage to stage of the regions of the cerebral cortex (the 'grey matter') associated with touch and sight, and partly also to the increase in the number of pathways connecting one part of the brain with another. The human brain is larger than that of other primates, both actually and in relation to body weight. A gorilla male, for example, may be nearly three times as heavy as a human male, but its brain is less than half as large.

Finally, the evolutionary trend of the primate order has been towards a steadily increasing life-span and a larger proportion of that life-span spent in the infantile and juvenile stages. Many kinds of prosimian mothers can leave their infants alone in nests soon after birth, and monkey infants can cling to the mother's fur from the moment they are born. Infant apes, though, cannot cling for at least the first month of life and must therefore be carried. Human children, of course, require many years of social learning in the family, from friends, and at school before they can become fully functioning members of their society. Females among non-human primates bear offspring right into old age. Human females, on the other hand, cease reproducing at menopause but usually live for several decades longer, during which time they can care for the last-born offspring and contribute to its survival. With monkeys and apes, the chances for survival of the last-born are much lower since they are usually left motherless while still immature.

The prolongation of the infantile, juvenile, and adolescent stages in humans is an evolutionary trend that is no doubt associated with the rise of complex culture. Humans must know much more than any other primate, and thus require extra time to learn it. Delayed maturity, though, has presented a social problem during the past several hundred years of human history. The need to develop technological skills has prolonged adolescent dependence well beyond the age of physical maturity. As a result, today's high school and college students are sexually and socially mature while technologically still juveniles. Denied the economic and social benefits to which maturity entitles them simply because they have not yet acquired all of the technological skills needed in the modern world, young people may become restless and antisocial in their behaviour. The situation would, of course, be improved if the trend were towards delayed sexual maturity – but during the past several hundred years it has been just the opposite. Improved diet and health care have steadily

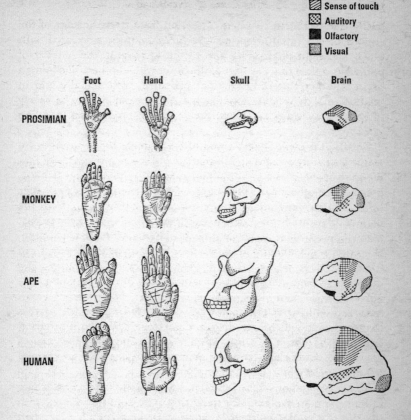

| | Foot | Hand | Skull | Brain |

Legend:
- Muscle control
- Sense of touch
- Auditory
- Olfactory
- Visual

PROSIMIAN

MONKEY

APE

HUMAN

THE MAJOR FEATURES OF PRIMATE EVOLUTION

This chart outlines the evolution, beginning with the prosimians, of features crucial to humankind: the feet and hands, the skull and teeth, and the brain. Humans have in general departed little from the basic primate pattern, yet in these drawings several essential refinements are clear. Human feet are adapted for walking on two legs; the thumb can move to oppose any of the other fingers and thus manipulate tools precisely; the shape of the skull has altered as a consequence of upright posture, a larger brain, and the decreased importance of the jaws and teeth; the size and complexity of the brain have increased enormously. Primates consume a wide variety of plant foods, insects, crustaceans, lizards, and tough meat with equal efficiency because of their array of different kinds of teeth: front incisors (used for cutting), larger canine teeth at the sides (for tearing and piercing), and the rearmost premolars and molars (for grinding and crushing). Note that similar regions of the brain in prosimians, monkeys, apes, and humans are shaded in the same way. This shading reveals a steady decrease in the proportion of areas devoted to smell and hearing, and an increase in the amount of uncommitted cortex (the 'grey matter' that makes apes and humans behave so intelligently).

lowered rather than raised the age of puberty. The onset of menstruation for United States females in 1900 occurred between ages fourteen and fifteen; now the age is closer to 12.6 years.

*

This chapter has so far emphasized the biological features of the primates that were especially important for the development of modern humans. In most instances these features are typical of generalized mammals. They represent refinements rather than such extreme alterations of structures as the giraffe's neck, the elephant's trunk, or the camel's hump. In their behaviour, though, the primates have not merely refined old ways but rather have developed radically new ways of responding to the environment. Although various mammals exhibit kinds of behaviour similar to those of primates, only the primates display the full constellation of these behaviours. Four major behavioural characteristics in particular distinguish the primates – social learning, tool-making, co-operation in hunting, and social organization – and all have had important implications for the later development of the human way of life.

Most mammals learn from experience. They modify their behaviour in response to events they have both participated in themselves and observed in others of their species. The anthropoids are notable for having carried this kind of social learning far beyond that found in any other mammals. From earliest infancy, primates spend considerable amounts of time simply observing behaviour: first that of their mother, later that of siblings, peers, and other members of the group. Eventually, the maturing monkey or ape enters into the group, which represents almost the entirety of its small and familiar world. Other kinds of animals, of course, also live together in groups, but none approaches the rich and varied social life of the primates. Thousands of ants inhabit the same nest, but their duties are determined at birth and they repeat the same behaviours day after day throughout their lives. Primates, by contrast, have exploited group living in a way that confers numerous adaptive advantages. The list of such advantages is long, but those of particular importance in understanding human behaviour are: the security of companions known since infancy; kinship ties with the mother and with siblings who can be counted upon for protection; the safety afforded by the continued presence of adult males; and the pleasurable social interactions of a predictable way of life.

Until the early 1960s, humans were thought to be the only animals that regularly made tools for specific uses. But close study of chimpanzees living under natural conditions at the Gombe Forest Reserve in Tanzania has revealed that humans are not unique in this respect. Chimpanzees were observed to make several kinds of tools, admittedly primitive ones but tools in concept nevertheless. They crumple leaves and use them as sponges to sop up water from holes in trees and to wipe dirt from the body. Chimpanzees also manufacture tools to capture termites for food. They first search for twigs or stiff grass blades of the necessary strength and size, rejecting many until they find the ones they want, much as the early hominids must have rejected many pieces of stone before finding suitable ones for their purposes. They then strip off leaves, bite off bent ends, and shape the width of the stems. They clearly display foresight by preparing the appropriate tools before going in search of a nest where termites have tunnelled near the surface. Having found it, a chimpanzee will scrape open a hole and insert the probe it has made. The response of the alarmed termites is to clamp their jaws onto the probe, after which the chimpanzee withdraws the tool gently so as not to dislodge the captured insects.♂♀

Chimpanzees also employ tools as weapons in a way that must be similar to that of the earliest hominids who ventured from the forests on to the grasslands. Some years ago, primatologists put together a realistic model of a leopard, which could be pulled from a concealed lair and whose head and tail could be moved by remote control. The chimpanzees reacted by hurling stones or by throwing long sticks, although with less effectiveness than human hunters use spears. As in human societies, males were the ones who used these weapons to defend the group. Such efforts against predators are grossly inefficient, however. Out of forty-seven instances of weapon use observed at the Gombe Reserve, the rocks or clubs actually struck their targets only five times.♂♀ Even so, the potential for making and using tools and weapons is well entrenched in the primate heritage of humankind.

Nearly all of the more than three million years since human history began has been spent following a way of life in which hunting for food was important. Anthropologists long believed that humans were the only primates to pursue game co-operatively and to share the kill afterwards, but recent observations of non-human primates in the wild show that is not so. During a decade of observations at

Gombe, approximately fifty chimpanzees killed ninety-five mammals and attempted to prey upon another thirty-seven that escaped. Other prey presumably was also killed but went unobserved by the primatologists. Such hunting was carried on almost exclusively by adult or pre-adult males; females were observed to hunt only when no males were in the vicinity. Evidence has accumulated as well that male chimpanzees not only co-operate in the chase but also distribute the kill afterwards. Normally, primates do not share food, not even females with their offspring. But for a short time after a chimpanzee makes a kill, the carcass becomes common property. Even chimpanzees that did not co-operate in the hunt are allowed to grab pieces of meat, and a single carcass is known to have been shared by as many as fifteen animals. Soon afterwards, though, the animal that made the kill hoards it, while others in the vicinity beg for a portion. Not every begging animal receives meat. Entreaties from an adult male sibling, a female with high status in the group, or a sexually receptive female are the ones most likely to be rewarded.

The recent studies of co-operative hunting and subsequent sharing have altered many previous notions about the behaviour of the early hominids. Anthropological dogma used to state that only humans displayed fully developed hunting behaviour – that is, co-operation between male hunters and their subsequent sharing of the kill. Such behaviour, though, was possibly already rooted in the primates before the emergence of humankind. As more and more primate species are observed in the wild, it begins to appear that hunting is not limited to chimpanzees. For example, during 1000 hours in which one baboon group was kept under observation by a primatologist, forty-seven small animals were successfully killed and eaten. Each baboon group apparently concentrates on only a few species – and the prey preferred by one group often differs from what is sought by neighbouring groups. A male baboon on the prowl for game ranges up to two miles from the rest of the group and, if he is unsuccessful, he might hunt the same prey repeatedly on subsequent days. Hominids obviously did not develop all at once and out of nowhere the hunting behaviours that remained a foundation of their way of life for several million years. The first apelike humans that ventured out of the forests on to the grasslands must already have exhibited such behaviour in rudimentary form. ♂♀

Learning, tool-making, and co-operative hunting have all been shown to be rooted in our primate heritage. The fourth important behavioural characteristic of the non-human primates – social organization – is difficult to generalize about because of the great diversity of primate species. Two aspects of this social organization, though, are exceptional. The first is that among the primates all social processes may occur at any time, whereas in most mammals specific seasons of the year are set aside for such events as battles between males, mating, birth, and migration from one habitat to another. Because these and numerous other events may take place at the same time in the primate group, individuals must learn to switch rapidly from one social context to another. The second way in which monkeys and apes differ from most other mammals is in being attached permanently to a social group. A solitary bear, elk, or beaver can survive very well on its own, but a solitary anthropoid is usually a dead anthropoid. While solitary animals are found in some primate species, in general group life is essential not only for protection against predators but also for maintaining the entire complex of social learning that is a hallmark of the primate way of life. These two features of primate social life have reached their fullest expression in humankind.

Individual monkeys, apes, and humans are all born into a social group that will be important to them for the rest of their lives. Each individual thus tends to accumulate a storehouse of subtle distinctions about members of that group, their particular status, and the identity of their friends and kin. Whenever two monkeys or apes approach one another, a fairly complex interaction inevitably takes place. Each must know whether it or the other is the more dominant, whether the other is of an easygoing or an irascible disposition, and whether it can immediately call upon the help of siblings if a fight should break out. A young male who is insensitive to the behaviour of other males will be harassed constantly. He may be forced to leave the group and live alone, thereby becoming easy prey for carnivores. If he remains within the group, he will have very low status and therefore be among the last to obtain food – the result of which will be weakness, disease, and a possible early death. Even if such a male should reach reproductive age, he probably will not be allowed by other males to copulate with females at a time when they are likely to conceive offspring. No matter what his exact fate, the genes of this insensitive male probably will not be passed on. Generation after generation of the elimination of the socially inept has produced an extraordinary ability in today's primate species – humans included – to evaluate complex social situations and to act appropriately.

\*

Some of the social behaviour that so distinguishes the human species – roles based on age and sex, the dominance of males, kin groups, and the bond between the sexes – can be found, at least in prototype, among the other primates. Nowadays many people condemn dominance behaviour because it is based on the threat of force; but among primates it has long been an adaptation that promotes social harmony. Adult males are almost always dominant over females (except for the individual male's mother), and females are ranked in their own dominance hierarchy. These hierarchies grow out of social experiences that begin shortly after birth, and that teach the young monkey or ape who can be dominated and who cannot. Eventually all members of the group learn their places in the hierarchy. ♂♀

Dominance was at one time believed to be a fairly simple arrangement, with animal A dominant over animal B, B over C, and so on. Primatologists have now found it to be more complex than that. Animal A may dominate animal B in aggressive interactions, but B might be bolder in obtaining food. Two brothers who individually rank around the middle of the dominance hierarchy sometimes team up and wrest the position of dominance from a more powerful but lone male. Nor is dominance automatically bestowed on the largest and the strongest male. Personality and temperament also play a part. Some monkeys and apes react speedily to threats, whereas others have placid dispositions that make them reluctant to enter into threatening situations. The importance of personality traits in establishing dominance is clear from the case of one male chimpanzee at Gombe. He had been low on the dominance hierarchy until the day when he learned that banging together empty kerosene cans stolen from the primatologists' camp could create a tremendous racket and scare off the more dominant males. He immediately rose in rank.

A stable hierarchy in which every male knows his place clearly affords adaptive benefits for animals that must live together in a group and interact numerous times each day. If such hierarchies did not exist, two males would have to fight every time they both desired the same piece of food or even a comfortable seat on a branch – with resulting social disruption, waste of energy, and the danger of wounds, which in the tropics easily become infected. In actuality fighting rarely takes place, since one of the males knows he is subordinate and therefore must defer to the other. The dominant males merely have to remind the subordinate males from time to time of who is who. These reminders may consist of no more than a yawn that subtly displays the canines, or a prolonged stare. Whatever has been said about the dominance hierarchies among non-human primates applies as well to many human situations. Any group composed of many individuals in potential competition – such as a business corporation, a club, or even a religious organization – would be inefficient indeed if squabbling for dominance went on constantly. Instead, everyone in the group is aware of both formal and informal hierarchies. All members know who has the right to sit in the most desirable place at meetings, who orders first at business lunches, whose approval must be obtained before an action can be taken. Such knowledge avoids time-consuming bickering and allows productive energies to be concentrated on the really important functions of the group.

Until very recently, most studies of primates in the wild emphasized the role of males, largely because of the drama of their competition for dominance. Nowadays, though, the basic interaction in primate social behaviour is known to be between a mother and her offspring. Most mammals expel their offspring soon after weaning, but among almost all monkeys and apes the attachment to the mother is lifelong and highly charged with emotion. A humanlike bond between the mated male and female is displayed in only a very few monkey or ape species, most notably the marmoset monkeys of South America, the hamadryas baboons of Ethiopia, and the gibbons of Southeast Asia. Such family units are an important adaptive device on the part of both males and females – the same sort of unconscious strategy that has worked so well in the human species. The female is assured of a male's constant protection for herself and her offspring, thereby increasing her offspring's chances of survival. From the male's perspective, this sort of arrangement also offers definite advantages. He is more likely to perpetuate his genes by protecting a small number of young he knows are his own than by impregnating a large number of females and never knowing which infants are his. ♂♀

This strategy, though, is very much the exception among primates. The female primate is sexually receptive ('in heat', or technically 'in estrus') for a few days before and after the egg passes from the ovary to the uterus. During this time she may copulate with as many as twenty adult males, thus ensuring fertilization – but making it virtually impossible to determine which male is the father. Although the human female has retained the menstrual cycle of other primates, she has suppressed estrus and presents no visible signs of ovulation (which in some primate females consists of a swelling of the brightly coloured skin in the area of the vagina). Instead, the level of human sexual activity remains consistent during the year – a behavioural and biological change that has undoubtedly strengthened the bond between human males and females, as well as given human sexuality a prominence and intensity unmatched in any other member of the animal kingdom. Once a monkey or ape female has conceived, on the other hand, she will not come into estrus again until her infant has been weaned.

Even this brief discussion of primate social organization makes plain that the adaptations of monkeys and apes sometimes diverge sharply from those of humans. Yet much of the social behaviour that so typifies humans obviously was entrenched in the primate line long before the appearance of the earliest hominids. The primates set the stage for human evolution – not only in physical structure but in behaviour as well – in a way that no other group of mammals could have done. In other words, humans are primates not by chance but by the direct outgrowth of adaptations long present in the primate line. ♂♀

*

The human way of life is also foreshadowed in the non-human primates by protoculture – a capacity not unlike the complex process of human culture for hitting upon novel ways of acting and transmitting them both to other members of the group and to subsequent generations. Protoculture was discovered quite by accident among Japanese macaques while they were being studied in their native habitat. (This is the species that is traditionally represented in carvings of the three monkeys miming the Buddhist proverb 'See no evil, hear no evil, speak no evil.') Primatologists put out various foods, such as wheat and potatoes, which were not part of the macaques' natural diet, to attract the animals to feeding grounds near the open seashore where they could more easily be observed. Within four hours after a dominant male in one group had sampled the wheat that had been left and then begun eating it, the entire group followed his lead.

Because a mound of wheat had simply been piled on the beach, the monkeys found it difficult to separate grains of wheat from grains of sand. Year after year, the monkeys painstakingly picked out the grains of wheat with their fingertips – until a young female arrived at the novel solution of scooping up a handful of the mixture and running on her hind-legs to the sea. When she opened her hands in the water, the heavier sand grains sank immediately while the wheat grains floated on the surface, where they could easily be scooped up. This method of sifting wheat eventually became a tradition within the group, much as it must have in human groups that early developed the cultural innovation of winnowing wheat to separate the chaff from the grain. Wheat-sifting by macaques represents true protoculture: a modification in behaviour different from that of other groups belonging to the same species and faced with the same potentials and limitations in the environment – one that is then transmitted throughout the group and from generation to generation.

Once a new tradition becomes established, it can affect other aspects of the protoculture. After the macaques began the traditions of sifting wheat and later of washing potatoes, they became more oriented towards the sea, an aspect of their environment they had previously ignored. Juveniles began to play in the water, and later some macaques learned to dive for seaweed. At least one monkey swam to a nearby island. In other words, the introduction of new food sources led first to the innovation of washing food, then to a new awareness of the sea, and finally to the exploitation of the sea as a place to find new foods and for travel. Other groups of Japanese macaques, which did not accept the foods that were offered them by the primatologists, failed to develop these behaviours. And they continued to ignore the sea even though it was within their sight much of the day. ♂♀

The development of new forms of behaviour within the small social groups of Japanese macaques is the closest approximation to human culture so far known in detail. Wheat-sifting, potato-washing, and swimming are, though, better regarded as protoculture than as the fully developed culture familiar to human beings. The macaque traditions became established by direct imitation or by experimentation with behaviours that won the approval of the dominant animals in the group. The establishment of traditions in this way differs from the human reaction to an invention. The person who invented the skateboard did not simply roll on it for months until some other human concluded that it offered rewards in entertainment and exercise, proceeded to copy it, and was in turn copied by still others. The human inventor works through legal institutions to establish proprietary rights to an innovation, then gives it a name, after which it is packaged, distributed, marketed, advertised, and publicized. At each stage, the human inventor uses symbols to bring about behavioural responses that hasten the spread of the invention throughout the society. In contrast, only four of the sixty Japanese macaques in one group took up potato-washing during the first year after the innovation.

Protoculture differs from human culture in the crucial respect that culture is transmitted by symbols, most often language. The traditions adopted by certain groups of Japanese macaques, on the other hand, did not involve symboling in any form. The Japanese macaques did not attach symbolic importance to the wheat or potatoes – as Christians do when they treat wine and bread as symbols of the blood and body of Jesus, or as Jews do when they eat unleavened bread to commemorate the exodus from Egypt. Nor did the macaques put the potatoes to any other use besides food, which is something humans do when they break bread in a symbolic act of friendship. No Japanese macaque or any other non-human primate deprives itself of food as penance or as a fast to protest social injustice. It does not endow substances with supernatural qualities, as humans do in the case of holy water or sacred mushrooms. A devout Moslem or Jew will suffer hunger in the presence of a nutritious food like pork that has been branded unclean by members of the culture, but no non-human primate does that either. All such cultural behaviours of humans are based on symboling – that is, the assignment to things and events of a set of meanings that extend far beyond what can be grasped through the senses – something that non-human primates display in only the most rudimentary ways.

\*

That humans are primates and not members of some other mammalian order has had an overriding influence in fashioning the kind of creature we are. More than half a century ago, the humourist Clarence Day speculated in *This Simian World* about the way in which humans might have evolved if they had been descended from the felines rather than from the simians (monkeys and apes):

A race of civilized beings descended from the great cats would have been rich in hermits and solitary thinkers. The recluse would not have been stigmatized as peculiar, as he is by us simians. They would not have been a credulous people, or easily religious. False prophets and swindlers would have found few dupes . . . None but the lowest dregs of such a race would have been lawyers spending their span of life on this mysterious earth studying the long dusty records of dead and gone quarrels. We simians naturally admire a profession full of wrangle and chatter, but that is a monkeyish way of deciding disputes, not a feline . . . What outrages [the simian] is to make him stop wagging his tongue.

The primate pattern both afforded potentialities and imposed limitations upon the development of the hominids. The primates display a remarkable diversity of social organizations, as would be expected from approximately two hundred species living under a wide variety of ecological conditions. These organizations range from monogamous pairs (gibbons and marmosets) through harem systems (certain baboons) to loosely organized kin groups revolving around the mother (chimpanzees). A basic difference does nevertheless exist between the human and the non-human patterns. The non-human primates display many kinds of social organization simply because the primates consist of many species – in contrast to the single human species, which exhibits all the kinds of organization found in the totality of other primate species. Humans have even gone beyond the diversity of other primates to develop one unique form of social organization, polyandry – that is, a group composed of a single female and several males, as occurs in places in India and Tibet and on some Pacific islands.

Non-human primates studied in the wild during recent decades have revealed an unsuspected potential for acquiring information and for developing innovative forms of behaviour. These accomplishments, though, are unimpressive when compared with those of humans, and even of some other mammals. Only when primates are brought into the laboratory in contact with human trainers does their potential for solving problems, co-operation in tasks, and symboling become clear. Laboratory chimpanzees have been taught, for example, to play a kind of slot machine that pays off in rewards of fruit. But they have learned on their own to hoard tokens of a certain colour because these could later be used to obtain particularly favoured fruits from the machine. Under laboratory conditions, the superior mental abilities of a primate over other tool-using animals, such as the California sea otter, become apparent. The skills of the sea otter are specialized and genetically fixed, while the skills of a primate are flexible and afford an enormous potential for developing new kinds of behaviour. No one has yet completely explained why these flexible skills, the very hallmark of the hominids, emerge in laboratory primates but not in primates living in the wild. One obvious reason, of course, is that in the laboratory situation primates are in contact with humans from whom they might learn. But even those laboratory apes and monkeys whose association with their human caretakers is minimal nevertheless display behaviours that have never been observed in the wild. Whatever the explanation, the fact is apparent that the earliest hominids from the outset used their flexible skills inherited from primate ancestors to create their unique pattern of life. ♂♀

# 3

# The Hominid Pattern

Despite their humanlike qualities, apes do differ anatomically from humans in major as well as trivial ways. The human female, for example, possesses large breasts, whereas only rarely do female apes have even slightly protruding mammary glands. As a result of very slight anatomical differences in the vocal tract, humans can speak, but no other primate can. Humans are also the only primates able to vary the pitch of sounds in melodious sequences, and thus to sing. We are the least hairy of the primates, but not the least hairy of mammals (the elephant, hippopotamus, and whale are more naked per square inch of skin). Inch for inch on our bodies, our hairs are as numerous as those of monkeys and apes, but most humans produce only a fine down rather than the long, coarse hair that covers the bodies of non-human primates. The hair the human male grows on the face, though, makes him hairier there than any other primate, and he has almost as much hair on the chest as a gorilla. Baldness in the mature male is thought by some to be exclusively a human trait, but it is actually characteristic of the primates. A tendency towards baldness in maturing males has been found in the chimpanzee, orangutan, and several kinds of monkeys.

The proportions of the human skull, face, and jaw are considerably different from those of the apes. The human skull is enormous because of the very large brain it encloses; the face is relatively much smaller than in the apes except for the very prominent nose. The teeth and jaw are also much smaller in humans, who generally eat softer foods or soften them by cooking. The huge canine teeth of male monkeys and apes are displayed as threats to other males and are used as weapons, but the canines of humans are small and lie flush with the rest of the teeth. Humans no longer need enormous canines for aggression or defence, yet they still regard baring the canines while smiling as a threat. Beware the broad smile of the villain in melodrama or movie – that 'smiling, damned villain', as

Shakespeare described the murderer Claudius in *Hamlet*. ♂♀ Along with the reduced size of the jaw, humans have lost the heavy brow ridges that serve in many primates as buttresses against the pull of their powerful jaw muscles.

Bone for bone, the basic pattern of a human skeleton and a gorilla's is similar. With a few minor exceptions, all of the gorilla's bones have approximately the same shape and are to be found in the same position as in the human skeleton. The major differences that do exist are in the face, in the proportions of certain bones crucial for human upright posture, for walking on two legs, and for the dexterity of the hands – most notably in the thickness and length of the bones of the limbs, the shape of the pelvis, and the curve of the spinal column. Because the gorilla walks by putting weight on its front knuckles, it has long arms and short legs, whereas all of a human's limbs are long. The gorilla's hands are long and slender and have a short thumb; human hands, in contrast, are short and stubby, with a long thumb that can form a precision grip with the index finger. Such differences, though, are of degree rather than kind, and reflect the different ways of life of apes and humans. Comparing a gorilla skeleton with a human one is somewhat like comparing a pick-up truck with a passenger car. Both are unmistakably vehicles of automotive transportation, but they vary in construction and performance because they serve different uses.

New biochemical methods that can determine precise evolutionary distances indicate still closer affinities between humans and apes than are suggested by anatomical comparison alone. In fact, at the biochemical level, humans and chimpanzees are as close as two species can be while still remaining recognizably different at the levels of anatomy, physiology, and behaviour. Very minor genetic changes apparently have had major consequences for the evolution of the human pattern of life. For example, a slight difference in the structure of the thumb has meant the difference between the monkey's ability to peel a banana and the human's extraordinary dexterity in wiring an electronic circuit.

No one will ever know, of course, precisely what the changes were that made humans today's masters of the planet and relegated apes to a few species dwindling in numbers and limited in geographical range. Anyone attempting to piece together even the barest outlines of hominid evolution immediately comes up against a number of insurmountable problems. The first is the extreme scarcity of well-preserved fossils whereby the exact sequence of that evolution might be revealed. A second is the difficulty in agreeing upon the exact point at which hominid evolution began. Scientists at one time searched for the 'missing link', the single fossil that would mark the unmistakable transition between humanlike ape and apelike human. Any search for such a missing link, though, is futile because no single form embodied the transition; rather, the hominids emerged over a long period of time from a diversity of humanlike apes. A third problem is deciding what constitutes a hominid. The qualities that are crucial for defining humanity do not leave their marks upon skulls and bones. No fossil can reveal to what degree the living organism was able to communicate, or what kind of social organization it took part in. Anthropologists have added still further to the confusion by not always employing the same criteria to define what is 'human'. To some it is the ability to walk upright; to others, the possession of dexterous hands; to still others, a large and complex brain.

Anyone who reads a book on hominid fossils will encounter a bewildering inventory of skulls, tongue-twisting names for fossil discoveries, disputes about dating, and other things of interest primarily to specialists. Readers who wish to enter this fascinating arena of contention can do so by consulting some of the books cited in the Notes and Sources section for this chapter. But the details are not essential to an understanding of the relevance of the hominid pattern of life to our behaviour today. The main thing to bear in mind is that between about twenty-five million and ten million years ago a wide variety of primates are known to have ranged from Spain to China and southward throughout much of Asia and Africa. Large portions of this region were heavily forested, but much of it consisted of open woodlands and tree-dotted grasslands (known as 'savannas') similar to those existing today in Africa. Numerous species of primates had ventured down from the trees and were attempting to exploit the food resources in these open areas. The savanna in particular must have provided a bonanza of foodstuffs for the venturesome primates that possessed generalized digestive systems. Many species undoubtedly failed to adapt themselves to life on the ground. But some were successful, among them the ancestors of the modern chimpanzees, gorillas, macaques, baboons – and humans.

The first milestone on the way to becoming human was the descent from the trees to exploit ecological niches on the ground not previously occupied by primates. The second was exploitation of the new habitat by travelling on two legs, thereby leaving the hands free for carrying food and for using tools. Chimpanzees and – as mentioned in the previous chapter – Japanese macaques occasionally run on two legs; but presumably the ancestors of humankind did so most of the time. These prehumans must have learned to run before they could walk, because running is considerably easier than slowly shifting balance from one leg to another – as is clear from watching any child take its first steps. Walking on two legs presented numerous problems, one of which was the narrowing of the birth canal and the resulting problems of bearing young. Another must have been disposal of body wastes. Some other mammals, such as cats and dogs, are genetically programmed to solve this problem by covering their dung. Non-human primates, though, merely drop their faeces wherever they happen to be, a method of disposal that presents few problems in sanitation because primates generally sleep in a different place each night. And because the non-human primates lack buttocks, their faeces drop away cleanly from the anal region. The musculature necessary for the humans' upright stance is also responsible for the buttocks. As a result of this development, the anal region is squeezed between the inner edges of the buttocks, causing faecal matter to stick to the skin. All human societies have solved the problem of waste disposal by designating specific places in the settlement as appropriate for defaecation and also by teaching children the culture's approved method of anal cleaning. We may like to suppose that the arts, such as dancing and painting the walls of caves, were early features of human culture, but they were very late developments; toilet training surely was one of the earliest.

The terrestrial, omnivorous, bipedal, tool-using primate that became established in the new environment of the savanna would have been rewarded with plentiful supplies of nutritious foods, free of competition from most other primates. It also would have encountered many new dangers from such predators as the ancestors of the lion, hyena, and jackal. Presumably, though, this terrestrial biped was little different from the human hunting bands of today, which are bound together by strong ties of co-operation. The tightly knit social organization that gives modern-day baboons on the African savannas protection from predators would undoubtedly have served this terrestrial biped just as effectively. The heritage of living in the trees – where instantaneous eye–brain–muscle co-ordination is essential – would also have enabled these ancestors of humankind to react quickly to danger. They undoubtedly were at least as venturesome, alert, cunning, and well co-ordinated as their potential predators, even though fossils indicate that they generally had small brains compared to modern apes and humans. Perhaps the most important of all the primate traits that these bipeds carried down with them from millions of years of evolution in the trees was a tendency to investigate, observe, remember, and then rapidly alter their behaviour in response to new information.

These pioneering bipeds apparently belonged to a group whose fossils are known as Ramapithecines. Ramapithecines were eminently successful. Their fossil remains have been unearthed in India, Turkey, Europe, and East Africa. Little is known for certain about them, but a few things can be inferred from the examination of their fossils and a knowledge of the climate during the time they lived. The environment inhabited by the Ramapithecines was not the tropical forest, which produces fruit and other soft plant foods throughout the year, that is inhabited by modern apes. In their subtropical forests, which produced only seasonally, the Ramapithecines would thus have found their food supply inadequate. Those that survived would have done so because they foraged on the ground and along the edge of the forest for such tough parts of plants as nuts and roots. They obtained their food differently from the way the other apes did. This hypothesis would explain the distinctive jaws and teeth that set the Ramapithecines apart from other apes of their time – and that also foreshadowed the skull and jaw of the earliest hominids. In any event, the Ramapithecines are humankind's most remote ancestors among the primates that can be identified with any degree of certainty. ♂♀

After the disappearance of the Ramapithecines from the fossil record some eight million years ago, a succession of their descendants presumably followed with more and more hominid characteristics. Finally, in the fossil remains dating to about five million years ago, the outlines of hominid evolution become less sketchy. Hominid skulls and bones – and with them, tools and the remains of animals presumably killed for food – appear with increasing frequency. They document the evolution of forms of life unmistakably possessing characteristics that set hominids apart from all other creatures.

From this time onwards, the fossils can conveniently be grouped into three main stages of human evolution: the earliest hominids, *Homo erectus*, and modern humans.

\*

Several lineages of the earliest humanlike primates had evolved by about five million years ago. Among them were two Australopithecines ('southern apes'): the large *Australopithecus robustus* and the much smaller *Australopithecus africanus*. Fossil discoveries of both have been widespread in Africa, probably because more of a search has been made there than elsewhere; apparently they inhabited parts of Asia as well. *Robustus* can safely be dismissed from consideration as a human ancestor. It weighed about as much as most modern humans, but its brain was no larger than that of little *africanus*. Its jaws were massive and, like the modern gorilla, it had a crest along the midline of the skull to support powerful chewing muscles. Presumably it consumed tough plant foods of the same sort as are eaten by gorillas today. Three other things argue against *robustus* as a human ancestor: Its leg bones indicate that it could run but not walk; it seems not to have manufactured tools; and its brain size did not increase significantly throughout the approximately four million years before it became extinct. Every bit of evidence suggests that *robustus* was a large, dim-witted vegetarian.

The other Australopithecine, *africanus*, is of considerably more interest. The great variety of tools and the remains of animal prey associated with *africanus* fossils indicate that it had already developed the hunting–gathering adaptation that was typical of all humans on the planet until about 12,000 years ago (and that is found today among isolated bands of Pygmies, Bushmen, Australian Aborigines, and various South American tribes). The leg bones of *africanus* show that it could walk as well as run, and its jaws and teeth were very much in the human pattern. Its brain was small, averaging less than 500 cubic centimetres, which is somewhat under the average for a modern gorilla and considerably under the 1450 c.c. that is average for a modern human. But such comparisons are misleading. Brain size must be judged in relation to body size, and *africanus* ranged from perhaps forty to ninety pounds in weight and from three to a little more than four feet in height.

Here was a small creature that apparently walked upright, hunted mammals larger than itself, and used tools to butcher meat. These, the earliest of hominid tools (known as 'choppers'), consisted of stones, usually smaller than a baseball, crudely flaked to a point by a few blows, that could be gripped in the palm of the hand with the cutting edge downward. Although choppers are obviously primitive, the accomplishment they represent should not be underestimated. Tool-making marks the hominids' third milestone, after the move on to the savanna and the development of bipedalism. The very fact that *africanus* manufactured an object in advance of its use implies the ability to project current desires into future events. To find a piece of stone and then shape it so as to perform a predetermined task is a truly creative act, no matter how crude the tool itself may have been.

*Africanus* the hunter apparently lived alongside *robustus* the vegetarian for several million years, each one inhabiting its own ecological niche and no more interfering with the other than do modern gorillas and chimpanzees. Until recently, most specialists in human evolution believed the course of hominid origins to have been a very straightforward one: *Africanus* simply kept evolving towards more modern forms of *Homo*. New evidence, though, makes it almost a certainty that *africanus* was merely a small-brained contemporary of the true human ancestor; both had apparently evolved from an earlier Australopithecine tentatively identified as *afarensis*. In 1972, anthropologists excavating along the eastern shore of Lake Turkana (formerly called Lake Rudolf) in Kenya unearthed a hominid skull that possessed an unusually large braincase – about half again as large as that of the average *africanus*. Some very humanlike leg bones that were also discovered left no doubt that this early form of *Homo* could walk upright. Most surprising was the undisputed antiquity of the fossil – more than two and a half million years old. It was thus contemporary with the same Australopithecines from whom it had supposedly descended.

Additional spadework at Lake Turkana has uncovered several more fossils with the same large braincase and the same modern shape of the skull – and these dated from an even earlier period, about three million years ago. In addition, numerous stone tools were found buried in the same layer of volcanic rock. Year by year, new excavations at Lake Turkana and also at other locations in East Africa have continued to uncover the fossil remains of the earliest hominids, whose teeth, skulls, and bone fragments show them to be true ancestors of humans and not merely humanlike apes. In fact, one nearly complete skeleton, found in Ethiopia and dated at more than three million years ago, has a pelvis, knee, and foot as well adapted to bipedalism as those of humans today. ♂♀

With this new evidence, a much clearer idea about the beginnings of the hominids has emerged (although it has not yet won unanimous acceptance from scientists investigating the problem of human origins). The parent stock of the hominids apparently arose about five million years ago. *Australopithecus africanus* was humanlike in that it walked on two legs and used tools, but from the neck up it was still apelike. On the other hand, the Lake Turkana fossils are of a creature that had a humanlike body from the neck down, and in addition a brain that was considerably larger than that of the Australopithecines. Even more significant, the *Homo* brain had gone on increasing in size, whereas that of the Australopithecines had remained the size of a chimpanzee's over a period of several million years. In other words, *Australopithecus robustus* and *Australopithecus africanus* were not transitional to the human line of evolution. They were instead related, contemporaneous forms that lived in the same environment as the true hominids over wide areas of Africa (and possibly Asia as well) at least three million years ago. Eventually, though, the competitive advantage given the early hominids by their large brain enabled them to exploit that environment more efficiently. The Australopithecines were gradually pushed into extinction, although some survived in Africa until as recently as one million years ago.

This new view of the earliest stage of hominid evolution appears to be the most logical explanation for the evidence that has been unearthed. Whatever precise details of the story may finally emerge, hominids were already entrenched on the African savanna almost four million years ago. They manufactured a variety of tools to hunt and butcher large prey. This stone technology, primitive as it was, opened up for exploitation a new environment that was far from the trees in which the ancestors of humankind had evolved. These earliest hominids were launched along a path that was strikingly different from the one taken by any primate before them. Once so launched, they would have had increasing difficulty in returning to the life of the forest. The very adaptation of walking on two legs that made hominids successful on the ground would have been a hindrance in the trees. Gradually, as these hominids increasingly perfected the new adaptation, they gained an advantage and replaced those whose adaptation to life on the ground had been less successful. ♂♀

\*

Some controversy still exists about the earliest stage of hominid history, but anthropologists are much more in agreement about the subsequent stage, *Homo erectus*, a species name that nowadays lumps together a wide variety of similar forms previously given such names as 'Java Man' and 'Peking Man'. The earliest of these fossils dates to about one and a half million years ago, and beginning about a million years ago *erectus* demonstrated its biological adaptability by expanding throughout the Old World continents. It also became increasingly modern in appearance. The earliest *erectus* brains were small in comparison to those of modern humans, but by 250,000 years ago brain size had increased to about 1100 c.c. (only slightly smaller than the smallest brains of normal humans today). Brain size is important, of course, but so is the internal structure of the brain. *Erectus* apparently lacked certain essential capacities of the brain of modern humans. The skull was pinched inward in those areas which in the modern brain are concerned with speech, thinking, and memory. Other primitive traits also remained – low forehead, heavy jaw, and large teeth – but in upright posture and bipedalism *erectus* was as fully developed as modern humans, and the same applies to the structure of the hand. That right-handedness was apparently established during *erectus* times is borne out by the discovery of some *erectus* tools, which are easier to hold in the right hand than in the left. A preference for the use of one hand over the other – the right-handedness that today characterizes from 85 to 95 per cent of the world's population – meant that the dexterity of the hominids had been further increased by its concentration in one hand rather than being divided between two hands.

Increasingly skilful hands are evident from some of the tools found with *erectus* fossils. During the previous few million years, virtually no progress at all had been made beyond the manufacture of crude chopping tools. Compared to the earliest stone tools associated with *Homo* and the Australopithecines, which had been merely chipped with half a dozen blows to form a cutting edge, the tools of *erectus* are varied and show superior workmanship. By about 500,000 years ago, *erectus* populations almost everywhere had developed the hand axe, which is not only a great refinement of the chopper but an important step forward conceptually as well. Flakes chipped off in making the hand axe were not simply thrown away; rather, they were used to make a range of other specialized tools for butchering and cutting. Technology improved in other ways as well. The *erectus* peoples expanded the range of materials used for manufacturing tools, apparently travelling considerable distances in search of what they needed. And for the first time, hominids began to make wooden spears whose points were hardened by fire.

Early hominids were exclusively tropical, but *erectus* expanded northward into the cooler regions of the Old World. This expansion of range was made possible by technological innovations: not only new and better tools, but even more the controlled use of fire. Evidence for the use of fire, both in making tools and for domestic hearths, has been found at several locations in Europe and Asia, dating from as early as 750,000 years ago; and its use seems to have spread rapidly thereafter. Fire kept away predators at night, provided warmth, produced chemical changes in wood to harden it, and stampeded animals into ravines, where they could be killed easily. The control of fire must have meant a marked improvement in the utilization of meat. Modern domesticated animals are bred to yield tender flesh, but the meat of wild animals is sinewy. Cooking, though, causes chemical reactions that break down tissues, thereby making possible new sources of food and also making utilization of previous sources more efficient  Cooking provides other benefits as well. It kills parasites that inhabit animal tissue and that otherwise would be transferred to humans; and it allows food to be stored longer without spoilage because it kills decay-producing micro-organisms. The controlled use of fire by *erectus* was a major accomplishment, second only to the manufacture of tools.

Fire also was used to evict large mammals – sabretooth tigers, cave bears, and hyenas – from the caves that were their dens, which the humans then proceeded to occupy. One such cave is at Choukoutien near Peking, China. Archaeological excavations reveal that it had long been inhabited exclusively by large mammals. Then, abruptly, comes clear evidence of fire, and with it traces of the mammals disappear and the first signs of permanent human occupancy are seen. Many of the human skulls unearthed at Choukoutien reveal that the base had been opened, presumably to extract the brain, and that the bones of the legs and arms had been split, apparently to remove the marrow. Such cannibalistic behaviour is looked upon with revulsion by people in modern societies. But cannibalism most often displays traits of humanity rather than the reverse. Excluding exceptional cases of starvation, groups that have practised cannibalism in modern times have rarely done so for the purpose of adding meat to their diet, but rather as part of a solemn ritual to express devotion to the dead, to obtain magically the qualities of the person whose body was being devoured, or to appease the gods.

*Homo erectus* was firmly established as a successful biological species somewhat less than a million years ago. By then its closest competitors, the Australopithecines and the early hominid forms, had already disappeared. Spreading far and wide out of the tropical cradle of humankind, *Homo erectus* had colonized an area extending from northwestern Europe across Asia to northern China, as well as southward into Java and southern Africa. It had learned to make tools in considerable variety, to co-operate in mass slaughters of giant elephantlike mammals, to put up dwellings, and to use fire. In its adaptation to hunting, *erectus* apparently developed something close to the technology and the co-operative social system that were universal among humankind before the development of agriculture, about 12,000 years ago. *Homo erectus*, though, was not yet *Homo sapiens*, either physically or culturally. The exact way in which the gap was bridged, at some time between about 250,000 and 100,000 years ago, is still unknown because not enough fossils dating from that period have thus far been discovered. One thing is certain, however: no *Homo erectus* mother simply gave birth to a *Homo sapiens* infant. The evolution of one species into another is always gradual, and certainly never an event perceptible at a particular time and place. Before the advent of the fully modern humans, hominids still had before them one brief but important stage which began about 80,000 years ago: the Neanderthals (whose name is derived from the Neander Thal or 'valley' of western Germany where the first specimen was found). ♂♀

\*

The Neanderthal is still pictured in the popular imagination as a stooped, beetle-browed cave-dweller who walked with a shuffling gait. This erroneous conception is based on an early Neanderthal skeleton, which recent re-evaluation has demonstrated to have been that of an old man suffering from an advanced case of arthritis of the spine, the jaw, and possibly the legs. The Neanderthals were in fact quite otherwise – and in brain size sufficiently like modern humans for biologists to classify them in the same species as *sapiens*. But they were sufficiently different in numerous minor ways to be assigned to a subspecies, known as *Homo sapiens neanderthalensis*. Some of the Neanderthals were very similar to the fully modern *Homo sapiens sapiens*, which includes all humans who have lived on earth for about the past 40,000 years. But others, particularly those inhabiting northern Europe, were notably different. The European Neanderthal had a skull that was flattened at the top, with heavy brow ridges and a massive jaw, and its build apparently was stocky, similar to that of the modern Eskimo – as might be expected of people inhabiting very cold environments, for the reason that a stocky build conserves heat better than a thin one.

The Neanderthals are notable for two major achievements in human history. The first is their expansion into new ecological zones: the northern forest and the Arctic tundra, where they adapted successfully to the harsh climate and hunted such formidable mammals as the woolly rhinoceros, musk ox, mammoth, and cave bear, and also exploited the vast herds of reindeer. The second is a sophisticated new concept of obtaining food, one that has been described as the difference between 'earned' and 'unearned' resources. Previous to the Neanderthals, hominids depended mostly on earned resources – that is, they hunted the game animals that shared the local environments with them, and which, being constantly present, were obvious targets. The Neanderthal peoples, on the other hand, by settling along the valleys used as migration routes by herds of mammals, were able to tap unearned resources: mammals that had grown fat by obtaining their food outside the Neanderthal's environment, and which were killed as they passed through. In other words, instead of exhausting the capacity of their own environments, the Neanderthals exploited game that had put on flesh elsewhere. ♂♀

The teeth of Neanderthal fossils reveal the same sort of wear that is seen in Eskimo teeth today, and which is caused by chewing animal skins to soften them. Neanderthal tools – which include such things as scrapers for cleaning animal hides, knives for cutting them, and gougers for boring holes so that the hides might be sewn together – confirm their dependence upon animal skins for clothing. Nowadays, clothing serves several obvious purposes: protection against cold, sun, or objects that might abrade the skin; modesty;

vanity; and for carrying things. Of all these uses, the most important must originally have been the last: the transportation of infants, tools, weapons, plant foods, and meat. Any device that would allow objects to be transported, and at the same time leave the hands free, would have had undoubted survival value. Possibly the first article of clothing was nothing more than a piece of animal skin or a few feet of vine draped over the shoulders or tied above the hips, those two natural projections of the human body that easily sustain weights. The waist belt – from which weapons, tools, pouches, and a breech-clout can be hung – is still one of the most widespread articles of clothing in use throughout the world.

The Neanderthals were responsible for yet another milestone in the development of human behaviour. Whereas the fossils of earlier hominids reveal that most died young as a result of injuries and disease, the Neanderthals are remarkable in that so many reached old age. Some did so after suffering severe wounds, clear evidence that they had been cared for and fed while disabled. In fact, one fossil shows that a Neanderthal had an arm amputated and yet continued to live for many years thereafter. The appearance for the first time on the planet of a startlingly different behaviour – care of the disabled and the elderly – gives proof of an entirely new outlook on the nature of human existence. This outlook extended to the Neanderthal's ritual disposal of the dead, the first examples in what is currently known of hominid history. Numerous Neanderthal graves show that often the interred were given elaborate burials and provided with tools and food. At one Neanderthal burial site in southern France, a man was found with his head resting on a pillow of flints and with other stone tools and animal bones placed nearby.

Neanderthal dead were also sometimes surrounded with wreaths of flowers. A recent analysis of the pollen from garlands found at a burial site in northern Iraq, dating from 60,000 years ago, reveals that the plants were not chosen haphazardly. Out of the hundreds of varieties of flowers that might have been gathered to make the wreath, all but one of those selected are known to have medicinal properties (and the one exception may have had a symbolic importance not presently understood). These plants have long been used in the Near East to heal wounds or cure dysentery, as stimulants or astringents, or as ingredients in various herbal remedies. The Neanderthals must likewise have been aware of the medicinal properties of these flowers, since the very survival of the people depended upon an intimate knowledge of the environment they inhabited. ♂♀

The Neanderthal concept of self as seen in the care of the sick and wounded and in ritual burials is confirmed also by the discovery of polished animal teeth and stones, apparently the earliest jewellery so far unearthed. Jewellery, though usually regarded as nothing more than baubles or trinkets, in fact had a profound importance in the development of human behaviour. When people form a social group, they must have some way to identify the different networks of kin to which they belong, and also to display their particular status. Such distinctions would not be visible if people went about stark naked. So they declare their social identity by placing symbols in the most obvious place: on the body itself. Probably the skin was used at first as a status billboard by colouring it with pigments in various designs. Later, ornaments were embedded in the skin or worn as bracelets, necklaces, earrings, nose plugs, and penis sheaths.

Roughly 40,000 years ago, the Neanderthals were replaced by the single subspecies of humankind existing today, the fully modern *Homo sapiens sapiens*. No one is certain about exactly what caused the extinction of the Neanderthals. Specialists in human evolution used to envision the shuffling, dumb Neanderthals as having been killed off by the wily Cro-Magnons, as they are in William Golding's novel *The Inheritors*. Anthropologists now know, of course, that the Neanderthals had fully modern bodies and that their brains were on the average slightly larger than those of the Cro-Magnons. No shortage of other hypotheses exists to account for the Neanderthals' extinction. One is that they may have become too specialized in their adaptation to living on the fringes of the ice sheet; when it retreated, along with the cold-adapted mammals they had hunted, the Neanderthals went into a decline also. Another possibility is that the tools of modern humans were so clearly superior that the Neanderthals simply lost out in the competition for resources. A tool that is more finely fashioned, better balanced, or more symmetrical will also be more efficient. A carefully manufactured tool does not have to be vastly superior to give its makers an advantage. A weapon that hits its prey only 5 per cent more accurately or more often will allow its makers to obtain considerably more meat. It therefore increases the likelihood that people with the improved tools will survive to produce offspring. If the slightly greater efficiency stemming from superior tools is maintained generation after generation, eventually the makers of such tools will supplant those who are less proficient.

One intriguing hypothesis concerning the decline of the Neanderthals is based upon the relation between body build and particular kinds of weapons. A spear obviously becomes more efficient as its velocity, and therefore its penetrating power, are increased. Such an increase can be achieved if the spearman possesses a long throwing arm and a long trunk, which together act as a lever. Here the Neanderthals would have been at a disadvantage because of their heavy build and their adaptation to power rather than to speed. This disadvantage must have been increased still more after the Cro-Magnons invented the spear-thrower – a thick stick or board between one and three feet long, with a groove running its entire length (as illustrated on page 59). The spear-thrower is held in one hand with the butt end of the spear resting in the groove, so that when the spear is hurled, the effect is that of an artificial extension in the length of the hunter's arm and thus a great increase in the velocity of the spear. ♂♀

The most probable explanation for the disappearance of the Neanderthals, though, is simply that they evolved into modern humans. Evidence that this might be so comes from caves in Israel, where many generations of Neanderthals lived less than 45,000 years ago, and where they left their fossil remains. The skulls found there reveal a great diversity of types, ranging from undisputed Neanderthals to others who would be virtually indistinguishable from humans today. The change from Neanderthal to *Homo sapiens sapiens* must have been imperceptible to the people concerned.

Truly modern humans appeared in the Near East and in Southeast Asia about 40,000 years ago, and only slightly later in Europe. Because more spadework has been done in Europe than anywhere else, the best-known early modern type is the European one, named Cro-Magnon after an archaeological site in France. But it should not be inferred from the great number of sites excavated in Europe in search of skeletons and skulls of early *Homo sapiens sapiens* that the process of sapienization was a European phenomenon. European claims for priority were widespread earlier in this century and were sometimes used to bolster arguments for the superiority of Europeans over other peoples of the world. The fact is that the process of sapienization occurred throughout the continents of Europe, Africa, and Asia in much the same way and at approximately the same time.

Europe is definitely not the 'cradle' of modern humans even though more fossils have been uncovered there than anyplace else.

Displays in many natural history museums still show reconstructions of Cro-Magnons standing tall and straight, with flowing blond hair, in contrast to the dark-skinned, slouching Neanderthals. Such reconstructions not only are false; they also are projections into antiquity of modern racial prejudices. Such idealized reconstructions of the Cro-Magnons are no more faithful to reality than saying that all modern Europeans are tall and thin and have blue eyes and blond hair. Individual differences among Cro-Magnons were apparently as great as they are among modern Europeans. Some were taller than others, some had broader faces or longer noses, and they probably displayed a range of skin and hair colours as well.

The anatomical contrasts between a Neanderthal and a Cro-Magnon might appear insignificant to the non-specialist, but the same cannot be said of their technologies. The Neanderthals improved tool-making somewhat, but it was the Cro-Magnons who brought about the really great advance. For several million years, no very startling changes in tool-making techniques had taken place, and stone had continued to be the basic raw material. But all at once, beginning about 35,000 years ago, a great variety of new tools appeared, using not only stone but also bone, antler, and wood. These raw materials had occasionally been employed by *erectus* peoples in Spain, but their everyday use in making a diversity of tools really begins with the Cro-Magnons. Their radically new techniques included the polishing of stone tools. Instead of leaving the surface pitted by the chips that had been removed, they devoted considerable time and patience to rubbing the tool with abrasives such as sandstone and emery. The additional effort meant that the tools were much more efficient and that they lasted longer, as an experiment in Denmark demonstrated. Three woodsmen who set to work clearing trees with axes using ancient polished blades succeeded in levelling an eighth of an acre of hardwoods in only four hours. And one of the blades proved so efficient that it did not need rehoning until after it had been used to fell about a hundred trees. ♂♀

Cro-Magnons undoubtedly exploited their environment much more efficiently in many other ways than did Neanderthals. They left behind bone fishhooks and harpoons that clearly indicate the expansion of their food-getting activities to the rivers and seacoasts.

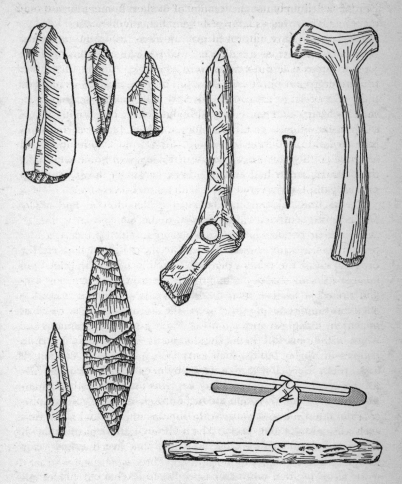

CRO-MAGNON TOOLS

The Cro-Magnons of Europe manufactured a marvellous diversity of specialized tools. Shown here (*clockwise, starting at top left*) are just a few kinds: scraper, knife, drill, a carved reindeer antler with a hole that was possibly used for straightening spears, an awl for the manufacture of skin clothing, a hammer made from antler, a carved spear-thrower, and points for attachment to spears. The inset sketch illustrates the way in which the spear-thrower served to extend the length of the hunter's arm and consequently allowed a spear to be hurled with greater force.

A variety of tiny points for attachment to short spears indicate that small animals as well as large ones were being hunted. And hunting efficiency must have improved greatly after the invention of the spear-thrower. Extensive evidence for Cro-Magnon shelters has been found in areas where no caves were available. Among these were semi-underground pit houses, in which overhead beams were made of the ribs of large mammals, covered with animal skins. Dome-shaped construction thus existed long before the popularity of Buckminster Fuller's geodesic dome; it has in fact been the most common form of housing throughout the world. The dome-shaped huts made by Pygmies, Bushmen, Australian Aborigines, and many American Indian tribes, among others, consist of flexible saplings bent over and then covered either with animal skins or with mats of grass, bark, and leaves. And, of course, the igloo built of ice blocks by some Eskimo groups is a self-supporting dome.

Another invention of the Cro-Magnon hunters is the bow and arrow, a marked improvement over the spear in that it stores the energy of human muscle in the drawn bow. Because the velocity of the arrow depends upon the energy in the taut bow, the most efficient archer is the one who has short arms with thick muscles – exactly the opposite physique from the linear build that is most efficient in hurling a spear. This difference probably explains the failure of the bow to become the dominant weapon among certain groups with linear builds, such as the East Africans, even though these groups are well aware of its use by neighbouring peoples. The archer's ideal body build possibly explains also the aesthetic standards for the male physique among Europeans. The typical European physique – a slim waist with broad shoulders and thick arm muscles – was the one preferred all through the age of archery, from Cro-Magnon times until as recently as five hundred years ago. ♂♀

The Cro-Magnons are the first peoples to leave a clear record of concern with music and art. When Russian archaeologists recently unearthed a Cro-Magnon site in the Ukraine, dating from 20,000 years ago, they found a structure that had been used as a centre for festive and ritual events. Inside it was an assortment of mammoth bones, many of them painted red and decorated with geometrical designs. From the way their surfaces had been worn down through use, they have been identified as a set of percussion instruments. One of them, an ivory bracelet made from flattened rings of mammoth tusk, is thought to have been worn by a dancer, whose move-ments would have caused it to rattle, making a sound like that of a modern castanet.

Chief among the artistic glories of the Cro-Magnons, though, were the superb paintings and carved bas-reliefs they left on the walls of deep caverns. Most of this wall art depicts the large herbivores and other game animals of the Ice Age. Human figures are usually absent, but in places the human presence is indicated by hand prints, by spears embedded in game, and by what appear to be symbolic representations of sex organs. When human figures do appear, they are often very stylized as compared to the realistic depiction of the mammals. Cave painting was restricted to a limited geographical area, primarily in southwestern France and northern Spain, and most of the known examples were executed between about 15,000 and 11,000 years ago, although some paintings have been dated to as far back as 30,000 years ago.

Sculptural representations of both humans and animals originated and flourished much earlier in eastern and central Europe than they did in the western part of the continent. Making three-dimensional representations is technically less complex than painting three-dimensional objects on a flat, two-dimensional surface. Sculpture is also conceptually different because it is portable. Some surviving ancient sculptures were apparently intended as realistic portraits of important individuals. One face, carved in ivory and unearthed in what is now Czechoslovakia, has a crooked mouth and brow such as would have resulted from damage to the left facial nerve. That this might indeed have been a portrait of an actual person is indicated by the discovery close by of the skeleton of an old woman whose skull shows damage on the left side. Because she had been buried with elaborate ritual, she (or possibly her husband) apparently was an important personage. Evidence from ancient cultures, and also from the art of surviving hunter–gatherers, indicates a long tradition of preserving likenesses of persons important to the group. The pre-servation of such likenesses after the death of the individual contributes to the unity and allegiance of the band or tribe. Also found at Cro-Magnon archaeological sites from France to Russia have been unusual figurines carved out of stone. Because of what seem to be grossly exaggerated breasts, buttocks, and pubic regions, they are thought to be fertility figures or earth goddesses. (Some pre-historians, though, have recently questioned whether such figurines

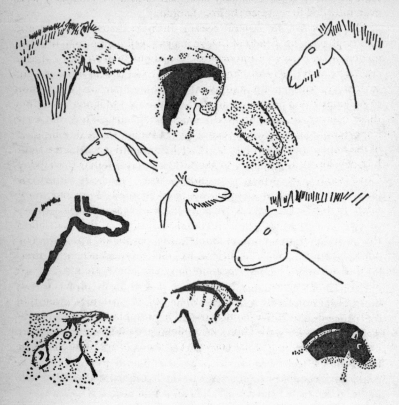

THE ARTISTIC VIRTUOSITY OF CRO-MAGNON

Between about 30,000 and 10,000 years ago, the Cro-Magnon peoples of France and Spain created a great number of paintings on the walls of caves. The truly remarkable diversity of styles and techniques is seen in these depictions of a horse's head from about ten different caves. Some are incised into the walls, others are bas-reliefs, and still others are painted in various shades of red, brown, yellow, violet, and black. No less remarkable is the inaccessibility of most of the paintings, which are either in deep chambers that can be reached only through tortuous passages or in small recesses where it is almost impossible to see them. Numerous explanations for these paintings have been offered: they were simply decoration, or a magical device for increasing success in hunting, or a commemoration of notable hunts, or a representation of myths, or a ritual adornment in chambers set aside for ceremonial use. Specialists have concluded that the Cro-Magnon cave art probably served all of these purposes — as well as others still not understood. ♂♀

were intended to serve fertility uses, and indeed whether they were even intended to represent human females.)

This early art, for several reasons, has fascinated scientists and philosophers alike. Study of the work produced over a span of about 20,000 years may give important clues about the origins of artistic creativity, a uniquely human trait. And because this art often appears to deal with ritual and the supernatural, those interested in the roots of religious belief find much to study in the Cro-Magnon caves. For those concerned with the total behaviour of humankind, the art is important because it marks yet another milestone in the development of the human pattern of life. It is the clearest evidence that the brain had developed the capacity to abstract in a way familiar to us today. Cro-Magnon art differs conceptually from the body ornaments found with Neanderthal remains – trinkets made from mammoth teeth and polished stones that were clearly associated with the wearer. In Cro-Magnon painting and sculpture, on the other hand, the pictorial representations remove the person or thing from its normal context. Such likenesses are the very essence of abstract symboling in that they transmit messages about things that are absent. Furthermore, any representation necessarily abstracts only a few characteristics, using these to suggest the complex thing they represent. A few dozen paint strokes, for example, clearly imply the millions of hairs on the body of a shaggy mammoth. To modern humans, Cro-Magnon art conveys the shock of recognition. These people are us.

# 4

# Becoming Human

No assessment of the hominid pattern can avoid giving overriding emphasis to the existence of human intellect. From the outset, the brain of the earliest hominids was larger and presumably more complex than that of equivalent-sized ancestors of the great apes, and it has remained so down to modern *Homo sapiens*. The human brain today is nearly three times the size of the gorilla brain, even though the gorilla weighs nearly three times as much as the average human. Size alone is an unreliable guide to intellectual ability. The heaviest brain ever recorded was that of the nineteenth-century Russian author Ivan Turgenev; it weighed four pounds, seven ounces. The smallest brain for a normal human being belonged to Anatole France, a contemporary and likewise a distinguished author; his brain weighed only about two pounds, four ounces. ♂♀ In most human adults, the brain weighs about three pounds. More important than size of the brain are its structure and its network of internal pathways. A human classified as a microcephalic has a brain about the same size as that of a gorilla. Nevertheless, microcephalics are humanlike and not gorillalike in their behaviour, and they have the capacity to speak and understand language. To extrapolate from the remains of a fossil skull the exact structure of the brain it once contained is obviously quite difficult. But it would seem that the visual, motor, and association areas of the brain of the early hominids had already moved in the direction of increased complexity. Such a brain would have given the hominids an undisputed advantage in competition with other primates. To be quicker to act, more inventive, and more adept at learning meant the opening up to the clever hominids of a whole new world that had been denied to the non-human primates.

The brains of the earliest hominids carried to an extreme the evolutionary trends already present in the primate brain: the expansion of uncommitted cortex, the shift from smell to sight, and a superior eye–hand co-ordination. These and other trends have produced the brain of the modern human, an organ so active that every minute an amount of blood equal to its own weight must be pumped through it. The adult brain accounts for only 2 per cent of the total body weight, yet it consumes about 20 per cent of the body's total oxygen supply and about the same percentage of the total sugar. If the blood flow to the brain is cut off for more than a few seconds, thus depriving it of oxygen and sugar, fainting occurs. This is an adaptive mechanism that lowers the head and makes it easier for blood to reach the brain without being pumped uphill. If even after fainting the supply of oxygen and sugar remains inadequate, death quickly follows. ♂♀

Ever since the Middle Ages, anatomists have remarked upon the resemblance between the human brain and a walnut. The nutmeat inside the walnut shell consists of two very wrinkled halves, connected by a thick stalk. Because the nutmeat is pitted and wrinkled, its surface area is many times greater than that of a ball with the same diameter. Similarly, the brain is constructed of two halves, the bulging cerebral hemispheres that are the most recent product of its evolution. The hemispheres are connected by a thick stalk of nerve tissue (the corpus callosum), and their outer surface (the cortex) is wrinkled and convoluted, just like the walnut's. Wrinkling and fissuring have evolved as a way to cram a tremendous amount of cortex into a limited area. If the cortex could be spread out flat, it would have almost the area of a page in a daily newspaper. So important have the hemispheres and the surrounding cortex become that they cover nearly all of the brain structures that had previously evolved in lower animals. In fact, together they make up about five-sixths of the human's total brain mass.

Many lower vertebrates, such as birds, lack a cerebral cortex, yet their behaviour can nevertheless be quite complex. Mammals do possess a cortex, but it is not essential to their general behaviour. A mammal whose cortex is removed experimentally will survive in the laboratory and continue to move about, feed, drink, and sleep. Its behaviour, though, will tend to be automatic, stereotyped responses that are not always appropriate to what is going on around it. That the ancient and medieval anatomists knew animals better than they knew humans is obvious from their failure to place much emphasis on a structure so prominent in humans as the cerebral cortex. Indeed, they often underrated the accomplishments of the entire brain

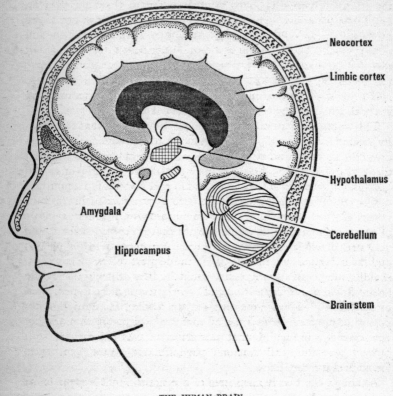

Neocortex

Limbic cortex

Hypothalamus

Amygdala

Cerebellum

Hippocampus

Brain stem

THE HUMAN BRAIN

The human brain can be thought of as something in the nature of an evolutionary onion, with the more ancient features buried in the centre and those more recently evolved making up the layers on the outside. Deep in the interior are certain primitive structures evolved by reptiles several hundred million years ago – such as the brain stem and the hypothalamus, which in humans are much diminished in relative size and buried under more recently evolved portions of the brain. These ancient bundles of nerve cells are associated with the powerful drives and emotions of hunger, thirst, fear, rage, pain, pleasure, and reproduction. Behind this ancient brain is the fist-sized cerebellum, one of the few brain regions to which neurobiologists can assign a specific function. It controls the precise muscular movements which allow a vertebrate to reach out and touch an object accurately, without knocking it over or missing it completely. (Disorders of the cerebellum commonly occur in the elderly and account for their hand tremours and loss of muscular coordination.) The early mammals evolved a primitive cortex, a thinking-in governing human behaviour. Aristotle, for example, believed that the brain was merely a cooling mechanism for the blood and that the heart was the seat of true thought. The awesome capacities of the human brain are now, of course, fully appreciated, even though still not fully understood. Recent research, enormous as it is, has not yet revealed the precise way in which the brain can transform a mere ten watts of energy and some chemicals into novel thoughts, memories of past experiences, creativity, feelings, and dreams – in short, the total awareness of our environment and of ourselves.

The cortex has been mapped by neurobiologists, who have learned, surprisingly, that most of it has nothing to do with such obvious brain functions as vision, hearing, or muscular movements. At least three-quarters of the cortex, made up of what are known as the 'association areas', is uncommitted to any specific task. Uncommitted cortex represents an essential difference in the human brain from that of all other vertebrates. Other vertebrates are, of course, capable of complex behaviour. A salmon swims in from the open sea to the very stream where it was hatched; rodents run complicated mazes; and birds engage in elaborate courtship displays. These behaviours, though, are mostly stereotyped – that is, they are wired into the brain. Some human behaviour, of course, is also stereotyped, such as the infant's search for the nipple of the mother. Humans, though, possess in addition large areas of uncommitted cortex that are not behaviourally pre-wired, that can associate past experiences with present problems, and that can put unrelated events together to form novel combinations.

Although the two hemispheres of the brain might appear to be

cap known as the 'limbic system', which surrounds the reptilian core. The mammalian brain is responsible for many of the intuitive reactions of humans (like identifying someone at a distance); it also plays a central role in memory and emotions. Associated with it is the amygdala, which is an important influence on aggressive behaviour. The key to memories lies in the hippocampus, a tiny structure only about an inch long. People who have suffered injury in this area usually retain information they acquired prior to the damage but they are incapable of remembering new things for more than a few minutes or at most hours. Short-term memory, though, remains unimpaired, and people who have suffered damage to the hippocampus can nevertheless repeat what they have just heard. The hippocampus obviously acts as a conductor in the transfer from short- to long-term memory. Finally, the outside layer of the brain consists of the most recent evolutionary innovation, the neocortex ('new' cortex) of the primates, which reaches its greatest size and complexity among humans.

mirror images of each other, in fact they are not. Modern brain research has disclosed that two very different capacities inhabit the two halves of our heads. The difference between them might be compared to the difference between a bookkeeper and an artist. For most people, the left hemisphere thinks sequential, analytical thoughts and is also the centre of language. The right half of the brain thinks intuitively. Its provinces are spatial relationships and form, and it performs much better in matching one pattern with another, in recognizing faces, and in perceiving the arrangement of objects in space. Strangely enough, the left hemisphere is concerned with the right half of the body and the right hemisphere with the left half – which means, for example, that damage to the motor area of the right cortex could result in manipulative ability in the left hand. No one knows for certain why such a curious crossover should exist. Though the brains of all vertebrates are built along the same basic pattern, only in the human brain has each hemisphere developed its own functions.

Almost all humans are right-handed, which means that this hand is controlled by the left hemisphere. The left hemisphere thus becomes the 'dominant' one. The speech centre of the brain will also be located there, while the equivalent regions in the right hemisphere remain functionally almost silent. The assignment of language and right-handedness to one hemisphere, which is almost always the left one, represents a basic reorganization of the human brain as compared with that of other mammals. It is thus equipped to carry out the very specialized and uniquely human acts of speaking and performing precise manipulations, while still leaving an area sufficient for other, no less complex, mental operations. ♂♀

The location of the language centre in the left cerebral hemisphere applies to all right-handed people but to only about 60 per cent of those who are left-handed. The rest either process language in the right hemisphere or else use both hemispheres. A right-handed person who suffers injury to the left side of the brain may thus lose the power of speech, but the same injury to one who is left-handed may not be so severe because that person's brain is less specialized in its hemispheric functions. Other parts of the brain are often quick to take over and restore the skill with words that has been only temporarily lost. Left-handers, though, pay a severe price for this recuperative ability. They suffer more from epilepsy, stuttering, dyslexia, and mental retardation than do right-handers. No significant relation has been discovered as yet between left- or right-handedness and intelligence, although the intelligence of the left-handed does appear to be of a different kind from that of those who are right-handed. Left-handed persons outperform the right-handed on verbal tests but do less well on spatial ones.

Considerable dispute still goes on among neurobiologists about the extent to which the two halves of the brain co-operate, inhibit, or compete with each other. Some clues have been obtained from volunteers who allowed electrodes to be pasted on the scalp to measure electrical activity in the two hemispheres. In right-handed people who were asked to write a letter, the left side of the brain produced rapid waves of electricity while the right hemisphere showed very little activity. The same results were obtained when these volunteers were asked simply to *think* about writing a letter – or to perform such mental tasks as reading, arithmetic, and thinking of words to form complete sentences. Exactly the opposite hemispheric activity was observed when the volunteers were asked to remember musical tones, arrange coloured blocks, and draw designs. Different tasks obviously utilize the hemispheres in different ways. During most activities they simply co-operate, owing to the 200 million nerve fibres of the corpus callosum that form a thick cable allowing communication between the two hemispheres. Speech and right-handedness are clearly, at least in most people, the domain of the left hemisphere, with creative abstraction the corresponding domain of the right. For many other human behaviours, though, the exact relation between the hemispheres is still unknown.

Numerous ingenious experiments have been devised to determine the extent to which the human brain is symmetrical. In one such experiment, a volunteer wears stereophonic earphones and thus can hear different signals through the right and left channels. The experimenter may, for example, at the same time send the word *boy* into the left earphone and the word *girl* into the right. When asked to identify what was heard in each ear, the volunteer is much more likely to identify words received by the right ear. This test has been performed repeatedly with different volunteers, using not only pairs of English words but also nonsense syllables. Greater accuracy has almost always been shown by the right ear – which is controlled by the dominant left hemisphere. Experiments of the same sort have also been performed with non-verbal sounds – musical notes, street noises, and laughter – instead of words. In these instances, the left

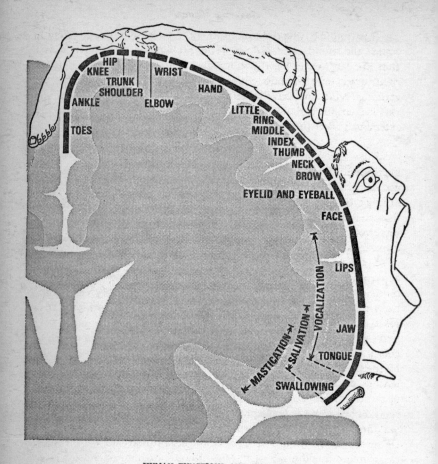

HUMAN FUNCTIONS AND THE BRAIN

This diagram in cross-section of a cerebral hemisphere identifies the various regions in the cortex controlling motor functions – and, through distortion, the relative importance of these regions in controlling various parts of the body. For example, the lips, tongue, and fingers are shown to have proportionately greater importance than the rest of the body put together; the emphasis given by the brain to language and tool use thus becomes dramatically evident in this diagram.

ear (controlled by the right hemisphere) proved much more likely to report the sound correctly. Experiments such as these have shown that the left hemisphere is not the superior one for processing all sounds, but only for those concerned directly with language. Whatever the exact process of separation of brain function between the two hemispheres, it begins at about the age of two and is virtually completed by the age of ten. ♂♀

\*

Equipped with this larger and more intricate brain, the hominid mentality followed a path of development that is extraordinarily divergent from that taken by any other primate. The distinctive feature of the human mind is its ability to create symbols: to bestow arbitrary meanings upon objects and ideas. Human hair, for example, has symbolic value in all human societies, although the exact kind of value differs from one society to the other. From a purely biological standpoint, hair has little utility in protecting the skin of modern humans against cold or injury. It is generally very scant except on the scalp, under the arms, and around the genitals. It is relatively inert, despite the metaphor of 'hairs standing on end'.

Nevertheless, humans have attributed great symbolic powers to this scanty, inert, and almost useless appurtenance of the body. In Western tradition, hair has long been a symbol of very high numbers; witness the New Testament statement of Jesus that 'the very hairs of your head are all numbered'. It has been used to represent extreme delicacy, as in such terms as 'hairsbreadth', 'hairspring', and 'hair trigger'. It is a symbol of uncouthness, as in the biblical contrast between the rough, hairy Esau and the smooth-skinned Jacob. Nowadays, many females make a point of not removing hair from their legs or from under their arms as a symbol of female liberation. These are only some of the many symbolic meanings conveyed by hair to Western minds. Similar lists could be drawn up for other cultures as well. ♂♀

No chimpanzee is capable of understanding the difference between holy water and ordinary drinking water, but human beings are. All humans re-create and transform the visual world around them. They decorate the body, they make drawings on cave walls and paintings on canvas, they carve and mould likenesses in stone and clay, and they rearrange slabs of rock into structures. But no chimpanzee outside the laboratory has ever been known to produce copies of existing or imaginary figures by drawing, carving, assembling materials, or any other means. From the ability to symbol stem all of those other complex behaviours that make up human culture: for example, the setting aside of a day as the sabbath and keeping it holy, or the use of coins or shells to indicate economic value in the marketplace, or the respect for a flag as a symbol of group unity. Until humans acquired the ability of symboling, culture obviously could not exist.

Because language makes possible all other cultural activities, it is the highest form of symboling. Language is a distinctly human attribute. Claims of linguistic competence have been made for about a dozen chimpanzees, several orangutans, and a gorilla, all of which have been trained to communicate by one means or another – but their accomplishments are minimal when compared to the scope of human language. No untrained apes have ever been observed, either in the wild or in laboratories and zoos, to use anything remotely resembling human language. In fact, after years of intensive training, one chimpanzee had learned the gestures for only a hundred or so words in American Sign Language, whereas a human child at an equivalent stage of development has a vocabulary of many thousands of words – and, more important, the human child can combine these into a huge number of grammatical patterns offered by the native language. A human can transform sentences from the active to the passive voice, make subtle distinctions between similar words, and use language to deceive – things beyond the capacity of any trained ape.

Apes are, of course, constantly communicating with one another through a whole matrix of vocal, visual, tactile, and olfactory signals. So far as is known, this matrix is not comparable to human language. For one thing, apes lack the cranial capacity, the neural development, and the association areas apparently necessary for language. For another, it is impossible for apes to speak because their vocal tracts are so constructed as to prevent them from sounding important vowels. This lack is not as trivial as it might seem. It can perhaps be better understood by the comparison of a giant computer with an inexpensive handheld calculator. Both use circuit elements of basically the same sort, but owing to the giant computer's speed of operation, its large memory storehouse, and its capacity to be programmed, it is able to do very many things the small calculator cannot. Human language is like the large computer in that it can process information very fast, and this in turn is so because the human vocal channel uses certain capacities for communication to which the non-verbal channels used by apes simply are not equal. Why this is so becomes clear when the nature of speech sounds is considered. Humans can count rapid pulses of sound made by certain electronic machines at rates up to ten per second. Beyond that the pulses fuse and are heard as one continuous tone. Humans, though, speak at a rate of about twenty pulses per second – and these do not fuse. It is the vowels attached to consonants that allow us to decode the sounds as speech signals; these vowel sounds are the very ones that the vocal tracts of the apes are unable to produce. ♂♀

Language allows humans to transcend the limitations imposed by their environment and by the process of biological evolution. That process required tens of millions of years to produce an amphibian like the ancestor of the frog, which could live on land or water. On the other hand, cultural evolution (which is ultimately based on language) in a matter of decades produced a different kind of amphibian, the astronaut, who is equally at home on the planet or in outer space. Biological evolution had to work slowly, through genetic changes and the gradual selection for survival of those amphibious forms that could live outside water. Cultural evolution, on the other hand, worked through the transmission of information from one generation to another, allowing that information to become cumulatively greater. Each human generation could thus begin, thanks to the storehouse of language, where the previous generation left off, instead of having to begin anew. Humans therefore did not have to wait for biological evolution to alter their anatomy so as to survive in space. Instead, they drew upon language to discover ways of supplementing anatomy and thereby making it spaceworthy.

The vocalizations of monkeys and apes are not truly communicative in the way language is. At most, they are expressive signals conveying an animal's emotional state at a particular moment. Human language, on the other hand, can not only express emotion but also convey information about the entire environment, seen or unseen, real or imaginary. When a foraging chimpanzee comes upon a tree laden with fruit, it responds to the discovery by giving a series of hoots. Such vocalizations in monkeys and apes used to be known as 'food calls'. Actually they are expressions of excitement, which are often associated with food but may also be associated with other things. From the intensity, duration, and frequency of the hooting, other chimpanzees can gauge the extent of the signaller's excitement. The direction from which the sounds come is a help to other members of the group in locating the forager, and thus the food source as well. But otherwise the chimpanzee has really communicated very little about its discovery. A human in the same situation might also emit a similar cry of excitement, such as *Yippee!* The human also has the option, as the ape does not, to say: *Everyone come here! I'm about twenty feet from the river. There's a tree full of ripe fruit. If we all pitch in, we can gather them in about fifteen minutes. But be on your guard coming here because I think I saw a leopard.* Information thus conveyed by human speakers obviously allows them to exploit their environment in a vastly superior way.

At its simplest level, symboling in language is based upon the ability to name things in the environment. Humans assign a particular sequence of sounds to an object – as when speakers of English use the word *book* – and then they form an association between the object and the sounds. The human brain has evolved to the point where it can make a huge number of such associations with ease. These associations are truly cultural symbols that differ from group to group and are not built into the human species as a whole. In contrast, the basic repertory of vocalizations by rhesus monkeys remains about constant, regardless of whether the monkeys are found in India, their native habitat, or have spent their entire lives as laboratory animals in the United States. Groups of human beings living in various parts of the world, on the other hand, are not compelled by their biology to speak in the same way.

Numerous attempts have been made to define exactly the ways in which human language differs from animal communication. One linguist has isolated a constellation of sixteen such features. Most of the sixteen can be found also in one animal species or another, but only humans exhibit them all. And several crucial features appear, on the basis of present knowledge, to be largely if not entirely exclusive to humankind. These have been identified as openness, arbitrariness, displacement, discreteness, and duality of patterning.

Human languages are 'open' systems, whereas animal call systems are closed. Language enables human speakers to be continually expressing things that they have never said before and that may possibly never before have been spoken in the history of the language. The preceding sentence, for example, has probably not been set down by me previously in exactly the same words – or, for all I know, by anyone else either. The same thing can be said of the next sentence, the one I have just written. In short, human language is a vehicle for infinite creativity. Because it is an open system, it therefore is also 'arbitrary'. Human beings apparently are born with an innate capacity to speak a language, but the one they actually use is arbitrarily determined by the group into which they are born. Furthermore, this group has arbitrarily assigned various combinations of sounds to stand for certain objects and ideas. Dogs of the same breed utter a bark that sounds very much the same whether the animal was born in the United States or Finland – whereas the language spoken in the United States has arbitrarily obliged a child to translate that bark into *bow-wow*, and the one spoken in Finland into *hau-hau*. People in English-speaking countries call a certain four-footed domestic animal a *dog*. People in French-speaking countries call it a *chien*, and in the Swahili-speaking countries of Africa a *mbwa*. These arrangements of sound used by various groups within the human species are all arbitrary, and have nothing whatever to do with the traits of the animal being spoken about.

'Displacement' is that feature of human language that enables the speaker to communicate information about times and places remote from the present one. Although a chimpanzee trained in sign language did demonstrate rudimentary displacement to the extent of giving the gesture for *dog* after hearing a distant bark, this example of displacement is assuredly trivial beside what humans can do. A chimpanzee is also manifesting a degree of displacement in its behaviour when it prepares a certain kind of stick in advance of probing for termites. This stick is probably manufactured according to the chimpanzee's recollections of past experiences with other sticks. The chimpanzee thus demonstrates a conceptual recall of past events and the anticipation of future events, but it does so behaviourally and not through language. Humans, in contrast, can recall their childhood or speak of approaching old age; they can anticipate that tomorrow, after the noisy party to be attended tonight, they may not feel well; they can speculate about hominid origins five million years ago and also about the future of their species.

Another important feature of language is 'discreteness'. A rhesus monkey when mildly alarmed will emit a growl somewhat like a dog's – a sound that is indefinitely continued whereas the English word *growl* is a discrete syllable, complete in itself, with a beginning and an end. Each word in a language is similarly a discrete message composed of an exact and limited number of sounds joined in similarly exact and limited combinations. These two components, the sounds and their particular combinations, are responsible for the final peculiarity of human language, 'duality of patterning'. First, the particular sounds that are the basis of each language set up fine distinctions that avoid confusion. The English language, for example, places great reliance on the distinction between the two similar sounds represented by the letters *p* and *b*. In itself, the distinction is meaningless. But the difference becomes essential to the meaning in such pairs as *pill–bill*, *pet–bet*, and *pat–bat*. Second, the sounds can be joined to form units or words, thus enlarging the possibilities for conveying meaning. Each language is limited to between a dozen and five dozen sounds out of the many thousands that human vocal cords can produce; English, for example, uses about forty-five of them. But owing to duality of patterning, each language can produce hundreds of thousands of common words out of the few and intrinsically meaningless sounds it employs. ♂♀

No one knows for certain when and how occurred the crucial reorganization of the brain that made language possible. Controversies about the origins of speech have for so long been heated that since 1866 the Linguistic Society of Paris has enforced a rule prohibiting all discussion of the origin of language at its meetings. Part of the problem, of course, is that since words leave no fossils, any discussion must be highly speculative. Also part of the problem is that language has been regarded as a single development, with no recognition of the distinction between its communicative and perceptual aspects. No reason exists, though, for assuming that communication and perception necessarily developed together. Hominids undoubtedly carried on vocal communication among themselves from the outset, just as many mammals and birds do today. Eventually the hominids would have developed an inherited, stereotyped communication system that used conventional signals, similar to the twenty-five calls used by chimpanzees. A small part of human communication still consists of such stereotyped exclamations: the *ouch!* when one is hurt and the *yippee!* of enthusiasm. A simple communication system of this sort might have developed even in the relatively small brains of the earliest hominids, as it has done in the much tinier brains of birds. Looked upon this way, language – as communication – could have originated early in the evolution of hominids, as a natural outgrowth of the primate adaptation.

The second aspect of language, however – the perceptual and cognitive – is something truly new in the history of life. And it could not have appeared before the existence of a large brain with complex neural pathways. A world of difference exists between the exclamation *ouch!* and the almost infinite number of perceptual–cognitive statements that might have been made, such as *I hurt my head*, *Please get me to a doctor*, or *That pun was just awful*. In other words, a different sort of brain is required to summon up mental images of past experiences, to explore causes, and to describe things perceived by the senses. That new capacity demanded an enormous amount of neural tissue, and it must have accounted for much of the expansion in size of the human brain. ♂♀

Some anthropologists date the origins of speech to the emergence of the first hominids, but such an early date is unlikely in view of the great amount of evolutionary time needed for the reorganization of the primate brain into the human one. Others believe that speech must surely have arisen by the *Homo erectus* stage because they cannot conceive of the possibility of co-operative hunting and tool-making in the absence of a sophisticated communication system. But non-human primates are able to hunt and to make tools of an elementary sort with a limited repertory of gestures, facial expressions, and vocalizations. And as the highly organized wolf pack demonstrates, language is not necessary for co-operative hunting. In fact, speech during a hunt might warn the quarry and thereby frustrate the enterprise. Instead of language, hunters who know one another intimately can rely upon such subtle cues as shifts of the eyes, facial expressions, and hand signals. The Bushmen of the Kalahari Desert, for example, have developed a very sophisticated communication system of hand signals, used while they silently pursue game. ♂♀

That language may have originated quite recently could be a possible explanation for the sudden flowering of culture that occurred at about the time of the appearance of *Homo sapiens sapiens*. Previously, over a period of some three million years, tool-making techniques had changed in only relatively minor ways. Suddenly, beginning not quite 40,000 years ago, new materials came into use and tool types became much more varied; the wholly new technologies that now developed were conceptually different from those used for so long in the past. Cave paintings and sculpture of great beauty suddenly appeared, as if from nowhere. At about the same time, notational systems came into existence in the form of patterns scratched on various objects. Although no one is as yet certain about the way to interpret these patterns, they obviously represent a major expansion in human mental abilities. Furthermore, at about this time, *Homo sapiens* populations were growing rapidly in numbers and invading the continents of Australia, North America, and South America – a vast area of the world where hominids had never previously trod. Something new and of major importance had obviously been added to our species – and that hitherto missing ingredient might logically be assumed to be language.

What is known about anatomy also suggests that fully developed speech could not have arisen in hominids earlier than *Homo sapiens sapiens*. Speech demands anatomical changes that did not occur until the emergence of fully modern humans: a decrease in the size of the jaw and a change in its position, and the exact balancing of the skull on the backbone. These changes caused rearrangements of the vocal chords, the larynx ('Adam's apple'), and tongue, all of which must be precisely co-ordinated to produce the sounds used in human speech. Lacking the smaller jaw and forward thrust of the chin that produced these modifications in modern humans, the tongue would not have had the necessary freedom of movement. And because the voice box has been shifted away from the soft palate and tongue, modern humans can emit certain vowel sounds which chimpanzees cannot. A computer study of Neanderthal skulls several years ago concluded that Neanderthals lacked these and other refinements, and therefore were incapable of fully developed speech. This study, however, is controversial because the small sampling of skulls included was probably not typical of all Neanderthals. Furthermore, a modern human is occasionally born with the same anatomical features that supposedly prevented Neanderthals from speaking – yet these modern humans do speak. Possibly the true explanation for the origin of language will turn out to combine aspects of both theories – the early and the very late origin. Hominids may have long possessed an efficient communication system which did not exhibit the perceptual–cognitive complexities of modern speech before the advent of *Homo sapiens sapiens*. ♂♀

*

The human intellect – with its capacity for symboling, for the creation of culture, and for communication through speech – undoubtedly was central in producing the hominid pattern out of the primate way of life. The intellect, though, did not expand in isolation from other crucial evolutionary changes, but rather from an interplay between anatomical and behavioural adaptations. Tool-making, for example, could not have become established in the absence of anatomical changes: a larger and more complex brain (which produced the specialization of right-handedness and superior eye–brain–hand co-ordination), walking on two legs (which freed the hands for the use of tools), and changes in the hands themselves (which allowed the thumb to be moved opposite any finger). The manufacture of tools furthermore became part of an array of cultural behaviours: ownership and sharing, co-operation in obtaining raw materials, the barter of tools, and rules restricting the use of particular tools by age and by sex.

A large and complex brain was essential for sophisticated tool-making, and so were upright posture and walking on two legs (bipedalism). The skeleton of a four-footed mammal is somewhat like the structure of a cantilever bridge. The mammal's backbone may be compared to the arch and the four limbs to the supports. The rib cage hangs downward from this arch, which also supports the internal organs of the trunk and abdomen. Such a skeleton cannot simply be up-ended into an upright posture because the cantilever construction, which thrusts all weight to the apex of the arch, would then become a drawback rather than an advantage. Instead, the weight-bearing stresses in bipedalism are downward – and so the single arch of the quadrupeds had to become the S-shaped curve of the human backbone. Furthermore, to support the weight of this vertical skeleton, the human foot had to abandon its dual function of both grasping and walking. Having lost the capacity to grasp, in its adaptation to walking it became one of the most specialized portions of human anatomy.

Humans are not, of course, the only animals in the present or past that have moved about on two legs. Birds, certain lizards, kangaroos, bears, and several other species are either exclusively or frequently bipedal, and so were some of the dinosaurs. Several kinds of non-human primates also occasionally switch to a bipedal gait. Humans, though, are the only animals that possess the other distinguishing primate traits and that walk upright all of the time. They also do so with extraordinary efficiency in contrast to a chimpanzee, which runs bipedally by slightly bending the hips and knees and, at the same time, spreading the legs. The chimpanzee's body weight then shifts

Walking on two legs freed the hands for the manufacture of tools – yet most people do not realize that the arms are still used in walking. With each stride, the arm on the opposite side to the forward-moving leg swings forward also to compensate for the twist of the pelvis. (This swing can be seen in the top drawing: A–A′ represents the axis of the body and B–B′ the axis of the pelvis.) Now imagine that both arms are immobilized, as occurs when a heavy object is carried in front of the chest (middle drawing). Immobilization forces both the axis of the body and the axis of the pelvis to be on the same plane. Much more energy must therefore be expended to overcome the twist of the pelvis that accompanies each stride. The female gait is usually similar to that shown in the middle drawing, owing to the wider pelvis of females and also to the belief in many societies that it is unseemly for females to swing their arms. In fact, the undulating swing of the female hips and buttocks while walking has become a sexual recognition signal in many cultures. The bottom drawing shows that efficient bipedal walking can be restored even while carrying heavy objects – so long as these objects are removed from the arms and placed in a backpack, cradle board, or sling, or are balanced on the head. The difference in gait between males and females may also explain why male and female students carry their books differently. Females almost always hold books with both arms in front of the chest; nearly all males carry them to one side, with the arm straight and swinging in unison with the opposite leg. Even though the arms are necessarily involved in efficient

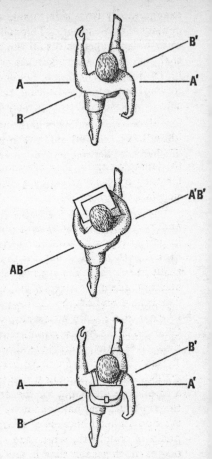

bipedal walking, the hands remain free – that is, they do not have to support body weight, as they do for monkeys and knuckle-walking apes. Human hands were therefore able to evolve independently of the arms and to excel in precise manipulation.

exaggeratedly from side to side as each foot successively comes in contact with the ground. This rolling gait is often seen in sailors, who must balance themselves on the tilting deck of a ship by spreading their legs apart to form a solid pedestal. When humans walk normally, though, the two feet are close together and the body weight tilts forward to the weight-bearing leg rather than being distributed from side to side. For all its efficiency, and even after millions of years of evolution, bipedal walking remains a precarious mode of locomotion for humans. People whose co-ordination is even slightly impaired – through illness, old age, alcohol, or drugs – are subject to damaging spills. Nor are the young and the healthy immune, for they are easily felled by a crimp in a carpet or by a crack in a sidewalk pavement. ♂♀

Upright posture and bipedalism have left humans with what some anatomists call 'the scars of evolution'. The human backbone is an imperfect support, particularly in the crucial lower region of the body that is both the pathway for the reproductive system and also the point at which the backbone, hip, and legs meet. Persistent backaches plague many people, and unusual movement of the body can cause the discs between the lowermost vertebrae to slip out of place, so that a delicate neurosurgical operation becomes necessary. Changes in the pelvis required for walking have given humans their distinctive waist; these have also increased the distance between the lowest rib and the top of the pelvis, thus weakening the abdominal wall and making humans prone to hernias. A further result has been a smaller pelvic outlet for the newborn to pass through, an evolutionary trend that has been more magnified by the increasing size of the human head because of a larger brain. One result has been the pangs of childbirth, which are suffered by the human female to a degree much greater than in any other mammalian species. Another result has been a limitation of the size of the head, which has produced jaws too small for the teeth. Teeth too large in proportion to jaw size are the cause of an imperfect 'bite' in many children, thus requiring visits to an orthodontist for braces. The mouth does appear to be evolving an adaptation to this problem by the gradual elimination of the rearmost molars (often called 'wisdom teeth'). ♂♀

In the face of so many disadvantages associated with bipedalism, why did it become the successful means of locomotion for the hominids? The obvious explanation is that the advantages it conferred far outweighed the disadvantages. Upright posture freed the hands and made them the chief organ of the sense of touch. In fact, the hand is at one and the same time a sensory and a motor organ. It can investigate the environment by touch and then, owing to its manipulative ability, immediately react to what it finds. And in probing the environment, it can do things the eye cannot. It can 'see' in the dark and also around corners because it is situated at the end of a long, flexible arm. Yet another function of the hand is gesturing. It can point out objects, issue instructions and directions, communicate thoughts, and express emotional states.

With these amazingly manipulative hands, hominids began to excel in another major area: technology. Other forms of life use tools, but only chimpanzees, certain monkeys in captivity, and humans make them. And humans alone manufacture tools in sufficient variety and quantity to modify their environment to any significant extent. Tools must have been a necessity to the earliest hominids on the savanna, where they were at a severe disadvantage defensively because they had neither fang nor claw, lacked an armoured skin, and probably moved slowly as a consequence of their imperfect bipedalism. But fangs, armour, and speed are trivial assets when compared to the advantages to be gained from technology. A hefty wooden club wielded by an intelligent hominid must have been vastly superior to a claw, and still better was a missile thrown with accuracy by the most dexterous hands in the animal kingdom. Hominids did not inherit built-in weapons and behavioural programming for the way to use them. Instead, humans were born with an unmatched inventiveness of brain and nimbleness of hand that allowed them to develop technologies that transcended their inherited structures.

The very tools that humans have devised for eminently practical purposes – to kill more game, to butcher meat, and to cut skins more efficiently – probably were superior from the outset because of artistic creativity. And the metallurgy that developed about 8000 years ago was originally not used for manufacturing tools but for making beads and ornaments of copper and lead. Not until more than two thousand years later were the same metallurgical techniques employed to make knives and other useful objects. The technology of welding, developed originally in ancient Greece and China, was used first not to make machines but to join together parts of bronze statues and ceremonial vessels. The earliest known ceramics are clay fertility figures that were hardened by fire; only afterwards was the process applied to making pottery for storage and cooking. The wheel was used first for religious objects and for toys, and only later for locomotion. The great advances in technology would obviously have been impossible without the human urge to explore new directions in artistic creativity. ♂♀

\*

Brain, language, bipedalism, and technology in themselves are still insufficient to account entirely for the special kind of animal that humans became. Many of the fundamental changes that went into the evolution of our species took place within a context of new social relations. Among the non-human primates, every individual (young and old, except nursing infants) is a complete subsistence unit. Once a monkey or ape infant is weaned, it must obtain all of its own food since mothers do not share food with their young. In contrast, human young are long dependent upon adults for food and for many other kinds of attention as well.

The prospects for human children of obtaining essential food and care during their long period of dependency were undoubtedly improved by the division of food-getting tasks between males and females. The designation of males as hunters of large and dangerous animals and of females as gatherers of plant foods can be explained by the two basic necessities for the perpetuation of the band: subsistence and the reproduction of a new generation. Adequate nutrition demands the addition to the diet of animal products, at least in small amounts, because certain nutritional requirements of humans cannot be met in any other way. No permanent society living on plant foods alone has ever been discovered, for the reason that survival is extremely difficult in the total absence of at least some animal protein. The plant foods gathered by females therefore had to be supplemented by meat. Male–female co-operation was also necessary to protect offspring during infancy.

Males who hunted co-operatively were much more likely to be successful than females hunting alone, or even than mixed hunting parties of males and females. Because of the different construction of the pelvis in males and females, males can run faster in pursuit of game; and males in general are somewhat more muscular than females. Furthermore, males who brought females along on the hunt might be distracted sexually. And finally, it would have been unwise to jeopardize the lives of females on dangerous hunts, since they were obviously the only ones who could bear children and nurse those already born. Probably no fossil discoveries will reveal whether any hominid bands regularly sent out mixed parties or even un-accompanied females to hunt. But it is reasonable to suppose that they did try it, since the inventive hominids seem to have experimented with every possibility. For the reasons just given, such bands would have been at a severe disadvantage while obtaining no compensating advantages. Eventually, it can be assumed, any such bands would have died out or would have realized their mistake and begun to restrict hunting to co-operating males.

Once division of labour by sex arose, it must have produced several immediate benefits for the early hominids. First of all, nutrition would have improved owing to a balanced diet of meat and plant foods. Second, each male or female would have become expert in only a part of the skills needed for subsistence and have increased his or her efficiency accordingly. Third, division of labour can work only if it is based on equitable sharing, and this in turn would have operated against the survival of antisocial individuals who attempted to obtain more than their share of food. Finally, the first signs of a tendency to settle down in a single place, even for a short time, must have appeared. Non-human primates are constantly on the move, but male hunters and female gatherers had to agree on a meeting-place where at the end of the day they could exchange the foods that each had obtained.

Closely associated with division of labour must have been that uniquely human institution, the family. Despite the diversity of family arrangements found in human societies around the world, all share one characteristic: specific males are in a more or less permanent relationship with specific females and with those females' offspring. Within the family context, males and females alike have obligations to one another and to the offspring as well – even though the male partner may not have actually fathered these offspring. The situation in which the sociological father is not the biological father is common today in simple societies as well as in highly industrialized ones. In both, divorce is prevalent and the new husband acts as father to the offspring fathered by the previous husband.

Male–female partnership would not have been possible except for certain changes that have occurred in human sexual behaviour. The females of all mammalian species undergo physiological and be-havioural changes around the time of ovulation that force them to seek mates. Among chimpanzees, for example, a few females in oestrus ('heat') will bring the entire group to an orgy of copulation, during which the females mate with most of the males in the group. Oestrus could be extremely destructive to the family if it occurred in humans the way it does in non-human primates. What male would go off hunting to provide for his family if females in heat were around the camp – or if he thought that his own oestrous female might be unfaithful? And how could the permanent male–female bond possibly survive? Humans have suppressed oestrus and substituted a continuing sexual relationship that is under the conscious control of both partners. Contrary to what many people suppose, though, human females have not completely curtailed oestrus. Most experience an increase in sexual desire around the time of ovulation, although a psychological rein is usually placed upon it. Nor have the phero-mones, those sexual odours which in other animal species play an important role in communication between the sexes, been complete-ly suppressed either. Tests have shown that humans can usually distinguish between male odours (which most of those taking part described as 'musky') and female ones (described as 'sweet').

Primate males, like human males, apparently experience an orgasm during mating, but human females seem to be unique among mammals in having an orgasm also. Almost entirely unique to humans, too, is face-to-face mating. (Chimpanzees and gorillas sometimes assume positions in which the female lies on her back and the male squats, but he does not actually lie between her legs.) Face-to-face mating may have arisen simply because lying full length is the natural resting position for the upright, bipedal human – but what-ever the reason, it contributes to closer emotional communication between the pair. This mating position was accompanied by the location of sexual characteristics at the front of the body: the beard of the male and the delicate facial features of the female, the pubic prominence in both sexes, and the female's rounded breasts.

Several hominid family units presumably lived together for pro-tection against predators and for co-operative hunting – though these were probably not the only reasons. Humans, like almost all of their anthropoid relatives, are gregarious animals. In fact, a ten-dency towards gregariousness is probably inherited as part of the human being's genetic make-up. That is because those hominids who lived together, sharing food and co-operating in defence, would be apt to survive longer and therefore to produce more offspring than those who tended to be solitary. The solitary hominids would be likely to fall prey to animals, or to lie sick and wounded on the savanna, without human care. More hominids with a gregarious make-up would thus survive, generation after generation, until eventually they replaced those who tended to be solitary. Since humans are highly gregarious today – and it is reasonable to speculate that they have always been so – it is difficult to believe that living under conditions of high population density in cities is injurious. On the contrary, humans seem to require the wide open spaces much less than they do close physical contact with their own kind. Even in the sparsely populated Kalahari Desert, where empty land is available as far as the eye can see, the Bushmen huddle together into tightly packed camps that are among the most congested places on earth. ♂♀

\*

Anthropologists used to debate which characteristic – a complex brain, language, bipedalism, tool-making, or social behaviour – marked the watershed between the non-human and the human primate. ♂♀ Nowadays, though, most anthropologists consider such debates unfruitful because they all ignore one basic fact about evolution. Adaptive changes do not occur in isolation but rather as entire complexes of change at many levels: anatomical, physiological, behavioural, and social. A change in one part of the adaptive complex inevitably leads to changes in the others. The development of bipedalism, for example, freed the hands for tool manufacture, which in turn made possible the weapons used in hunting to obtain meat. The resulting improvements in diet gave an advantage for survival to those individuals who were steadiest on their legs, and presumably contributed to their mastery of bipedalism – thereby freeing the hands still further for the use of tools. At the same time, since the improved ability to make and use tools also required better eye–brain–hand co-ordination, a premium would have been placed on those hominids with larger brains. But a large brain and a female pelvis adapted for bipedalism meant that human infants had to be born less mature than other primates if their heads were to squeeze through the narrow birth canal. As a result, the period of infant dependency increased and social institutions arose to protect the helpless infants.

All these changes, and still others, eventually went into the mosaic that forms the human pattern of life. Very early in hominid history they produced the particular kind of adaptation – the hunting and gathering of wild foods – that prevailed everywhere on earth until about 12,000 years ago (one that still prevails for a very small part of the present population of the world, such as the Eskimos, the Australian Aborigines, and the Pygmies and Bushmen of Africa). Much of what humans are today stems directly from the more than 99 per cent of their history that hominids spent as hunter–gatherers.

# II: Human Adaptations

# 5

# The Hunting–Gathering Adaptation

Perhaps a total of 100 billion humans have walked the planet since the appearance of the earliest hominids. Of these, about 6 per cent have been agriculturists, fewer than 4 per cent have lived in industrialized societies, and all the rest – approximately 90 per cent – have lived as hunters and gatherers. Only during the past 12,000 years in a few places, and for less than 5000 years in most of the world, have humans domesticated plants and animals, lived in settled villages, developed complex societies, and harnessed other sources of energy besides human muscle. The 12,000 years since the earliest agriculture represent only about five hundred human generations, surely too few to allow for overwhelming genetic changes. Therefore the origins of the intellect, physique, emotions, and social life that are universal to human beings must be traced to pre-agricultural times. Humans are the evolutionary product of the success of the hunting adaptation, even though almost all of *Homo sapiens* alive today have abandoned that way of life. The traits acquired over millions of years of following this adaptation continue to provide the basis for human adjustment to the modern world. Still influencing us today is the fact that hunting and gathering is more than simply a particular means of subsistence. It is a complete way of life: biologically, psychologically, technologically, and socially.

Humans have evolved physically as organisms adapted to hunting wild game and gathering wild plants – an existence that demands versatility, endurance, and strength. Of all living things, only a human is capable of swimming a mile, then walking twenty miles more – scampering over boulders along the way – and finally climbing a tree. Humans about equal chimpanzees in the capacity to pull loads, and pound for pound they are superior to the donkey in toting heavy weights on their backs (as witness the Sherpas of the Himalayas). Many mammals can run faster than humans, but they lack the humans' great endurance. Probably no other land mammal can equal the stamina and the sustained speed of the marathon runner, who averages about twelve miles per hour over a course of twenty-six miles. Nor does any other species equal the human ability to adapt physiologically to the stresses of diverse environments: very high and very low altitudes, extremely hot and extremely cold climates, the virtually sunless floor of tropical forests and the sun-baked desert. Each of these environments yields strikingly different plant and animal foods, yet the human digestive system has no difficulty in coping with any or all of them. And added to this re-remarkable physical flexibility is a quickness to learn, a superior memory, and the gift for creative thought. A human is thus the only animal that can run down a horse or an antelope simply by tiring it over a period of several days – and afterwards decide whether to ride it, paint a picture of it, worship it, or eat it.

Although we certainly would not have become the kind of crea-tures we are today had the early hominids not evolved as hunter–gatherers, modern humans living in industrialized societies are now paying a penalty for the bodies that evolved in this adaptation. During the long ascendancy of the hunting–gathering adaptation, the human body developed certain biological responses to emergency and stress. The large capacity of the lungs and heart, for example, allows a rapid transport of oxygen to the muscles. In the polluted atmosphere of megalopolis, that capacity becomes a disadvantage because the pollutants enter and remain in the lungs. The adrenal glands became adapted to mobilizing the entire body to immediate action, whether that action was to flee or to fight. Hormones, poured into the bloodstream, still release fatty products that once produced energy for muscles fatigued by battle or by attacks on game. These responses are no longer appropriate in today's urban world. A social premium is nowadays placed on those people best able to control their impulses and actions rather than those equipped to mobilize them for physical exertion. As a result, the fat in human tissues is not used up. Instead, it circulates in the bloodstream, where it clogs the arteries and contributes to such stress-related diseases as arterio-sclerosis. After all, the kind of aggressiveness required today to make a successful businessman, labourer, or even soldier is no longer that of a bruiser. With increasing populations and the spread of in-dustrialization, more and more of the world's societies are defining uncontrolled physical actions as deviant behaviour, and ostracizing, imprisoning, or confining to mental hospitals those who cannot suppress these actions.

The hunter–gatherers maintained the primate dependence upon fruits, nuts, roots, and other plant foods, meanwhile increasing the proportion of protein-rich meat in their diet. They thus became adapted to a diet that could be varied within wide extremes. Today, human populations range from those that are almost entirely meat-eating (some Eskimos) to others living almost entirely on plants (some South American Indians). But even the near-vegetarians are not so by choice (aside from religious orders like the Jains of India), for they consume large amounts of meat whenever hunting is successful. The hunter–gatherers who still survive in various places on the planet will gorge themselves for days after being fortunate enough to kill a large mammal – and then go without any meat at all when luck in hunting changes. This 'hunter's appetite', associated with the over-consumption of food when it becomes available, has persisted into modern societies even though it is no longer appropriate. People still overeat as if anticipating a period of scarcity, such as rarely occurs in industrialized societies. Sustained overeating – combined with physical inactivity – is, of course, responsible for obesity and related diseases, which are virtually unknown among today's hunter–gatherers. ♂♀

Because of the metabolism of the human body, at least some animal products are essential to the diet. The reason is that nine (and possibly ten) of some twenty amino acids, which are the building blocks of protein, cannot be synthesized by the human body. They must therefore be obtained from the diet. Simply eating foods that contain one or another essential amino acid does not solve the problem because an adequate diet must provide the entire spectrum of the essential amino acids. Furthermore, they must be consumed in the proper balance and at the same meal if the body is to receive the full benefit from them. Numerous kinds of plants do, of course, contain a number of the essential amino acids, but a strictly vegetarian diet will seldom provide all of them, and at the same meal, as it must do if the body is to have sufficient protein for growth and survival. A vegetarian meal that lacks even one of these amino acids is useless from a protein standpoint, because the absence of that single one prevents the body from utilizing the rest. None of these objections apply to such animal proteins as meat, eggs, and milk. Any one

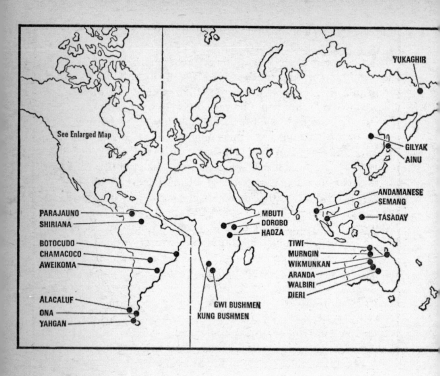

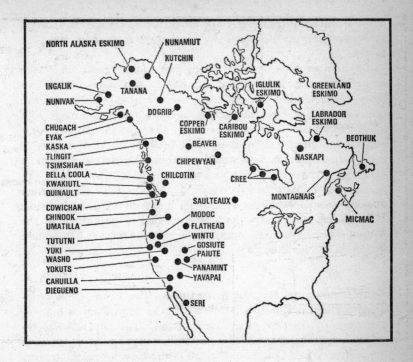

WHERE THE HUNTER-GATHERS ARE

These maps show the distribution of some of the hunter-gatherers who survived long enough into historic times for their cultures to be described by explorers and anthropologists. Most of the groups shown here have already abandoned that way of life, so quickly is it disappearing from the face of the earth.

A survey of the world's known societies several years ago turned up only 74 in which hunting, fishing, and gathering plant foods provided at least three-fourths of their subsistence. The number of surviving societies is considerably smaller today, and they decrease yearly.

of them contains all of the essential amino acids in exactly the correct proportion for the human body to convert them into necessary protein. ♂♀

Yet another development among the hunter–gatherers was a richer and more varied sexual life than in any other mammalian species. The hunting–gathering adaptation probably could not have been successful without the basic change in sexuality that made both males and females continually receptive to sexual intercourse. After all, a long-lasting bond was essential between the male hunter of meat (whose quest for food would not always be successful) and the female gatherer of plants (whose food quest almost always was). The sexual bond assured the unsuccessful hunter that when he returned to camp a female would be waiting for him with the plant foods she had gathered. Similarly, the female needed to be assured of the faithful return of the male, occasionally bringing meat rich in protein for herself and her offspring.

\*

Some 12,000 years ago, the human population of the globe numbered perhaps ten million people and all of them lived as hunter–gatherers. By the time of the birth of Jesus, agriculturists had replaced hunter–gatherers over at least half of the populated portion of the planet. When Columbus arrived in the New World 1500 years later, an estimated 15 per cent of the inhabitable surface of the earth was still occupied by societies following this adaptation, but in numbers they accounted for only about 1 per cent of the world's population. Hunter–gatherers declined rapidly thereafter, and today a mere 0.005 of 1 per cent of the approximately four billion people alive still follow that way of life. The more powerful agriculturists, and after them the still more powerful industrialized societies, have taken over with impunity the lands of hunter–gatherers. Hunting–gathering peoples have been exterminated directly by advanced weaponry or indirectly by the destruction of their foraging grounds, as well as by exposure to new diseases and various other kinds of stress. Many former hunting–gathering peoples have been reduced to dependency on reservations, and still others have been coerced into making the transition to a life based on agriculture and urban labour. The few that still survive around the world have mainly been relegated to marginal areas where agriculture is very difficult or uneconomical: the Kalahari Desert of Africa and the Great Central

Desert of Australia, the tropical rain forests of the Congo and South America, and the arctic regions of Siberia and North America.

In the minds of most people, hunter–gatherers seem precariously balanced on the edge of survival. They supposedly awaken every morning not knowing whether they will eat that day. The quest for food is thought to make their life one of unremitting toil, which would mean that they do not have the leisure to produce art or even to develop agriculture. Their lives are said to be short, forever subject to sudden death from attacking animals or to a lingering one as a result of famine and disease. Thomas Hobbes in his *Leviathan* (1651) offered the classic view of wretched hunter–gatherers: 'No arts, no letters, no society, and, which is worst of all, continual fear and danger of violent death, and the life of man solitary, poor, nasty, brutish, and short.' ♂♀ In this entire description, however, only one generalization turns out to have been accurate: the absence of letters. It is true that no society of hunter–gatherers has ever developed a system of writing – but the same is also true of many of the world's agricultural societies.

Such false ideas about hunter–gatherers may have originated in the deep-rooted prejudice of the earliest farmers against the hunters. The archetypal example, of course, is the spread of the descendants of the farmer Jacob at the expense of the hunter Esau, who as elder son should rightfully have been the heir of Isaac. The Roman philosopher Lucretius took the same dim view of the hunting–gathering way of life, and so did Mark Twain. In *Roughing It* (1871), written at a time when the United States government was uprooting the hunting–gathering Indian bands from the territory between the Rocky Mountains and the Sierra Nevada, he described the Gosiute of western Utah as a people

... who produce nothing at all, and have no villages, and no gathering to-gether into strictly defined tribal communities – a people whose only shelter is a rag on a bush to keep off a portion of the snow, and yet who inhabit one of the most rocky, wintry, repulsive wastes that our country or any other can exhibit. The Bushmen and our Goshoots [that is, Gosiutes] are manifestly descended from the self-same gorilla, or kangaroo, or Norway rat, whichever animal-Adam the Darwinians trace them to. ♂♀

Whatever the origins of this attitude may be, it has persisted down to the present day and is revived whenever an agricultural society wishes to justify its expropriation of the hunters' land.

The facts about hunter–gatherers are quite different from what

Hobbes and Twain supposed. Even though the surviving groups have been pushed into marginal areas, these peoples are nevertheless 'the original affluent society', as one anthropologist has described them. ♂♀ As a consequence of their knowledge of their native flora and fauna equal to that of ecologists, most hunter–gatherers find it quite easy to obtain the food they need during much of the year. They therefore have abundant leisure, much more than farmers or factory workers – and they do spend it in the creation of pictorial art, literature (oral rather than written), music, and dance. North American or European labour leaders who boast of having achieved a forty-hour week for workers are comparing today's conditions to the dismal life of the worker in the last century. These leaders are not describing an advance over the work schedules of hunter–gatherers, who would regard even a forty-hour week as inhuman. Hunter–gatherers work a mere twelve to twenty hours a week, and for many weeks or months throughout the year they do no work at all. Furthermore, the diet of most hunter–gatherers is abundant and nutritious. They are among the best-fed people on earth, and also among the healthiest. Under natural conditions they fall prey to few epidemics such as periodically decimate populations in more complex societies. The mass deaths from disease that have occurred among some hunter–gatherers were due to new forms of infection, against which no immunity had been built up, introduced by contact with Europeans. Predation by wild animals is virtually non-existent. Nor do hunter–gatherers engage in unremitting warfare: the practice of war is so little known among them that often they do not even have a word for it.

That we nevertheless look down upon hunter–gatherers is a result of our own culture-bound conceptions of the good life. We assume that such peoples are on the edge of starvation because their varied diet may include lizards, snakes, termites, grasshoppers, and other foods that we judge repulsive and inedible. We condemn their lack of foresight when they eat through all of the food in their camp, rather than storing some for a future time of need. But why should they store, when the earth has been so prodigal of its bounty for these people who know intimately every plant that grows and the habits of every animal they see? Father Biard in *The Jesuit Relations* (1616) recorded his wonder at the ease with which the Micmac Indians of New Brunswick, Canada, obtained an abundance of food: 'Never had Solomon his mansion better regulated and provided with food . . . their days are all nothing but pastime. They are never in a hurry. Quite different from us, who can never do anything without hurry and worry.'♂♀

Frugality, thrift, providing for a rainy day – these are modern North American and European concepts, not those of hunter–gatherers. When well-intentioned missionaries suggest to hunter–gatherers that they be less prodigal, that they store nature's bounty against a time of want, the response is likely to be laughter at such a ridiculous suggestion. Most hunter–gatherers lack the technology to store meat to prevent spoilage (except, of course, the Eskimos, who live in a natural deep freeze). Nor can plant foods usually be stored, because these peoples lack the pottery jars that would protect such foods against rodents and insects. Were some foolish hunter to follow the missionaries' advice, he would lose out in one of two ways. Since his society demands that every hunter share what he has killed, he would find himself working night and day to feed the rest of the camp members, who would be content to live off his efforts. Or, were he to take the second course and refuse to share his surplus, he would be regarded as guilty of a serious breach of custom for hoarding it, and thus find himself socially ostracized. Indeed, sharing itself is a form of food storage. A hunter who shares with another has earned the right to be repaid at some future time when he has been un- successful in killing game. Efficient storage for hunter–gatherers, therefore, is not in pottery containers or in larders but rather in the stomach of another hunter, who is aware of his obligation to repay in kind.

The fashion has recently arisen among romantic North Americans and Europeans to envy the existence of hunter–gatherers as people who are not faced with inflation and recession, decaying cities, pol- lution, and loss of personal identity. Hunter–gatherers do assuredly live in a harmony with their environment unknown in any other adaptation. Notwithstanding Hobbes's opinion that hunter– gatherers lack 'society', the social group is extremely important to them; much of their abundant leisure time is spent reinforcing the social bond by visiting relatives and friends. And they behave much more rationally than we do when interpersonal disputes erupt. Judging by detailed studies of Pygmies, Bushmen, the Hadza of Tanzania, and others, the principals in a conflict usually part com- pany rather than allow a dispute to erupt into violence. Such avoid- ance is particularly important in hunting–gathering societies because they lack rulers, judges, courts, police, or any other institutions for settling disputes.

Whatever temptation may exist for hunter–gatherers to shift to an agricultural way of life, many have attempted to resist it. Having observed the labours of a neighbouring farmer or herder, they have sensibly concluded that such hard work is unnecessary. Hunter–gatherers feel no pressing need to switch to a more complex economy, which would be based upon scarcity in the marketplace, whereas their own economy is very rationally based on abundance for all. When they are hungry, they simply share in the kill of another hunter or walk a short distance to gather some nuts and roots. When one of them needs a tool, he or she finds it easy enough to borrow one, since they are little hampered by the concept of 'mine and thine'. Nor is status in hunter–gatherer societies based on the accumulation of wealth – as was demonstrated after the discovery in 1971 in a Philippine rain forest of a cave-dwelling people, the Tasaday. The Filipinos tried to press gifts upon them, laying shiny knives on the ground and encouraging each male to help himself. After each Tasaday had taken one, a single knife remained. Urged to take that also, the Tasaday refused, explaining that each male now possessed a knife, and that anyone with two knives would be a disruptive influence because he would be set apart from all other men in the band. ♂♀

The hunter–gatherer's life is thus assuredly not the 'nasty, brutish, and short' one that Hobbes imagined. Drought or other natural disasters might cause the death by starvation of millions of agriculturists and pastoralists – as has recently occurred in Sub-Saharan Africa and the Indian subcontinent – but such events usually affect hunter–gatherers only slightly. They can pack their few possessions and move to areas that have escaped the drought. If they decide to remain, some food can always be found for their small numbers even in the most drought-ridden environment. Such mobility allows hunter–gatherers to regard all of nature as a storehouse capable of providing at least some sustenance, no matter what disasters may occur. One basic flaw, though, is built into this adaptation. Hunter–gatherers are seriously afflicted by what has been called 'the imminence of diminishing returns'. ♂♀ Even a small band numbering only a few dozen persons will eventually over-harvest the food resources within convenient range of the camp. The band may remain at that camp anyway, but it will pay a penalty in decreasing returns for its food-collecting efforts. The people will be forced to work longer hours without the same assurance of success, and each day they will have to travel farther afield to seek new foraging areas. Sooner or later, diminishing returns will force them to go somewhere else.

Mobility for hunter–gatherers, therefore, is ultimately not a choice but a necessity. And migration to new foraging grounds will only transfer the same problem of diminishing returns to a new location. Food will at first be abundant once more. The people will have long stretches of leisure during which they might manufacture a great number of tools, invent new kinds of utensils, and accumulate many of the conveniences of life. But the knowledge that they will soon have to move again makes such possessions a burden rather than a boon. The overriding standard of portability is applied with ruthless objectivity to every possession. All hunter–gatherers inevitably must place strict limitations on their material possessions. And some prune out members of the group who are not mobile on their own: infants, the aged, and the infirm. Since a foraging female can carry only one infant with her at a time, a second born before the first has been weaned must be killed at birth, as are all but one infant resulting from a multiple birth.

*

The best documented of all surviving bands of hunter–gatherers are the Bushmen of the Kalahari Desert in the southern African countries of Botswana, Namibia, and Angola. This is because since 1963 they (in particular one group of them, the Kung) have been intensively studied by an interdisciplinary team of cultural anthropologists, archaeologists, linguists, psychologists, and specialists in such fields as nutrition, medicine, and child development. In 1963 only about 9000 Kung still followed the hunting–gathering way of life; today even that small number has been drastically reduced. Those who abandoned hunting and gathering have gone to work on Bantu and European farms, have taken up farming themselves, or have drifted into towns and cities where they work as labourers. ♂♀

More than a decade of study has demonstrated beyond any doubt that the Kung Bushmen have access to a reliable food supply based on a wide variety of plants and animals, even though they inhabit one of the bleakest deserts on earth. The Kung know when the berries or nuts of a particular kind of plant are likely to ripen; they can detect the thin sliver of a dried leaf that indicates an edible underground tuber; they know when each kind of animal is likely to come to waterholes to drink. Such skills are the common possession of every adult Bushman. Exhaustive knowledge of the environment, though, is only one explanation for the reliability of their food supply. Even more important is the dependence upon plant foods rather than upon hunting as the foundation for their subsistence. In fact, plants provide between 50 and 80 per cent of all foods eaten, depending upon the season of the year. Game animals are scarce at times and the success of the hunt is always unpredictable. But plants are rooted in place and produce season after season – for those who know where and when to look, and what to look for.

The plants that are collected most often by the females are remarkably nutritious. The mongongo nut, which is the mainstay of the food supply, is nutritionally very near the equivalent – in vitamins, proteins, and iron – of such important domesticated food sources as beefsteak, rice, and soyabeans. The Bushmen consume millions of these nuts every month of the year, yet they remain so abundant that millions more are left on the ground to rot. Even more nutritious, although not so abundant, is the marula nut; its inner kernel contains 31 per cent protein and has extremely high concentrations of calcium, magnesium, phosphorus, sodium, and potassium. Mongongo, marula, and other plant foods are particularly valuable because they contain high levels of protein and fats that take the place of meat when game is scarce. So abundant are the plant foods during most of the year that the Kung can be extremely selective about which they gather out of the more than a hundred species that are usually collected. They select only the foods they prefer because of taste or ease of collection, and leave the rest. No wonder that when a Kung was asked why he had not become an agriculturist, he replied, 'Why should we plant, when there are so many mongongo nuts in the world?'

Since the game hunted by males plays a role only secondary to the plant foods gathered by females, one wonders why it has traditionally been so much emphasized. Even though a Bushman hunter's chances of success are increased by the use of poisoned arrows, he considers himself very fortunate if he manages to kill six large animals of any kind in a year. The average kill for the Hadza of Tanzania is lower still. About half of the adult males fail to kill even one large animal a year, and some hunters have not killed a single large animal during their entire lifetimes. The important thing, though, is not the dramatic success of bagging big game but the total weight of meat of all kinds obtained by the hunter. Looked at this way, hunter–gatherers are very well supplied with high-protein meat. Each person in a typical band receives an average of nearly seven ounces of edible meat per day. A human group that regularly eats meat will be healthier than one that does not because it is thus supplied with all of the essential amino acids necessary for body growth and cell replacement. Such a group will produce more offspring, who in turn will have a better chance to survive to the age of reproduction. Furthermore, the social values of hunting are nearly as important as the meat itself. In the absence of hunting, many specifically human behaviours – division of labour between the sexes, co-operation, the permanence of the male–female bond, and so on – would probably not have developed, at least not in the distinctively human way they have.

A nutritious diet, co-operation, and freedom from stress have made the Bushmen among the healthiest people on earth. No evidence exists of high blood pressure, coronary heart disease, high cholesterol, or obesity; no malnutrition, neurological diseases, or attempts at suicide have been recorded; nor do the Bushmen suffer from varicose veins, haemorrhoids, or hernias. Respiratory diseases are very common, however, undoubtedly because of the Bushmen's addiction to tobacco, which they obtain from neighbouring farmers and which they smoke constantly from about the age of ten. The life expectancy of adults is longer than that in many more complex societies, even though the Bushmen suffer higher infant mortality and a higher death rate from accidents because of the absence of doctors and hospitals. About a tenth of the Bushmen studied by the interdisciplinary team were older than sixty years – or approximately the percentage of the elderly in many agricultural and industrialized societies where medical care is available. ♂♀

Nor, of course, do the Bushmen have to work very hard. Males are not expected to hunt until after they have been married (usually between the ages of twenty and twenty-five) and have a family to feed. So, on a typical day, healthy young men spend their time visiting at nearby camps or resting at their own, while their older relatives provide food for them. And most males retire from active hunting in their fifties. The combination of carefree adolescence and an unstrenuous old age means that about 40 per cent of the population contributes virtually nothing to the band's subsistence. Both males and females use their leisure for a variety of projects, such as cleaning the camp or making tools, apparel, and jewellery. But most of the time is spent resting, visiting at other camps, entertaining visitors, or holding frequent ceremonial dances. And an amazing amount of time is spent in simply talking:

The Kung must surely be among the most talkative people in the world. The buzz of conversation is a constant background to the camp's activities: there is an endless flow of talk about gathering, hunting, the weather, food distribution, gift-giving, and scandal . . . Often two or three people will hold forth at once in a single conversation, giving the listeners a choice of channels to tune in on. ♂♀

Much of this talk, however, is argumentative. Bushmen argue in particular about unfair sharing, niggardliness in gift-giving, and the failure to reciprocate hospitality. Over a period of a few hours, arguments will steadily increase in intensity, and soon open accusations fly back and forth. Tempers flare – and just as suddenly, without either participant's seeming to give ground, they are extinguished. A few minutes later the disputants are chatting and laughing together. Part of the pleasure of arguing, it appears, is in laughing about it afterwards. Sometimes, though, an argument becomes serious and may require the intervention of peacemakers. A result of a serious argument is that within a day or so one of the parties to the dispute finds an excuse to leave the camp. In fact, many of the transfers of allegiance from one camp to another can be explained by the strained relations growing out of serious arguments. People simply pack up and go away rather than risk a fight. They have an intuitive fear of violence because they know the social disruption it can cause in a small group. And they know that because of the poisoned arrows always at hand, an argument can quickly turn into a homicide. This explains why the Bushmen attach no honour or glory to fighting and aggression. Their culture is without tales of bravery, praise of aggressive manhood, ordeals of strength, or competitive sports. The violent, competitive, aggressive personality is a misfit in Bushman society.

Bushman personal property is easily portable, and so families can move from one camp to another without effort. The total weight of a Bushman's possessions is usually less than twenty-five pounds, and all of it can be stowed into two leather bags the size of overnight cases. Because they are not chained to the land by the farmer's fixed investment in a home, barn, heavy tools, fences, and cultivated fields, they tend to move away rather than to squabble over property rights. They are free to go where and whenever they choose – to avoid interpersonal conflicts, to join friends and relatives, or to take advantage of the growth of a favoured kind of food. A lean-to can be thrown together anywhere in a few hours, and even a more substantial shelter for the rainy season requires only a day's work. Moving about, though, has had one serious drawback for the Bushmen, and for the other hunter–gatherers as well. Whenever they have come into contact with settlers from more complex societies, their initial response has usually been to abandon the land rather than to fight. By the time hunter–gatherers have learned that they must make a stand to defend the natural storehouses that sustain their way of life, they have already been pushed on to marginal lands. Even the non-aggressive Bushmen did eventually put up a brave fight against European colonists and native African farmers – but by then it was too late.

*

The adaptation of other hunter–gatherers naturally differs somewhat in detail because of differences in their respective cultures and environments. Nevertheless, the Bushmen seem typical of hunter–gatherers in the relative importance of meat and plants in the diet. The typical diet of the hunting–gathering groups of the world consists of about 35 per cent meat and 65 per cent plant foods – almost exactly the proportion found among the Kung Bushmen. A common feature of hunter–gatherer subsistence is a base of reliable plant foods, with meat consumed whenever it becomes available. A joint American–Australian expedition to Arnhem Land, a region in northern Australia set aside for the Aborigines, reached conclusions similar to those summarized here about the Bushmen. The Aborigines were well nourished; adults worked less than four hours a day in food-connected activities; the environment produced much more than the Aborigines used and therefore served as a natural larder; and the people had enormous amounts of leisure time. The same things were true also for the Great Basin Shoshone Indians who so offended Mark Twain by their seeming indolence. Their staple food consisted of the abundant nuts of the piñon pine, which are high in protein and essential nutrients. These and other plant foods were supplemented by co-operative hunts for pronghorn antelope and rabbit; when larger game animals were scarce, the Shoshone obtained their protein from lizards, snakes, and insects. ♂♀

Studies of the surviving hunter–gatherers make it clear that many behaviours characteristic of all human societies developed during the ascendancy of this adaptation. These include some things that have already been mentioned: division of labour between males and females, co-operation, sharing, planning, intensive exploitation of the environment, and specialized technological skills. But other aspects of the hunter–gatherers' behaviour – the ways in which they view their world – have not yet been mentioned. Perhaps the most important of these is the difference in attitude towards space among non-human primates and hunter–gatherers. Monkeys and apes have excellent vision, which is aided by their ability to climb to a vantage-point high in a tree. Yet most of these animals spend their entire lives within an area of from perhaps five to fifteen square miles. They make no attempt whatever to explore the horizons that open before their eyes. Human hunters, in contrast, explore not only the lands they can see from their camp but also those far beyond. In the course of only a few days' hunting, a Bushman will have traversed a wider area than most monkeys and apes cover in a lifetime. Such curiosity about what lies beyond the horizon has liberated humans to take advantage of foods in different environments at different seasons; it has allowed them to flee from areas of drought and other natural disasters; and it has offered the opportunity of finding new raw materials and of obtaining inventions from other groups.

A second important aspect of the world-view bestowed on us by our long history as hunter–gatherers is an altered relationship with the rest of the living world. Monkeys and apes usually move freely among other species of animals, feeding alongside them and sharing the same water-holes. But with the development of systematic hunting by hominids, this peaceful relationship was destroyed. The world became, in the human view, divided into two opposing sides: humans and everything else. Modern humans continue to feel that it is 'natural' to prey upon other animals. Although hunting wild game for food has been an anachronism in Europe for hundreds of years, the wealthy and the aristocrats still maintain reserves where they can kill wild animals for sport. In North America, hunting remains a pastime for millions of people; national and local governments spend enormous sums of money each year to increase the populations of game animals and to stock streams with fish. On weekends, people flee the cities to hunt deer and other game, to fish from riverbanks, and to dig clams at the seashore. They do for pleasure what hunter–gatherers do for survival.

Finally, the hunting–gathering adaptation would not have been successful without the development of an attitude that placed high value on the welfare of others. The social bonds existing in the non-human primates have become even more tenacious in humans. Hunter–gatherers could not have survived their initial ventures on to the unfamiliar African savanna, and afterwards spread into totally new environments around the globe, without the assurance they would be cared for when ill, wounded, or hungry. Although countless hunter–gatherers throughout hominid history undoubtedly died from neglect, disease, and injury, many others must have owed their lives to those who cared for them when they were unable to forage for themselves.

*

This chapter has been concerned with a way of life that is rapidly disappearing. Within a few generations it will undoubtedly be gone forever, except for those reservations and preserves where a handful of hunter–gatherers will be allowed to act out for modern tourists a pitiful simulation of their past achievements. Yet hunting–gathering was eminently successful during the millions of years that it lasted. For the very few survivors today, it remains so – but only for as long as they are willing to maintain mobility, portability, and low populations. If they desire to break free from these constraints, then they must take the steps towards agriculture. Hunter–gatherers, however, find it extremely difficult to adjust to the life-style of this more complex adaptation. Agriculturists cannot be mobile, for they are as much domesticated as the crops and animals they raise. Possessions abound and their differential distribution in the society bestows more status on some people than on others, in sharp contrast to the egalitarian society of the hunter–gatherers. Violence and warfare become commonplace when property in the form of fertile fields and herds must be defended, or are taken by force from others. Once the constraint of 'the imminence of diminishing returns' has been done away with, culture becomes increasingly complex and free from environmental limitations. Eventually the agriculturists become so proficient that they can put new environments into production by irrigation, feed great cities – and even explore outer space, an environment where natural conditions for agriculture are totally absent.

# 6

# Food Production and Its Consequences

*The pastures are clothed with flocks; the valleys
also are covered with corn; they shout for joy, they
also sing.*

— PSALM 65

In the few thousand years before the Psalmist wrote these lines, large areas of the Near East had been transformed from the diverse environments of hunter–gatherers to the uniformity of fields entirely planted to the same crop. The production, rather than the mere collection, of food represented a major reorganization in the human way of thinking about the environment, a reorganization that occurred in widely scattered areas of the globe: the Near East, southeastern Europe, China, Southeast Asia, Mexico, and Peru. That food production arose independently in each of these areas there can be no doubt, since in each of them the environment was strikingly different, and the plants domesticated in each were markedly so. Millet was domesticated in cold northern China, rice in tropical Thailand, wheat and barley in the hot and dry Near East, corn (Indian maize) in the cool and dry uplands of Mexico, and potatoes in the high mountains of Peru. Everyone has learned in school that food production became the base on which were erected such great civilizations as those of Sumer, dynastic Egypt, the kingdoms of Israel and Judah, Crete, and China. In dealing with these dramatic examples, a more important fact is often overlooked. In most of the world, food production did not develop beyond an inefficient subsistence level until the beginning of the Industrial Revolution, about two centuries ago. Even in today's industrialized world, more than half of all humans earn their daily bread through the practice of a very simple agriculture. Although this adaptation is as much as 12,000 years old in a few parts of the world, it is considerably more recent in most. Yet in a matter of only several thousand years, it has had major consequences for the human body and intellect as well as for technology, social and economic systems, and political and religious institutions. In fact, this adaptation probably brought about as many fundamental changes in the human way of life as occurred in the preceding several million years.

Food production could not have occurred without domestication, which is based on a two-way relationship between humans (the domesticators) and a small number of favoured plants and animals (the domesticants). The domesticators profit by obtaining larger quantities of specific foods, and of such new raw materials as wool, than would otherwise have been possible. By encouraging the growth and reproduction of those domesticants whose traits are of value to humans, the domesticators can eventually produce species with useful characteristics. Before they were domesticated, sheep had little wool, the jungle ancestor of the chicken laid eggs only seasonally, and the wild cow or aurochs produced milk only while nursing young. ♂♀

The domesticants may be said to have profited also by achieving greater biological success: sharply increased numbers and a more widespread geographical range. Wheat and barley, for example, once grew wild in only a few environments of the Near East – but as domesticants, they have been spread by food-producers to all the temperate regions of the world. The domesticants have 'made' their human domesticators do for them what they could not do for themselves. Humans clear away competing vegetation and extirpate predatory animals; they furnish living space, water, and fertilizers; and they care for domesticants that have been attacked by diseases or pests. So intertwined have the relations between domesticators and domesticants become that most of the latter would find it difficult to continue to prosper without human intervention. And some plants – corn, banana, and date palm, to name three – would die out completely because they have lost the capacity to disperse their seeds without human assistance.

Beginning about 20,000 years ago, the hunting–gathering adaptation was marked by two tendencies that made possible the transition to food production. First of all, hunter–gatherers began to harvest a broad spectrum of new foods – including wild grains, fishes, and molluscs – which were found at approximately the same places year after year. Humans thus showed themselves willing to experiment with new food sources, which also meant that they were able to settle down for longer periods in semi-permanent camps. Second, a technology was developed for exploiting the new foods. At about this time an important tool, the microlith, appeared in the Near East. It reflected both a part of the broad-spectrum adaptation and a new ability to manufacture complex tools. Microliths were tiny, sharp

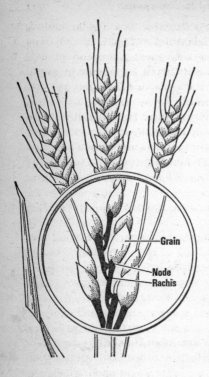

**WILD AND DOMESTICATED WHEAT**

This illustration shows in diagrammatic form a typical spike of wheat or barley. The black, vertical column represents the rachis, composed of many individual nodes to each of which a grain (or seed) is attached. In the wild wheat plant, the grains separate easily at the node and one by one fall to the ground or are blown away by the wind. The brittleness of the rachis is thus a beneficial trait for wild wheat because it disperses the seeds gradually, thereby ensuring that at least some will be released at the optimum time for survival. This trait, though, worked to the disadvantage of humans attempting to harvest wild wheat, which shattered at the touch of a sickle and blew away.

Wheat does from time to time produce mutations with spikes that do not shatter because the rachis is tough rather than brittle. These mutations do not survive under natural conditions because the entire head falls to the ground in a single place. As a result, large numbers of the grains are not covered by soil, and the rest sprout in a dense mass of competing seedlings. Having presumably recognized the advantage of non-shattering ears that would remain on the stalks for weeks, the harvesters must have unwittingly encouraged the spread of plants with the tough-rachis mutation. Since these plants still had grain on the stalks after most of the brittle ones were bare, a disproportionate quantity of seed from plants of the tough-rachis mutation would inevitably have been collected and brought back to camp. Some of the seeds must have spilled and taken root easily in the bare patches of earth that existed around prehistoric camps. We would seriously underestimate the intelligence of our ancestors if we did not also suppose that they, as practical ecologists, could very well have planted some of these seeds around the camp intentionally. In either event, the result would have been the same: an almost pure stand of the plants with the tough, non-shattering rachis. This sequence of events, although hypothetical, would reasonably account for the biological changes that took place in domesticated varieties of wheat and barley. These events would obviously have had to occur over and over again in many places, for by about 9000 years ago the tough-rachis varieties of wheat and barley had appeared in numerous sites from Israel to Iran.

blades of flint, which were mounted in a row on a handle made of wood or bone, thus forming an efficient sickle. That a forager using one of these sickles could harvest an enormous amount of wild grain was demonstrated by a United States agronomist in south-eastern Turkey, where wild wheat still grows in thick stands as it did thousands of years ago. Using microliths, he succeeded in harvesting more than five pounds of grain in an hour. He estimated that a family of four, working throughout the entire three-week period during which this kind of wild wheat became ripe, could easily harvest about a ton – more than enough food to last the family for a full year. Furthermore, chemical analysis showed this wild wheat to be highly nutritious, containing 24 per cent protein as compared to the 14 per cent in the modern wheat grown in North America for making bread. ♂♀

The gradual shift from nomadic hunting–gathering to food production is demonstrated clearly by the ancient Natufians (named after an archaeological site in Israel). Their culture flourished over a wide area, stretching from southern Turkey to the Nile, between about 12,500 and 10,000 years ago. The Natufians hunted wild gazelle, deer, wild cattle, goats, and other large mammals. They also harvested a variety of foods – such as fishes, crustaceans, turtles, and snails – from rivers and lakes. And although the Natufians remained hunter–gatherers in their orientation, they obtained a large proportion of their diet by harvesting wild cereals with microliths. Stone mortars and pestles, which had been developed originally for grinding nuts and other wild plant foods, were now used for grinding the grain, at least some varieties of which were to be domesticated. Even more important, the Natufians lived in permanent settlements which began as small camps but soon developed into towns numbering several hundred people.

Food production was once thought to have made life in permanent villages possible, and thus to have been responsible for the resulting large populations, the rise of political institutions, the emergence of differences in social status, and increasing complexity of culture. Now, though, evidence from the Natufians and others in the ancient Near East – and also from a few contemporary hunter–gatherers – has shown that permanent settlements can sometimes predate agri-culture. One example is the Northwest Coast Indians who inhabit the Pacific shore between California and southern Alaska, where they harvest the rich bounty of the seas, rivers, and forests. Their food supply is both abundant and storable. Acorns are easily collected and stored as flour after grinding; fish is smoke-dried and preserved in wooden boxes. Because of the reliability of their food supply, the Northwest Coast Indians are able to live in permanent villages with populations as high as a few thousand each. They are particularly notable for having established an elaborate culture based on the simple adaptation of hunting and gathering. They are the only such group known to have developed a political hierarchy of chiefs and nobles, a complex social system in which everyone was assigned a particular rank, unequal distribution of wealth, defence of territory, and warfare to gain the lands and goods of neighbours. And their technological accomplishments – as seen, for example, in intricately carved totem poles, large boats, and magnificently decorated utensils and clothing – testify not only to their organization of leisure time but also to their ability to feed artisan specialists who produce no food.

Both the ancient Natufians and the present-day Northwest Coast Indians show that humans themselves were already domesticated before they turned to domesticating plants and animals. Sedentary hunter–gatherers were as surely tied to their villages as they would have been if they were in fact food-producers. They could not easily move their settlements because that would mean abandoning their investment in houses, in bins and underground silos built to store wild grain and other foods, and in heavy grinding stones used to process them. People who make so large a commitment of time and resources clearly display a new attitude: a willingness to bank on the future productivity of a single location to which they have become rooted.

The Natufians and other settled hunter–gatherers are said to be 'preadapted' to food production. (A preadaptation in this usage denotes a behaviour pattern that develops at one time but that may later become more advantageous as conditions change.) Preadaptations can be known about only in retrospect, of course. People who made innovations that came to be of major importance later on did not consciously plan ahead, but were merely filling their present needs. Hunter–gatherers had developed grinding stones for wild plant foods long before the Natufians used them to remove the tough husks from cereal grains. Similarly, the bins and silos that were essential for storing the surplus from food production originated as containers to store such wild foods as nuts and, surprisingly, snails, which were an important food source. Perhaps the most important preadaptation to food production was the hunter–gatherers' profound knowledge about a wide variety of plants and animals, along with their willingness to develop tools and techniques to take advantage of new food sources.

By about 9000 years ago, people in many parts of the Near East were experimenting with domestication of both plants and animals. At Beidha in southern Jordan, for example, archaeologists have discovered wheat seeds that varied greatly in size, indicating that this was a transitional period between the gathering of wild wheat and the domestication of it. The archaeologists also unearthed the bones of a large number of goats which had served as food. Close examination of the bones revealed the significant fact that all the goats were of approximately the same age. Obviously, young animals were being slaughtered for food while older animals were being allowed to breed.

One of the best known early farming villages dating to this time is Jarmo in northeastern Iraq, a cluster of about twenty-five houses which were inhabited by an estimated 150 people. Archaeologists have unearthed a variety of sickle blades, grinding stones, and other tools used to harvest and process barley and wheat. The presence also of bones of domesticated forms of sheep and goats disproves the notion that humans first domesticated plants and only later turned their attention to animals. In the Near East – and apparently in southeastern Europe, China, and Southeast Asia as well – the domestication of plants and of animals proceeded at the same time, part of a single adaptation. Animal domestication helped solve the problem of storing the surplus produced from domesticated plants. It could be fed to farm animals, which thus became stores of meat and wool on the hoof – 'living larders and walking wardrobes', as an archaeologist once put it. ♂♀

By about 7000 years ago, food production was well under way in the Near East, northern China, Southeast Asia, Europe, Mexico, and possibly Peru as well. Sheeps, goats, pigs, and cattle had already been domesticated in the Near East and in Europe, and the guinea pig in Peru. Pottery, which was important for storage because insects and rodents could not eat through it, had been invented in several places by at least 8500 years ago. Farming villages became not only more common but also larger. Forests were levelled and burned; deserts were made to blossom by water brought to irrigate them. Domesti-

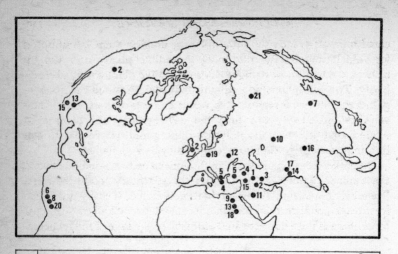

| 1 | SHEEP  Zawi Chemi Shanidar, Iraq (9000 B.C.) |
| 2 | DOG  Jarmo, Iraq (9000 B.C.)   Jaguar Cave, Idaho (8400 B.C.)   Star Carr, England (7500 B.C.) |
| 3 | GOAT  Ali Kosh, Iran (8000 B.C.) |
| 4 | PIG  Cayönü, Turkey; Greece (7000 B.C.) |
| 5 | CATTLE  Thessaly, Greece; Anatolia, Turkey  (7000 B.C.) |
| 6 | GUINEA PIG  Ayacucho Basin, Peru (6000 B.C.) |
| 7 | SILK MOTH  Hsi-yin-t'sun, China (3500 B.C) |
| 8 | LLAMA  Andean Highlands, Peru (3500 B.C.) |
| 9 | ASS  Nile Valley, Egypt (3000 B.C.) |
| 10 | BACTRIAN CAMEL  Southern U.S.S.R. (3000 B.C.) |
| 11 | DROMEDARY  Saudi-Arabia (3000 B.C.) |
| 12 | HORSE  Ukraine, U.S.S.R. (4350 B.C.) |
| 13 | HONEY BEE  Nile Valley, Egypt (3000 B.C.)   Mexico (? B.C.) |
| 14 | WATER BUFFALO  Indus Valley, Pakistan (2500 B.C.) |
| 15 | DUCK  Near East (2500 B.C.)   Mexico (? B.C.) |
| 16 | YAK  Tibet (2500 B.C.) |
| 17 | DOMESTIC FOWL  Indus Valley, Pakistan (2000 B.C.) |
| 18 | CAT  Nile Valley, Egypt (1600 B.C.) |
| 19 | GOOSE  Germany (1500 B.C.) |
| 20 | ALPACA  Andean Highlands, Peru (1500 B.C.) |
| 21 | REINDEER  Pazyryk Valley, Siberia, U.S.S.R. (1000 B.C.) |

cated animals grazed the hilly uplands, making them inhospitable for wild herbivores by consuming the edible plants, and also by causing the land, now stripped of its protective plant cover, to erode badly. The wild plants and animals that had sustained the hunter–gatherers were now regarded as weeds or crop-robbers – and they were extirpated. By this time the environment had become so altered that it was impossible for these people to return to the hunting–gathering adaptation, even if they had wanted to.

One other adaptation was long thought to be transitional between the nomadic hunter–gatherers and the sedentary food-producers. 'Pastoral nomadism', as this adaptation is called, is really not in the least transitional; rather, it is an unusual adaptation all its own. Pastoral nomads raise domesticated animals for the sake of milk, cheese,

### EARLY EVIDENCE OF DOMESTICATED ANIMALS

The first animals to be domesticated were often the ones most commonly hunted. They were also generally the most docile ones (such as wild sheep and goats), as compared with species that were difficult to pen or to tame (such as deer). Cattle are an important exception. The wild ox or aurochs was dangerous and unmanageable, which explains why cattle were not domesticated until comparatively late; and then the original impetus seems to have been their use as sacrificial animals and in other religious ceremonies rather than for meat or milk. The domestication of animals should not be looked upon as a process divorced from the cultivation of plants. The two were part of the evolution of the single food-producing adaptation. As wheat and barley gradually became cultivated grains, wild sheep and goats must have come increasingly close to human habitations. No longer would hunters have to go after meat, now that the animals soon to be domesticated came nearer to graze.

This map shows the areas where archaeological evidence for very early domestication of animals has been unearthed. The comparatively late domestication of the dog is surprising, since for today's hunter–gatherers it is an important help in increasing the number of kills, and presumably the situation was the same for ancient hunter–gatherers. A date of at least 11,000 years ago has recently been obtained for dog bones found in Iraq, but domestication probably took place earlier than that. Archaeologists once believed that domesticated sheep, goats, pigs, and cattle competed with the humans who were attempting to domesticate plants, but that does not appear to be true. These animals thrive on stubble and the inedible portions of domesticated plants. They could be kept out of the fields until the grain was harvested, and then allowed to browse on the portions not used for food by humans. In that way, the domesticated animals would also manure the fields, increasing their productivity. The simultaneous domestication of plants and animals developed very early. Remains of wheat and barley, as well as of domesticated goats, that have been found at Ali Kosh, Iran, date from about 9500 years ago.

and, in East Africa, small amounts of blood that are drained from punctures in the necks of cattle and then drunk with milk; only rarely do they keep animals for the meat. The nomads have almost completely abandoned hunting–gathering, but they have not taken up agriculture because they nearly always inhabit cold or arid regions that are inhospitable to farming. Instead, the nomads wander about with their flocks and herds in the sparser regions of the earth, taking advantage of green pastures wherever they find them – which is something that food-producers, tied to their lands, cannot do with their own domesticated animals. The nomads have never been able to sever completely their links to the settled villages, however, because of the constant need to obtain supplementary grain. A symbiotic relationship often develops between a group of pastoral nomads and particular villages, whose inhabitants exchange their grain for hides, cheese, and other animal products obtainable from the nomads. Sooner or later, though, the nomads usually realize that they have little reason to trade, since they can simply take what they need from the villagers. After all, they possess the military advantage because they are mobile and can launch sudden attacks astride their horses or camels. The Mongols of Asia and the Arabs of the Near East so systematized their raids that they eventually exerted control over vast areas and ruled over cultures much more advanced technologically than theirs. ♂♀

*

Because of the long history of intensive archaeological field-work throughout the Near East, the development of the food-producing adaptation is better known for that region than for any other. Half a century ago, the story seemed a simple one. Food production, it was thought, originated in the Near East and from there slowly diffused throughout the world. The influential British archaeologist V. Gordon Childe went so far as to declare: 'Europe is indebted to the Orient [that is, the Near East] for the rudiments of the arts and crafts that initiated man's emancipation from bondage to his environment.' ♂♀ This notion of the diffusion of food-production techniques to the rest of the world is now outmoded. At least six major centres of domestication arose independently within several thousand years of one another: the Near East, Europe, China, Southeast Asia, Mexico, and Peru.

Numerous hypotheses have been put forward to account for

domestication, and one after the other they have been discredited. The eureka hypothesis is the oldest and least sophisticated. In one version or another, it attributes food production to a sudden blessing bestowed either by a god or by chance. According to the ancient Egyptians, humans were meat-eaters until the supreme god Osiris tutored them in the agricultural arts. The Greeks associated the origins of food production with the goddess Demeter, to whom the Romans gave the name Ceres (whence the English word *cereal*). After mythological origins went out of fashion, the eureka hypothesis reappeared in the new form of the dump-heap hypothesis. Foragers supposedly carried back wild grain to their camps, a few seeds dropped on the rubbish heaps of ancient camp-sites and there took root. Such heaps, being rich in nitrogen, would have produced vigorous plants which the foragers would inevitably have noticed, thereby inspiring the people to plant seeds intentionally. This explanation, though, cannot account for the crucial fact that all hunter–gatherers alive today, no matter how isolated they have been from agricultural societies, possess a botanist's knowledge of the growth habits of plants. That seeds sprout was assuredly common knowledge among hunter–gatherers, and no sudden discovery need be postulated.

The oasis hypothesis also was once in favour. Its proponents maintained that the withdrawal of the last ice sheet caused the climate of the Near East to become much drier, forcing humans, plants, and animals alike to become concentrated around the permanent water-holes at oases. There, an intensive interaction was believed to have taken place and to have led to domestication. Recent botanical and geological field-work, however, makes clear that such climatic changes did not occur in the Near East during that period; in fact, rainfall in many places actually increased. Finally, the hilly-flanks hypothesis holds that humans first domesticated plants and animals in the upland areas of the Near East – but it fails to explain how and why they did so. Nor is it likely that domestication would arise in the very areas where wild plants could be harvested most easily.

Nowadays most archaeologists subscribe to one or another of the various ecological hypotheses. Basically, these all assume that food production could not develop until people had become preadapted to it – a process that began about 20,000 years ago in the Near East, when hunter–gatherers broadened the spectrum of their diet to include small river animals (such as crayfish and frogs), snails, cereal grains, and other foods that were easily gathered, transported, and stored. This shift to a broad-spectrum subsistence would have been accompanied by the other preadaptations already mentioned: sedentary populations, widespread use of grinding stones, and storage bins. Once the people were preadapted for domestication, any change in the relation between humans and their environment was likely to tip the balance towards food production. Just such a change probably occurred when human populations increased in one of the major environmental zones of the Near East: the rich intermontane valleys. This is the zone in which wild wheat, barley, and other plants later to be domesticated grew in great abundance.

The densest human populations would thus have become concentrated in this favourable zone before food production began about 12,000 years ago. It was not here, however, that domestication began. Rather, the increase of population in this zone would have forced some people into less favourable ones: high plateaus, foothill grasslands, and deserts. There the migrants attempted to re-create the broad-spectrum pattern that had been so successful for them in the rich intermontane valleys – and the only way they could do so was by domestication. They would have obtained the seeds of grain from the valleys where they were native because the people in the various zones were in regular contact through trade. Asphalt (used as an adhesive in making tools) was available only in the foothill grasslands, but from there traders took it to other zones; copper and turquoise entered the trade network from the high plateaus; obsidian used for making spear points and ornaments was mined only in certain places and salt was mined in others. Once wheat and barley had been transplanted into new environmental zones, changes in the plants themselves must have occurred rapidly, resulting in varieties of grain that were better adapted to these less favourable regions than were the wild kinds. The ecological hypothesis asserts the futility of searching at any single location in the Near East for the origins of domestication, since it must have originated at the same time in several zones throughout a large area. ♂♀

But what is the reason for that initial increase in population, an event on which the ecological hypothesis hinges? The Bushmen provide at least a partial explanation. A typical female walks about 1500 miles each year while foraging. Because a mother carries her infant with her during its first three or four years of life, her offspring would obviously have to be spaced that many years apart so that the older child could walk by itself by the time a new infant was born. A further advantage of such spacing of births is that the mother is better able to care for each infant individually. And such spacing is exactly what happens with most females among the Bushmen – apparently owing to the long period, at least three years, during which the infant is breast-fed. Lactating females can maintain an active sex life without conceiving again, a reason being that ovulation does not resume until the percentage of body weight consisting of fat passes a critical threshold, between 20 and 25 per cent. Only then has the mother stored enough reserve energy to accommodate the demands of a growing foetus. A nursing mother, though, finds it difficult to amass this fatty reserve because her infant drains about a thousand calories a day from her body. So, as long as the infant is being breast-fed, ovulation is not likely to resume, unless of course the diet is unusually high in fats. Whenever wide spacing between offspring does not occur naturally, the Bushmen must resort to the birth-control practices that are common among all hunter–gatherers: infanticide and abortion.

Bushman infants are nursed for so long because soft, easily digestible foods that might substitute for milk are unavailable in the usual hunting–gathering diet. Among farmers and herders, though, the mush and milk on which infants can be weaned early are available. Mothers will thus nurse their infants for a shorter period, and as a consequence ovulation is suppressed for a shorter time. The effect of a soft diet has already been observed in those populations of Bushmen who in recent years have abandoned nomadic hunting and gathering to settle down as farmers and goat-herders. The interval between births in these populations quickly dropped to between thirty-three and thirty-six months, as compared to the forty-eight months among Bushmen who still maintained the nomadic life. A decrease of even one year in the spacing of births can have a major cumulative effect upon population growth. The female still following the hunting–gathering adaptation might bear a total of only four or five children during her lifetime, whereas the same female engaged in the production of food, with a shorter spacing between offspring, might bear five or six. Thus in the course of only a few generations, a food-producing population would – in theory – have grown to twice the size of a hunting–gathering one. ♂♀

Whether or not such a hypothesis fully accounts for the population increase that accompanies a sedentary life, there can be no doubt that human numbers soared. In the interval from 10,000 to 6000 years ago – a mere 160 human generations – the population of the Near East is estimated to have increased from less than 100,000 people to more than three million. With each increase, additional pressure was placed upon the food-producers to domesticate new species and to invent new technologies, such as those based on the plough and on irrigation. Human beings now found themselves on a treadmill from which to this day they have not been able to get off. They are still plagued by the basic paradox of food production: intensification of production to feed an increased population leads to a greater increase in population.

An ecological approach to the origins of food production answers one question that has long plagued those attempting to account for this momentous change in the human way of life: Why did not food production develop earlier? After all, stands of wild wheat and barley presumably grew in the rich intermontane valleys of the Near East long before domestication began. And excavations under what is now Mexico City show that wild corn was growing there at least 80,000 years before it was domesticated. Furthermore, sheep, goats, and cattle had long before evolved digestive systems enabling them to feed on grasses and other plants high in cellulose and low in protein. The plants and animals were obviously ready for domestication, but humans were not. Some of the essential ingredients for production that were missing until between 20,000 and 12,000 years ago have already been mentioned: a broad-spectrum utilization of the environment, an increase in population, more or less permanent settlements, and a preadapted technology – one that included microliths for harvesting, stones for milling grain, and bins for storing a surplus. Once all these conditions existed, food production could become an actuality.

Many signs point to an increased population as the real spur to food production. Both archaeological evidence and studies of modern hunter–gatherers show that human populations – unlike those of many other mammals, which usually remain in natural balance with the environment – tend to increase in numbers because they have the cultural ability to surmount environmental limitations. For hunter–gatherers, an increase in population would mean an increased work load and the threat of a decline in the quantity and quality of food. The band then has several possible choices. If it is to maintain its hunting–gathering way of life, it might limit population growth by infanticide, abortion, and contraception; indeed, the chances are that the hunter-gatherers are already doing just that. If the band's numbers still increase, it may also search for food over a wider area or move camp more often. These responses, though, demand an increase in the expenditure of labour – and, of course, one band trying to expand its range will eventually come up against competition from others that are doing the same thing.

Usually, in the end, the band has only one feasible option: it must artificially increase the density of edible plants within the gathering area. This can be done through one or more of the techniques with which its members must certainly be familiar: the removal of competing plants by weeding, the protection of plants from crop-robbing mammals and birds, hoeing to improve growing conditions for the desired plants, and the selection of those that are most productive. *In toto*, these techniques add up to a subsistence based on food production. Apparently, however, the techniques were adopted piecemeal over a period of several thousand years. Each one of them must have been adopted reluctantly because it demanded an increased investment in labour. Yet the techniques were adopted, simply because they were the least objectionable among the options available.

During the past decade, social scientists have abandoned as myths many long-cherished ideas about food production. In contrast to hunting–gathering, for example, food production does not provide a superior diet, a more reliable food supply, or greater ease in obtaining it. Exactly the opposite is true. Production provides an inferior diet based on a limited number of foods, is much less reliable because of blights and the vagaries of weather, and is more costly in terms of the human labour expended. Hunter–gatherers made the transition to food production only because it does provide one certain benefit: the ability to harvest more food from a given acreage. Hunter–gatherers long maintained their superior diet by roaming over tremendous areas and by keeping their populations low enough so that the resources would replenish themselves naturally. Fenced into small areas, they would starve to death – and indeed this is what happened in the last century, when American Indians were forced on to reservations that were much smaller than their former hunting grounds.♂♀

What caused food production to begin suddenly in half a dozen isolated portions of the globe, all within the remarkably brief span of no more than several thousand years? The answer is that obviously, at long last, the human species was ready for it. By the time that pattern of subsistence emerged, the relation of humans to their worldwide environment was a different one from anything that had gone before. The species had at last occupied all of the land areas of the globe and, more than that, had filled all the major ecological zones on the continents. In the New World, for example, by about 10,000 years ago the ancestors of the modern Indians had already occupied the forests, deserts, grasslands, river valleys, seacoasts, and tundra from the Arctic to the southernmost tip of South America. In other parts of the world as well, hunter–gatherers had occupied the habitable places of the earth. As their populations continued to multiply, the technology for increasing food supplies through production would develop as a matter of course – especially since earlier production involved no techniques unfamiliar to hunter–gatherers. These same basic techniques for encouraging the growth of particular plants are known to all modern hunter–gatherers, even though they do not themselves practise food production. In at least half a dozen major regions of the world, the hunter-gatherers had evolved to the point where food production not only had become necessary but was at the same time a natural outgrowth of the success of the hunting–gathering adaptation itself.

*

This discussion has so far been limited largely to the Old World, but many similarities in the origins of food production exist between the Old World and the New. In both hemispheres, strikingly different environments – valleys, plateaus, grasslands, and deserts – were to be found, often not very far apart. In both hemispheres also, the foragers passed through a transition to broad-spectrum collecting that preceded food production. But in neither the Old World nor the New did any 'agricultural revolution' take place, as was once believed. Rather, the shift to food production developed slowly, over thousands of years. Nor did that development take place in isolation from the rest of what was happening in human societies. Populations increased, technology became more sophisticated, settlements grew in size and permanence, specialized occupations appeared, and social inequalities became more evident.

One major difference in food production as practised in the two hemispheres, though, was the nearly complete absence in the New World of domesticated animals. The only one domesticated for food over a large area – throughout the southwestern United States, in Mexico, and in Central America – was the turkey. All of the large mammals of the New World either had become extinct (possibly through over-hunting) or else, surviving, had proved difficult to domesticate. The bison, pronghorn antelope, deer, mountain goat, and mountain sheep were not as tractable as the mammals of the Old World. The horse had once been native to the New World, but ancestors of the American Indians helped bring about its extinction before food production developed; and the ox was absent altogether from the western hemisphere. The absence of such large domesticated mammals as horses and cattle meant that it was impossible for Indians to use ploughs to dig up the virgin grasslands. The dog was early domesticated by Indian hunter–gatherers and it was sometimes consumed for food, but its value for this purpose was limited because it is itself a carnivore and thus in direct competition for food with humans. Similarly, the domestication of the turkey in the New World was relatively unimportant because it consumed the very grains that humans needed. The three most important mammals that were domesticated fairly early after the development of food production were all South American species. Although the Andean civilizations obtained some meat from their domestication of both the llama and the alpaca, the llama was primarily a pack animal and the alpaca was bred for its wool. The main source of meat was the domesticated guinea pig, which reproduces rapidly and is easily kept.

A second major difference between Old World and New World food production was the crops grown. In the Caribbean and South America, the staple domesticants in addition to corn were such root crops as potatoes and manioc, as well as tomatoes and peanuts. North American and Mexican agriculture was based on the nutritionally valuable triad of corn, beans, and squash. When eaten together, they provided a balanced diet of proteins and essential vitamins, even in the almost complete absence of meat. The most important of the three was corn. Domesticated in Mexico from teosinte, its wild ancestor, it spread from there throughout much of both the temperate and tropical regions of the New World (although it may have been domesticated independently in Peru). The achievement of the Indians in domesticating corn was really quite extraordinary. In it they produced the greatest change in any crop in the world, and also the widest adaptation to geographical conditions. ♂♀

Nowadays corn produces massive ears bearing many rows of large kernels, but its ancestor was an inconspicuous grass, with ears about the size of the filter-tip on a cigarette. From this small beginning emerged – through mutation, hybridization, and selection for favourable traits by humans – some 150 modern varieties which grow bountifully in a wide range of climates around the world. Today corn is so thoroughly domesticated that it cannot reproduce itself without human help in scattering the seeds, owing to the tough rachis that holds the kernel and the husk that envelops the entire ear. Teosinte still grows abundantly as a weed on soils that have been disturbed. Hunter–gatherers who returned to a campsite they had cleared the previous year would probably have found a teosinte field. No conscious act of planting would have been necessary. The ancestors of the Indians have further been extolled for developing the nutritionally balanced combination of corn, beans, and squash. Wild beans and wild squash, though, grow naturally under the same soil conditions as teosinte, and the beans even twine around the teosinte stalks. In this the Indians merely had to copy a natural model. ♂♀

The origins of food production in the New World were long the subject of conjecture and wild speculation, simply because so little archaeological evidence suggested an independent origin in the New World. Finally, though, a team of archaeologists and botanists who in the early 1960s had begun exploring the highland caves of central Mexico uncovered, in the Tehuacan valley 150 miles south of Mexico City, the sequence of steps in the development of the most important crop of the New World. Domestication had begun there about 9000 years ago, with such crops as teosinte, squash, chilli pepper, and avocado providing about 6 per cent of the diet. The fossil remains of these plants show beyond any doubt that food production was indigenous to the New World. And it had slowly increased until by about 5000 years ago the people of Tehuacan were obtaining a quarter of their food by that means, were already concentrating on the nutritionally balanced triad of corn–beans–squash, and had actually developed hybrid varieties of corn. Earlier sites in which plants were domesticated will probably some day be found in the New World, but for now Tehuacan offers clear evidence of the entire sequence of food production, beginning with the wild ancestors of present-day crops. The claim used to be made that voyages had been undertaken to the New World by boatloads of ancient Phoenicians,

Lost Tribes of Israel, Egyptians, Chinese, Japanese, Greeks, Irish, Welsh, or Polynesians to convey the benefits of agriculture. If such voyages indeed took place, whoever made them would undeniably have been served meals from a wide variety of already domesticated New World crops. ♂♀

\*

More changes in the human way of life took place in the period between 10,000 and 5000 years ago than had occurred in the preceding three million years. Following the initial rise of the hominids as bipedal, tool-making hunter–gatherers, the first great dividing line in human history was the adaptation to food production. Almost everything familiar to us in the modern world came as an outgrowth of it. This adaptation gave humans the basic freedom to develop in new ways – and as a result, the tempo of biological, technological, social, and intellectual change became extraordinarily rapid.

Agriculture transformed *Homo sapiens* from a rare to an abundant species because the need for the labour of even the very young provided an incentive to produce numerous offspring. A juvenile hunter–gatherer is almost useless in the quest for food, but among food-producers even young children can perform chores. An increased population, however, brought with it the scourges of epidemic, famine, conquest, and unremitting warfare. Little wonder that St John put these scourges, which he represented as horsemen of the Apocalypse, astride a domesticated species. As humans increasingly lived together in crowded settlements, in towns, and later in cities, new health hazards appeared. Certain parasites could now become established under conditions that permitted the constant reinfections of their human hosts. Cultivated plots of land which humans trod over and over again to produce crops became a focus for disease-spreading rats, ticks, fleas, and mosquitoes. The birds that humans had domesticated, or which were attracted to the fields, spread bacteria, protozoa, viruses, helminths, and other parasites. Even cattle presented a health hazard. Human pulmonary tuberculosis must have arisen after animals were domesticated, since the most common type is easily acquired from cattle via their meat or milk. ♂♀

The high-carbohydrate, low-protein diet of agriculturists brought with it beriberi, pellagra, rickets, and other vitamin and amino-acid deficiencies. The new diet also produced obesity and widespread dental decay because of the high intake of sugars. A liking for sweets is an ancient trait which humans share with other primates. A cave painting in Spain, dating from perhaps 20,000 years ago, shows people using ropes to reach a beehive with its store of honey. Pygmies, Bushmen, Australian Aborigines, and other contemporary hunter–gatherers also prize honey. This carbohydrate, though, existed in only small quantities in the pre-agricultural environment. It was usually so difficult to obtain that it could not do much damage to human health – until the practice of agriculture made it abundant.

Populations in agricultural regions that had been subjected to periodic crop failures developed the typical 'famine-adapted' small body size, requiring fewer calories and less protein. The human physique also became increasingly adapted to wielding a hoe. The hoe and other agricultural tools used to break the soil depend on different physical features from the long arms of the spearman and the concentrated muscular power of the bowman. The amount of work accomplished with a hoe is in direct proportion to the amount of sustained muscular energy applied during long hours of back-breaking work. The most successful food-getter in the agricultural adaptation is therefore neither the long-limbed spearman nor the broad-shouldered archer, but rather the wiry peasant of small or medium build. ♂♀

Food production both caused and accompanied drastic changes in political, social, and economic life. Without this adaptation, complex societies – the state, the empire, and later the industrialized nations – could not have developed. This adaptation also brought with it a new attitude towards material objects and possessions. Hunter–gatherers shared food, raw materials, and lands – but with the rise of agriculture, the sower insisted on being also the reaper. Sharing became restricted to the family; ownership became paramount; and behaviours previously unknown appeared, such as possession for exclusive use, staking out and defending territories, and the inheritance of property. Since some people had access to more land than others, the egalitarian society of the foragers gave way to increasingly greater differences in wealth, power, and status. For the first time, societies became divided into the rulers and the ruled, the rich and the poor. Wealth and power did not merely appear for the first time; they also became hereditary. They thus gave certain people in the society political authority and social privileges that had little reference to their abilities.

In contrast to the diversity of skills possessed by every hunter–gatherer, the food-producing adaptation compartmentalized skills in the form of highly specialized occupations. Had such specializations been absent, the technological achievements that developed as part of this adaptation would have been impossible. Even a partial listing of the technological achievements emphasizes the debt the modern world owes to the inventors of food production: many new kinds of architecture (temples, pyramids, palaces, irrigation dams and canals, farm buildings and corrals, roads, fortifications), town planning, ploughs and other agricultural implements, spinning and weaving, ceramics, metallurgy, wheeled vehicles, calendars, weights and measures, and record-keeping. This adaptation early contributed techniques that altered the internal properties of natural substances. Clay, earth, and ore were modified to produce pottery, glazes, and metals. If clay, for example, is heated to a high temperature, it is transformed into pottery and ceramics, substances that can no longer be returned to their original state. The humans' new ability to change the very nature of matter must have profoundly enhanced their intellectual awareness and their confidence in being able to serve their own needs. Domestication, after all, involved simply guiding normal biological processes, whereas the new technology involved a control over matter itself. ♂♀

Humans were unquestionably so changed by food production, right from the outset, that they could not have returned to a simpler existence. No foraging economy could have been re-created in the transformed environment from which most game animals and wild plant foods had been eliminated. And the new political, social, and economic fabric was so tightly woven that each individual was inextricably enmeshed in the society. Once under way, the food-producing transformation could not be halted; its own momentum prevented any turning back. Humans had been seduced into what one ecologist has called 'those first fatal steps towards the primrose-lined, ambition-greased chute of civilization'. ♂♀

People in our threatening century often tend to look back with envy on the seemingly idyllic past of leisured hunter–gatherers or simple agriculturists. But since turning back is impossible, we must live today with all the consequences – whether good, evil, or neutral

– of innovations stemming from the development of food production. Our path today is still laid out for us by those innovations, made so many thousands of years ago. The population explosion, the shortage of resources, the pollution of the environment, exploitation of one human group by another, famine, and war – all have their roots in that great adaptive change from foraging to production. We are severely hampered in coping with the ills of today's world by the paradox that the human brain evolved during the hunting–gathering adaptation, whereas our deepest moral and philosophical convictions were moulded early in the adaptation to food production. On the other hand, it was food production that permitted the cultural potentiality of the human species to develop freely. Having become liberated from the limitations and constraints dictated by the environment, the innate capacities of our species could now be expressed much more fully.

Several years ago I stood at an archaeological site in the Near East that dated back to the beginnings of food production. The archaeologists had not unearthed anything spectacular: a small hamlet, in its heyday probably sustaining no more than several dozen people. Some shards of crudely decorated pottery, a few bones of domesticated sheep and goats, a scattering of dried-out cereal grains, tools, and trinkets – these were all that remained after the dust of thousands of years had been cleared from what could never have been more than a backwater in the rush of human history. Yet, undeniably, this is what it was like; this is where our modern world began.

# 7

# The Perennial Peasants

Not all peoples on the face of the planet necessarily pass through the same sequence of adaptive stages. For example, not all hunter–gatherers become food producers before they move to cities; the Aborigines who have drifted into the cities of Australia show that. And just as numerous different kinds of adaptations to the physical environment are possible, so are there adaptations to the social, political, and economic environments such as peasants have made. Few people are aware of how widespread peasantry was until the Industrial Revolution began to convert small farms into large rural factories. Even today, more than half of the world's population – notably in Latin America, Asia, eastern Europe, and North Africa – maintain the peasant way of life. The Spaniards and Portuguese introduced the peasant system of feudal times into Latin America, where their descendants have continued it even after the nations there achieved independence. In El Salvador, 65 per cent of a total population of five million are classified as peasants. The country has long been dominated by a few families who own all the best farming land. The peasants either own unproductive plots on eroded hillsides or grow the food they need on the fertile valley plots which they rent from large landowners. The peasant family could grow enough corn on a rented plot two or three acres in size to feed themselves for a year – if they could keep all of the harvest. But this they cannot do, because a third of the crop must be paid to the landlord for rent. To supplement their income, peasants must labour for the landlord at exploitive wages – for example, cutting sugar cane for only $1.25 per day.

Most North American readers of this book are only a few, or at most several, generations removed in descent from peasant ancestors (either born abroad or born in North America during the time when sharecropping flourished). Much of the behaviour of certain North Americans today – particularly as shown in such traits as suspicion of outside authority, conservatism, and the profligacy of the poor – can be attributed to the cultural influence of recent ancestors who laboured as peasants. In a period of little more than a hundred years subsequent to 1815, the United States received as emigrants from every part of Europe some thirty-five million peasants (or ex-peasants who had left the land to work temporarily in mills and mines). Well over four million of these came from Great Britain, between four and five million from Ireland (particularly after the potato famines that began in 1846). They were soon joined by two million Scandinavians who had fled crop failures and the commercial agriculture that expropriated the small land-holdings of peasants. And still the mass exodus from the land continued: six million Germans, five million Italians, three million from the southern Balkans and Asia Minor, and eight million East Europeans who were displaced by the large-scale agriculture that took hold in the Austro-Hungarian Empire and in tsarist Russia. These tens of millions of peasants came either directly from the land or from the expanding cities where they had tried to make a living for a generation or so. No history of North America or of Europe could possibly be complete if it ignored the attitudes, prejudices, fears, and hopes of today's populations that stem directly from the peasant heritage.

Although peasants are widely scattered throughout the world, owe allegiance to many nations, speak a variety of languages, and display dissimilar customs, they nevertheless share certain fundamental traits. For this reason they often give the impression of being – as Karl Marx once declared with some exaggeration – as alike as the potatoes in a sack. ♂♀ The apparent similarity of all peasants, living at different times and in different places, is of course illusory. Peasants have shown remarkable diversity in the details of their lives, due both to ecological conditions and to such historical events as wars, revolutions, famines and plagues, and religious conversion. The life of a Russian serf under a feudal system in the thirteenth century obviously was not the same as that of a Russian peasant under a Soviet bureaucracy in the twentieth century. In medieval Europe, peasants were legal inferiors who obtained their land through social relationships (that is, by serving a lord or through kin affiliations). By the twentieth century, peasants were legally free and could purchase or rent land – but they were in actual fact still social inferiors, still poor, still semiliterate, backward farmers who lived in near-isolation from their nation's cultural and political life.

Even though it is impossible to make statements that apply equally to all peasants, past and present, in Europe, Asia, the Middle East, and Latin America, a number of general similarities do emerge – simply because as legal and social inferiors in the context of powerful external rulers, peasants everywhere have had to make certain adaptations. For example, large numbers of peasants around the world are associated with four major religious traditions – Buddhism, Christianity, Hinduism, and Islam – all of which differ in their doctrines and in the nature of their religious observances. Yet widely scattered peasants who subscribe to these different traditions often carry on very similar practices. In a large sample of peasant communities from diverse parts of the world, more than half of the peasants have developed closely comparable social systems, inherit land through the male line, base the family on the presence of three generations living together, and carry on similar kinds of interpersonal relationships within the family. They have also developed religious observances that are very similar, including family shrines and rituals that reinforce close ties between the family and the land.♂♀

Almost anywhere that peasants are encountered, they are likely to give the same impression of being conservative, individualistic, prone to suspicion, jealous, violent, superstitious, and unthrifty. Nearly all of them carry on agriculture at least some of the time, although they may also be traders, pottery-makers, and weavers. Their agriculture is of a kind that is unfamiliar to most food-producers in the modern world. To the peasant, the farm is a household rather than a business enterprise designed to turn a profit, as are most farms in North America and western Europe today. The household-farm barely provides subsistence for the family after the obligations due the owners of the land and the wielders of political power are met. Peasants are unlike modern farmers also in that they do not rely on machinery, modern techniques of plant science, or hired labour. The extreme inefficiency of their methods can be compensated for only by long hours of back-breaking labour. Even so, they cannot survive by agriculture alone. In Jamaica, for example, the male peasant tends the crops while his wife travels far and wide as a trader. At harvest time the Indian peasants of Guatemala and the Andes descend to the coastal plantations, where they serve as wage-labourers, and Mexican peasants go northward to the United States to work as braceros.

Even these statements do not precisely define what a peasant is, for many of them can be applied, for example, to the garden-farmers in Sub-Saharan Africa, who are not peasants. The essential difference between peasant agriculture and all other kinds is this: people engaged in it are inextricably tied to a role that is subordinate to external sources of political, economic, and social power. Unlike those tribal groups around the world who practise a simple agriculture, peasants always exist within the framework of a complex society. And they produce the food that makes the society possible. Their labours support the political and religious rulers who are there to protect them against enemies, foreign and domestic, real and imaginary, but who also keep the peasants powerless. Peasants are fated to obey all the arbitrary exercises of power that affect their very existence. They are rarely permitted to participate in national decisions but rather must accept the authority that flows from the society's administrative centre. Peasants are kept personally in the role of the underdog through taxes, military conscription, forced labour, rent, high interest, and low economic return on their produce. The desperate plight of the Chinese peasant was described in the 1930s by a British historian:

... the rural population suffers horribly through the insecurity of life and property. It is taxed by one ruffian who calls himself a general, by another, by a third and when it has bought them off, still owes taxes to the government ... There are districts in which the position of the rural population is that of a man standing permanently up to the neck in water, so that even a ripple is sufficient to drown him. ♂♀

Such has been the lot of peasants in almost all societies since complex civilizations arose about 6000 years ago. No precise record of the origins of this adaptation exists, but it is clear that as states and then empires emerged in the ancient world, they inevitably reached out and offered protection to the nearby farming villages. At first the protection was no doubt welcomed, but not the price that sooner or later had to be paid for it: tribute in food, goods, and obligatory labour on public works. Eventually, when even these were judged to be insufficient, the rulers virtually expropriated both the land and the persons of the food-producers. Formerly independent farmers, they now had to labour long and hard to make their small parcels of land produce enough for both themselves and the ever-increasing tribute they were forced to pay for the privilege of working someone else's land. Institutionalized poverty, generation after generation, became the peasants' way of life; it was on the foundation of that poverty that Sumer, Babylon, Egypt, Greece, Rome, and other empires were erected.

Here and there, in futile attempts to make a fresh start, free of domination by the all-powerful state, the peasants would flee into the wild domains still held by the remnant hunter–gatherers. In the process, the peasants took over the lands of the hunter–gatherers and the herders, killing off some of these people and incorporating the remainder into their way of life, thereby incidentally hastening the decline of the hunting–gathering adaptation. Their freedom was at best only temporary, though, as it has always been since there were peasants. They are forever merely the vanguard, the pioneers who make it easier for empires to expand into the lands the peasants themselves have subdued at the cost of great personal effort. This is the scenario of what took place during historical times in the North American West, and that is seen being repeated today in the Amazon basin of Brazil.

The peasant is distinguished from both the simple food-producer and the modern farm operator by a single, crucial characteristic: outside power is exercised in the form of 'rent', which must be paid in cash, in a share of the crop, or in labour. Peasants are thus at the mercy of whatever outside power has first claim on their production. The outside power might be a political ruler, the nobility, a religious organization, or a wealthy landlord. In any event, the power of the state stands behind the peasants' overlord and will use force to compel the payment of rent in whatever form is traditional. This is as true of peasants in communist societies as in capitalist ones. Peasants in today's Soviet Union, eastern Europe, the People's Republic of China, and elsewhere find the managerial bureaucracy just as despotic as in feudal times. The communist state continues to set production quotas, fix prices, and extract rent in the form of both produce and conscripted labour.

The economic lot of what has come to be regarded as the 'typical' peasant of Europe is documented in the records of a small farm in Mecklenberg, northern Germany, during the fifteenth century. This forty-acre farm produced an average of 10,200 pounds of grain each year – at first thought assuredly more than sufficient to feed a large family. But 3400 pounds had to be set aside as seed for next year's crop and 2800 pounds to feed four horses, leaving only 4000 pounds. Even this relatively small amount of grain was not destined for consumption by the peasant family because more than two-thirds

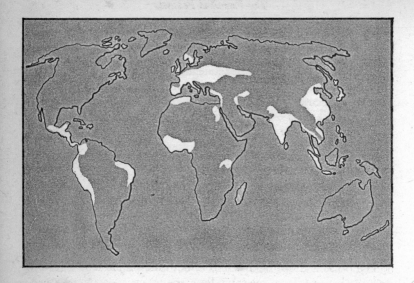

WHERE THE PEASANTS ARE

As the modern world reaches towards outer space, more than half the planet's peoples are still peasant villagers tied to impoverished soils. Physically trapped in a way of life that offers a bare subsistence and little freedom, peasants are also mentally trapped inside a cocoon of customs, prejudices, and beliefs that to outsiders often seem irrational or self-defeating. Shown in white on this map are the major peasant regions of the world today. By far the largest number of peasants is found in China, with India in second place. Even in Europe, the region where the industrial revolution first took hold, peasant life has persisted to this day, particularly in areas around the Mediterranean, in northern Spain, and in parts of eastern Europe. Here peasants endure a low standard of living, put in long hours of work, and spend whatever leisure they may have in trying to supplement farm income with handicrafts. Strictly speak-

ing, peasantry has not existed in most of Sub-Saharan Africa as an indigenous adaptation. Simple agriculture is, of course, widespread there, but before European and Arab colonialism, the vast majority of the population remained outside the control of a wider economic system. (Exceptions are the complex civilizations of West Africa, such as Benin, and those of east-central Africa, such as Buganda.) After the conquest of Africa by colonial powers, rural populations in many places were transformed into a peasantry, but that was an imposed transformation rather than an indigenous adaptation. Although the map shows no peasants in North America, they still exist in isolated pockets – and formerly they were widespread as sharecroppers in the southern United States, in French-speaking Canada, and on the reservations inhabited by some Indian tribes.

had to be paid as rent to the lord who maintained jurisdiction over the land. A mere 1300 pounds of the harvest remained to feed the family, which meant a daily *per capita* ration of only 1600 calories, far below the minimum daily requirement. To sustain life, therefore, the peasant was forced to seek additional sources of calories, such as working yet more hours in his own garden. ♂♀ No wonder that the life of peasants is unremitting drudgery as they try to produce enough to feed themselves, pay rent to an overlord, put aside seed for next year's crop, and feed domestic animals.

No wonder, either, that over the centuries peasants have been of small stature, simply because those most likely to survive have been those with a low requirement of calories. The peasant diet is unique among the basic human adaptations in that it contains almost no animal protein. The idea of a peasant having meat was a revolutionary one in 1589, when Henry IV promised his subjects on being crowned king of France, 'If God grants me the usual length of life, I hope to make France so prosperous that every peasant will have a chicken in his pot on Sunday.' Promises to peasants, though, are rarely realized. Though King Henry lived for twenty-one years more, longer than usual for his time, what he gave to France was mainly a succession of wars – for which the peasants supplied the cannon fodder – and the absolute monarchy whose vices led to its fall in 1792. But at least King Henry did recognize that the peasant family was in real dietary difficulties, as it still is. A peasant family might occasionally have an egg or a small piece of meat, but on the whole it subsists on plant foods, which rarely contain the full allotment of the essential amino acids. The problem of diet is further compounded by the kind of crops peasants must grow. Corn, potatoes, and bananas are well adapted to growth in the environments in which peasants are most numerous, but by itself each of these crops is a poor source of essential amino acids. The lack of a suitable diet is made even more acute by the intestinal parasites many peasants harbour as a result of inadequate sanitation and medical care. Their basically poor diet, accordingly, must feed not only themselves but the parasites inside their bodies as well.

The human body adapts to protein deficiency by a delay in the growth of the skeleton and a slower maturation. The lack of protein eventually produces the small, wiry physique seen in peasants around the world, but it acts through different mechanisms in males and in females (apparently because of their different hormones). Males do not reach mature growth until their middle twenties, in contrast to the maturity by age nineteen seen in North America and western Europe. Peasant females are at least as malnourished as males but, strangely enough, their growth curve more closely follows that of the well-nourished in other adaptations. They attain physical maturity at an early age and they even maintain a reserve of amino acids in their muscles, thus making possible the carrying of a foetus despite the lack of sufficient protein in the diet. They can, therefore, reproduce at an early age – so long as they remain small and thereby lessen their demands on the meagre protein supply. Those peasants with the greatest chance to survive and eventually to produce children of their own are thus the smaller individuals. With time, the greater reproductive success of the smaller members of the peasant population over the larger results in populations of almost uniformly small size. ♂♀

*

Some historians and economists have asserted that duties, rights, and obligations are balanced between the peasant and the external power – in other words, that peasants receive benefits approximately equal to the payments made. In the fourteenth-century English allegorical poem *Piers Plowman*, the mutual privileges and obligations between the lord and the peasant are stated by Piers, who promises to 'sweat and sow for us both' so long as the lord continues to 'keep holy church and myself from wasters and wicked men'. During feudal times in Europe, the lords indeed offered numerous services to peasants: military defence against invaders, police protection against crop-robbers, a system of justice to resolve disputes with other peasants, use of the lord's land for raising crops, emergency provisions of food in times of crop failure, and presents at Christmas and other holidays. The obligations of the lord were certainly numerous, but they failed to include the one thing that would have afforded the peasants more than a miserable existence: land free from the payment of rent. So long as an outside power maintains – in the name of the state, of privileged nobles, of a religious organization, or of large landowners – a monopoly on free access to land, then peasantry must exist. A genuine land reform that distributes ownership of the land to the peasants would solve almost all of their problems – but throughout history very few such reforms have been made.

Peasants at all times and in all places, almost without exception, have had an inferior status – legally, politically, socially, and economically. In medieval Europe, for example, they were prohibited from changing their place of residence and restrictions were placed on the kinds of weapons, clothing, and adornments they could use and wear, and even on the foods they were allowed to eat. Peasants were not allowed to grind their own grain, to sell their own beasts, or to give their own daughters in marriage without first obtaining permission of their lord. This subservient position of peasants in society has produced behaviour that often appears irrational, uneconomical, and ultimately self-defeating. Any North American who visits a foreign peasant community immediately becomes aware of an almost total lack of public-spirited undertakings. There is no equivalent of the Red Cross, the Community Chest, the Future Farmers of America, Boy and Girl Scouts, Rotarians, or other such service organizations. No Chamber of Commerce proposes betterment projects and no church group sponsors a benefit for a local charity. Some children in peasant villages do go to school, but among their elders no such thing as a Parent–Teacher Association exists. ♂♀

Peasants frustrate all attempts by national governments to get them to increase agricultural production through the use of modern technology. And while seemingly making no attempt to lift themselves out of inherited poverty, they even worsen the situation by rejecting birth-control measures. Furthermore, they allow a large percentage of the children they produce to die prematurely by stubbornly refusing to accept health services provided by the national government. Many of the ills besetting them could obviously be cured by co-operation and the exercise of local leadership, but the peasants remain tenaciously individualistic. Well-intentioned outsiders – such as Peace Corps or United Nations workers who come to the village and attempt to provide such leadership – are viewed as potentially dangerous, criticized, and gossiped about, and sometimes assaulted. A widespread peasant strategy in contacts with outsiders is to play dumb, preferring this to being swindled by a representative of the external powers. Or an outsider will be replied to in words that mean 'Yes, I'll do it tomorrow'; with Spanish-speaking peasants it is *mañana*, with Italian ones *domani*, with German ones *morgen*, and the Amhara of Ethiopia say *eshi naga*. As if all this were not irrational enough, one further thing bewilders outsiders. As soon as peasants have acquired a small surplus through hard work or good fortune, they spend the entire amount profligately on one grand fiesta or ceremonial.

Why is it, we may wonder, that the peasants do nothing to better themselves? Some scholars have concluded that they are too desperately poor to have time for social co-operation or for political agitation. Others have attributed the inaction to their being as impassive as their donkeys and oxen. Still others explain that the peasants have been exploited for so long by the upper classes that they would never join their social superiors in any venture, for fear of being cheated. Each of these statements is true to some extent, but none by itself can account for the peasants' disregard of their own welfare. The peasants may be poor, but each could afford a day or so of voluntary labour for such community projects as repairing a schoolhouse. Impassive they may be also, but they are far less so than is usually thought. Scarcely a peasant can be found who in private conversation is not articulate about the ills of this world and about what steps might be taken to correct them. And if the peasants so mistrust the upper classes, why then do they not band together? Obviously, none of the above explanations entirely accounts for their acting as they do.

Their behaviour is not irrational at all, given the realities of their existence. In fact, the attitude of peasants is probably the only one possible for them. A modern observer of peasant life has defined their adaptation in terms of 'the image of limited good'. ♂♀ In other words, peasants view their total environment as one in which all the good things of life – land, wealth, power, friendship, sex, health, and honour – exist in only limited quantities. As they see it, the limitation exists for two reasons: there are more of themselves than there are of good things, and they consider themselves powerless to increase the quantities available. Peasants have unconsciously extended a truth about the limited nature of their arable land to include all aspects of life. Like the land itself, good things can be divided and their ownership changed – but they cannot be increased.

Because not enough good exists to go around, a peasant family can improve its position only at the expense of other families in the community. A family that actively works to improve its lot thus represents a threat; whatever extra good it obtains must inevitably be taken from someone else. Peasants consequently regard modern farming techniques as ways to deprive others of their rightful share of wealth rather than as ways to increase productivity and thus to create new wealth. Even enlightened peasants realize that they cannot modernize, although they understand the advantages in doing so, simply because the other villagers would see it as taking unfair advantage if they were to augment their share of the limited good. The peasant belief that everything desirable is limited lies behind the social behaviour that to outsiders often appears ludicrous, pathetic, or maddening.

True friendship is included among the scarce goods, and to ensure at least a minimum of it peasants try to form a long-lasting relationship with a close friend. Similarly, honour and manliness (the well-known *machismo* of Latin American peasants and the *philotimo* of Greek peasants) exist only in limited quantities. Constant vigilance is therefore required to prevent loss of any amount of manliness – which explains the male peasant's sensitivity to insults and his violent reaction to real or imagined affronts to his honour. The list of goods that are considered scarce is a long one, and it even includes health. The supply of blood itself is thought to be limited, and thus to give a transfusion would mean that the donor had parted with a non-renewable good.

No wonder, then, that peasant behaviour is characterized by extreme individualism and the absence of co-operation. To co-operate, peasants would have to delegate authority – but no one wishes to assume leadership lest gossiping neighbours complain that their own share of authority is being taken away from them. In thus shirking community responsibilities that might thrust them into prominence, peasants deprive their own community of the leadership essential for breaking the cycle of poverty. They pay no immediate penalty for their lack of co-operation, as do hunter–gatherers (whose very survival may depend upon it) or people living in modern societies (whose complex political, social, and economic systems could not function without it). The peasant family can manage very well without co-operation because it is a nearly self-sufficient unit. It produces almost all of its own food, uses only family members for labour on the farm, makes its own clothes and most household utensils, and carries its own produce to market. Most families feel that rather than waste time on co-operation they should spend it in vigilance to make sure that they obtain exactly their share of the scarce good things. The family must not fall behind, but it must also not appear to improve its relative position lest that arouse suspicion and jealousy. Outsiders who visit a peasant village are usually struck by what appears to be uniformity of housing and attire (such as the plain black dresses of Spanish, Italian, and Greek peasant women and the trousers and shirts of white cotton twill worn by Latin American men).

Peasant families make a desperate effort to guarantee for themselves their proportionate share of the limited good through the sheer number of children they produce. From the standpoint of the peasant, it makes eminent good sense to have many children. In fact, almost everything in their experience goes against the opinion that small families are advantageous. Because the mortality of peasant children has traditionally been high, large numbers of them are a form of insurance that at least some will survive. Even young children can do chores both inside and outside the house. As the younger children grow up, some of the older ones can be spared from the land to take up employment elsewhere and contribute their wages to the family's well-being (as do the braceros who annually cross into the United States from Mexico). The peasant couple realize that the more sons they produce, the greater the chance that a few will survive to care for them in sickness and old age. In the process of producing many sons, of course, many daughters might also be brought into the world. But daughters will eventually marry and provide a wide network of sons-in-law, who with their kin can be called upon for support in time of need. From almost every point of view, the peasant's logic is unassailable: the rich agriculturist can invest in farm machinery but the poor peasant can invest only in children. ♂♀

Numerous children do not represent the crushing financial burden to peasants that might be imagined. The high cost of having children is a Western phenomenon; quite the opposite is true in the rest of the world, where children produce economic benefits while still young. A study of Javanese peasant families has shown that children from large families actually accomplish more productive work in agriculture than those from small families. Even at an early age, they can care for and feed animals, keep birds away from crops, and cut grass or gather firewood. In other words, the more children a peasant has, the more work that is found for them to do and the more productive they become. This increased productivity is accounted for by two things. A young child with older siblings is encouraged by them to perform tasks at an earlier age than might otherwise be expected; and the elder siblings, because younger ones can relieve them of chores around the house, are freed to engage in more productive agricultural work.

For such reasons, birth-control campaigns – aimed at proving to the Javanese peasant that limiting the number of children benefits the parents – have been doomed to failure. The contention simply is not true – and the peasants know it. No comparable studies have been made of productivity when the Javanese peasant family migrates to the city. At first thought, it might seem that the children would have fewer avenues for productive labour in the city. A family with many children would therefore apparently be penalized because the children's productivity does not equal the cost of their keep. Yet the impression of visitors to Jakarta and other cities is that the streets are teeming with young children who shine shoes, collect cigarette butts for 'recycling', sell old magazines and other items, or simply beg. ♂♀

But what if peasants were made to understand that child mortality need not be? What if the national government provided rural hospitals and doctors? Aside from the fact that most governments where peasants are numerous cannot afford the necessary social programmes, any such attempt would immediately encounter the underlying suspicion of peasants against anything done for them by outside powers. Rather than go to a hospital, peasants will stay at home, ailing with a disease that could easily be cured, and wonder what trick their overlords were plotting when they decided to build a hospital. Peasants have been victimized for so long that little hope exists of getting them to believe in any programme designed for their benefit. Their suspicions prove true often enough to confirm them in their reluctance to trust outsiders. Peasants in an Indian community in Ecuador finally overcame their suspicion of the national government and adopted a new breed of sheep superior to the kind that had traditionally been raised there. Wool production did indeed improve markedly – to such an extent that the more dominant mestizos (people of mixed European and Indian descent) began stealing the sheep from the peasants, who thus soon found themselves much worse off than before. ♂♀

*

An economic system in which it is impossible for a landless family to obtain land, or for a small landowner to become a large landowner, will obviously place no premium on thrift, hard work, and other capitalistic virtues. Such virtues are clearly irrelevant in a peasant society. Why be thrifty when the economy rarely produces a surplus – and if you know, moreover, that even when it does, your wealth will provoke suspicion and envy? Why exercise foresight and plan for a rainy day in a world subject to the caprices of outside powers? The peasant who yearns to become rich must either leave the land and place himself at the mercy of those powers, or remain a peasant and find ways to tap the wealth of outsiders. Wealth acquired from outside the village does not arouse suspicion and fear because, having been brought in from elsewhere, it does not reduce the limited quantity of good things in the peasant's own village. The wages brought back each year by hundreds of thousands of Mexican peasants who go to work on farms in the United States is not criticized since clearly it was not accumulated at the expense of anyone in the village.

The second way to accumulate wealth is through luck. Clever peasants seek to put themselves in a position where luck might strike – which explains the popularity of the national lottery among peasants (and also of off-track betting and 'playing the numbers' among the poor in industrialized societies). Peasants often try to be where the rich tourists are in the hopes of selling a handicraft far above its usual price, of performing a service and being rewarded, or of stealing a camera or a transistor radio. Sometimes, though, peasants whose thrift, intelligence, or hard work has made them wealthy concoct a story to explain away their good fortune and thereby avoid suspicion. Such explanations often take the form of fanciful tales: the discovery of buried treasure, a reward from a rich tourist, or a gift from a supernatural being. Treasure tales have thus become a staple of peasant societies around the world; the sophisticated parents in North America and Europe who today read folk stories to their children are seldom aware of the peasant roots of these tales.

Whatever the origins of a peasant's newly gotten wealth, subtle sanctions are soon brought to bear in the community to restore the balance. Gossip becomes widespread, and accusations may be made of trafficking with demons or of other preternatural goings on. Pressure will be exerted for speedy consumption, for sharing the new wealth with relatives and friends and even with mere acquaintances from neighbouring villages. The surplus wealth must be syphoned off in such ways because the village lacks any mechanism to direct it towards the production of benefits for the entire community. Most commonly, a prosperous family will find itself obliged to subsidize an elaborate feast, at which the wealth vanishes down the gullets of the villagers and into thin air in the explosion of fireworks. In a Mexican peasant community, the role of *mayor-domo* ('sponsor') at a fiesta is pressed upon the wealthiest male, who must then dissipate his savings on food, fireworks, candles, and musicians. The savings are quickly gone – and the village is rid of a potentially divisive surplus. Thus wealth taken from those who have makes all the villagers once again have-nots.

The caprices of the external world, to which peasants have always been subject, have become even greater with the expansion of modern transportation and international trade. As more and more middlemen and processors enter the picture, the peasant is increasingly removed from direct contact with markets and sources of supplies. Peasants in Colombia, for example, do not understand why the coffee they grow fetches a lower price when people in far-off North America or Europe switch their preference to a different brand. Nor do they understand why, though the market price for their coffee may drop, they must still pay more for machetes and other products manufactured in the industrialized world. Instead of a traditional economy in which prices were governed by local customs and by the local marketplace, peasants find themselves subject to forces of international supply and demand that they cannot possibly control or even understand. At the very time that worldwide inflation increases prices for the things peasants buy, they are losing markets for the handicrafts they sell. Industrial nations have pumped vast quantities of cheap, mass-produced products into peasant markets. These may be paid for in pennies, but there are enough peasants throughout the world that the cumulative return to the industrial nations is enormous. As a result, peasant crafts – usually worked on during spare time to supplement the family income – can no longer compete with these less expensive and flashier foreign goods.

Two obvious solutions come to mind whereby peasants might break their cycle of poverty: either increase production or curtail consumption. Both alternatives have been tried, and neither has been successful. To increase production, peasants need capital – but they rarely can accumulate any beyond that required for paying rent and provisioning their own households. Only in times of political disorder, when the external powers are too weak to syphon off the full measure of rents, are peasants able to accumulate a surplus. That happened with the yeomen of sixteenth-century England, the rich peasants of Nationalist China, and the kulaks of Russia just prior to the Soviet revolution. Much more common is the alternative of curtailing consumption. Peasants set up their households as bastions against the temptations of the outside world. They buy little, instead manufacturing almost everything themselves; they cut down what they eat to the minimum needed to sustain life; they strenuously resist the distraction of innovations. This strategy does not produce a lasting solution either. The unwillingness to accept innovation is self-defeating because it eventually results in decreased production. And any modest surplus that the peasant might achieve in this way is soon drained off by obligations to the community.

Much more successful has been the strategy of entering into associations and coalitions that enable peasants to share the hazards of their adaptation: a crop blighted by disease or ravaged by weather, the envy of other villagers, the exploitation by overlords, and the seemingly irrational behaviour of outside powers. The association might be as simple as a formal tie of friendship, such as that of the *compadre* ('co-parent') that is found throughout Latin America and also, with variations, around the Mediterranean, in the Balkans, and in India. Two people who are not related by ties of blood become *compadres* when one of them sponsors the child of the other at a baptism, communion, or marriage. In addition to the resulting tie between godparent and godchild, a more important union is formed between the two sets of co-parents and their families. Once two people have become *compadres*, a fiction of kinship between the families is created. They use special terms of address with each other, extend mutual aid, and in general display the rights and obligations of kin.

Godparent–godchild ties of a different sort are formed in some Mediterranean countries. These ties are between parties greatly unequal in status and power – for example, the one between patron and peasant that sustains the Mafia of Sicily. The patron proclaims himself the protector, both physical and economic, of the peasant against outside powers by becoming the godfather of his child. The peasant reciprocates by supporting the patron with votes, by keeping the patron informed of gossip and plots, and by generally praising him at every opportunity. The Mafioso system was extended into Sicilian cities by peasant migrations and has been transported nearly intact to the Americas, where it today still flourishes among some Italian–Americans.

Yet a different kind of association grew up among the peasants of China, particularly in the southern regions where intensive rice cultivation made wealth possible. A family who had begun to accumulate profits would join a coalition based on kinship, known as a *tong* or *tsu* ('clan'). As its member families increased in wealth, they would hold clanwide ceremonial gatherings, endow a clan temple, and hire genealogists to seek out distinguished family members. The *tsu* eventually grew into a far-flung corporation based upon the recognition of descent from a common ancestor. Those *tsu* members who left the land and entered the bureaucracy or the gentry would maintain their affiliation with their clan. Those peasants who remained poor also received direct benefits from membership. Poor relatives were likely to receive more fertile land and they could pay rent directly to the *tsu* bureaucrats rather than to unrelated landlords. Such favouritism partly accounts for what Westerners saw as widespread corruption in the ranks of Nationalist Chinese officials. Under the best of circumstances, no more than about 40 per cent of the taxes collected by bureaucrats ever reached the central government. The People's Republic of China has understandably attempted to abolish these large descent groups and to introduce communes which shift loyalties from the *tsu* to the national government.

That Chinese peasants were better able to improve their lot than is the rule for peasants in other countries came about largely because the ruling dynasties constantly assembled a vast pool of talented males from among whom bureaucrats and administrators could be recruited. Competitive examinations were given throughout the realm to hundreds of thousands of ambitious youths. Success in these examinations conferred enormous prestige, meanwhile giving the state a monopoly on the talent of young males. The entire system was described by one specialist on China as 'a giant roulette game in which local communities are trying to toss up into the bureaucratic apparatus a candidate for office who will hit a winning bureaucratic slot and return benefits to his locality'.♂♀ Among those benefits were the power to protect the local group and to further its interests. The successful scholar was honoured in his home community, thereby exercising a claim on any wealth, power, and prestige he acquired. To counteract this debt of allegiance, the Chinese rulers forced bureaucrats to serve in areas far from their home villages – a measure that did not succeed, however, for the scholar–bureaucrat merely syphoned off wealth from more distant communities for the benefit of his own. Much the same situation prevails today among the talented offspring of Sicilian, Greek, East and South Asian, and Puerto Rican peasants who succeed in the city or in some foreign country – and who then send back part of their wealth for the benefit not only of their relations but of the whole village they left behind.

\*

Associations, though, are of only limited effectiveness in solving the peasants' basic dilemma. The *compadre* association often proves temporary because it can become unequal; one friend in the relationship might consistently give more than he receives. Similarly, the patron–peasant relationship is fragile because one patron may be deserted in favour of another who promises greater protection. And peasant coalitions that attempt to bypass the national government are vulnerable to retribution once the state reasserts its authority. Little wonder, then, that from time to time the accumulated frustration of apparently supine and docile peasants has erupted in violent uprisings. Revolts, large and small, occurred throughout Europe during feudal times when the peasants rebelled against the worldly excesses of the clergy and the wealth of the nobility. Such a revolt, often called a 'jacquerie' – the term derived from the name Jacques Bonhomme ('Jim Goodfellow') that was disdainfully applied by the nobility to the French peasants who revolted in 1358 – is usually of extreme violence. The excesses of the peasants as they loot, burn, and kill inevitably produce a bloody reaction by the more powerful overlords.

Perhaps the bloodiest of all jacqueries was the Taiping Rebellion (1850–65), which was a foreshadowing of the peasant-based, communist-led revolution of the twentieth century. Its strength was centred in the southeastern provinces around the port city of Canton (later to become the centre also of communist power); its leader was a local peasant (as was Mao Tse-tung). The Taiping Rebellion was eventually suppressed by government troops, with the loss of an estimated twenty million lives. But many of the reforms advocated by the Taiping Rebellion were remarkably similar to those later advocated by Mao. Rule by the gentry was to end and the entire society reorganized into peasant–soldier cadres. Each family was to receive land which its members would work but not own, and any surplus above that required for local consumption would be transferred to the public granary. Equality would be granted to women; traditional religions, ancestor worship, and the use of literary languages in place of every-day ones were all prohibited; opium, concubinage, and prostitution were outlawed. Many of these same reforms were later put forward by Mao, who based his strategy on mobilization of the peasants (in contrast to Chiang Kai-shek, whose support came mainly from merchants and city-dwellers). Mao's success in recruiting the peasantry was such that by 1949, when the communists took control of all mainland China, about 80 per cent of the party members were peasants.

The violence and cruelty of a peasant uprising often startles outsiders because it appears so out of keeping with the peasants' traditional passivity. Yet under a stolid exterior, while they went on dutifully paying their rents, peasants have always nourished an animosity towards representatives of the outside powers, such as the tax collectors and the militia. Peasants' songs and tales glorify those who oppose by force the social order that exploits them: Robin Hood in England, William Tell in Switzerland, Pancho Villa in Mexico, the Samurai in Japan, and various bandit–heroes in China. Chinese peasants above all depart from the image of peaceable endurance portrayed in Hollywood movies and by popular myth. They have long revered bloodthirsty heroes who steal from the rich and give to the poor. One classic Chinese novel, translated into English by Pearl Buck under the title *All Men Are Brothers*, tells the story of more than a hundred of these bandit–heroes. ♂♀

Mao Tse-tung's peasant rebellion is one of the very few in world history to have succeeded over a large geographical area. Almost all other peasant uprisings have been doomed to failure because of a built-in handicap – namely, the peasants' inability to unite and form stable coalitions. Any temporary victory they gain by force is usually crushed with at least equal violence – while their grievances remain unredressed. In Russia the astonishing total of 1186 unsuccessful peasant uprisings occurred during just the thirty-five years between 1826 and 1861. ♂♀ Karl Marx understood the potential value of the peasants in helping to overthrow governments, but he also understood that once they obtained land they would cease to be a revolutionary force. And he was correct. In 1910 Emiliano Zapata led his peasant masses out of the highland villages and eventually seized Mexico City itself. But after only a few years his army had been reduced in size from 70,000 to a mere 10,000 because of mass desertions. What the peasants wanted was land – and once the land had been seized, they no longer saw any reason to fight.

In this century, peasant revolutions have been unsuccessful or only temporary in many places, among them Guatemala, Bolivia, Peru, Chile, and Indonesia. In others they succeeded, but the peasants soon lost control. The only change was in the authority to whom they paid rent: an all-powerful state (as in Russia, China, and Yugoslavia) rather than a private landowner. Peasant revolutions in Cambodia and Cuba appear to have succeeded, but these nations depend heavily on China and the Soviet Union for protection and economic support. All in all, peasant revolts in the twentieth century have been little different from those of the past. The peasants have furnished their bodies and shed their blood – but in the end they find themselves still landless, still subordinate to a capricious outside power to which the fruits of their unceasing labour must be rendered.

*

Peasants today are rapidly being drawn into the modern world. Although some social scientists predict the total disappearance of their way of life in the new technological order, its end is by no means inevitable. For an indication of just how tenacious the peasant adaptation is we may look to the Soviet Union, where nearly half of the population still lives in rural communities, only about a tenth of the agricultural production is fully mechanized, and most cultivation is still carried on by primitive hand techniques. The persistence of the peasant way of life is to be explained not as stemming from any desire on the part of rulers to perpetuate its inefficiency nor from the conservatism of the peasants themselves, but rather, from one inescapable reality: it is not only for the peasant that physical resources are limited; the same is true for peasant and non-peasant alike.

At the very time that peasant populations are exploding, those resources are in fact becoming fewer for greater and greater numbers of people. Of all the goods produced today, the industrialized 30 per cent of humankind consume some 80 per cent; and they are doing all they can to increase their material affluence still further. As a result, not enough resources are left over for the peasants to modernize after the modern nations have exploited them. The heralded 'green revolution' (which increases yields through intensive agriculture) is capable of wonders, but these depend upon vast reserves of energy not available to the peasants. The green revolution is based upon large amounts of water, which must be pumped with fuel-hungry machines, and large quantities of chemical fertilizers, which are themselves derived from oil. Intensive agriculture is possible only when one crop is harvested swiftly and another is planted, so that the land yields several crops a year. This cannot be done without machines that consume vast amounts of energy. The use of tractors and other farm equipment means that there must be factories to produce them plus transportation networks for distributing both machines and petroleum – all of which require natural resources that are in short supply in most of the nations where peasants are to be found. The magnitude of the problem can be seen in the fact that 2500 tons of water are needed to manufacture just one ton of the rubber that goes on to the wheels of these machines – and that water, at every step from locating it to finally pumping it into the factory, likewise uses up tremendous amounts of energy.

Why cannot the developing nations imitate the history of the modern nations and transform inefficient peasant operations into efficient ones? First of all, the modern nations control most of the world's capital, industries, transportation, and resources; they are not likely to decrease their own standard of living willingly so that other nations can modernize food production. Second, the modernization of the countries of North America and Europe was a slow evolutionary process that spanned more than two centuries; even Japan's unprecedentedly rapid industrialization required nearly a century. Beset with the high birth rate of their peasants, the developing nations simply cannot risk that much time. Finally, these nations find unacceptable the ruthless methods – such as subjugation of native labour and the exploitation of foreign resources – that were previously used by colonial powers and without which the industrialization of Europe and North America would have been impossible.

Given these obstacles, it is a wonder that the peasant-ridden nations can modernize to even a modest extent. And the reason that they have been able to do so turns once again on the contribution of the peasants themselves. They must pay at every stage for the modernization of the entire developing economy. They finance it directly by their rent for use of the land. They support it indirectly by providing a pool of cheap labour. Most important, they pay by existing as a segment of the developing society that is neglected in the provision of such services as education, public health, and transportation while the nation is accumulating the capital necessary for investment in modernization. And in the end, the peasants pay the ultimate price. Once agriculture becomes mechanized, they become surplus labour. They are driven from the land into the cities. There they are maintained on pittances doled out by the government as they make an often futile attempt to adapt to urban life. Urbanization, the subject of the next chapter, cannot be understood without understanding the contribution made to it by the peasants. ♂♀

# 8

# Urban Influences

Throughout the nineteenth century, and indeed until only a few decades ago, scholars visualized an evolutionary path in human history that led in a straight line from the 'savagery' of hunter–gatherers to the 'agricultural revolution' and finally to the 'urban revolution' that produced the great civilizations of Mesopotamia, Egypt, India, China, Mesoamerica, and classical Greece. The urban revolution was supposed to be easily identified by a cluster of traits, including dense concentrations of people, production of a food surplus, a central political authority, social inequality, monumental architecture, writing, and trade. But archaeological work in the past decade or so has shown that these ideas about the rise of complex civilizations, which have long been taught in schools, are based on general assumptions which simply do not apply. Several of the best-known civilizations, for example, lacked cities. The elaborate ceremonial centres built by the Maya went unoccupied (with certain exceptions) for most of the year. The major settlements during the first 1500 years of Egyptian civilization were the temporary ones that sprang up during the process of building the shrines and pyramids each of the pharaohs ordered erected in honour of himself. In many parts of the Near East, writing was not invented until after cities had flourished for thousands of years. Some cities, such as Jericho in the Jordan valley, even managed to exist without surplus agriculture; instead, they obtained most of their food supply by trade. Social inequalities based on differences in wealth and status existed in many civilizations, but by no means in all.

On the other hand, some societies that were not urban display many of the criteria of urban civilization. The Northwest Coast Indians, the Maori of New Zealand, and the native Hawaiians were characterized by such things as dense populations, central political authority, a food surplus, monumental architecture, social inequality, and trade – without developing such other urban criteria as cities, agriculture, or writing. Monumental architecture is undoubtedly the hallmark of many complex civilizations, but the 'barbarians' of ancient Europe built the monumental structures found at Stonehenge and in many stone tombs thousands of years before they developed urban centres or other hallmarks of the urban revolution. Some of the tombs, using massive slabs of stone that often weighed several tons, may have been erected 2000 years before the Egyptian pyramids. Nor is writing the acid test of civilization. People in a small farming village in Rumania wrote on tablets about 4500 years ago, not much later than writing was supposedly invented by the urban civilizations of the Near East. ♂♀

Neither is it true, moreover, that the urban revolution originated at a single place – usually said to be the 'nuclear area' of Mesopotamia – from which it diffused throughout the Near East, eastward to the Indus valley and China, westward to Europe, and finally across the Atlantic to the New World. Rather, urban civilization is now known to have developed independently in many regions of the world. In fact, the substitution of many nuclear areas for a single one in Mesopotamia is itself an oversimplification. Whereas the Sumerians of Mesopotamia were thought to have created the first urban civilization – one answering all the criteria – which then diffused throughout the Near East, archaeologists now know that a major hallmark of Sumerian civilization, monumental architecture, had already appeared at several other places in the Near East. Recent archaeological discoveries do not confirm Sumer as the 'inventor' of urban civilization but rather show that many Near Eastern civilizations in Mesopotamia, Turkey, and elsewhere were developing distinctive patterns of urban life as early as 5500 years ago. Five hundred years before the supposed diffusion from Sumer of its brand of civilization, these distinctive civilizations were in contact through trade and were influencing one another in various ways. Yet each retained its distinctive characteristics – which explains why no single set of criteria can account for all urban civilizations. Each had resources, inventions, and ideas to contribute – and the dialogue among all of them must have stimulated further developments.

After so many erroneous ideas about the rise of cities have been overturned, it is little wonder that the most sacrosanct notion of all should finally come under attack. Archaeological theory long assumed that the practice of agriculture developed first, followed by farming villages, then towns, and finally cities. Agriculture had been visualized as the 'basic' adaptation, and cities as merely parasitic upon it. So it has indeed been in many areas. Yet the curious fact has now emerged that some of the earliest cities grew up far from the areas in which agriculture had developed. The great civilizations of Mesopotamia, for example, arose in the lower reaches of the Tigris and Euphrates rivers, many hundreds of miles from the upriver areas where very early evidence of food production has been discovered. In fact, at some archaeological sites, striking examples of large settlements appear before any clear indications of food production. Shanidar in Iraq was already growing as an urban centre, and even producing artistically wrought metal, about 11,000 years ago, before plant and animal domestication was of importance there. Tell Mureybit in Syria was established as an urban centre about 10,000 years ago, but more of its residents were apparently traders than farmers. Growth from a farming village is obviously not a precondition for the rise of a city. Cities can become established without any preceding smaller settlement based on agriculture – and can survive in the absence of agriculture owing to trade or manufacture, or as the seat of political and religious authority. ♂♀

How, then, is urban civilization to be defined? It does, of course, adhere to most of the criteria already discussed, but it is not some rigid checklist of these. Nor does any single criterion, or set of criteria, exist that can be used to account for every urban civilization. The urban phenomenon arose in different ways in differing parts of the world. It may have been foreshadowed by those hunting–gathering peoples who practised ritual burial. The first humans to have a permanent dwelling place were the dead. Their burial sites were the revered places to which the living wanderers periodically returned. In other words, the cities of the dead predate the cities of the living; necropolis comes before metropolis. It was the attraction of the necropolis that drew the ancient Hebrews towards the Promised Land; they claimed it because it held the graves of their forebears. In later civilizations, ceremonial centres grew up surrounding the necropolis, and hordes of people came to these to worship and to do the bidding of the gods. Today the cities of Rome, Jerusalem, Mecca, Benares, Peking, Kyoto, and Mexico City still remind us of the ancient attractions exerted by the ceremonial centre upon people sharing a religious belief. ♂♀

Another need that impelled people to live together in cities was trade, often underestimated until recent archaeological excavations showed its importance. Dense populations settled near sources of raw materials to defend their rights to these materials, to fashion them into items that could be traded, and to exchange them for agricultural products. Jericho was one such town. By a little less than 10,000 years ago, it covered about ten acres and was fortified by a wide moat and an encircling stone wall complete with towers, one of which is thought to have been at least 28 feet high. (The walls that Joshua was to destroy were built much later, about 3200 years ago, and they were even more imposing: a double ring of them, each about six feet thick and 30 feet high.) Such defensive works obviously could not have been constructed in the absence of a political power strong enough to muster the workers, who were drawn from a population estimated at about 2000 people. Since food production had not yet developed in Jericho at this time, the defences were apparently meant to protect Jericho's trade in salt, bitumen, and sulphur from the Dead Sea.

Jericho was not some isolated exception. Urban centres recently discovered in Iran, Turkey, and southern Russia traded such raw materials as lapis lazuli, obsidian, and copper. These and other materials were in demand throughout the ancient world, and farmers were willing to bring agricultural products to the cities to obtain them. Furthermore, the cities grew by trade among themselves. Jericho could supply salt but lacked obsidian; Catal Huyuck in south-central Turkey had an abundance of obsidian but no asphalt; the Mesopotamian cities provided grain but needed lapis lazuli. The result was a system of trade in the ancient world whose scope remained unsuspected even a few decades ago. And along the same trade routes travelled inventions, skills, and beliefs – probably the first major exchange of ideas in human history. In the midst of this intellectual ferment, the leaders of the early cities found ways to grow more powerful, to impose their authority in ever-widening arcs, and to develop those numerous criteria of urban civilization that were discussed at the outset of this chapter. ♂♀

Trade, though, meant potential plunder. For several thousand years after Jericho's walls were built, other urban centres also found it important to erect defensive works. By 6300 years ago, a major change had already taken place in the Near East. Not only fortresses were being built but soldiers' barracks as well. Barracks present clear evidence that a specialized class of soldiers had arisen who would make warfare become rampant in the Near East over the succeeding millennia. Historians used to believe that the catalyst for warfare in the ancient Near East was rivalry between urban centres, agriculturists, and pastoral nomads. The accumulation of wealth and the control of strategic sites for the exploitation of trade, however, are sufficient in themselves to explain the sudden rise in organized hostilities. And the political organizations that developed to handle trade relations were probably a prerequisite of the centralized control necessary for warfare.

The course that such warfare took is typified by Sargon of Akkad, who about 4500 years ago overran much of Mesopotamia. Because of the Akkadians' need for raw materials that were lacking in Mesopotamia, Sargon conquered the trade routes leading through Lebanon to the Mediterranean; he penetrated as far north as Turkey and as far south as the city-states of the Persian Gulf that controlled trade to India and northeastern Africa. More conquests ensued as Sargon found himself obliged to make his trade routes secure – much as in later periods the Hudson's Bay Company, the East India Company, and the European enclaves in Chinese ports would have to be supported by military power. Thus, early in the history of urban civilization, the economic imperialism more recently practised by Europeans was already foreshadowed.

War and domination were built into the ancient city as inescapably as the very mud-bricks and stone that went into the physical structures themselves. Each city vied with others in its armed might, under the leadership of a divine king who spoke in behalf of a wrathful god. Violence itself was not new under the sun. Hunting–gathering peoples feuded with one another, and ancient farmers captured and sacrificed human victims whose blood was thought to ensure the fertility of the fields. In no previous adaptation, though, had one society rallied massive armed power to subdue or annihilate another. The oppressive economic weight of maintaining an army always on the ready, the burden placed upon agriculturists who had to supply both the food and the sons for foreign conquests, the vast military bureaucracies that grew up – all these consequences of warfare worked against the survival of urban civilizations, and ultimately brought them one by one to ruin.

The ancient cities had locked themselves into a behavioural pattern in which war fostered more war. Victory in battle meant plunder and rule over the economy of a conquered city–state, but the resulting wealth made the victors a natural target for depredations by still others. The physical form of the city, and even its very social life, was thus shaped from the outset by the demands of war. Walls, ramparts, watch towers, gates, and moats characterize cities from antiquity down to the eighteenth century in Europe (and to this day in a few other parts of the world). So it was with the acropolis (literally, 'high point of the city') – those elevated, fortified sections of Athens and other ancient Greek cities – and so it was with Rome, Paris, London, New York, Pittsburgh (originally, 'Fort Pitt'), and San Antonio ('The Alamo'). As Plato wrote in *The Laws*, 'Every city is in a natural state of war with every other.' ♂♀ One might think that eventually humans would have abandoned attempts to survive in cities that were constantly under siege or in the process of besieging others. Yet every year the cities were replenished by the fresh arrival of young peasants, full of rural simplicity yet wise enough to know that the military offered them the one clear path out of their poverty. The peasants came to kill and be killed, and the cities continued to prosper despite appalling casualties. Without the peasantry, the city would soon have been literally drained of its life. No wonder the citified poets wrote bucolic odes to the peasant villages while ignoring the misery to be found there.

With the rise of the urban centres, warfare became an industry which, with only certain exceptions throughout history, increasingly transferred power from the peasant–citizen to the specialized military. Previously, in simpler adaptations, the weapons of battle were not much different from the weapons of the hunt. Any male could manufacture them himself, and the raw materials for them were distributed more or less uniformly throughout the environment. But urban specialization changed that. The cost of manufacturing bronze weapons, and later those of iron, put them beyond the reach of peasant agriculturists. Furthermore, the ores were not freely available but rather had to be extracted and refined by specialists. Even so, the mass production of metal weapons eventually made these available to the citizenry, who thus could stand up to the elite on horseback or in chariots. The peasant army was once more rendered ineffective by the invention of armour for knights and for horses and of the iron stirrup. Smithies and artisans had to be maintained for their manufacture, something only the military specialists could afford. But the development of the crossbow and the longbow – with which English troops cut down the French armoured knights at the Battle of Agincourt in 1415 – restored the supremacy of the peasant infantry over the cavalry. The development of small guns and later of artillery once again put weaponry beyond the reach of the individual. The production of artillery was a heavy industry and its deployment required large numbers of horses and men to operate the weapons and to transport the heavy shells and gunpowder. From that time forward, the weaponry of war has remained an exclusive possession of national governments and of the allied industries that manufacture it.

*

Urbanized society brought into existence social units of a size and complexity that must have been inconceivable to food-producers. Society became divided into rulers and ruled, powerful and weak, rich and poor. A marked change also took place in the status of females. So long as females were gatherers or simple food-producers, they shared equally with males in the quest for food. In an urban civilization, though, females had little more to do except to produce ever more offspring, providing the city with soldiers and replacing the workers who constantly succumbed to disease and unsanitary living conditions. Just as the female's digging stick became outmoded when ploughs were invented, so the female goddesses of fertility yielded to such male gods of ruling force as Mars and the Egyptian Ptah (whose greatest glory was said to be that 'he founded cities').

The rise of cities also meant a new kind of interpersonal relations that allowed dense populations to coexist. No longer was it possible to move away from squabbles, as people did in the hunting–gathering adaptation. Populations closely packed together had to learn to get along with one another, and so new standards of conduct were established, including civility and mutual courtesy. Part of the reason for this great social upheaval was that certain individuals came to exercise a disproportionate amount of political authority. What at first must have been only a slight political advantage soon developed into the concept of the divine ruler, a government holding sway over an organized territory, a political and religious bureaucracy, a standing army to enforce authority, and the inheritance of wealth and power. Behaviour was codified into laws that were imposed from above, in contrast to the customs and social pressures that had operated as sanctions in less complex adaptations Urban societies, in which face-to-face interactions with kin or with known neighbours are sharply reduced, require that laws be spelled out, clearly setting forth the consequences of alternative courses of action. For example, a law might threaten the peasant with such and such a punishment if he failed to pay rent, but the law also had to reassure the peasant that if the rent were paid, his family would continue to receive the protection of the state. The ancient laws were remarkably precise. About 3250 years ago, Moses the lawgiver presented the Israelites with the Ten Commandments as well as the biblical books of Leviticus, Numbers, and Deuteronomy, which dealt with almost every conceivable facet of conduct pertinent to the times.

Laws can be effective only if they are made known to all of the people concerned, and in an unambiguous manner. Such purposes are best achieved by setting down the laws in writing. The great civilizations eventually developed or adopted writing systems, at first to record economic transactions; but very soon writing was being used to give permanence to laws and administrative decisions. The Incas did both by means of a memory system that used, instead of writing, sequences of knotted, coloured cords known as *quipus*. The system fell into complete disuse almost immediately after Pizarro's conquest of Peru, and so exact details about it are not known. At least some *quipus* almost certainly represented a numerical system based on decimals. The arrangement of knots at various positions and the use of differently coloured cords probably also had stereotyped verbal meanings. The Incas are known to have rapidly transmitted bureaucratic decisions throughout their realm, and the only possible method woulad hve been through information contained in the *quipus*.

The writing systems more familiar to people in Western societies originated in a wide arc that extended from Mesopotamia through the northern Near East and southward to Egypt. At first, about 5000 years ago, these systems consisted only of pictographs – that is, realistic symbols used to convey meaning, such as a crude picture of a house to stand for the actual house. Very soon afterwards, though, a new development took place: ideographs or idea–symbols that used pictographic elements to suggest abstractions. Whereas in simple pictography a circle might represent the sun, in ideographic writing the circle might also stand for heat, light, a god associated with the sun, or the word *day*. The Egyptians eventually expanded this dual system to include some symbols that stood for sounds; but even so, their hieroglyphs were clumsy and limited in the information they could communicate. A system somewhat similar to the Egyptian developed early in China and is still in use, with certain modifications; it is capable of conveying both scientific data and the subtleties of poetic expression.

The Phoenicians and other Semitic-speaking peoples developed, about 3500 years ago, a purely phonetic alphabet in place of one combining pictographs, ideographs, and sound signs. The word *alphabet*, by the way, is itself derived from the first two letters of the Semitic alphabet, *aleph* and *beth*, later to be called *alpha* and *beta* by the Greeks. The Greeks improved upon the Semitic alphabet by writing out the vowels that formerly had been merely understood. The Romans in their turn eventually modified the Greek alphabet so that it applied directly to their own spoken language. Theirs was the one finally adopted throughout most of Europe and much of the world. Tracing the spread of writing is a fascinating scholarly pursuit, but that very fascination has sometimes obscured the significance of writing as a milestone in human history. For the first time, knowledge and experience could be put into a form that would endure beyond the life-span of an individual speaker and of those who

1.  ꝺꟾ.ꝼ ꛭ ꟿ.ꝛ ꞁ ꟿ.ꝺ ꞁꟿ ꟾꟿꝛ.ꝺꝼ.ꝺꟾ ꝍꝏ ꟿ.ꝛꝼ ꝺ

2.  ꛭ ꞁ ꝛ.ꟿ ꝏꝏ.ꝺ ꝛ.ꝛꟿ ꟿ ꟿ ꞁ ꝺ.ꟿꞁ ꝛ.ꟿ ꛭ ꝺ

3.  ꞌN K · M S ᶜ · B N · K M   S M L D · M L K · ꞌ B

4.  ꞌAN°Kⁱ MᵉShᵃᶜ  BᵉN  KᵃM°ShMᵃLD  MᵉLᵉK  M°ꞌAB

5.  I   Mesha    son-of Kamoshmald    king-of Moab

THE EVOLUTION OF A WRITING SYSTEM

About 2800 years ago, King Mesha of Moab erected a huge stone to commemorate his victory against the kingdoms of Israel and Judah. The message inscribed on it has provided a clear example of an early (although not the very earliest) Semitic alphabet. In these drawings, the first line shows the inscription as originally written; it is read from right to left, as has been the custom in Semitic languages. In the second line the same message is reversed so as to read from left to right. The next line translates the Semitic letters into the modern alphabet. The fourth line includes the unwritten vowels to show pronunciation, and the final one is the English translation.

listened. Speech sounds fade away almost instantly, and the memory of spoken words dies with the listener – but in writing, those words endure, keeping events of the past as fresh and alive as though they were happening today. ♂♀

In the ancient city, as in that of today, every individual filled a very exact niche as servant, craftworker, merchant, bureaucrat, or member of the religious hierarchy. Occupational specialization was quite different from the generalized behaviour of hunter–gatherers, each of whom was about equally qualified to hunt, fish, chip flint, make snares, dig roots, and perform other tasks as the occasion demanded. That one person year after year should have only a single job to perform would be unimaginable to most hunter–gatherers, who to this day resist specialized work whenever they are forced or gulled into it by outside exploiters. Few Native American hunting–gathering or food-producing tribes provided their European conquerors with labourers willing to perform repetitive jobs on a fixed schedule – and so the Europeans imported slaves from more complex African societies that had long trained their people to work for others at assigned tasks. In the ancient urban civilizations, the people who succeeded were those who became full-time specialists. As a result, they achieved an excellence in their work that would have been impossible without concentration on a single task. The development of specialization increased production many times over – and led to innovations that were probably the direct result of ideas such as would have occurred only to a full-time tinkerer accustomed to manufacturing a single product. Another consequence was the appearance of neighbourhoods in which particular crafts were practised, and each governed by its own special rules of behaviour and standards of conduct. Sumer, Babylon, Athens, Rome, and other urban civilizations of the past had their equivalents of today's professional neighbourhoods: the Broadway theatrical district, 57th Street art galleries, Wall Street financial district, Madison Avenue advertising agencies, Fleet Street newspapers, and Harley Street physicians.

The rise of the city brought a new shift of emphasis in human attitudes. The hunting–gathering people had been above all in close relation to their total environment. This ecological continuity was maintained by those who took up food production, but with a technological shift. The emphasis was now placed on a few favoured domesticants rather than on the total environment. Urbanization brought into prominence a relationship that previously had not been developed to any real degree: that of one human to another. In other words, the relations of urban life are primarily social rather than ecological or technological. Social skills that had been successful for maintaining harmony in the band and the simple farming village were no longer sufficient. In the city, humans found themselves no less dependent upon their social environment than the hunters and gatherers had been upon their physical environment. Violence arising from arguments or from family feuds was now forbidden by the authorities. Religious observances were no longer directed to personal household gods, but instead consisted of public expressions of obeisance to whatever gods were then ascendant.

For the first time in human history, a very small minority dominated not only the majority living inside the city but also those living in the vaster territories around it. Until the rise of the city, human history had been anonymous. No one knows the names of the discoverers of fire or of the Cro-Magnon cave painters. But with the rise of the city, history begins to celebrate the small minority while the overwhelming majority of humankind continues to labour in the same anonymity as before. The success of the ruling minority in making itself prominent, begun in antiquity, has persisted to this day. Anyone who tries to imagine the civilizations of the past will tend to think of Babylon, Jerusalem, Athens, Alexandria, Rome, and other great cities. Yet such a city almost never contained more than 10 per cent of the people of the civilization it represented, and often still fewer than that. How can we have fallen victim to such a misapprehension? The explanation is that history has been written by people who lived in cities and towns and who recorded the life they knew: that of the ruling classes in the major population centres, not the illiterate, anonymous peasants toiling in the fields.

\*

For thousands of years, people who lived under varying political systems and who held widely divergent beliefs nevertheless did not differ greatly in the actual physical designs of their cities and the institutions they created to govern them. Not only did the ancient Near Eastern cities physically resemble those that grew up more recently in Europe; the former were often superior, item by item, to their more modern counterparts. In the ancient cities, streets were better paved, sewer systems were more efficient, water supplies safer and more plentiful, neighbourhoods better planned, and public buildings and monuments generally larger. Mohenjo-Daro, built about 5500 years ago on the banks of the Indus River, was every bit as elaborate as the Paris of Louis XIV. The similarity extends from physical layout to the activities that went on inside their walls. Wherever they were located – the Near East, the Indus valley, China, Europe – cities were alike in assimilating migrants from rural areas, in developing a broad economic base, in the manufacture and exchange of goods, in occupational specializations, and in the creation of such bureaucratic institutions as a unified political system and a state religion.

Until recently, the city remained what it had been from the beginning: a collection of small villages, with garden plots and barnyard animals, small workshops, market streets, and the grander dwellings of the wealthy, all growing up side by side. People of the same neighbourhood knew one another, were linked economically or by kinship ties, shared the same well, and were frequently buried in the same graveyard. To some extent, this mixture and diversity can still be found in a few cities in North America and Europe. As one economist has written:

Rich and poor live literally in the next streets to each other in a Chelsea [London] or a Montparnasse [Paris] or Brooklyn Heights [New York City]. This is the essence of what Doctor Johnson and James Boswell felt to be the greatest gift of cities – 'the whole of human life in all its variety' – the possibility of mixing cultures and experience and even dimly perceiving, under all the quirks and oddities of human behaviour, an underlying shared humanity which is enriched, not endangered, by sharing the same community. ♂♀

Some parts of New York, Boston, London, and Paris have maintained the character of village life within this wider scale. And some, such as Greenwich Village in New York, have even clung to the old name.

People went on building replicas of the ancient city for thousands of years – until, beginning a century or two ago, the very concept of city life was altered radically under the pressure of industrialization. The new mill city – like Manchester and Birmingham in Britain, Pittsburgh and Wilmington in the United States – was something completely different. These either lacked previous villages embedded in them or else the character of the embedded villages had been obliterated. Differences based on wealth and social position had always existed in the urban centres, but now these became magnified as the gap between classes widened, until almost no contact took place between mill owners and mill workers. A symptom of that drawing apart was the suburb. Such a thing had never existed until in the 1790s people began leaving Manchester to find fresh air, greenery, and open spaces. By the middle of the last century, almost every industrial city was ringed with suburbs inhabited by the newly enriched middle classes. The process has continued until almost every major city in an industrialized nation today shows the same pattern: the poor living in squalor close to the industrial section or else inhabiting a blighted inner ring consisting of earlier suburbs from which the more privileged have long since departed.

And so in no more than a century or two, and about 12,000 years after humans first began to live in permanent settlements, the character of this adaptation has been drastically altered. Through all those thousands of years, until the Industrial Revolution began in 1775, about 90 per cent of the world's population lived not in urban settlements but in such smaller units as hamlets, villages, or farm compounds. By the time the Industrial Revolution was well under way, the urban population still accounted for only about 15 per cent of the world total. But by 1960, one person lived in a city for every two who lived in the country. By the year 2000, the world will undoubtedly have more urban than rural inhabitants.

Not only are more cities being established at an accelerating rate; the older cities are also becoming larger. Before the beginning of the nineteenth century, a large city rarely numbered more than 100,000 people. Among the few exceptions were Imperial Rome which at one point may have numbered a million people, and Hankow, China, which in the thirteenth century, according to Marco Polo, had a population of several million. At the time of the American Revolution, which is contemporaneous with the beginning of the Industrial Revolution in Europe, only Boston and Philadelphia had populations of even 50,000. Then the explosion in city size began. London's population reached a million in the 1820s. Eleven such cities existed by 1900, seventy-five by 1950, and by 1985 the figure is expected to be about 275.♂♀

Much of the difference between life in today's cities and that in ancient ones is due, of course, simply to this bigness. Assume that a city person can travel ten miles in any direction in a day; the distance

encompassed is a circle with a total area of 314 square miles. Assume
also a population density of about 8000 per square mile, a fairly
representative figure for metropolitan areas in the United States. In
a single day, each person in such a metropolitan area will potentially
be exposed to contact with up to 2,512,000 people. The number of
actual contacts will be increased by a phenomenon most people have
an intuitive feeling about: the pace of life in big cities *is* faster than it
is in small towns. A study of fifteen communities in six countries
indicated that the larger the city, the greater the speed of walking.
People in Brooklyn, New York, walk at the brisk pace of 5 feet per
second, just slightly less rapidly than people in the heart of Prague,
Czechoslovakia, who bustle ahead at 5.8 feet per second. Both
Brooklyn and Prague have populations in excess of a million people.
In contrast, the villagers of Psychro, Greece (population 365), amble
along at a mere 2.7 feet per second, and those in somewhat larger
Corte, France (population 5500), move at 3.3 feet per second.

That people in big cities walk faster seems to have little to do with
national attitudes or culture. The explanation apparently lies in the
human response to the increased number of contacts in cities. People
seem to believe that faster walking will help them get through the
commotion more speedily and without becoming involved in the
affairs of passers-by. Such behaviour, though, would appear to be
self-defeating, since an increase in walking speed merely increases the
number of people with whom one will be in contact in any given
moment of time. ♂♀

Personal contacts not only are much more numerous in cities but
are also of a different nature. In a small community, most contacts
are with people whose behaviour and habits are already known, the
result of years of close association. Contacts in modern cities, on the
other hand, are apt to be much briefer, less personal, but more
utilitarian. People who live in cities obviously could never know the
other inhabitants as intimately as they would know their neighbours
in small settlements. Nor could they possibly wish to; they would be
under agonizing stress if they were to attempt becoming involved
emotionally with the hordes of people whom they encounter in
passing. So the only feasible way for urban dwellers to cope with the
huge numbers of strangers is to keep them at an impersonal distance,
to recognize their roles rather than their personalities. The person at
the supermarket check-out counter is usually only an anonymous
being who adds up the total, not a human made of flesh and blood

with a conceivably fascinating personal life away from the super-market.

Coping with the large numbers of people that a city-dweller is likely to encounter suggests an analogy from cybernetics: systems overload, or the inability of a mechanical or electrical system to process inputs because they occur too rapidly. An overloaded system adapts by setting priorities. Input A, for example, might be processed while B is delayed – and C might have to be sacrificed altogether. Living in cities represents a continuous encounter with overloads, and some of the behavioural adaptations to them are:

Disregard low-priority inputs. The city-dweller reserves time and energy for a few close friends and virtually refuses to acknowledge the existence of strangers, even when they need help.

Shift some of the inputs to other parts of the social transaction. Harried bus drivers no longer make change for passengers; the responsibility for having the exact fare has been shifted to the passenger.

Block off inputs before they can enter the system. Many city-dwellers evade incoming telephone calls by leaving the receiver off the hook, by employing an answering service, or by using an unlisted number.

Create specialized mechanisms to absorb inputs. Welfare agencies care for the indigent who might otherwise block the streets as they beg from passers-by.

Ruthlessly sacrifice some inputs. Fellow citizens are often sharply divided into two categories: those needed for some personal gain and those who can safely be disregarded. The result is an unwillingness to become involved with people who have no personal claim on one's time or energies. ♂♀

Experiments with animals have shown that rats, mice, and rabbits are adversely affected by crowding, and the same thing has long been assumed to be true as well of humans crowded into cities. Clear evidence of such harmful effects on humans, however, is lacking and, all in all, crowding seems to be a neutral influence. The experimental literature on crowding in humans has been reviewed by one psychologist, who concludes:

First, high density (crowding) does not have generally negative effects on humans . . . It does not produce any kind of physical, mental, or social pathology. People who experience high density are just as healthy, happy, and productive as those who experience lower density. Second, high density does have effects on people, but these effects depend on other factors in the situation. Under some circumstances, high density makes people more competitive and aggressive, but under others it has the opposite effect. High density can cause people to be friendlier and also less friendly. And under certain conditions, the reactions are different for men and women. ♂♀

Such conclusions would appear to run entirely contrary to common sense, yet much of the fear of cities stems from a misinterpretation of statistics. Statistics tell us that the crime rate in the United States is five times greater in large cities than in small ones, and eleven times greater in cities than in rural areas. Major crimes do occur most often in areas of high population, but that is not the same as to say that they occur in crowded areas. Population densities in the hundred largest metropolitan areas of the United States show a tremendous range: from as few as forty people per square mile to as many as 13,000. Generalizing about crime in 'crowded' cities is therefore difficult. But density does not appear to be as important a variable in crime as other factors, particularly social and economic status. When neighbourhoods with people of approximately the same socio-economic status are compared, the crime rate is about the same, even when one neighbourhood is densely populated and the other only sparsely so. Crimes against persons (such as murder, assault, and rape) might be expected to be more common *per capita* in crowded areas, but that is not true either. Nor do the neighbourhoods that are the most densely populated have the highest rate of infant mortality, mental illness, venereal disease, or other pathologies as compared with areas having considerably fewer people per square mile.

Something about cities, though, does seem to foster certain kinds of antisocial behaviour. Since 1964 the notion of 'bystander apathy' has become a sociological commonplace as a result of the publicity surrounding the murder of Kitty Genovese in New York City. As she was being attacked in front of the apartment building where she lived, her cries of terror brought thirty-eight of her neighbours to their windows. She fought off the killer for more than half an hour, yet in all that time not one of the neighbours came to her aid or even bothered to call the police. Such a complete failure of human compassion inevitably leads to the question: Why did no one intervene? Many explanations were offered: apathy, fear, lack of concern, and the depersonalization of city life. Each of these explanations contains a partial truth, but the full answer is undoubtedly more complicated.

Most people assume that as the number of bystanders increases, so does the likelihood that at least one of them will give aid in an emergency. Studies of reactions among witnesses to a violent domestic quarrel, a robbery, or a fire have revealed just the opposite. When only a single bystander is present in such a situation, the choice is very simple: the bystander will either act or not act. When a crowd is present, though, responsibility is diffused among many bystanders and focuses on no single one of them. Each member of the crowd assumes that someone else will take action, with the inevitable result that no one does. Bystanders fail to act for yet another reason: the high-cost, low-benefit ratio of doing so. The cost is usually quite high because danger is involved, and intervention usually means a considerable loss of time. Anyone rushing to aid a fellow citizen under assault would probably be assaulted also. Moreover, anyone who intervened would later have to give testimony to police, prosecutors, and judges in a case that might conceivably drag on through years of hearings, trials, and subsequent appeals. In return for taking such a risk, the rewards are discouragingly small. A general failure to intervene, as in the Genovese case, may make front-page news, but intervention usually does not result in an equivalent degree of favourable publicity. In the final analysis, the only reward the bystander who intervenes can expect is a statement of gratitude. The ratio of cost to benefit is quite different in a hunting–gathering band or in a farming community. The rewards for rendering assistance are very high: prestige, a reputation in the community for bravery, and acquiring in the kin of the beneficiary a set of allies who at some future date can be called upon to repay the debt. ♂♀

\*

Urban existence has gone far towards reversing a major evolutionary characteristic of hominids: generalized behaviour. Over a period of several million years, our species remained unspecialized. Humans could thus easily put aside behaviours as they became outmoded and develop new ones as the need arose. Those individuals who succeeded in the urban adaptation, though, did so through committing themselves entirely to a specialized life-style. In most urban societies previous to industrialization, craftworkers were apprenticed to a hereditary calling at an early age, while their bodies were still growing. The physical traits of city-dwellers thus became as much badges of occupation as the clothes worn: the stout legs of the military man, the massive upper body and stubby legs of the blacksmith, the hump and bent neck of the tailor or goldworker. Changes occurred also in certain sensory skills that had been valuable to hunter–gatherers but were less so in an urban setting. City-dwellers cannot equal the visual acuity of the Bushmen, who can see four moons of Jupiter with the unaided eye and can hear a single-engined light plane seventy miles away.

The biological consequences of urban life are usually not so apparent as the social changes, but they assuredly do exist. Few people realize the extent to which cities, even in industrialized nations, have been ravaged by epidemics of disease. Only a century or so ago, the London water supply was so primitive that it was polluted by cesspools and graveyards, and epidemics of water-borne diseases were periodic occurrences. In urban areas of England, as a whole, the death rate was a third higher than in rural counties. The increased population density and the greater number of interpersonal contacts in cities allowed infectious diseases to thrive: cholera, smallpox, mumps, measles, chicken pox, rubella, and many others. Permanent settlements produced accumulations of wastes, thereby setting up ideal conditions for bubonic plague, leprosy, hook-worm, and dysentery.

Many of the infectious diseases that now ravage humankind appeared for the first time with the rise of cities because these diseases multiply and persist whenever people live at the high densities found in cities. Infections by salmonella bacteria (which are responsible for typhoid, 'food poisoning', and other diseases of the gastrointestinal tract) are likely to be prevalent only among city-dwellers. A hunter might occasionally have picked up salmonella bacteria from an animal he had killed, but the bacteria would probably not have survived long enough to produce an epidemic because of the relatively few human contacts that would take place during the brief time the bacteria were still infectious. Only after cities developed, with their high densities and their communal water supplies, could salmonella have become established in a population.

One of the most terrible plagues ever to strike urban populations began in A.D. 540 in Egypt and within a few years had spread throughout much of the Byzantine Empire. This bubonic plague reached Byzantium (now Istanbul) in 542 and soon the death rate approached 10,000 each day. Graves could not be dug quickly enough to bury the dead. The plague spread so rapidly that half of the inhabitants of the empire are estimated to have succumbed within twenty-five years. Still the plague returned, sparing not a city or town in the empire, until it finally abated about the year 590. (Interestingly enough, contemporaneous accounts state that more males than females died – yet another example of the relatively higher mortality of males when both sexes face the same threat to life, a subject to be discussed in Chapter 10.) Before the plague, Emperor Justinian extended the Byzantine Empire to its farthest boundaries and ushered in an era of imperial splendour and learning. When he died in 565, he left an empire considerably weaker than when he had mounted the throne. Many cities, towns, and villages were wiped out or abandoned, agricultural production fell drastically, and panic swept the empire, leaving it open to depredations by Huns, Slavs, and Persians.

Even more lethal than the plague of Justinian was the Black Death of 1346–61. This bubonic pandemic attacked people throughout Europe; it reached southward into Africa, eastward to China, and northward to the Scandinavian countries. A witness to the epidemic in 1348 in the French city of Avignon reported that only a quarter of the population had survived. Scarcely a tenth of the people were left alive in some of the densely inhabited areas of England. Those fleeing the cities spread the plague to rural towns and the countryside, but the populations there were too sparse for the disease to become established after it had taken its initial toll. The devastation wrought in Scandinavia might well have influenced the European colonization of the New World. Erik the Red had established settlements in Greenland in A.D. 936, and from there his successors had gone on to colonize parts of eastern Canada. But ships carried the plague to these settlements in the fourteenth century, weakening them to the extent that they could not withstand attacks by Eskimoes and Indians. The last Norse settlements in the New World disappeared early in the fifteenth century, leaving behind only a few house foundations and some pieces of iron.

Nor could such viral diseases as chicken pox, smallpox, poliomyelitis, measles, and the common cold have spread without the great number of interpersonal contacts typical of life in cities. The measles virus, for example, demands a minimal number of contacts that far surpassed those found in small, isolated populations of hunter–gatherers or food-producers. To survive, either it must exist in a population dense enough to maintain a reservoir of the virus, or that virus must be continually reintroduced by infected individuals from elsewhere. Both conditions are common in dense cities that constantly receive new migrants. Epidemiologists have determined that a reservoir of measles virus is maintained when a population exceeds 300,000, which means that a minimum of from 4000 to 5000 people will contract it every year. At lower levels of population the virus simply dies out. Few of the ancient cities of Mesopotamia, the Indus valley, or China had populations of even 100,000 people, yet measles probably was already an urban disease. The explanation is that many of these smaller cities were in regular contact through trade, war, and migration, thus providing the minimal population necessary to harbour the virus. ♂♀

The disadvantages of life in cities probably have been evident from the first. Yet, down through the millennia, more and more cities have been built and the older ones have grown larger. Every year, in all parts of the world, migrants flock to cities to make their fortunes and to escape intolerable existences as peasants. The urbanization of humankind has resulted in a striking redistribution of the world's population. At no time before the previous century did city-dwellers ever compose more than 5 per cent of the total human population on the planet. Even by the year 1800, the number of people living in cities of 20,000 or more represented only 2.5 per cent of the world total. That percentage has now increased elevenfold. Humans are not only increasing in numbers, but are also huddling together in ever smaller portions of the planet's surface. Settlements in excess of 100,000 first began to develop around the Mediterranean several thousand years ago. Thereafter concentrations of humans increased rapidly. Cities larger than a million people had developed by about the year 1800; only 150 years later, cities in excess of ten million had appeared. Cities that two decades from now, in the developing regions of the world – Asia, Africa, and Latin America – are expected to pass the twelve million mark include: Mexico City, São Paolo, Buenos Aires, Rio de Janeiro, Lima, Bogotá, Cairo–Giza, Teheran, Karachi, New Delhi, Bombay, Calcutta, Shanghai, Peking, Seoul, Bangkok, Manila, and Jakarta. Most of these cities are already horrendously overcrowded and unable to provide services for the people living there. Nearly a tenth of Calcutta's inhabitants, for example, sleep in the streets every night and almost half of the population lacks sewerage facilities. Yet new migrants continue to arrive in these cities every day, willing to exchange the certainty of poverty and starvation in rural areas for the uncertain prospects of city life.

The growth of cities in the United States is even more striking. When the first census was taken in 1790, the urban proportion of the population was only 5 per cent; now it is about 75 per cent. In 1800 not one city in the United States exceeded 100,000 inhabitants. Both Philadelphia and New York were small towns compared to the 800,000 people living in London or the 500,000 in Paris. But only sixty years later, New York City (not even including Brooklyn) was already the third largest city in the world, after London and Paris, and Philadelphia had surpassed Berlin in numbers. By 1880, a score of United States cities exceeded 100,000 people. Now, of course, in some places in the United States, the borders of one city meet with those of the next, producing megalopolises with tens of millions of inhabitants.

Because disease and famine have caused higher death rates in urban areas than elsewhere, cities have been able to increase in size only by constantly drawing upon new migrants. The perennial trade-off between cities and rural areas has been the production of people in the countryside and the consumption of them by the cities. Poor rural people have almost always wound up as poor urban people. The history of United States cities as recipients of inflowing migrants has been little different from that of cities at other places and other times. Until recently, when the urban birth rate finally exceeded the infant mortality rate, growth in United States cities had not been generated internally but rather as a result of the influx of rural people. Black Americans, for example, began to pour into northern cities from the rural South in search of jobs just after World War I. Because of their poverty and the discrimination they suffered, these migrants were forced into dilapidated and crowded tenements that had only recently been vacated by previous migrants from else-where. In 1910 nearly 75 per cent of Black Americans still lived in the rural South, but so rapid was the migration that only fifty years later almost exactly the same percentage resided in urban areas.

In most urban areas, increases of population cannot be generated naturally from within for two reasons. The first is high infant mortality as a result of unsanitary living conditions. In the slums they inhabit, the migrants make an unsuccessful attempt to transfer country ways to a new environment. Garbage disposal, for example, presents no major problem in rural areas. Waste from a farmhouse, thrown out of the back door into the yard, will be promptly disposed of by pigs, chickens, and dogs. In the city, though, the same practice encourages the breeding of rodents, roaches, and disease organisms. The second is that most cities of the world are inhabited by an enormous preponderance of males, particularly those at the height of the reproductive age, between twenty and forty. This distortion in the normal sex ratio is caused by the multitudes of male peasants who flock to the cities for work, hoping eventually to save enough money so that they can send for their wives. Most of them never do rise above urban poverty, and so the females remain in the country-side – thus leading to a low birth rate in the cities and to social dis-ruption in the rural areas that have been depopulated of young males. ♂♀

Rapid urbanization through migration inevitably places strains on the entire social order. The typical migrant is from a homogeneous society in which the rules of behaviour have been unconsciously assimilated since childhood. In the city, though, migrants are faced with a bewildering diversity of customs, brought in by large numbers of migrants from other places. The world they enter is an unfamiliar one of few family ties, impersonal contacts with strangers, and rules of conduct that often seem arbitrary, along with general din and con-gestion. The migrants must adapt quickly to unfamiliar ways if they are to make a living; but they lack skills for city work, are almost always illiterate or semiliterate, and are not accustomed to fixed working hours. As if all this were not discouraging enough, the migrants for the first time encounter the unmistakable difference between haves and have-nots. The differences are not so striking in rural areas, nor are they usually what sociologists call 'felt differences' since the people with whom one associates are equally poor. In the city, though, the migrants feel the inequalities deeply, and the feeling adds to their misery, frustration, and unrest.

*

This chapter began with the rise of the first cities, each of which to its inhabitants must have seemed to be the whole world. Some 10,000 years later, the whole world is fast becoming one city. Much of this chapter has dwelt on the misery and the darkened human condition brought about by urban civilization. Paradoxically, as the world has become more urbanized, distrust of the city has increased. The people in the United States who found themselves in a position to deal with urban affairs have often been the very ones who mistrusted the urban environment. In 1787 Thomas Jefferson wrote to James Madison: 'I think our governments will remain virtuous for many centuries as long as they are chiefly agricultural; and this will be as long as there shall be vacant lands in any part of America.' That attitude has persisted down to this century. Frank Lloyd Wright wrote of the urban human that '. . . if he is properly citified, the citizen has long lost sight of the true aim of normal human existence. He has accepted not only substitute means but substitute aims and ends.' ♂♀

We can nevertheless look beyond the urban blight that today so degrades the spirit of humankind and see the beneficial effects of urban existence. In the cities, the human species for the first time was able to control its physical environment. Floodwaters were channelled, water was stored against drought, habitations were made impervious to the weather, and streetlights turned night into day. Transportation networks were constructed over which people, and with them a host of ideas and innovations, could be moved rapidly. The urban civilizations, with all their drawbacks, wove a social fabric of law and justice that allowed huge numbers of people to live together in relative harmony. The city has enlarged the scope of human activities. Through the development of libraries, archives, and museums, the city was able to store the ever-accelerating accumulation of knowledge and to transmit it intact to future generations. The city has taken random human activities and given them form and direction. But primarily it has transmuted human energy into complex culture and into new kinds of social institutions.

Nevertheless, the urban pattern of existence has arrived at a point where it no longer offers humankind advantages in survival. We persist in minor tinkering with urban problems by planning, zoning, and slum clearance, whereas it may turn out that the only permanent cure for urban ills is to rid ourselves of the outmoded idea of the city itself. We obviously cannot return to hunting–gathering or to primitive agriculture. Something new is needed, something that could scarcely have been imagined only half a century ago. We are already in the process of developing the next human adaptation: modernization. ♂♀

# 9

# Modernization: Towards the World City

Nearing the end of his life, Henry Adams – historian, novelist, and direct descendant of presidents and statesmen – reflected on the changes he had seen. He felt in particular an inability to cope with the new technological age because by his time in the early twentieth century '. . . a nineteenth-century education was as useless or misleading as an eighteenth-century education had been to the child of 1838 [the year in which Adams was born]'.♂♀ In no more than a century or so, human life in all its aspects has altered more rapidly and extensively than throughout the previous 10,000 years. So rapidly have changes been occurring that the familiar world of youth has become an alien one by the time a person reaches old age. The inability to cope with a dynamic society is a root cause of the confusion and discontent all around us: social frictions, disruption of the family, and cleavage between the generations. Massive change is occurring everywhere. No human group, whether of Eskimos north of Hudson Bay or of the most traditional peasants in India, has been able to escape the extraordinary changes of this century. Philosophers used to seek the ideal society in some 'golden age' of the past; more recently, many people have tended to believe that the ideal society, if it was ever to be found, would be in the future. As a result, in the past few centuries a new value system has equated change with progress, and society has rewarded those who encourage or achieve rapid change. From all indications, the old adaptations are coming apart and a new one is being fashioned.

Modern changes are often referred to as 'Europeanization', 'Westernization', or 'industrialization' because they accompanied the rise of the Industrial Revolution in western Europe. These labels are misleading; the changes are more than a mere transplantation of European institutions or even a simple diffusion of European ideas. They are, rather, what many social scientists describe as 'modernization'. This rapidly evolving adaptation is being witnessed in both European and non-European societies and appears destined to produce a new world civilization. A major characteristic of modernization is that changes wrought in the political, social, and economic systems accelerate. In England and Wales, for example, the change from 10 per cent urban to 30 per cent urban required seventy-nine years. Equivalent urbanization required only sixty-six years in the United States, thirty-six in Japan, and twenty-six in Australia.

One measure of this worldwide modernization is the number of people an individual knows directly or at least knows about – in other words, the total experience of a member of our species concerning other members. A century or so ago, an individual in the United States probably knew directly a few hundred kin, neighbours, trades-people, and friends in nearby communities. Aside from these, very few other people were known about except for a small number of national leaders. Nowadays, the number of people an individual knows directly probably remains very much the same. A revolutionary increase has taken place, though, in the numbers of people known about, largely through the world communications network. To a modern North American, the faces of a foreign head of government, a champion tennis player, a leading artist or musician, or an Indian guru are often better known than the faces of neighbours living only a city block away.

The quickened pace of transportation and communication has permitted people to be in almost instantaneous contact for the transmission of goods or of ideas. Some 3500 years ago, the fastest transportation available to humans was the chariot, which was capable of about twenty miles per hour for short distances. The chariot, though, was a specialized implement of war; the fastest average speed at which most people and goods could be transported over long distances was eight mph by camel caravan. The first mail coach, which began operating in England in 1784, bettered that speed by only two mph – and the first steam locomotive, introduced in 1825, managed a top speed of only thirteen mph. After that, speeds increased rapidly. The hundred-mph barrier was broken around 1880 by more advanced steam locomotives, and by 1938 aeroplanes were travelling at more than 400 mph. Nowadays, of course, supersonic airliners travel at speeds in excess of 1250 mph. ♂♀ Like the transport of goods, the transport of information was once limited to the speed of human and animal foot-power. Today, though, electronic communication via telephone, satellite, and computer network has allowed a new invention in New York or London to be known about almost immediately in Japan.

The keys to modernization are a continuous expansion of knowledge, the application of this new knowledge to technology, and the use of increasingly large amounts of energy. New sources of energy, and its use in novel ways, in particular distinguish a modern society from any previous kind. Under modernization, energy has been put to work out of all proportion to population growth. Worldwide consumption of energy in the form of coal, oil, gas, and hydro-electric power increased by more than five times in the past half century alone. Such statistics, usually presented in terms of metric tons of coal or ergs of energy, are often difficult to comprehend. A better way to visualize energy consumption is in terms of pharaonic power – that is, to convert these units into units based on human slave labour. The amount of energy each individual in the United States consumes is thus equivalent to owning the labour of more than two hundred hard-working slaves. These slave-machines perform for their owners the services that slaves have always had to perform. In the shape of such things as bulldozers they carry out the back-breaking tasks of earth-moving; vacuum devices clean the house; automatic ovens and other appliances replace human menials required to gather firewood, keep fires stoked, and laboriously prepare vegetables; power mowers tend lawns and snow-throwers open up blocked driveways and roads. Television, telephone, satellite, and computer networks transmit messages faster and more reliably than any slave messengers ever could. And, of course, in the form of the automobile these slaves carry their masters about in greater splendour than any despotic pharaoh who was ever paraded on a royal litter.

In hunting and gathering, humans depend directly upon other living organisms for their energy requirements. They tap this energy in three ways: they feed on plants, they eat an animal that has eaten the plants, and they burn the energy stored in such plant materials as wood and peat. In short, hunter–gatherers simply transfer energy from plants and animals to themselves. Food production does not basically alter this process of transfer; it merely concentrates it selectively on a few domesticated species. Advanced agricultural systems, though, tap additional sources of energy: wind power to operate irrigation works, water power to grind grain, and animal energy to pull ploughs. The modern society taps the entirely different sources of energy that exist in combustible and atomic fuels. By 1900 in the United States, coal had surpassed wood as the dominant fuel and provided more than half of the total energy needs. By 1950, the reliance upon wood, coal, and hydro-electric power had fallen behind oil and natural gas. Shortly afterwards, nuclear energy was introduced – and by the year 2000 it is expected to supply the United States with as much energy as all other forms together provided in 1940. ♂♀

Modernization is usually thought of primarily in industrial terms, but its effects have impinged on all previous adaptations. Modern agriculture turns dairy farms into factories with mechanized production lines and mass-produces wheat on tens of thousands of acres. Nor is the difference between modern agriculture and simple food production solely one of scale. A peasant agriculture – which relies on hand tools, maintains soil fertility by letting a portion of the acreage rest each year, and depends upon rainfall rather than irrigation for water – produces perhaps ten calories of energy for each calorie expended. By contrast, an industrialized corn farm in Iowa can produce 6000 calories for every calorie of human labour expended by the farmer. But the seeming efficiency of the modern farm turns out to be illusory. Enormous amounts of human energy are put into agricultural production in addition to the obvious input by the farmers themselves. When this energy from outside sources is added up, United States farms turn out to be using, on a per acre basis, 15 tons of farm machines, plus the 22 gallons of gasoline required to operate them, and 203 pounds of fertilizer – a total per acre of nearly three million calories. Put another way, a total of 2790 calories of energy are expended to produce and deliver to the consumer in the United States just one can of corn containing 270 calories. The production of beefsteak demands an even more prodigious deficit of energy: 22,000 calories to produce an amount of meat (about four ounces) that contains the same 270 calories.

In other words, for each person physically present on the modern farm, other 'farmers' are at work in the factories that manufacture machines and chemical fertilizer, on railroads and trucks that haul grain and livestock, in canning plants, and in oil refineries. Modern agriculture's accomplishment has been not so much a reduction in the work force as a process of taking it off the farm and integrating it into the rest of the economy. The farmer was once regarded as the

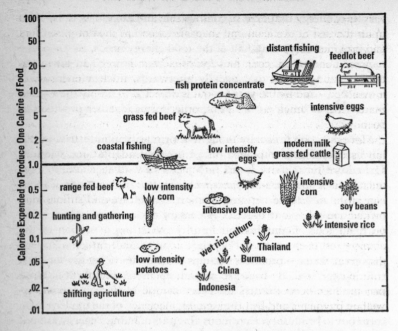

THE ENERGY BALANCE OF MODERN AGRICULTURE

The number of calories of energy necessary to produce a single calorie of food depends upon the nature of the crop and the kind of agriculture practised. The expenditure of merely a single calorie of energy can sometimes yield many calories of food – as the examples in the bottom half of this chart show. In Indonesia, simple agriculture based on rice and the water buffalo yields fifty calories for every calorie expended. In modern societies, as shown in the top half of the chart, just the opposite is true: many calories must be expended to yield a single calorie of food. Modern agriculture, in contrast to pre-modern agriculture, thus consumes more energy than it produces. From this point of view, modern agriculture is obviously much less efficient than simple agriculture. The advantage of modern agriculture over simpler systems lies not in caloric output but rather in the reduced calories of *human* energy required. The modern farmer, who may expend merely one calorie of human energy for every 400 calories obtained, consumes many times those 400 calories in mechanical and electrical energy. The deficit is made up by energy sources other than the human farmer's muscle: machinery, chemical fertilizers, pesticides, and such fossil fuels as coal and petroleum. The use of energy sources other than human muscle has been the trend in North American agriculture. In 1910 United States farmers obtained slightly more than one calorie of food for each calorie expended. But by 1970 an average of nearly ten calories of non-human energy was being expended for each calorie harvested. Modern agriculture has achieved its high productivity only very model of self-sufficiency. Now farmers are no less dependent upon the rest of the economy than are office workers in New York City or London. ♂♀

Almost as soon as modernization took hold in northern Europe at the beginning of the nineteenth century, the dehumanization of agriculture began. Peasants by the millions were forced from their small plots of land, as wealthy landowners switched to intensive farming and stock-raising. In this century, owing to mass production, the lowered cost of machinery has permitted landowners to work the land economically without the labour of peasants. In the southern United States, sharecroppers thus became less efficient than mechanical cotton-pickers and other machinery, and today the same thing continues to happen around the world wherever wealthy landowners can obtain the capital necessary for modernization. Every year, millions of small farmers and peasants are driven from the countryside to make room for machines. These vast armies of the dispossessed have no place to go but to the cities, where their lack of training for a modern society makes them unemployable. These become members of a depressed urban proletariat that survives on welfare payments and by begging and thievery.

*

The Industrial Revolution should not be looked upon as a sudden upheaval, any more than should the food-producing revolution that began around 12,000 years ago. Rather, the emergence of the new adaptation is best described as a slow evolution. Many of the important components of the Industrial Revolution – water power, metallurgy, and machines – had long been known in other parts of the world before the Industrial Revolution began in Europe. Two questions arise: Why was modernization so long in developing? And why did it finally begin in western Europe, one of the least likely places?

Before these questions can be answered, two kinds of political–social–economic systems – those of China and of western Europe –

by squandering the energy stored in fossil fuels. Developing nations cannot easily adopt these techniques because they cannot afford to be prodigal of fuels. Their agriculture remains inefficient in terms of the human labour necessary – but in terms of calories harvested for each calorie expended it is extremely efficient. ♂♀

must first be contrasted. Anyone alive in A.D. 1700 might have safely predicted that modernization would begin in China, where technological accomplishments had long overshadowed those of Europe. The Chinese had already invented or exploited watermills, gunpowder, paper, mechanical cranks, the iron suspension bridge, canal gates, spinning machines, and many other technological innovations. Furthermore, the Chinese had available the human resources necessary to exploit their technology: a very large population, skilled workers, and a highly organized bureaucracy. The Manchu dynasty, which took control of China in the middle of the seventeenth century, created an empire that was more densely populated and more powerful than any the world had ever seen before. It occupied most of eastern Asia and ruled more than 300 million people, about a third of all humans alive at that time. Yet instead of leading the world to modernization, Chinese power during the next few centuries was gradually eroded and then destroyed by small numbers of Europeans.

The seeming might of China in the seventeenth century turned out to be a weakness from the point of view of modernization. Under the Chinese political–social–economic system, two crucial features of modernization, change and the possibility of choice, were hampered. The Chinese system's wealth and burgeoning populations had been made possible by government control over an extensive system of irrigation works. To recruit the millions of labourers needed to construct and maintain these works, and to apportion the water to tens of millions of peasant farmers, an imperial bureaucracy had come into being. So, because of the ready availability of labour and the rigid organization of the bureaucracy, no need existed for change, such as using the machines that had already been invented as a substitute for human labour. And of course the people themselves were given no choice about this. Under such conditions, capital accumulation could occur only rarely. Rich merchants and large landowners often found their profits syphoned off by a corrupt bureaucracy or seized by despotic rulers. Furthermore, the entire Chinese system was so vast and so immovably entrenched as to be virtually beyond reach of alteration by any new technology.

The European system contrasted sharply with the Chinese. European agriculture depended upon the vagaries of rainfall, rather than upon a reliable supply of water from irrigation works. This basic inefficiency, though, saved Europe from falling under the control of a single centralized government, as had happened in China. Farming based on rainfall did not involve the same massive co-operation for irrigation projects under despotic authorities empowered to coerce the entire nation. For all his powers, the European ruler possessed nowhere the authority of the Chinese despot. In England, the Magna Carta extracted from King John by the barons prevented the rise of a centralized power and assured the individual barons of their supreme authority in their own castles. The European rulers were further limited in their authority by other members of the landed nobility, by the Church, by the guilds of artisans, and by the bourgeoisie of the cities. Instead of a centralized national rule, each little feudal entity in Europe developed what later came to be called 'capitalism' – the accumulation of wealth in the hands of a few entrepreneurs. The very essence of capitalism is the choice that was denied the Chinese: the possibility of using wealth in any one of several ways to produce additional wealth. During the Middle Ages, each little fiefdom became a centre of capitalism, and each one competed with others in the production and distribution of goods. Such an economic environment – in which *choices* were constantly being made about the most productive use of capital – inevitably encouraged *change* because any venture that might increase capital found ready support. ♂♀

The explorers in the fifteenth and sixteenth centuries, for example, were no less entrepreneurs than were the merchants of the time. Their voyages were usually financed by risk capital; the ships were built in private yards and outfitted by private companies; the crews were hired by the entrepreneurs. Sometimes a monarch or religious leader would also invest, for reasons of national prestige but of personal enrichment too – as when Columbus was backed by Ferdinand and Isabella of Spain. The privateer Sir John Hawkins numbered Queen Elizabeth among his investors when he made a slave-run in 1564 from Africa to the West Indies. He bought and sold 400 Africans – and the queen made a profit of 60 per cent on her investment. Cardinal Richelieu set up a company which controlled the French fur trade in North America in the first half of the seventeenth century and which also bartered guns to Indians.

The answer to the questions posed a few paragraphs ago – Why did not modernization begin sooner, and why did it begin in western Europe? – now begins to emerge. Modernization could not take place until societies had, first of all, accumulated the necessary capital. England did so through what has come to be known as the 'tri-

angular trade'. English manufactured goods were first transported to
Africa to pay for the purchase of slaves. These slaves were then
shipped to the New World plantations where they were exchanged
for sugar, cotton, molasses, and other products – the processing of
which created new industries when they were brought back to England on the last leg of the triangle. By 1750 hardly a trading or manufacturing town in England was not connected in some way with the
triangular trade, from which were derived the profits that financed
the Industrial Revolution. ♂♀

To modernize, societies also had to develop a scientific technology,
a capacity for self-sustained growth, and a production-oriented economy. The towns and cities of western Europe around the end of the
Middle Ages were unique in that all three essentials came together.
China, by contrast, had a highly developed technology but lacked
the capacity for growth and the incentive for production. The Aztecs
of Mexico lacked an adequate technology, and though capable of
growth, their production differed from the European in being
oriented towards consumption, supporting a religious bureaucracy,
and sustaining a large army to obtain victims for sacrifice. In Europe,
on the other hand, production tended to be for its own sake, as when
machines were manufactured which could in turn be used to manufacture still other machines. European craftworkers were citizens
with full rights; they were at the very heart of the town economy,
whereas in China, Aztec Mexico, and other pre-modern states,
craftworkers were subservient to rulers, to the religious hierarchy, or
to the landed elite. European wealth was based on trade and industry and was centred on the artisan and merchant classes, thus
giving priority to non-military sciences. In contrast, pre-modern
societies based their wealth on land and booty; they bestowed power
upon soldiers and priests; and they gave priority to the military
applications of technology.

Two facts about modernization leave little room for argument.
Modernization began in Protestant nations, and they have been the
ones to reach the highest level of economic development. So it has
been argued, notably by the German sociologist Max Weber in *The
Protestant Ethic and the Spirit of Capitalism* (1905), that the rise of
capitalism owed much to the religious outlook of Protestant sects,
particularly the Calvinists and the Puritans. Part of the value system
known as the Protestant Ethic puts forth the beliefs that hard work is
rewarding in itself, that individual initiative is desirable and thrift

praiseworthy. By its very nature, therefore, Protestantism would have given religious support to forms of behaviour that were likely to result in business 'success' and 'progress'.

Any correlation between Protestantism and modernization, though, actually tells us very little, because the two phenomena apparently derived from common sources. To say that Protestantism gave Britons a capitalistic advantage over Catholics in Europe fails to explain why Britons adopted Protestantism in the first place. Neither Calvinism nor Puritanism preceded capitalism. Rather, those who gave their support to these movements were already urban merchants and craftworkers – in other words, incipient capitalists – who happened to be concentrated in such commercial centres as Geneva, Antwerp, Amsterdam, and London. Although Protestant sects did not produce capitalism, nor capitalism produce Protestantism, there must nevertheless have been a feedback between the two. Merchants who professed adherence to the new sects would certainly have been encouraged to view business as an honourable calling and vindicated in their desire to seek maximum profits. But it would be cruel in the extreme to project this feedback into a view that blames the poverty of the underdeveloped nations on their failure to adopt the Protestant Ethic. Underdevelopment is not to be explained by a lack of the Protestant virtues of thrift, hard work, and individual responsibility. Its cause is to be found, rather, in the harsh realities of political, social, and economic life – realities which in these countries tend to work against the accumulation of capital, retarding production and growth and thus lessening the possibility of change. Protestantism has in and of itself virtually nothing to do with the problem of development or underdevelopment. As a matter of fact, the virtues we associate with the Protestant Ethic can be seen most clearly in such non-Protestant countries as China.

\*

During the brief time since James Watt's commercial production of the improved Newcomen steam engine in 1775, a revolution unparalleled in human history has occurred at all levels of society and has penetrated all aspects of culture. The technological innovations are, of course, dramatic, but equally important are the biological, political, social, and economic consequences of modernization. From a biological perspective, the most important consequence is the extension of the human life-span and the growth in human numbers. In

One way to interpret the history of humankind is to look upon it as a series of technological conquests over sources of energy other than human muscle. Accordingly, this table highlights some milestones in the utilization of energy. (The first dozen milestones are dated only approximately because they are based on archaeological evidence, which is subject to constant revision; subsequent dates are more precise because they are based on historical evidence.)

The table shows that humans had mastered the basic principles of machines more than 1000 years before the Industrial Revolution finally came into being. And prototypes of machines that were later to replace human energy had been invented even earlier by the ancient Chinese, Egyptians, Greeks, and Romans. These inventions could not be exploited because no political, social, and economic institutions were yet ready for the task.

| | | |
|---|---|---|
| 750,000 | **B.C.** | Controlled use of fire |
| 10,000 | | Domestication of the dog |
| 8000 | | Emergence of food production |
| 7000 | | Domestication of the ox |
| 4350 | | Domestication of the horse |
| 3500 | | Use of the wheel |
| 3500 | | Metal-smelting |
| 3000 | | Domestication of the camel |
| 2600 | | Seagoing ships |
| 2500 | | Domestication of water buffalo and yak |
| 1200 | | Iron technology develops |
| 300 | | Invention of pulleys, levers, screw, pump, and water wheel |
| **A.D.** 650 | | Windmills first used in Moslem world |
| 850 | | Gunpowder bombs (China) |
| 852 | | Burning of coal for heating (England) |
| 900 | | Widespread use of watermill for grinding grain (northern Europe) |
| 1250 | | Watermill applied to making cloth, sawing wood, and extracting oil from vegetable seed |
| 1250 | | Coal used by smiths as a source of energy |
| 1386 | | Mechanical clock (installed in Salisbury Cathedral, England) |
| 1448 | | Gutenberg Bible printed with movable metal type (Germany) |
| 1606 | | Experimental steam engine (Italy) |
| 1709 | | Use of coal in iron industry |
| 1712 | | Commercially successful steam engine invented by Newcomen (England) |
| 1765 | | Modern steam engine invented by Watt (England) |
| 1787 | | Steamboat (USA) |
| 1790 | | Sewing machine (England) |
| 1800 | | Electric battery (Italy) |
| 1812 | | Practical steam locomotive (England) |
| 1831 | | Generation of electric current (England) |
| 1852 | | Passenger elevator (USA) |
| 1859 | | First oil well drilled (USA) |

| 1862 | Dynamite (Sweden) |
| 1874 | Chain-driven bicycle (England) |
| 1874 | Telephone (USA); four-cycle gasoline engine and carburettor (Germany) |
| 1880 | Patent of electric-light bulb (USA) |
| 1882 | Commercial use of hydro-electric power (USA) |
| 1887 | Gasoline-powered automobile (Germany) |
| 1892 | Diesel engine (Germany); gasoline-powered tractor (USA) |
| 1900 | Rigid airship (Germany) |
| 1903 | Flight of Wright brothers (USA) |
| 1923 | Bulldozer (USA) |
| 1926 | Rocket fired with liquid propellant (USA) |
| 1926 | Television (Scotland, USA) |
| 1937 | Jet engine (England) |
| 1945 | Nuclear explosion (USA) |
| 1946 | Electronic computer (USA) |
| 1951 | Hydrogen bomb (USA) |
| 1954 | Nuclear power plant put into operation (USSR) |
| 1957 | Artificial satellite (USSR) |
| 1958 | Laser (USA) |
| 1969 | Astronauts land on moon (USA) |
| 1975 | USA and USSR astronauts link in space |
| 1976 | Scheduled flights of supersonic aircraft (USSR, Britain–France) |

the past two centuries, life expectancy has nearly tripled and the population of our species has multiplied five times over. The most striking political consequence has been the almost complete disappearance of hereditary governments, to be replaced by systems that are more democratic or that at least make some gesture in that direction. With democracy has come the expansion of governmental responsibilities and of the bureaucracy. Perhaps the major social change has been the dilution of loyalties to family, place of birth, and social group. Loyalty to home town, kin, region, and even nation has been largely replaced by loyalty to one's professional colleagues around the world and to the governmental, industrial, or religious bureaucracy of which one is a part. That a truly global culture has emerged in all the modern nations is evident from the worldwide similarities in dress, music, art, language, and even beliefs that now prevail. The economic success of modernization is to be seen in the enormously increased production and consumption of goods; the *per capita* rate of both is at least ten times greater in modern than in agricultural societies. ♂♀

These changes probably could not have occurred without an accompanying basic change in human personality. People have had to make a psychological adjustment to the occurrence throughout their life-span of sudden, unexpected, and seemingly irrational changes at an ever-accelerating rate. Many of these changes are beyond individual knowledge or control; but many others concern the individual personally. For example, most modern corporations move large numbers of their employees to different parts of the world every few years; a quip among employees of IBM is that the company's initials stand for 'I've Been Moved'. Geographical mobility is now a way of life also for the contractors and consultants employed by these corporations, for people engaged in education and research, and for members of a new international bureaucracy. During the course of a working life, a modern individual may have lived in more than half a dozen different places on several continents. The ability to adjust every few years to new superiors and new tasks, a new home, new schools for the children, and often a new language demands a particular kind of personality – one that can withstand unexpected changes without the stress and anxiety that usually accompany change in pre-modern societies.

No wonder that under modernization the nuclear family (that is, parents plus their offspring) has assumed an importance it has not had since hunting and gathering prevailed. The modern family must be nearly as mobile as a Bushman nuclear family. About a third of all Bushman families shift their allegiance from one camp to another each year – about the same proportion as change their cities of residence among employees of a modern corporation or of some United States agencies. An employee who must be prepared to move within a few months from Texas to Iraq or Indonesia cannot be slowed down by elderly parents, unmarried uncles and aunts, or other members of an extended family – any more than a hunter–gatherer can be weighed down with excess baggage. The old people go into nursing homes and senior-citizen housing, and the children are often sent to boarding school. A further cause of the dilution of kinship ties in a modern society is that kin provide only limited benefits. Among hunter–gatherers and food-producers, a brother-in-law was someone who shared food and gave support in times of distress. In modern society, though, no one asks who your kin are when you buy groceries at the supermarket or bring your automobile to be repaired. Nor does job advancement usually depend upon help from kin. Promotions are awarded on the basis of competence, tenure, or personality, and only rarely because of kinship (except, perhaps, for people closely related to someone illustrious).

Modernization is being forged today out of all the conflicts, inequities, and seemingly contradictory behaviour around us. Some trends are clear; others can as yet be only dimly perceived. Five general components of this new adaptation go far towards explaining the often confusing modern world:

*A new kind of labour force.* Under modernization, relatively few people are engaged directly in producing food or in manufacturing goods. Rather, they perform services: communications, finance, government, trade and transport, education, research, recreation, and health. White-collar workers in the United States now outnumber blue-collar workers nearly three to two, and the increase accelerates each year. The United States has become the first nation in which the performance of services accounts for more than half of the labour force and for more than half of the gross national product; other modern nations will soon pass the halfway mark. In other words, under full modernization, much less effort will be expended in actually producing things than in making plans about their quantity, diversity, distribution, and use.

*The rise of a professional and technical elite.* An important change has already occurred within the ranks of the growing number of white-collar workers. An increasing proportion of them are now highly trained professional and technical workers, who require education throughout their lives to keep up with the expanding technology. They now make up about 15 per cent of the United States population, and the promise of high prestige and financial reward, together with the increasing need for the co-ordination of production and services, means that the proportion will continue to grow.

*The primacy of theoretical knowledge.* Every adaptation demands knowledge. The hunter must know the habits of game; the farmer, soils and weather; the industrialist, raw materials. In the modern society, a change in the character of the required knowledge has taken place. It is now theoretical rather than practical, abstract rather than concrete. The period in human history during which lone inventors could develop a new technology is past. Nowadays the inventor must not only be knowledgeable, skilled, and creative, but also have the ability to get along with a team of other innovators and planners.

*The planning of technology.* The Industrial Revolution introduced new technology without any attempt to assess its long-range effects. The automobile, for example, has undoubtedly proved more efficient than the horse-drawn carriage, but it has fouled the air with pollutants, taken the best agricultural lands out of production to make room for highways and shopping centres, and greatly increased the mortality due to accidents. In a modern society such abuses of technology will no longer be condoned. Modern societies tend more and more to assess the consequences of a new technology before it becomes widespread, as in the continuing debates about potential hazards from pesticides, food additives, pharmaceuticals, factory pollution, nuclear power, and supersonic aircraft. No such debates took place at the time when previous innovations, such as X-rays, were being introduced. For the first time in human history, technological change is being consciously planned rather than allowed to work its haphazard way.

*The creation of a new 'intellectual' technology.* In early modernization, the first great invention was the very method of inventing, which produced the railroad, telephone, automobile, aeroplane, and many other technological marvels. Nowadays the fully modern technology deals with entire systems. Cybernetics, information theory, automation, and studies of social interaction are examples. Hundreds of millions of citizens of modern societies every day are making trillions of decisions about what to buy, what to eat, where to go, and what to do on the job. Any single decision is unpredictable, yet intellectual technology is attempting to make sense out of this aggregate behaviour – and thus to form a basis for decisions about housing, employment, nutrition, recreational facilities, and the production of goods. In other words, even though modern society has become extraordinarily complex, modern science is developing the tools to see it whole and to make rational decisions about it. ♂♀

\*

Today the world is changing with unprecedented rapidity as it adapts to modernization. Older citizens in modern societies are overwhelmed by change and even youthful technocrats find themselves overtaxed in coping with the acceleration of events. 'In the three short decades between now and the twenty-first century,' begins one examination of modernization, 'millions of ordinary, psychologically normal people will face an abrupt collision with the future. Citizens of the world's richest and most technologically advanced nations, many of them will find it increasingly painful to keep up with the incessant demand for change that characterizes our time. For them, the future will have arrived too soon.'♂♀ As if all this were not enough, the higher standard of living that modern changes appear to offer still seems elusive to hundreds of millions of people, even in the modernized societies of North America, Europe, and Japan. And modernization meanwhile has scarcely reached the peasants, the simple food-producers, or the hunter–gatherers. In the highlands of New Guinea, in the Kalahari Desert, on the slopes of the Andes, modernization is not yet a direct concern – although it is encroaching rapidly.

In concluding this section, one is tempted to glance backwards over the adaptations made since the earliest hominids and to draw some sweeping generalizations. To do so would be largely repetitive because the preceding chapters have already indicated certain milestones in the human adaptation to life on the planet. One major generalization, though, can be made: the pace of change has been accelerating with each human adaptation. In fact, humans are the most extraordinarily dynamic species the living world has ever seen, in their relations both to the physical environment and to one another. People used to practise sorcery and demonology to assure themselves a long life or love or wealth. Anyone so inclined today would presumably wish to strike a different Faustian bargain: a life long enough to witness the marvels, as yet almost unimaginable, that will occur in the next century as modernization becomes a worldwide human adaptation.

# III: The Infinite Variety of Humankind

# 10

# Male and Female

A look at the diversity of human beings inhabiting the planet today reveals people of many sizes and proportions, with notable variations in such things as skin colour, the texture of the hair, and the shape of the eyes. We are usually impressed by the great physical differences between, let us say, Tutsis of Central Africa (extremely tall and lanky, with very dark skin and hair) and the people of northern Spain (short and stocky, with light skin and hair). Such a disparity, though, can be applied to Tutsis and Spaniards only in general. And the differences, at least to most people, will seem much less than the similarity between a female Tutsi and a female Spaniard. One of the first things that children everywhere learn is that the sexes differ in size and strength, in the appearance of the genitals and other sexual characteristics, and in reproductive roles – and that these differences apply to all human groups. In other words, our perception of the diversity of human life would appear to yield before the basic division of persons into the two categories of male and female. In a description of any individual, the first characteristic to be mentioned will usually be that individual's sex. The four chapters that follow will discuss many aspects of human diversity – physical and mental differences, individual abilities, and 'race' – but overriding them all is the basic distinction between male and female.

The anthropologist Margaret Mead spent the years 1931–33 in New Guinea studying the contrasting attitudes of societies towards the sexes. Among three groups – the Arapesh, the Mundugumor, and the Tchambuli – living within a radius of only about a hundred miles, she found strikingly different ideas about masculinity and femininity. Among the Arapesh, men and women are regarded as equally gentle and are equally likely to initiate sexual relations. In fact, parents are more inclined to warn their sons than their daughters against getting into situations in which they might be seduced. Males take as much delight as females in those many aspects of parenthood that the North American and European stereotypes regard as 'maternal' behaviour. So little distinction is made between parental roles that the Arapesh verb which translates as 'to bear a child' refers equally to males who have become fathers and to females who do the actual bearing. When Mead remarked to a group of Arapesh that a certain middle-aged male was handsome, they agreed, and then one added, 'But you should have seen him before he bore all those children!'

The nearby Mundugumor also apply the same standards of behaviour to both sexes, but their ideal is the direct opposite to that of the gentle Arapesh. Both male and female Mundugumors are taught from infancy to be independent and competitive. As adults, females are expected to be every bit as aggressive in sexual encounters, and no less violent, jealous, and quick to avenge insults than the males. Among the third group, the Tchambuli, the sexes do exhibit definite behavioural differences, but with an exact reversal of the roles expected of them in most other societies. The males spend much of their time playing the flute and cultivating the arts; they take care in choosing their attire each day and in adorning themselves with jewellery; and most of the work they do consists of shopping and trading. The females, on the other hand, are assertive and practical; they show little interest in clothing or jewellery; and it is they who, by fishing and by manufacturing utensils for trade, largely provide for the family. ♂♀

The point of Mead's study is that human culture is responsible for radically moulding any basic physical and mental distinctions to be found between the sexes. People anywhere in the world are likely to agree that the sexes behave differently, though the exact standards of behaviour proper for each sex are defined variously from one society to another. A real difficulty thus exists in attempting to isolate the universal characteristics of each sex from the matrix of cultural and societal influences. The most clear-cut evidence for male and female dissimilarity might seem to come from biology, yet even here much of the evidence is ambiguous. Rather than falling into two obviously separate biological entities, males and females have the same basic physical design. And the sexual differences are more apparent than real, since the basic plan in embryonic development of the sex organs is common to males and females.

The sex of a normal individual is determined at the moment of conception by the male sperm. During the following nine months of gestation, though, numerous influences are brought to bear on the embryo. Until about the sixth week of prenatal life, the genitalia show no distinction. Both male and female embryos possess a single external opening that leads to the bladder and to the internal genitalia, along with a tissue that will develop into either the penis or the clitoris (the anatomical equivalent of the male organ). If the embryo is a normal male, this rudimentary tissue will enlarge to form the penis and the scrotum, into which the testes descend just before birth. (Remnants of the female womb are carried in structures in the male urogenital system, where their existence usually passes unnoticed until old age, when they may cause enlargement of the prostate gland.) If the embryo is that of a normal female, radical changes do not occur. The rudimentary tissue simply becomes the clitoris, and the urogenital opening the female's external labia.

The male and female gonads not only develop in the embryo from a common structure; they also produce the same chemical hormones. The relative proportions of these hormones, though, are different for the developing males and females – and these proportions are crucial for determining whether further sexual differentiation will take place. The dominant male hormones are the androgens, whereas the female hormones are estrogens and progesterones. The foetus, regardless of whether it is genetically a male or a female, is at first exposed only to the female hormones, which are transmitted to it through the mother's placenta. Unless this feminizing influence of the mother's hormones is counteracted by a flow of male hormones at a critical time, the developing foetus will form female reproductive organs – even though it was genetically determined at conception to become a male. In other words, nature first sets out to produce a female, regardless of the sex that was determined at the time of conception, and only by hormonal interference at certain times in the life of the foetus will a male be produced.

Once the hormones have been released at the critical times, a great number of distinctions between male and female begin to appear. Some of these distinctions are trivial. For example, at birth a female usually has a second finger longer than the fourth. The major differences between the sexes have to do with the male's somewhat greater size and weight and heavier musculature. (The tendency in most primate species for the male to be larger and more powerful than the female is technically known as 'sexual dimorphism'.) Human males at birth weigh about 5 per cent more than females; by the age of nineteen, the disparity in weight has increased to about 20 per cent. Girls are from about 1 to 2 per cent shorter at birth and throughout childhood; at maturity, males are some 10 per cent taller. The muscular strength of both sexes is about equal in the very early years, except for the weaker hand grip of girls; by the age of eighteen, though, females have roughly 50 per cent less muscular strength than males. Other differences between the sexes observed at the outset have to do with the fact that female infants tend to be more sedentary and to sleep more. They thus breathe less air and have a lower sustained output of energy, which is why they usually require less food than a male infant of the same weight and age.

Some of the statistics in the previous paragraph, which represent averages from wide samples of people in many societies, may nevertheless be misleading. Part of the disparity in physical strength, for example, can be accounted for by boys' greater participation in physical play at an earlier age. Furthermore, in most societies male infants are treated preferentially, given more attention and care, and fed better. When food was scarce in Nigeria during the 1970 Biafran War, the female children in the family often suffered from severe malnutrition while the sons were adequately fed. Finally, sexual dimorphism is not equally striking in all human societies. Clothed male and female Balinese, for example, can scarcely be told apart. Members of the two sexes weigh about the same and both have broad shoulders; males generally lack well-developed muscles and females usually lack large breasts. Physical conditioning accounts for at least part of this similarity between the sexes. Balinese females work very hard, both in the fields and around the home, while males traditionally do little heavy work. When males do labour as coolies, though, they develop the heavy musculature usually regarded as a male characteristic. In societies like that of Bali, where males do not work hard, the difference in physique between males and females is therefore not very striking.

\*

The somewhat greater size and strength of males leads most people to think that males are biologically superior; but just the opposite is true. In the modern nations and in the cities of developing nations, males throughout their lives are more likely to die than are females of the same age. More than 125 males are conceived for every 100 females, but the proportion of males born alive is much less than that; in the United States and Britain, the figure is about 106 males to 100 females. Several causes are behind the disproportionately high loss of males between conception and birth: the greater number of male foetuses that are spontaneously aborted, the greater likelihood that a male will die from birth trauma, and the unusually large number of males who suffer from congenital abnormalities. Males continue to die at a greater rate throughout their lives. During the first year of life, about fifty-four males die for every forty-six females; by age twenty-one, the figure is about sixty-eight males for every thirty-two females of the same age. Decade after decade male mortality rises – until about age seventy-five, when the proportions are reversed, simply because so few males older than that are still living.

Of the sixty-four specific causes of death listed by the United States census, fifty-seven show a lower rate among females at all ages. Of the remaining seven causes, five can be ignored because they include things which do not affect males, such as childbirth and uterine cancer. The only two causes of death which take a higher toll of females than of males are diabetes and pernicious anaemia. ♂♀ Similar statistics are recorded for other modern nations of the world. The situation is quite different in the rural areas of the developing nations, where females are overworked and underfed, have a greatly inferior status – and thus a higher mortality than males. In India, for example, the doctor called in to treat a sick female is likely to be a less competent one than the doctor called in to attend an ailing male. In rural Guatemala, because of the subordinate position of their sex, female infants are breast-fed for a considerably shorter period than are male infants. The life expectancy of females rises markedly when they move to urban areas where they can take advantage of health and welfare programmes.

No simple explanation for the disproportionately high number of male deaths has yet emerged. Part of the explanation lies in the preponderance among males of certain genetic disorders, but that does not account for the high death rate of males from diseases to which both sexes are susceptible. Epilepsy, for example, attacks males and females in approximately equal numbers, but the death rate from it is about 30 per cent higher in males. And females suffering from the same infectious diseases as males die at a much lower rate. A comparison of groups of males and females who smoked equally large numbers of cigarettes showed that females generally were more resistant than males to such deleterious effects as lung cancer and heart disease. Females obviously possess some superior capacity for survival that has little to do with the kinds of lives they lead.

Some researchers have been tempted to search for the explanation of female biological superiority in the influence of male and female hormones, but in doing so they have oversimplified very complex physiological processes. Although hormones have been studied for decades, little is known with certainty about their effects, which may vary with the amount produced, the age of the individual, and the previous actions of hormones. Actually, to identify the androgens as 'male' hormones and the estrogens as 'female' hormones is somewhat misleading because females also produce androgens and males also produce estrogens – though normally each sex produces more of the hormone identified with it. Nor is it proper to speak of these as 'sex' hormones since more than one bodily function is influenced by them, and the influence even on sexuality is indirect. Furthermore, these hormones are produced not only by the ovaries and testes but by the adrenal glands as well – thus accounting for the ability of a male to maintain an active sex life after castration.

The interaction of hormones is best understood as they affect the menstrual cycle of the female. At the start of the cycle, estrogen is produced at a very low level. The amount produced rises to a high peak at midcycle – that is, around the time of ovulation – then dips, rises once again, and finally falls sharply at the beginning of menstruation. Another hormone, progesterone, similarly shows a rapid rise about the middle of the cycle. Such fluctuations in hormone levels during each cycle must inevitably produce emotional changes. And indeed, predictable monthly swings take place in the personality of the female that correlate closely with her menstrual cycle. The intensity of these swings, though, may be affected by cultural attitudes towards menstruation and also by the individual's own temperament and predispositions. In other words, emotional changes during the female's monthly cycle are an objective fact related to changing hormone levels, but the actual direction those changes take is influenced greatly by the culture and by the individual's own previous experiences.

The best known of these personality swings is undoubtedly the 'premenstrual tension' syndrome. It begins a few days before menstruation and continues through the first day or so. In some societies, the emotional changes in females at this time are not very marked. But for many women in North America and Europe, it is predictably a period of depression, anxiety, irritability, sensitivity to personal slights, and an increased need for affection and approval. About half of all females admitted to hospitals are in these few days of their monthly cycle. Statistics indicate that about half of the females involved in serious accidents had been in that phase of the monthly cycle at the time, and that suicide and acts of violence by females also are at their peaks during the time of premenstrual tension. Female anxiety extends as well to other members of the family. Studies have shown that mothers are more likely to bring their children to the doctor for minor or imagined ailments during these few days than during the entire rest of the monthly cycle.

Such behaviour could account in part for the widespread folk beliefs and taboos that isolate menstruating females from certain activities. The Roman author Pliny the Elder wrote of menstrual blood: 'Contact with it turns new wine sour, crops touched by it become barren, grafts die, seeds in gardens are dried up, the fruit of trees fall off, the edge of steel and the gleam of ivory are dulled, hives of bees die, even bronze and iron are at once seized by rust . . .' ♂♀ The superstitious caution against walking under ladders probably is a carryover from a time when people would not walk under bridges, trees, or cliffs if a menstruating female was about, lest some of her blood fall on them. In many societies, menstruating females are prohibited from touching objects of value and are blamed for accidents and the destruction of property. Since males do not usually know when a female is menstruating, some taboos have been extended to prohibit females from important activities at any time. Newfoundland fishermen, for example, will not go out on the water if a female set foot in the boat that day. In light of what we now know about hormone fluctuations during the menstrual cycle, everyday experiences, greatly exaggerated, might have been the origin of these folk beliefs. ♂♀

Strikingly different behaviour is exhibited around the time of ovulation, when the production of estrogen and progesterone is high. Most females describe their emotional state at that time as outgoing, active, alert, permeated by a sense of well-being, with an increase in sexual fantasies and dreams. The hormones apparently are preparing the female, both physically and emotionally, for intercourse at the time of the month that she is most likely to conceive. Even though human females do not display the rampant sexuality of other primates during estrus, human culture has not suppressed altogether the hormonal interactions that produce estruslike behaviour. One study of nearly a hundred females showed that their rates of intercourse and orgasm were several times higher around ovulation than at other times in the monthly cycle. Ovulation apparently mobilizes the entire psychosexual system for conception and the resulting pregnancy. ♂♀

Such mobilization is readily understandable simply on the basis of an ancient principle in the mammals: nature intends the egg to be fertilized. Previous to the evolution of the hominids, a mammal's egg was normally fertilized every time ovulation occurred; a female would then not ovulate again until pregnancy and nursing were concluded. In the rare instances when for some reason or other fertilization did not occur, all of the uterine changes that had taken place during the first half of the monthly cycle were for nought, and menstruation resulted. The lining of the uterus, newly made ready for the fertilized egg, had to be discharged along with the increased uterine blood supply and the unfertilized egg. If hominids still lived the sexual life of their primate relatives, menstruation would be a very unusual and even 'unnatural' event. But through the intervention of human culture, menstruation takes place more often than not – and the various cultures have developed different ways to handle this unnatural event. For some, such as the Arapesh of New Guinea, it is a negligible inconvenience – as is not the case with a majority of North American and European females, who experience premenstrual tension, apparently because it is expected of them.

The fact that females are subject to emotional changes throughout the menstrual cycle has sometimes been used as an excuse for denying them positions of leadership. But statements that the menstrual cycle interferes with female capacity to make rational decisions are misleading. Even though the menstrual cycle is a biological fact, cultural attitudes towards it can be altered to minimize the emotional and physical effects. A menstruating female is, by definition, in her most vigorous adult years. Any slight emotional changes that she might suffer during the menstrual cycle are probably insignificant when compared to the greater proneness of males to illness and accidents. And after menopause, of course, females are as stable or as unstable as males their age. Statistically, older females are not as subject to the physical and psychological ailments of the elder males who have traditionally served as leaders in government and industry. In the United States, two recent presidents, Lyndon Johnson and Richard

Nixon, have been the victims of severe emotional problems during their terms of office. The handicaps under which 'elder statesmen' of other nations have operated are also well known: the paranoia of Stalin, the cancer of Chou En-lai, the senility of Franco and Salazar, and the delusions of De Gaulle.

The biology of sex differences is still incompletely understood, but nevertheless more is known about it than about mental and psychological differences. Females lag behind males in achievement, a fact that used to be attributed to the smaller size of their brains. (Female brains are smaller on the average than those of males, but brain size is proportional to body size – and females have smaller bodies.) Now it is beginning to be acknowledged, of course, that female underachievement represents a self-fulfilling prophecy. Societies place females in subservient roles and then rationalize their inferior status by pointing to their lack of accomplishment. Girls consistently perform better on IQ tests than boys do. Yet studies of gifted children of both sexes have shown that whereas boys with high IQ scores almost always achieve prominence as adults, high-scoring girls do not, even though as children the two groups appeared equally gifted. In one such study, two-thirds of the gifted girls became housewives or menial office workers. Female proneness to underachievement usually becomes apparent around puberty, a time when the sexes are being initiated into their adult roles of female conformity and male achievement. Such initiations are carried out either overtly through puberty rites, as in many simple societies, or more subtly through pressures and expectations, as in modern societies. One study of college women in the United States, for example, showed that well over half of them pretended to be intellectually inferior to their male friends. ♂♀

Even a cursory reading of the vast scientific literature on mental and psychological differences between the sexes would inevitably convince a reader that myths and contradictions abound. In a painstaking recent analysis of this literature, two psychologists have separated the few differences that are possibly supported by scientific evidence from the numerous myths. ♂♀ They emphasize that their findings should not be taken as the final word. Nevertheless, their conclusions about sex differences, which first appear in childhood, are probably as reliable as can be expected at the present time. For example, the widely held belief that girls are more social than boys appears to be unfounded – as are the assertions that boys are more analytical and better at forming abstract concepts, and that girls are better at rote learning and repetitive tasks. The psychologists also discovered no evidence that girls 'naturally' lack motivation for achievement or that they are more the slaves of their heredity than boys. In all, the authors identified only four traits in which sex differences seem to exist:

(1) Girls apparently have greater verbal ability than boys. The sexes are very similar in this ability until about the age of eleven, at which time female superiority appears and following which it continues to increase during the high-school years. This verbal superiority is seen at all levels: understanding of language, fluency in the native tongue, comprehension of difficult written material, and creative writing.

(2) Boys apparently excel in visual–spatial ability. Male superiority in such areas as seeing patterns in meaningless lines or drawing three-dimensional objects on two-dimensional paper is not evident in childhood; but it appears in adolescence and continues throughout adult life.

(3) Boys apparently excel in mathematical ability. The sexes perform equally well in mathematics throughout grade school; but by about the age of twelve, the mathematical skills of boys increase faster than those of girls.

(4) Males apparently are more aggressive. This conclusion is supported by observations from almost all societies in which aggressive behaviour occurs. (Some societies place no premium on aggression, and so sex differences will not be observed clearly there.) This sex difference appears as early as social play begins, around age two, and it is probably attributable to the male hormone.

A note of caution must now be sounded about these four apparent distinctions between the sexes. Regarding the first two – verbal ability and visual–spatial ability – the disparity observed between boys and girls might simply be related to physical maturity rather than to any essential male–female differences. Females generally attain maturity at an earlier age than males. Earlier development of the speech centres in the left cerebral hemisphere could therefore explain the female's superior language abilities. The development of the speech centres might also interfere with the development of visual–spatial abilities, thereby accounting for male superiority in these abilities. Such a hypothesis has recently been supported by the study of a sample of early- and late-maturing individuals of both sexes. Early maturers (regardless of whether they were boys or girls) scored better on verbal problems, whereas the late maturers (again, regardless of sex) scored better on visual–spatial problems. The implication is clear: the reported sex differences in these two behaviours seem to reflect maturity (which is generally earlier in females) rather than any basic difference between the sexes. The slower maturing of males would also account for the observations that the male's superiority in visual–spatial abilities does not appear until adolescence.♂♀

The apparent superiority of boys in mathematical ability might thus be explained by the greater visual–spatial abilities of late-maturing boys. Cultural influences cannot be ruled out, though, since the magnitude of difference between the sexes in mathematical ability varies from one society to another. A survey of students in southern California showed no difference between boys and girls in the lower grades in regard to whether mathematics was liked. The further along in school that the students progressed, though, the clearer became the sexual stereotypes that established mathematics as a male domain. Teachers' attitudes also contributed. Those who taught mathematics to these children often held the stereotyped belief that boys are better at the subject than girls, and not one believed the same to be true of girls. That leaves only the greater aggressiveness of males as a trait clearly distinguishing between the sexes. Since aggression is important for understanding sex roles, it will be discussed more fully later in this chapter.

\*

None of the findings about biological and psychological differences between the sexes would seem to account adequately for the dominance of males in all societies. A fair reading of the scientific literature does not explain why males everywhere are destined at birth to enjoy economic, political, social, and sexual privileges. In India, for example, ancient Hindu laws that are still largely observed prescribe that a female must obey males at every stage of her life: first her father, then her husband, and in old age her sons. Even in modern societies, obedience to males continues to characterize female behaviour. Quite the opposite conclusions should be expected. The long-lived, more healthy, less accident-prone, and equally intelligent females should be the dominant sex. True, males are somewhat larger and stronger, but that should be irrelevant in a species that has always substituted technology for the fangs, claws, teeth, and armoured skin possessed by other species. Hominids from the outset have compensated for their lack of built-in weapons by developing a suitable technology. In a species that has won out over huge and ferocious predators by the use of cultural artifacts, assuredly the female of that species could have devised weapons to compensate for the slightly larger size and heavier musculature of human males.

Even if females did not wish to engage in open physical combat to put an end to male dominance, they could have conquered by the use of psychological and cultural weapons. After all, females have traditionally had absolute control over the birth, feeding, care, and early training of the young. As undisputed rulers of the nursery, mothers could have sharply decreased the number of males in the next generation by allowing considerably more male than female children to die in infancy. And the mothers could have countered the male's aggression by rewarding their female children for aggressive behaviour while rewarding their male children for passivity. Eventually, the mothers would have reared a new generation consisting of numerous aggressive females and a small number of passive males whose function was to impregnate them. Female domination of the entire society would then have been assured. They would have had control of leadership positions in such institutions as government, education, and religion, thus perpetuating their domination.

None of these things has occurred in the several thousand societies around the world which have been studied by social scientists. The great paradox about male dominance is that females have allowed it to exist when they could so easily have undermined it. The word *matriarchy* can be found in all dictionaries, where it is usually defined as female domination of a society's political and social affairs. That definition notwithstanding, no example of matriarchy has ever been discovered. The Iroquois probably came as close to being a matriarchy as any people known about; but although Iroquois females did play a central role in the election of chiefs, these chiefs were always males and no females had a place in the supreme council of the Iroquois League. A small number of societies trace kinship through the female line; but that is not matriarchy, since it does no more than substitute a different male (the female's brother) for the authoritarian figure of the female's husband. Humans have devised societies with an extraordinary range of political, social, and economic institutions. Yet not a single society has ever been known to bestow leadership and authority on females rather than on males.

Patriarchy is universal, without any exception whatever. Even in those cases where a queen rules, as in Great Britain today, she does so only because no male high in the line of succession is available. A queen who assumes a male role in the absence of a male heir is usually regarded as an aberration; that is dramatically demonstrated by a sculptured portrait of Queen Hatshepsut of Egypt, who ruled about 3500 years ago. She is shown wearing a beard, as though to stress that her position of authority is one normally held by a male. A few African societies have been ruled by 'queen mothers', but these have been subordinate to a male king or chief in whom the ultimate power resided. India and Israel in recent years have both given the highest position of governmental office to a female. Even so, authority in these two societies continued to be associated with males. While Golda Meir served as prime minister of Israel, all of the other eighteen ministerial positions were filled by males. ♂♀

We might expect that the position of females in hunting–gathering societies would be at least equal to that of males because females provide most of the food. Certain extreme forms of female maltreatment such as exist in more complex societies are indeed absent among hunter–gatherers: savage physical punishment or death for female adultery, denial of divorce to females, and physical isolation in harems. The much more equal status of females in hunting–gathering societies stems from the fact that subsistence depends upon reciprocity between males and females rather than upon the monopolization and exploitation of resources by males alone. Male dominance is nevertheless very much present, although it is more subtle than in complex societies. Among the Mbuti Pygmies of the Congo, authority must sometimes be invoked for the good of the band, and it is always done so by the best hunter or by an elder male. Males achieve high status for their skill in hunting, but females achieve no such high status for their skill in gathering. And the most important rituals are reserved primarily for males. ♂♀ Male hunter–gatherers also monopolize all of the weapons. Although these are rarely used against females, the mere possession of them represents a threat. And in even the most egalitarian of hunting–gathering bands, males ultimately control life and death. When old people or infants must be killed to decrease the number of mouths to feed and thus ensure the band's survival, the men do the killing – and they usually kill females first.

Even sweeping political and social changes do not usually alter the dominance of males over females. After the establishment of the Soviet Union, Lenin boasted that 'except for Soviet Russia, there is not a single country in the world in which there is complete equality between men and women'. Equality for females has remained a fundamental aspiration of the Soviet Union ever since, and it has been achieved to a limited extent. Soon after the revolution of 1917, a sharp break with the old system of morality and sex roles took place; females were suddenly granted freedom from the secondary status traditionally imposed upon them by parents, tsarist laws, and the Church. Previously, the male head of the family had almost absolute authority over his spouse, children, and other relatives living in the household. Sons could eventually escape this tyrannical rule and set up their own familial dictatorships, but females were permanently bound to a subordinate role by fathers and then by husbands. Females had no voice in political affairs, nor could they inherit an estate from the father; both divorce and birth control were prohibited.

Much of that changed after the 1917 revolution. Females could then leave the family for the cities, terminate unwanted pregnancies, exercise individual choice in marriage, and obtain divorce from an undesirable partner. Females are now represented in all occupations and professions and in the bureaucracy; they perform physical labour on construction sites and they serve as administrators. Appearances, though, are deceptive. Females were allowed to fill some male roles largely because decades of internal disorder, war, and reconstruction limited the number of males available. But females are employed mostly in the lower ranks and at lower pay. Slightly more than 70 per cent of secondary-school teachers are females, but 72 per cent of the principals are males. Furthermore, the pendulum has swung back to the old order. Beginning with Stalin's assumption of complete power in the late 1930s, divorce became increasingly difficult to achieve and the life of the female again focused upon child-bearing and the performance of domestic labour in behalf of a dominant male. Distinguished service in baby-production was rewarded, ranging from the Maternity Medal for five children up to the title of Mother Heroine for ten or more offspring.

That the Soviet Union has more female doctors than male doctors is often pointed to as an example of the equality of the sexes. About 70 per cent of the doctors in the Soviet Union are indeed females, but the heads of hospitals are almost always males. The great number of doctors who are females is explained by the lack of desire on the part of males to enter the medical profession because of the low pay. The earnings of doctors are less than three-fourths the wages of the worker in industry. Medicine is not the high-prestige occupation that it is in the United States and in many other countries. Nor have females achieved high positions in the Soviet government. Although females are heavily represented in the membership of the Communist Party, males hold all of the important posts. The most powerful governing body is the fifteen-member Politburo, which at the time of writing included no females. In fact, only once since 1917 has a female served as a member, and then for a mere four years. The ninety-nine ministers and heads of government committees also are males. Females have obviously been allowed to enter every segment of the economy and the bureaucracy, but only in inferior positions. Furthermore, working females are still expected to assume the primary responsibility in caring for children, cleaning house, and preparing meals. This double burden of employment and housekeeping thus makes equality an illusion.

Males in one society or another fill every occupational role that humans have devised. In addition, males maintain their exclusive control over such roles as warfare and hunting. The same things cannot be said about females. No occupation exists that is universally female. ♂♀ When males join armies, they serve as nurses, launderers, housekeepers, and cooks – occupations that Western cultures traditionally regard as 'feminine'. But when females join armies they seldom fill masculine positions, such as those of fighter pilots or paratroopers.

Men may cook, or weave or dress dolls or hunt hummingbirds, but if such activities are appropriate occupations of men, then the whole society, men and women alike, votes them as important. When the same occupations are performed by women, they are regarded as less important. ♂♀

A striking example of the way in which societies assign a job to one sex or the other – and then make the male-assigned job much more rewarding – comes from New Guinea. Females there grow sweet potatoes, and males grow a similar vine with an edible tuberous root known as a yam. Little difference is seen between the two crops or in the effort needed to grow them, yet the male-grown yam is the prestige food. What is true of yam-growing in New Guinea is true also of many sex-defined roles in Western societies, in which the male's tasks are given prestige, higher pay, more excitement, or other rewards. When a culture develops a tradition of *haute cuisine* in contrast to ordinary domestic cooking, as occurred in France, then the chefs are always male. We can be certain that if males menstruated, they would brag about it rather than interpret it as a clear sign of infirmity, inferiority, and irrationality. Females have become so hopelessly subjugated by this state of affairs that in various surveys anywhere from five to twelve times as many females as males have said they wished they were of the opposite sex.

What accounts for the fact that high-status roles and positions are always the province of males? The most common explanation is simply that male dominance is rooted in our biological heritage. Males are indeed dominant in virtually all monkey and ape species. Those who espouse the biological explanation state that this is as it should be, because primate males are significantly larger and stronger. The early hominid females are presumed to have devoted themselves to caring for offspring and gathering plants, while the larger, stronger males hunted dangerous game and fought enemies. This argument cannot be supported, for several reasons. First, sexual dimorphism in humans is a reality, but it is not as extreme as in many monkey and ape species; the males of certain baboons, for example, weigh twice as much as females. Second, some of the differences in strength between the human sexes are apparently due to male physical conditioning from the earliest years. As a matter of fact, athletically trained females are not dramatically inferior to athletically trained males in certain physical abilities. Johnny Weissmuller gained fame in 1924 by winning the 400-metre free-style swimming event at the Olympic Games (and was soon to gain even greater fame for his portrayal in the movies of the sexist Tarzan). Yet the current female world record for this event is about 20 per cent faster than Weissmuller's. Third, in many societies females perform the more onerous physical labour, carry the heavier loads, and walk while males ride. And still the males dominate females in those societies.

A more recent explanation emphasizes the male's greater aggressiveness, which itself is the result of the male's production of androgen hormones. ♂♀ Because this trait is the clearest example of sex differences in childhood (as stated earlier), the explanation for male dominance might seem to reside in the hormones. Experiments with non-human primates appear to bear that out; for example, female monkeys injected with androgens usually become much more aggressive. But what is true for children and for monkeys is not a suitable explanation for adult human behaviour. Male dominance among adults is almost never based on overt aggression. In fact, no human society permits physical aggression against other members of the group as a habitual practice. The childhood bully who carries such behaviour into adult life is likely to be executed by his community (as among the Eskimoes), to be shot with poisoned arrows (as among the Bushmen), or to be put either in prison or in a mental institution (as is the custom of most modern societies).

The biological explanation, whether based on sexual dimorphism or on hormones, does not stand up under close analysis. Nor does the economic explanation: that male hunters held a monopoly over the supplies of meat and from there extended their dominance to the political, social, and sexual spheres. The major flaw in this reasoning is that females rather than males are the primary producers of food in numerous societies that nevertheless cast their female sex in subordinate roles. Females in New Guinean horticultural societies grow almost every bit of the food, but the female is never dominant over the male or even equal to him. A sexual explanation – that males are the sexual aggressors and that females exist as prizes for them – also has been offered but it does not have much merit. Supporters of this theory have argued that rape is committed only by males and that sexual assault by a female on an unwilling male is impossible. Further support is asserted because of the high value placed on female chastity in many societies and the double standard of sexual conduct for males. The sexual explanation, however, fails to account for the numerous societies in which males dominate but in which females nevertheless are the sexual aggressors and in which no premium is placed on female chastity. Other explanations that cannot stand up under observed facts or logic are the Marxist argument that in the beginning females held power but had it seized from them by males, and a psychoanalytic one that males envied the female reproductive power and therefore they acted in concert to control it. ♂♀

Probably the most reasonable hypothesis is one attributing the origins and perpetuation of male dominance to physical combat. This chapter has already mentioned the great paradox of male dominance: females, as rulers of the nursery, could easily tip the balance in the next generation towards the production of large numbers of aggressive females and a small number of passive males whose primary function would be to inseminate them. Why has not this strategy been accepted anywhere in the world? Imagine a social group in which females entered into a conspiracy to fill the roles formerly filled by males. Within a generation or two, the females would have created a matriarchy in which they equalled male competence in all roles – with the sole exception of hand-to-hand combat. Even though the physical strength of trained males is not much greater than that of trained females, a difference does nevertheless exist. Females are equalling Olympic records set by males only a decade or so ago, at least in swimming events; but they do not do as well in others requiring them to run far and fast, lift weights, or hurl the javelin and shot putt. At the 1976 Olympics, females were about 20 per cent slower than males in the 400-metre dash; one male threw the javelin (the Olympic version of the spear) almost a third farther than any female. And because of their somewhat heavier musculature, males can wield a weightier club and bend a stronger bow. More important, females would be considerably slower in advancing towards an enemy to attack or retreating after a defeat because their running speed is reduced by the wider construction of the pelvis that allows for the birth canal.

A matriarchy that bred few males and took over their roles in battle would, therefore, find itself at a decided disadvantage. The matriarchy would be doomed to extinction by neighbouring societies in which males still did the fighting. Once the members of a society realized that its survival depended upon breeding large numbers of strong and aggressive males, then those members would tend to give preferential care to male offspring, to practise female infanticide, and in general to elevate males to superior roles. The females would acquiesce in this arrangement, even though grudgingly, for the simple reason that if they did not, they would have doomed themselves, their offspring, and their entire group to extermination. The Iroquois provide an example. Females had total authority over the upbringing of children and they even occasionally accompanied males on hunts. Yet they never participated as armed combatants. ♂♀

Unlike the biological, economic, Marxist, or psychoanalytic explanations, the hand-to-hand combat hypothesis answers the crucial question: Why do females go along with a system unjust to them and which they could easily subvert in the nursery? Only because of the need for male protection are females willing to perform heavy labour, provide most of the food, bear the children, do the housekeeping – and nevertheless receive a lesser share of society's rewards. This state of affairs certainly was not arrived at consciously. Any societies of dominant females that failed to produce combat-ready males would have been at a disadvantage and would have died out. The ones that survived would have been those that bred large numbers of strong and aggressive males. And once males were given a pre-eminent position as warriors, such a system would necessarily be self-perpetuating. The society would have to encourage aggression in male children. It would also have to reward the successful warriors – and the most obvious ways to do so would be with high prestige and with sexual access to many females. Such male sexual privileges could not exist unless females were reared to fill passive and submissive roles.

The constant belittling of female work and the exaltation of male roles would gradually extend throughout the entire society: leadership, control of property, and the tracing of descent much more often through the male line than through the female. The effectiveness of males in combat would be enhanced through participation in competitive sports and mock combats like wrestling and duelling. Once male dominance became established in these ways, it would be almost impossible to change because it would tend to feed on itself:

The fiercer the males, the greater the amount of warfare, the more such males are needed. Also, the fiercer the males, the more sexually aggressive they become, the more exploited are the females, and the higher the incidence of polygyny – control over several wives by one man. Polygyny in turn intensifies the shortage of women, raises the level of frustration among the junior males, and increases the motivation for going to war. The amplification builds to an excruciating climax; females are held in contempt and killed in infancy, making it necessary for men to go to war to capture wives in order to rear additional numbers of aggressive men.

The feedback situation just described has been well documented among the Yanomamo Indians in southern Venezuela and northern Brazil. An anthropologist who has been studying them since 1964 has labelled them 'the fierce people' because their culture is built around persistent conflict. Yanomamo battles are waged solely to capture females or to retaliate for such capture by neighbouring villages. Yet, absurdly enough, the Yanomamos practise female infanticide on the grounds that males are more valuable to a people who are always fighting. Female infanticide in turn causes marriageable females to be scarce, and it is their scarcity that leads to chronic combat. Though such a system may seem ideal for males, one should remember that they pay a severe price. They constitute the bulk of the victims of the fighting that keeps the system going. About a quarter of all male Yanomamos die in battle.

The combat hypothesis might be objected to on the basis that in modern warfare the importance of males is greatly diminished. But it should be recalled that armed conflict has remained overwhelmingly hand-to-hand despite the recent invention of nuclear weapons and guided missiles. Witness the millions killed in the trenches during World War I, the enormous casualties during landings on Pacific atolls and the beaches of Normandy during World War II, and the losses among the infantry in Vietnam. Hand-to-hand combat has been the only kind for all but the past few decades of the hominids' three-million-year history. The fact that such combat is no longer standard in a few modern and developing nations does not lessen its significance for the millions of years that went before. ♂♀

*

Whatever the true explanation for male dominance, males and females in every society have been clearly defined according to sex stereotypes – those constellations of traits that are perceived as distinguishing the two sexes. The 'unisex revolution' of the 1960s in North America and Europe has had a negligible effect on these stereotypes, even among some supposedly liberated college students. Surveys have indicated that large segments of the educated population still perceive females as less competent, less independent, less objective, and less logical than males. Furthermore, the surveys have shown that females as well as males regard male traits as more desirable. Females are thus placed in a double bind by the impossibility of living up to the standards that have been set for them as females on the one hand and, on the other, as adult members of their society. Females who behave in ways that are regarded as desirable for all adults in the society (that is, who follow the preferred male stereotype) risk censure for failing to act in ways that most people consider appropriately feminine (that is, less competent, less independent, less objective, and less logical than males). But if they act as stereotypical females, then they merely confirm that females are less competent, less independent, and so on than males. Either way, they lose. ♂♀

In virtually all societies that have been studied, a child's ability to identify his or her own sex occurs very early, usually around the middle of the second year. Once sex identification has become established, it is usually irreversible except in cases of homosexuality, transvestism, and sex-change operations. Some societies show much more tolerance towards deviant sex roles than does that of the United States. A survey of sexual behaviour obtained data on homosexuality in seventy-six societies. Forty-nine of the seventy-six regarded homosexual behaviour as normal. Some societies have institutionalized homosexuality to a remarkable extent, as for example those of ancient Greece and the Mohave Indians in southern California. On the other hand, Kinsey's studies of sexual behaviour in the United States during the 1940s showed homosexuality to be quite rare. About 4 per cent of males surveyed had been exclusively homosexual throughout their lives, and the percentage was approximately the same for females. Considerably higher percentages were reported for people who were not exclusively homosexual but who had had overt homosexual experiences leading to orgasm: 37 per cent for males and 13 per cent for females. The much rarer occurrence of homosexual experiences among females is accounted for by two facts. First of all, females in United States society have traditionally been less promiscuous than males, whether the females are heterosexual or homosexual. Second, female homosexuality seems to be characterized more by emotional attachments than by explicitly sexual ones. In one survey of 1200 females who said they had had intense emotional experiences with other females, only about a quarter admitted to genital contact as part of the experience. ♂♀

Sex-role stereotyping begins before birth – when the expectant parents wonder whether the infant will be a boy or a girl – and it accelerates from the moment of birth. The obstetrician's usual sequence of information to the waiting father is, first, the condition of the mother, then the sex of the infant, and finally the health of the infant. The second piece of information sets in motion the long process of making clear the sex role the infant will later fill. A pink or a blue layette is purchased, a name is chosen from the appropriate category, and the pronoun *he* or *she* is used. Gradually, ever so gradually, the child is nudged and cajoled towards the role expected of him or her. First the parents, then relatives, friends, and teachers constantly remind the growing child that 'brave boys don't cry' or that 'nice girls don't do that'.

Studies that have been made in the United States to discover parental attitudes about bringing up each sex show a remarkable uniformity in the ways parents sex-type their children. For boys, the emphasis is on achievement and competition, control of feelings, and obedience. For girls, the same parents emphasize close personal relationships with themselves and the display of affection and emotions. Sex-typing is not exclusively a United States phenomenon. A study of university students in six countries (the United States, England, Finland, Norway, Denmark, and Sweden) compared their respective ideas about the ideal male and female. The students were in general agreement that males are more assertive, dominating, competitive, and self-controlled, and females more affectionate, impulsive, sympathetic, generous, and sensitive. Subtle differences among the national groups were nevertheless observed. In Denmark and Sweden, two countries with a long history of concern for social equality, somewhat less emphasis was placed on sex stereotypes. And in the United States, both males and females were distinguished from those of other countries in three important ways: a greater emphasis on sex-typing; more emphasis on competitive achievement; and less importance given to control of aggression in males. ♂♀

The cultural stereotypes of the 'passive' female and the 'aggressive' male have been carried over into discussions of human sexuality. Sometimes these stereotypes refer solely to the bodily gyrations of males and females during intercourse: the male as the actor, the female as the instrument acted upon. In any event, the female's receptivity is not just a matter of her open vagina. In the folklore of sexuality, her receptivity is supposedly related to her behaviour as a passive and submissive vessel for the male phallus. Such stereotypes, though, are difficult to sustain for our species as a whole simply because societies around the world exhibit a wide range of sexual behaviour. Unlike most mammals, in which mating behaviour is largely inherited, human beings have invented almost all of the details of their sex lives. Any pair of dogs will perform the same series of actions before, during, and after mating – but humans are unique in the tremendous variety of their sexual behaviour.

Sexual signals, caresses, foreplay, words, bodily positions, and frequency of intercourse all vary greatly among humans, both from culture to culture and from individual to individual within each culture as well. As a result, generalizations are almost impossible to make about the sexual behaviour of the human species as a whole. Certain sexual behaviours are generally typical of the male and female in a particular society at a particular time – yet differences still can be found according to age group, social class, and religious background. People in Western societies in particular find it difficult to make generalizations that encompass both their sexual behaviour and that of various other peoples. Take, for example, the Mangaians, a Polynesian people inhabiting an atoll south-west of Tahiti. To a Westerner, they would at first appear extremely prudish. Husbands and wives show no affection in public; even young children are not allowed to hold hands; parents never discuss sex with their children. Nevertheless, the Mangaians are intensely preoccupied with sex, possibly more so than any other group whose behaviour has been studied.

Their obsession is with the genitals; they are so totally unresponsive to the rest of the human body that a Mangaian male would find bewildering the interest of North American and European males in the female breasts and buttocks – whereas he will show an equal concern with the size, shape, and hair texture of the female's pubic mound. Young Mangaian females are equally knowledgeable about the male organ. Sexual intercourse begins well before puberty; after puberty, when Mangaians carry on intercourse with exuberance, it becomes extremely sophisticated. Young males compete in the number of orgasms achieved, and females boast about the succession of males they have received throughout the night. The Mangaian female shows virtually no interest in romance, protestations of affection, or physical foreplay. Least of all does she look for love in a partner. Sexual intimacy is not achieved by first demonstrating personal affection, as is usually the case in Western societies. The reverse is true. A man who can achieve many orgasms proves both his own virility and the female's desirability, and only then does he qualify to become an object of affection. So intense is Mangaian sexuality that eighteen-year-old males are reported to average three orgasms per night, every night; by the age of twenty-eight the number decreases somewhat, to an average of twice for nearly every night of the week. ♂♀

Or compare the Mangaians' behaviour with that of Asiatic Indians, who engage in sexual relations much less freely than people in most societies. I am aware that this statement runs counter to a commonly held notion that India's soaring population is due to a preoccupation with sex – a notion bolstered by the popularity of the *Kamasutra* and other ancient Indian sex manuals. In part the Indians' lack of interest in sex is, of course, due to poor diet and insufficient food; malnourished people lack the energy to be all that sexy. The major cause, though, is cultural. Hindu scripture regards the conservation of semen (called the 'vital force') as essential for physical, mental, and spiritual strength. Semen is believed to accumulate slowly, so that every orgasm means a loss of the vital force that has taken so long to create. Among devout Hindus, the surest way to find God is to take a vow of celibacy, as may be done even by a man who is married. As a result of poor diet and cultural inhibitions combined, Asiatic Indian females have sexual relations only about a quarter to a half as often as females in the United States. ♂♀

Even if continent societies like India are taken into account, the human species participates in sexual activity to an extent unequalled by any other mammal or even primate. The rampant sexuality of the non-human primates is a myth. A female chimpanzee has intercourse during a period of less than two weeks every two years, the time when she conceives. She does not become sexually receptive again until she has gone through the stages of pregnancy, birth, nursing, and finally weaning the offspring. Not only do humans engage in sexual activity much more frequently than non-human primates, but they appear to find it more pleasurable. The females of non-human primate species do not seem to experience orgasm, although males apparently do. Among most non-human primates, as among mammals in general, the duration of the sexual act is extremely short, often a matter of only ten seconds or so. Only among humans is the sex act a protracted experience. And humans mate at any season of the year, during advanced pregnancy, shortly after the birth of offspring, and at any stage of the female's monthly cycle (although in many cultures intercourse is avoided during the days of menstrual flow).

Most adults have a recurrent need for stimulation of the sex organs and the satisfaction of an orgasm. The source of this need is not really understood. In males, sperm continually produced by the testes accumulates and must be released from time to time. The quantity that accumulates, however, is small, and no sensory receptors are known about that detect its pressure in the way that pressure is felt in the urinary bladder. Since no similar accumulation of fluids occurs in the sexual organs of females, some other explanation must obviously be found for the female sex drive. Apparently the sexual urge for both males and females originates in the hypothalamus portion of the brain, but the pituitary gland and hormones also seem to be involved. As yet unknown is the exact mechanism whereby the brain causes the individual to become sexually responsive and to seek satisfaction through the sexual organs. A bewildering variety of physical and psychological stimuli can trigger sexual activity: stimuli originating in the sex organs themselves or in secondary sexual characteristics such as the beard or the breasts, the style of hair the tone of voice, and even 'A sweet disorder in the dress' that Robert Herrick stated 'kindles in clothes a wantonness'. Many scientists are increasingly convinced that scent plays an important part, whether in the form of natural body odours or of perfume (which usually includes extracts from the sex glands of mammals). Experiments have shown that male monkeys are attracted to females by olfactory signals, known as 'pheromones', which are produced in the vagina by estrogen hormones – and the same thing might be true of humans as well.

Sexual activity, though, is rarely governed solely by the physiological state of the participants. Frequency of intercourse, for example, almost never is regulated entirely by desire, by the stimulation which the individual experiences, or by potency. Every society, even the most permissive, imposes at least some restrictions upon sexual activity and at various times enforces an abstinence that has nothing to do with a person's capacity to respond and to perform sexually. Premarital relations are permitted for both sexes in a clear majority of human societies, but female adultery is almost universally condemned. Most societies also prohibit intercourse during at least a portion of the wife's pregnancy – although the Mangaians copulate right up to the onset of labour pains. In fact, some Mangaian males prefer intercourse late in their wives' pregnancy because they describe the female genitals at that time as 'wetter, softer, fatter, and larger'.

Cultural intervention in the individual's sex life over a long evolutionary span has undoubtedly produced the striking contrasts between the sexual behaviour of humans and of non-human primates. Perhaps the most remarkable of these differences is the greater control exerted by the cerebral cortex of humans as contrasted with the overriding role of hormones in the non-human primates. An aroused human can forego the sexual act if thoughts interfere, but a chimpanzee (which probably also has thoughts) cannot. Closely related to this evolutionary shift is the prevalence of indirect and non-biological stimulation to excitement in humans, such as the sound of music, sweet words of love, and even the promise of marriage. With other primates, excitement seems to be due completely to sensory stimulation and genital manipulation. Humans differ from the other primates in additional ways, particularly in the greater variability of their sexual practices and in their assignment of sexual activities to the parts of the day least active in other respects: night, early morning, and during the hours of siesta in tropical countries.

*

A major transformation has taken place over the past several decades in the relations between the sexes, in sex roles, and in sexuality generally. The situation in North America and Europe has been much publicized, but a sexual revolution appears to be occurring in other parts of the world as well. For example, the policy of the Soviet Union had been very prudish during the first half century of its existence. Premarital sex was sharply condemned by public opinion and appears to have been an unusual occurrence. But nowadays one out of every ten births in the Soviet Union is illegitimate, and in some Soviet cities the figure is one out of every three births. Extramarital sex is becoming the norm rather than the exception. Increasing numbers of young Russians are even avoiding matrimony altogether because of the greater opportunity for sexual relations outside the marriage bond. The new atmosphere of sexual permissiveness is being widely condemned by the authorities, though on economic rather than moral grounds. The Soviet government regards such permissiveness as a threat to the family and a contributor to the falling birth rate, both of which jeopardize plans for economic development. [37]

Social scientists differ widely in their evaluation of the sexual revolution. Some have perhaps exaggerated it, whereas others have declared that any revolution that may have taken place has been limited to the educated middle class. Two studies provide a basis for judging the extent of the revolution, at least in the United States. The first is that made by Alfred Kinsey and his colleagues in the 1940s and the second is one made in 1972, from a careful sampling by age, education, occupation, urban as opposed to rural background, geo-

graphical location, and ethnic identity of the United States population above age eighteen. ♂♀ A comparison of the two studies leaves
no doubt that sexual activity has undergone a dramatic transformation in three decades. Frequency of copulation has increased markedly, not only in the young and the unmarried but also among
married couples. Three decades ago, Kinsey reported that married
couples in the 25–35 age bracket had an average frequency of intercourse of 1.95 times per week; by 1972 the average figure had risen to
2.55 times. For the group aged 55 and over during the 1940s, intercourse averaged once every two weeks; by 1972, that rate had
doubled for those in the same age group.

Not only is sexual intercourse more frequent, but its practice is
becoming more varied. The percentage of college-educated married
males who reported that their wives used fellatio with them rose
from 43 per cent in 1938–46 to 61 per cent in 1972. Among those
with less education, the increase was even more marked: from 15 to
54 per cent. Comparable rates were reported by females for cunni-
lingus within marriage. Three decades ago, only a third of couples
had experimented with the female-above position, whereas by 1972
three-quarters had. And almost all males and females in the 1972
survey believed strongly that it is appropriate for females as well as
males to initiate sexual intercourse. Not only are married couples
having intercourse more often, with greater experimentation, but
they are also spending more time at it. The females in the Kinsey
studies reported an average of twelve minutes of foreplay; in the
1972 sample the average was fifteen.

A marked change in attitude has accompanied the revolution in
the purely physical aspects of sex. The people who responded to the
1972 survey tended not to find various sexual behaviours objectionable, even though they might not themselves have engaged in them.
Eighty-four per cent of males regarded premarital sex as acceptable
for both sexes, so long as they are emotionally involved with their
partners – thus almost completely doing away with the traditional
double standard. An unequivocal stand against homosexuality has
existed in Western cultures since early Christian times; yet nearly
half of the sample believed that it should not be treated as unlawful
conduct. About four-fifths of both sexes did not regard masturbation
as wrong. Mate-swapping has long been strongly disapproved of in
the United States because it violates entrenched ideas about marriage and the family. The 1972 survey showed that mate-swapping is

still regarded as deviant behaviour by a majority of the population, but, surprisingly, not an overwhelming majority: nearly a third of the males and a fifth of the females considered it acceptable.

Changing sex attitudes have given both males and females the option to express a part of their humanity that society has long caused to be repressed. Not all social scientists, though, see the new permissiveness as an unmixed blessing:

This parade of statistics, though important, ends up being mildly depresssing. One can conjure up visions of these legions of couples fiddling and fooling with each other in this tremendous forward leap of marital eroticism – and yet, if I am right, one price paid for this new capacity to explore one's sensory responses has been the abandonment of a meaningful emotional life outside the home. Another price is a vastly increased instability in marital relations. A final price of the eroticization of the couple's life, both before marriage and after, is the disintegration of a sense of the lineage of the family. Nothing is free in this world. ♂♀

Nor does sexual liberation necessarily indicate a change in the subordinate role of the female. The new sensual freedom for females in the bedroom has not been accompanied by equal political, social, and economic freedom outside it. Sex roles and the status of females are still inextricably meshed into the workings of the entire society.

Females today are, nevertheless, considerably more liberated from male dominance than they were in industrializing nations a century ago. Actually, the suppressed status of females was a temporary aberration brought on by the unusual circumstances that accompanied the early stages of the Industrial Revolution. Previously, the economic interdependence of husbands, wives, and offspring operating small family businesses or family farms had given females a measure of economic and social power. The husbands who went to work in the new factories became increasingly independent of economic contributions by their wives and children. Work had been removed from the family environment. And whether or not a husband earned an adequate living depended completely upon himself rather than upon the co-operative family unit.

Many wives and children eventually followed adult males into factories and mines, but they did so out of the necessity brought on by poverty. The social programmes of the late nineteenth and early twentieth centuries – such as free schools for children and laws prohibiting females from performing heavy work – alleviated the situation somewhat. But, ironically, these well-intentioned programmes worked against the freedom of females by imprisoning them in the household and leaving economic life the exclusive province of the male. And at the very time when the female's role was restricting her to the household, and her life was becoming centred on home and children, a drastic decline in the birth rate was taking place in all the industrializing nations – thus diminishing the household obligations for which she now had the time.

The Victorian era in Britain, and somewhat later in the rest of Europe and in North America, saw an ideological change that made a virtue out of the necessity of male economic power. The domestic encapsulation of females became rationalized in various ways. Female personality and biology were said to be weak, and thus suited only for a housebound way of life. Females whose mothers and grandmothers had laboured in the fields alongside their husbands were now pictured as fragile creatures who swooned before the harsh realities of life. The end result was that after only a few generations, females had been effectively socialized for submission while their husbands were being socialized for achievement. The attitudes towards male and female roles fostered by industrialization became too well entrenched to have been quickly overridden by the changes that are now occurring. Modernization offers females the opportunity, at the very least, to resume the freer and more open relations with males that had been lost during the Industrial Revolution.

# 11

# A Diverse Species

Beginning in the fifteenth century, the early explorers encountered peoples of diverse appearance and customs who presented them with the question: Was it possible that these 'savages' were cut from the same pattern as themselves? Such exotic peoples threatened the traditional definition of how a human looked and behaved. So the initial reaction of Europeans was to deny membership in the human species to those whose strange body sizes and shapes, unusual skin colours, shameless sexual behaviour, and heathenish superstitions ran counter to all the beliefs about humankind that had been cherished by the societies of the West. Pope Paul III nevertheless declared in 1537 that the American Indians (and, by extension, other 'savages') were indeed human, possessed souls, and thus were eligible for conversion to the Christian faith. No longer could the white, Christianized Europeans regard themselves as the sole standard for all humanity. ♂♀

As they learned about more and more diverse peoples, Europeans began to realize that they themselves represented only one small branch on the tree of humankind. Two explanations were put forth to account for the diversity in appearance and customs of exotic peoples: 'nature' (that is, heredity) and 'nurture' (environment). One or the other has been fashionable at varying times. The 'nurture' explanation predominated around the end of the seventeenth century, when it was given its classic expression in John Locke's *Essay Concerning Human Understanding*. Locke held that each infant came into the world as a *tabula rasa* (a 'blank slate', devoid of heritable factors) on which the environment wrote by means of experiences. The explanation favouring 'nature', or heredity, became paramount after the discoveries of Charles Darwin were simplemindedly applied to all biological, sociological, and psychological differences between peoples. Wealthy Europeans claimed that their superior heredity justified their exploitation both of the poor at home and of alien peoples abroad. These notions were challenged by Karl Marx, who believed that children of rich and poor brought up in the same environment would end up equally successful or unsuccessful. Many people who agreed with little else that Marx preached agreed with him about this. So complete was the environmentalists' victory over 'nature' in the early decades of this century that an influential United States psychologist wrote in 1925:

Give me a dozen healthy infants, well-formed, and my own specified world to bring them up in, and I'll guarantee to take any one at random and train him to become any type of specialist I might select – a doctor, lawyer, artist, merchant-chief, and yes, even beggar-man and thief, regardless of his talents, penchants, tendencies, abilities, vocations and race of his ancestors. ♂♀

Nowadays, of course, most scientists believe that nature and nurture are not opposing concepts, but rather that they are interwoven to form what may be envisioned as a lattice of interactions. Either one might be of paramount importance in a particular instance, but in other instances heredity and environment may combine to produce consequences greater than the mere sums of their separate effects. And in still others, environment and heredity may be in conflict and thereby to some degree each will nullify the influence of the other.

The difficulties involved in sorting out such influences are demonstrated by human adaptation to high altitudes. Perhaps 12 per cent of the world's population today live in mountainous regions, among the last environments on the planet to be occupied by humans. Lowlanders who travel to high altitudes often experience certain physical effects, commonly known as 'mountain sickness', which are the result of a decreased intake of oxygen: fatigue, sleeplessness, headaches, stomach cramps, rapid pulse rate, and inability to manage even slight physical exertion. Some people never adapt to the mountains and must return to lower altitudes. For most, the distress lessens after a week or two, as they become acclimated – primarily by an increase in the number of red blood cells whose haemoglobin transports oxygen from the lungs to the body's tissues.

Living at high altitudes would thus seem to be strictly an environmental problem, a matter of getting used to the mountains. But it is not. No matter how successful a newcomer's adjustment may appear to be, it is never as complete as the adaptation of those who are native to high altitudes. Indians living in the Peruvian Andes are biologically quite different from Indians belonging to related groups whose home is in the lowlands. Those native to the mountains have less need for oxygen because of their small size, lower pulse rate, and lower blood pressure while engaging in physical activity. And their disproportionately huge chests, their large hearts, and the corresponding larger amounts of blood in their lungs enable oxygen to move more rapidly to all parts of the body. Most highlanders also grow and develop more slowly than neighbouring lowlanders, thus requiring less oxygen during the crucial early years of life. The growth of both males and females in the Andes continues beyond the twentieth year, and differences in size between the sexes do not appear until about the age of sixteen.

People from low altitudes who seemingly have adjusted after many years in the high mountains really turn out in fact not to have done so. Females run much greater risks of miscarriage or of producing children with birth defects. The infertility of domestic animals in the mountains was early observed by the Spanish conquistadors, and was one reason that Pizarro transferred his capital from Jauja (at an altitude of 10,824 feet) to Lima, only a little above sea level. After Spaniards had settled in the Andes and brought over Spanish wives, it became apparent that high altitude caused infertility in humans as well. A Spanish priest observed:

The Indians are healthiest and where they multiply the most prolifically is in these same cold air-tempers, which is quite the reverse of what happens to children of the Spaniards, most of whom when born in such regions do not survive. But where it is most noticeable is in those who have half, a quarter, or any admixture of Indian blood; better they survive and grow; so that it is now a common saying based on everyday experience that babes having some Indian in them run less risk in the cold regions than those not having this admixture. ♂♀

At the high-altitude mining centre of Potosí, Bolivia, fifty-three years would pass before a Spanish female gave birth to a living child. And for long after that, it continued to be so unusual for a Spanish child to be born at high altitudes that any such birth was attributed to a miracle-working saint. The Indian population of the high Andes, in the meantime, reproduced with customary vigour. These Indians had inhabited the Andes for at least 9000 years. During that time, any females unable to produce live infants had obviously been replaced by those whose inheritance allowed them to do so.

High-altitude adaptation clearly is too complex to be reduced to a question of nature *v.* nurture. Actually, three different kinds of adaptation may be distinguished: in those who have made a short-term adjustment and do not suffer from mountain sickness; in those born in the mountains, whose growth and development show modifications to high-altitude conditions; and finally, in those born of parents who already possess an inherited adaptation to high altitudes. Nor do these adaptations themselves exist in isolation. Human beings display much plasticity in response to the environment; they either may or may not develop adaptations to high altitudes. Those who are born in the mountains and who do adapt will acquire during their growth and development the enlarged lung volume, high red-cell count, increased haemoglobin, and lower blood pressure that are the physical characteristics of high-altitude natives. Those individuals, on the other hand, who lack the inherited potential, can still achieve most of these characteristics by residing for a long time at a high altitude, so long as they begin to do so when very young.

What has been said about high-altitude adaptation is true as well for adaptations to other environmental stresses. All humans respond to cold by shivering (thus producing heat), but some populations seem better able to endure cold than others. Eskimoes can keep their hands immersed in icy water for extremely long periods of time, much longer than most people of European ancestry. The hands of Eskimoes generally stay warmer, a greater amount of blood flows through them, and they possess a superior ability to perform precise manipulation under icy conditions – all of which seems to indicate the importance of heredity. But Newfoundland fishermen who have spent years at their occupation do nearly as well, thus indicating that it is possible to become hardened to cold water by constant exposure. So the ability to withstand cold apparently derives both from inheritance and from acclimatization during the lifetime of the individual. Eskimoes who moved to a temperate climate for nine months were much better able to bear cold when they returned to the Arctic than European mountaineers who had become acclimatized – an indication that something in the Eskimo inheritance affords adaptation to cold. That a non-inherited component must exist also, however, has been demonstrated in a comparison of two groups of Australian Aborigines. Members of one desert-inhabiting group do not suffer discomfort from the bitterly cold nights there, even though body temperature and metabolic rates drop markedly. But coastal Aborigines, who had never been exposed to similarly low temperatures, are less able to bear the cold than desert Aborigines or even than Europeans who have become acclimatized to the desert. ♂♀

\*

The most obvious diversity found among human beings is in regard to size. The extremes in males, when those suffering from gigantism and dwarfism are included, are a height of 8 feet 11 inches on one hand and of 2 feet 2 inches on the other. The human physique ranges from extremes of lean to obese. Common-sense belief has long held that body proportions and personality go together. Tall people are supposed to be kindly and short people aggressive. The opinion that fat people are jolly and lean people are dour is one that Shakespeare put into the mouth of Julius Caesar:

> Let me have men about me that are fat,
> Sleek-headed men, and such as sleep a-nights.
> Yon Cassius has a lean and hungry look;
> He thinks too much: such men are dangerous. ♂♀

Common sense was given the stamp of scientific approval in the nineteenth century, when ways were supposedly devised to determine a person's character from physical clues. An Italian physician, Cesare Lombroso, expounded a theory by which a 'born criminal' could be identified. Any person who displayed five characteristics from a long list that included a receding forehead, a flat nose, large ears, a projecting chin, left-handedness, and a deficient sense of smell was said to belong to that category. This theory, which took into account no environmental influences whatever, was still influential several decades ago and even had the support of a prominent Harvard anthropologist. The belief in inherited criminality lingers on to this day, though no scientific evidence at all supports it. ♂♀

A very ambitious scientific attempt was made in the 1940s and 1950s to determine whether there is indeed a relation between physical traits and personality. The physiques of thousands of males were examined to arrive at basic types, of which three were eventually designated: endomorphy (characterized by a preponderance of digestive viscera and thus of body fat), mesomorphy (an abundance of muscle), and ectomorphy (a predominance of skin and thus a lean build). The classification was further refined by rating the individual in question on a seven-point scale for each of the three types, with 1 being the lowest rating. On such a scale, Abraham Lincoln – who was very low in endomorphy, very low in mesomorphy, and very high in ectomorphy – would thus have had a body type rated 1–1–7. The next step in the project was to rate large numbers of males for such personality traits as moodiness, tenseness, sluggishness, nervousness, and joviality. The personality traits were then compared with the basic body types. The researchers claimed to have discovered a number of correlations, such as between the endomorphic (or visceral) type and a personality that was jovial, relaxed, and given to such visceral satisfactions as eating. The muscular mesomorph was said to be competitive, aggressive, and energetic, and the lean ectomorph was described as thoughtful, sensitive, and restrained.

Strong objections have been raised to these studies, even though they wear many of the trappings of science. For one thing, the body types and the personality traits were both determined by the same investigators, thus producing a built-in bias towards certain hoped-for results. For another, a person's body type is affected in a major way by such environmental influences as diet, stress, and amount of exercise. Gains or losses of weight may thus occur several times during the course of a life without altering behaviour and personality in any predictable way. On the other hand, the common-sense beliefs on which this research was based continue to be valid to some extent. A person whose body shape or size is unusual (such as someone grossly obese or severely dwarfed) will usually develop compensating personality traits. ♂♀

Physique and size, for most humans, are not far removed from what would appear to be optimum for the species. In a survey of more than a thousand European females, for example, the numbers in each height category were as shown in the table on page 228. In other words, if a large sample is studied and the heights are then plotted on a graph, those of most people will tend to cluster near the midpoint of the height range. (Such a graph forms what statisticians call a 'bell-shaped curve', here indicated verbally by writing out the numbers falling into each category.) In this sample, therefore, more than 70 per cent of the females measured fall within the narrow range of 5 feet 1 inch and 5 feet 6 inches. ♂♀

The body size of humans is just about right for the pattern of life that the hominids developed. If humans were ant-sized, they would be capable of almost none of the cultural activities that have made us human. The problem is mainly one of physical laws. The smaller in size an animal is, the greater will be its surface area in proportion to volume. An ant therefore lives in a world in which it must constantly fight against surface adhesion – which is why it so easily becomes mired in a few drops of water. An ant-sized human might be able to put on clothes, but surface tension would prevent their being taken off. Furthermore, no ant could possibly light a fire and live, because even the smallest of flames would reach out farther than the length of its appendages and incinerate it. On the other hand, because of physical laws, for humans to be twice as tall as they are would be disastrous. In a human who was, say, eleven feet tall, a spill would have some thirty times the impact it has for one between five and six feet.

Evolutionary pressures have evidently kept humans within the appropriate size range. In one survey of thousands of births, of the approximately 4.5 per cent of those infants that were stillborn or who died in the first few weeks, almost every one was either exceptionally small or exceptionally large. Noticeable differences in size among human populations do, of course, exist. Among the Tutsi of Central Africa, males average about 6 feet 1 inch, whereas

| STATURE | NUMBER OF FEMALES OF THIS SIZE |
|---|---|
| 72″ | One |
| 71″ | Four |
| 70″ | Eight |
| 69″ | Seventeen |
| 68″ | Thirty-four |
| 67″ | Seventy-seven |
| 66″ | One hundred and ten |
| 65″ | One hundred and fifty-two |
| 64″ | One hundred and ninety-one |
| 63″ | One hundred and thirty-eight |
| 62″ | One hundred and eighty-one |
| 61″ | One hundred and forty |
| 60″ | Ninety-eight |
| 59″ | Forty-one |
| 58″ | Fifteen |
| 57″ | Eleven |
| 56″ | Three |
| 55″ | Two |

among the nearby Pygmy groups the males average only 4 feet 6 inches. Although size in both groups can be affected by numerous environmental influences – diet, stress, climate, and disease during growth – an important inherited component must nevertheless exist. Even with the best possible diet, Pygmies apparently could not grow to be very much larger than they do. ♂♀

The human physique is not correlated with what has been called 'race', as many people believe, but rather with evolutionary adaptations to climate. The tallest populations in the world include representatives from many racial stocks: Europeans (in Scotland), North American Indians (eastern tribes, some of the buffalo hunters of the Great Plains, and a few groups along the Colorado River), Central Africans (at the headwaters of the Nile), and some Australian Aborigines and Polynesians. The same thing can be said about very short populations: the Lapps of Scandinavia, some Asiatic Indians and Ceylonese, African Pygmies and Bushmen, American Indians of Labrador, and Negritos of Southeast Asia. Among tall populations, a thin build is typical of those in the tropics (such as the Tutsi), and a heavy build more typical of inhabitants of cold climates (Scottish highlanders). Similarly, short people native to cold areas are usually stocky (Eskimos) whereas short people native to hot regions are slight (Melanesians). In other words, regardless of whether they are tall or short, people are likely to be of heavy build in cold climates and of lean build in hot ones.

The explanation for these variations of physique with climate hinges upon heat control. Even when humans inhabit a temperate climate like that of southern California, they use more than 80 per cent of the energy contained in the food they eat merely to maintain a normal body temperature of 98.6 degrees. In an arctic climate, obviously, a person with the body proportions of a southern Californian would have to consume enormous amounts of food just to keep the body temperature up. The evolutionary solution to heat loss in cold climates (both for humans and for other mammals) has been the development of a stocky build, since a spherical shape exposes a smaller area of skin to the cold in proportion to volume than an attenuated one. Eskimos, for example, are short by North American and northern European standards, but they are also very stocky. The situation is just the opposite in the tropics, where both humans and warm-blooded animals must get rid of heat rather than preserve it. The evolutionary solution in tropical climates has usually been a

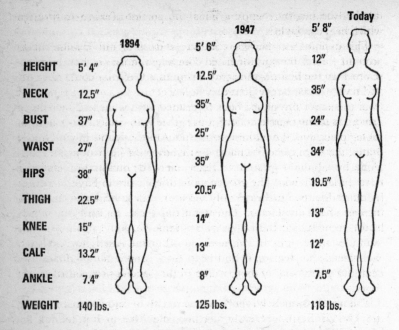

| | 1894 | 1947 | Today |
|---|---|---|---|
| | | | 5' 8" |
| | | 5' 6" | |
| HEIGHT | 5' 4" | | 12" |
| | | 12.5" | |
| NECK | 12.5" | | 35" |
| | | 35" | |
| BUST | 37" | | 24" |
| | | 25" | |
| WAIST | 27" | | 34" |
| | | 35" | |
| HIPS | 38" | | 19.5" |
| | | 20.5" | |
| THIGH | 22.5" | | 13" |
| | | 14" | |
| KNEE | 15" | | 12" |
| | | 13" | |
| CALF | 13.2" | | 7.5" |
| | | 8" | |
| ANKLE | 7.4" | | |
| WEIGHT | 140 lbs. | 125 lbs. | 118 lbs. |

THE CHANGING UNITED STATES FEMALE

In 1894, the manufacturers of a soft drink known as White Rock used a label on their bottles that depicted a goddess of purity. At that time the typical United States female (whom the label represented in idealized form) stood only 5 feet 4 inches, weighed 140 pounds, and was plump in her dimensions. By the time the company redesigned its label in 1947, the dimensions of the average female in the United States had changed, as shown in the centre drawing. She was now two inches taller, had lost weight, and was thinner in all parts of the body except the ankles. Another redrawing in 1975 (right) showed still a further increase in height, a shedding of seven more pounds, and a generally slimmer build. Although part of this transformation represents a change in aesthetic judgments about the ideal female figure, in part it is due also to the increase in human stature that has taken place around the world.

thin body shape, thus exposing a high proportion of skin area through which heat can be lost.

This explanation for variations in stature is still insufficient to account for all the known facts. The average size of hominids remained approximately the same for hundreds of thousands of years, and had increased very little until a few centuries ago – as is evident from the small size of the beds in historic homes and of the suits of armour seen in museums. But a rapid increase in stature has been taking place over the past few centuries. Among people in the United States, the average height has increased over the last two generations alone by about 1.5 inches. Even more dramatic are statistics from Japan showing the average size of children to have increased by more than two inches in only ten years. Clear evidence that such increases have accelerated emerges from those countries in which health records have been kept over a long period. In Norway, for example, the height of the average adult increased by 0.06 inch each decade between 1760 and 1830, by 0.13 each decade during the next fifty years, and by 0.25 in each of the decades between 1880 and 1940.

The trend towards larger size appears to be coming to an end in the United States, possibly because the inherited potential for growth has just about been reached. Between the beginning and the end of the last century, average stature in the United States increased by a total of four inches. But such steady growth in size ceased several decades ago among people in the highest socio-economic range – and it is now slowing down considerably among children belonging to the lower economic classes. The environmental factors in human growth – such as diet, sanitation, and freedom from childhood diseases – apparently are now making their maximum contribution. Growth will soon depend upon inherited potential alone.

Improved nutrition obviously has played an important role in the increased height of humans, but it does not entirely explain what has been happening. Increased stature is an adaptation not so much to the better quality of food as it is to quantity – that is, to the current propensity for over-eating. Statistics compiled by life-insurance companies in the United States show that people of normal weight live longer than those who are overweight, and that underweight individuals live longer still. A large body size, therefore, is advantageous for people who over-eat because the additional bulk metabolizes excess calories before they turn into fat. In other words, those people with an inherited potential for growing tall had a better chance to survive in an environment in which increased consumption of calories had become common. Such an adaptation is the reverse of the one long observed to occur among peasants, who must survive on a diet low in calories. Their small size makes fewer demands on the scant supply of calories available. The children of Mexican peasants who migrate to the United States grow considerably taller than either their parents or their relatives who remained at home – a result due at least in part to the greater number of calories available to growing children in the United States.

Stature is obviously the result of an interplay between inherited and environmental influences. Other examples of human diversity similarly do not support either nature or nurture exclusively. Yet for various specific traits, such as intelligence or mental illness, heredity must surely be more important in some cases and environment in others. Some scientists have investigated what at first appeared to be a very promising way to sort out the differential effects of heredity and environment. They could do just that, they reasoned, through studying two individuals whose heredity was exactly the same; thus any differences between the two would inevitably have to be the result of environment. Just such pairs of individuals were to be found in identical twins which used to be born about once in every 250 births (the figure is higher now because of the use of ovulation-inducing drugs and hormones to combat sterility).

An adult female normally produces a single egg about once a month. Two unfertilized eggs are occasionally released by the ovaries at the same time and are both fertilized by different sperm cells. The resulting twins can be of the same or of the opposite sexes. These 'fraternal twins', as they are called, are genetically no more alike than any other brothers or sisters born years apart would be; they differ from ordinary siblings only in having grown together in the womb and having been born at almost the same time. A rarer event is for a single egg to be fertilized by a sperm and then to divide into two eggs. Both eggs may become implanted in the uterus and grow into separate individuals, producing what are commonly known as 'identical twins'. Little inherited difference can be seen between populations around the world in regard to the frequency of identical twins. Most populations show an average of four or five identical twins per 1000 births. The birth of fraternal twins, though, apparently is influenced greatly by heredity, since a wide variation in frequency occurs from one population to another. Nigerian females, for example, produce about forty fraternal twins for every 1000 births, whereas in Japan the frequency is just slightly above two per 1000. This wide disparity appears to be due to the female's inheritance of genes that control the hormones which in turn control ovulation.

Since pairs of identical twins originate from a single fertilized egg, in theory their heredity should be exactly the same and they should show exactly the same behavioural traits. Any failure of both twins to exhibit the same trait would thus seemingly be explained on the basis of environment. For example, when one identical twin suffers from alcoholism, the other member of the pair will also be alcoholic about 65 per cent of the time. Presumably the 35 per cent of the cases in which alcoholism does not develop in the second twin could be attributed to the effects of environment, as in religious and ethical beliefs, social and economic class, and different individual experiences of each twin with alcoholics. The same thing apparently holds true for certain other behaviours, which show correlations of 98 per cent for male homosexuality, 86 per cent for schizophrenia, 50 per cent for vocational interests, and only 6 per cent for suicide.

Separating out the exact proportions of influences from heredity or environment, though, is difficult because identical twins share not only genes but also a common environment within the family: food habits, attire, speech, health care, and educational aims. Some environmental influences are clearly inherited, such as, most obviously, wealth. In most cases, though, the cultural inheritance is not always easy to distinguish from the biological one. From the day of their birth, twins are usually dressed alike, wheeled in the same carriage, treated the same way, and referred to as 'the twins', as though they lacked individual personalities. It is no wonder that almost all pairs of twins are very similar in behaviour – but to what extent that is the result of heredity or environment cannot be said with certainty. ♂♀

\*

The nature–nurture controversy in recent years has centred on mental traits rather than on biological ones. Is intelligence inherited or is it determined by the environment? And is it really true that certain ethnic groups are smarter or less so than others? The basic problem in answering questions about intelligence is that no one knows for sure what it is. Most psychologists agree that it entails the ability to learn and to adjust to new situations, two traits that humans share with many of their primate relatives. Attempts to isolate the specific characteristics of human intelligence have been unsuccessful. One psychologist claims to have identified eight mental abilities that enter into it; another believes he has discovered 120 different variables whose interactions go to make up intelligence. Obviously, too little is known about intelligence to be certain even whether the subject is being discussed intelligently. ♂♀

Much more knowledge is available, though, about one aspect of mental ability that can be measured by various tests: IQ. Contrary to what most people believe, tests of IQ – 'Intelligence Quotient' – do not measure overall intelligence. Rather, they were designed to measure the ability to learn the skills that are taught in North American and European schools. They might more accurately be called AQs, 'Academic Quotients'. The world of IQs is often an unreal one. IQ scores do accurately correlate with grades obtained in school, but to give them absolute value is to be guilty of circular reasoning, since IQ tests are based on nothing more than what is taught there. Studies dealing with a wide variety of occupations have shown that the correlation between the proficiency of workers in the same occupation and their IQ scores is no more than 4 or 5 per cent. Nor do IQ scores have much relevance to people who were not brought up within the middle-class Western tradition. An alert Australian Aborigine who has the traits usually associated with intelligence by his own society – that is, who remembers a vast literature of myths and proverbs, who learns quickly and can apply what has been learned to new experiences, and who is adept with tools – will fail miserably on an IQ test, even when it is administered in the Aborigine's own language. The skills that have allowed the Aborigine to survive in the Great Central Desert are simply not the skills that would predict survival in the environment of a school.

People who devise IQ tests have been brought up within a particular culture and therefore could not possibly be free from the cultural assumptions under which they have operated since childhood. These tests, furthermore, could not possibly be fair in measuring differences between people of varying social and economic backgrounds even in the same city. A child reared in an upper-class family will speak a different dialect, have a different value system, and give priority to different skills from a child reared in the family of an unskilled worker; that they both happen to live in the same city will have little or no relevance. The same IQ test administered to both would thus not be fair. Some psychologists have worked hard to develop 'culture-fair' tests, but theirs has often been a fruitless exercise. No psychologist, living from birth in a particular kind of cultural environment, could possibly cancel out the effects of this up-bringing on his or her own ideas, mental habits, perception and cognition, and judgments about right and wrong. ♂♀

IQ tests are, therefore, of value only in establishing differences in academic ability among members of homogeneous populations. Despite this limited usefulness, they do provide interesting data about the nature–nurture controversy. For example, the superior achieve-ment of firstborn children has long been a perplexing phenomenon. Firstborns are over-represented in *Who's Who in America* and in *American Men and Women of Science*, among Rhodes Scholars, and in the ranks of university professors in North America. More than half of the presidents of the United States – including Lyndon Johnson, Richard Nixon, and Jimmy Carter – have been firstborn sons. That firstborns also score generally higher in IQ has recently been shown by a study of the IQs of 400,000 Dutch males who took tests to de-termine their fitness for military service. Firstborns (excluding in-dividuals from one-child families) consistently scored higher than secondborns, secondborns scored higher than thirdborns, and so on. Various explanations have been offered, such as that parents spend less time with each additional child as the family becomes larger or that mothers produce offspring of lesser abilities with each subsequent birth. Both of these explanations have been investigated; the first appears to have little validity and the second none at all.

One thing is certain: the firstborn phenomenon does not admit of an explanation based on heredity. No mechanism is known whereby inherited characteristics can be associated with birth order. The total heredity of any offspring consists of a random contribution of traits from each parent – and this randomness is not affected by birth order. In other words, a fifthborn child has as much chance as the firstborn to inherit the traits that produce high IQ scores. Obviously, the relation between birth order and IQ is entirely environmental. Perhaps the most reasonable explanation is psychological. The firstborn child who must suddenly cope with competition from younger siblings has been likened to a dethroned king. The loss of the monopoly on parental attention apparently arouses a need for approval and recognition which the child (and later the adult) seeks to earn through achievement. Firstborns thus are likely to enter occupations that offer recognition, attention, and approval, and to be motivated to do well in these. ☌♀

The exact extent of the inherited component in IQ has been a matter of considerable dispute. The tendency towards high or low scores does appear to run in families, and could be due to heredity. The tendency might also be explained environmentally, since off-spring share a specific environment with each other and with their parents. Much of the claim for a large inherited component is based upon studies of identical twins. Such twins who are brought up in the same household show a correlation of approximately 85 per cent in IQ. The correlation drops only 10 per cent in cases where, because of death in the family or the inability of parents to care for many children, identical twins have had to be separated in childhood and have been brought up in different households. Such a small drop would appear to indicate that twins, who share the same inheritance, will thus be almost equally intelligent whether or not their upbring-ing is exactly the same. Statistical analyses of the IQ of twins have led some psychologists to assert that between 70 and 80 per cent of IQ is inherited, with the remainder due to environmental influences. Such statements have often been repeated, even though they have no basis in fact. They rely upon studies of a mere sixty-nine pairs of identical twins in the United States, Britain, and Denmark; one other study has been made, but it has been so severely criticized as to be scientifically inadmissible. Of the sixty-nine pairs, a careful ex-amination shows that thirty-eight of these were actually raised by close relatives who presumably offered environments that were very similar. That leaves only thirty-one pairs. Clearly, in so small a sample the chances of statistical error are overwhelming. ☌♀

False beliefs about inherited intelligence have led to stereotypes regarding various national groups: ingenious Japanese, clever French, stupid Germans, sharp-witted Jews, dim-witted Poles, and so on. Almost every nation on earth has minority populations who are repeatedly labelled with the stereotype 'innately inferior in intelligence' – which is then used to justify, political, social, and economic discrimination against them. People with a particular ancestry have been condemned at birth to poverty, poor housing, the drudgery of menial labour, and early death because of these mis-taken notions about 'innate' intelligence.

The State of Israel has a Jewish population that is the result of migration there by two different groups: generally well-educated Jews of European ancestry and semiliterate Near Eastern Jews. The Near Eastern Jews not only have a lower social and economic status; they have also seemed to be less intelligent because they scored poorly on IQ tests. The European and Near Eastern Jews in Israel provided an ideal set of experimental conditions for evaluating the effect of environment on IQ. Here were two groups who differed greatly both in background and in IQ scores. If their environments could somehow be made equal, then it could be seen whether their IQs became similarly equal. Psychological researchers set about using exactly this experimental strategy. They centred their attention on the kibbutzim (agricultural co-operatives). Because each kibbutz was founded with a particular social or political aim, all members therefore share the same utopian ideals. The environment in the kibbutz is the same for all children, whether their ancestors came from Europe or from the Near East. This equality begins even before birth, because all expectant mothers eat the same food from communal kitchens and are given the same medical attention. Equality of environment is maintained throughout childhood in communal nurseries, children's houses, and schools; the children live together and visit with their parents for only a short time each day.

The method followed by the study was to evaluate the progress made by pairs of children – one of each pair Near Eastern and the other European – from the same kibbutzim who were of the same age and in the same class at school. Data were eventually gathered on about 600 such pairs. Despite striking differences in inheritance, equality of environment produced equality in IQ scores. The average IQ of Near Eastern children was exactly the same as their European counterparts, and the same proportion of Near Eastern children achieved scores that placed them in the 'exceptional' range. ♂♀

The old debate about whether heredity or environment has the greater effect on intelligence is clearly a misleading one. Even the more recent view – that heredity establishes the broad range of an individual's score, and environment determines the precise score within that range – is probably much too glib. Other influences than simple heredity or simple environment must be at work to account for some of the IQ data, but research on the interaction between the two has only recently begun. An interaction, though, must necessarily take place. Studies have shown that individuals whose upbringing encourages the traits that measure high on IQ tests will score well above the national average – while individuals with the same score initially will measure only sixty-five ('retarded' category) if intellectual growth is hampered. Such a fantastically wide range cannot be explained by any known genetic mechanism. ♂♀

\*

Diversity has been crucial to the survival of humankind as a species. If human beings had not had a high potential for variability, they could not have colonized all the environments from the Arctic to the tropics. Populations with certain physical and mental capacities could survive in the face of such environmental stresses as cold, heat, famine, or disease, while other populations with different traits were killed off. Beginning about 12,000 years ago, though, technology has greatly lessened the importance of diversity in ensuring the survival of populations. The ancestors of the Eskimos, for example, were able to colonize the Arctic because they did not wait the thousands of years it would have taken them to adapt biologically. Rather, they proceeded to create a liveable environment by means of such innovations as igloos, sleds, snowshoes, insulated clothing, goggles, and lamps that burn blubber oil. What is true of the Eskimos has likewise been true in more recent times of those Europeans who established colonies on every continent and applied technology to the wide range of environmental conditions they found there. Similarly, modern challenges to the human organism are met more by technology than by biological adaptation. In the past, only certain people with inherited resistance would have survived various diseases. Nowadays, the inheritance of resistance is no longer such a great advantage because of the widespread use of modern drugs. Even so, technology has not annulled the laws of evolution, and these laws continue to influence our genetic make-up. We still inherit most of what we are.

# 12

# The Inheritance of Variation

Shortly after Leonardo da Vinci died in 1519 at the age of sixty-seven, his younger half-brother Bartolommeo set out to reproduce a living duplicate of the great painter, sculptor, engineer, and author. Since he and Leonardo were related, the father that Bartolommeo chose was himself. He chose as his wife a woman whose background was similar to that of Leonardo's mother: she was young and came of peasant stock, and had also grown up in the village of Vinci. The couple produced a son, Piero, who was then carefully reared in the same region of the Tuscan countryside, between Florence and Pisa, that had nurtured Leonardo. Little Piero soon displayed an artistic talent, and at the age of twelve he was taken to Florence, where he served as an apprentice to several leading artists, at least one of whom had worked with Leonardo. According to Giorgio Vasari, the leading art historian of the period, the young Piero 'made everyone marvel ... and had made in five years of study that proficiency in art which others do not achieve save after length of life and great experience of many things'. In fact, Piero was often referred to as the second Leonardo.

At the age of twenty-three, however, Piero died of a fever and so it is impossible to predict with certainty what he might have gone on to achieve – though there is some indication in that Piero's works have often been attributed to the great Michelangelo. Nor is it possible to say positively how much of Piero's genius was due to heredity and how much to environment. Full brothers share, on the average, 50 per cent of their genes, but Bartolommeo and Leonardo were half-brothers and so would have had only about a quarter of their genes in common. Piero's mother and Leonardo's mother do not appear to have been related, but in the closely knit peasant village of Vinci it is quite possible that they had ancestors in common and thus shared genes. On the other hand, a strong environmental influence cannot be ruled out. The young Piero was undoubtedly aware of his acclaimed uncle; and certainly his father, Bartolommeo, provided every opportunity that money could buy for the boy to emulate him. But Bartolommeo's efforts to give the world a second Leonardo by providing a particular heredity and environment might, after all, have had little influence. Piero possibly was just another of the numerous talented Florentines of his time. ♂♀

Nevertheless the attempt was a bold one, considering the lack of knowledge in the sixteenth century about the mechanisms of inheritance. These mechanisms were not generally understood until early in the present century, and even Charles Darwin propounded his theory of evolution in total ignorance of them. Nowadays, inherited traits are known to result from combinations of genes which are passed from generation to generation in predictable ratios. No certainty exists as to the number of genes a human possesses, but estimates range between 6000 and 40,000. Each of these may consist of tens of thousands of instructions, which contain, in the form of the chemical DNA, the information needed by the organism for its proper growth and development. As in other sexually-reproducing animals, these genetic codes are transmitted by the sperm and egg. The female egg, fertilized by a male sperm, eventually develops into an adult individual by proliferation and by differentiation. The egg proliferates by first forming two cells, then four, eight, and so on into the billions, to produce the embryo. During the process, the cells also differentiate according to genetic codes into skin cells, nerve cells, muscle cells, blood cells, and the specialized cells that make up the kidney and liver, to mention just a few. In fact, each organ of the body seems to have its own characteristic type of cells, whose development is determined by the information in the genes.

The genes are carried within the nucleus of each cell on threadlike structures called 'chromosomes' (literally, 'coloured bodies', because they become very conspicuous when the cell is stained). The number of chromosomes for each species is fixed: it is forty-eight in chimpanzees and gorillas, forty-four in gibbons, and forty-six in humans. Within the fertilized egg is contained all of the hereditary material that bridges the generations: twenty-three chromosomes from each human parent to make up the total complement of forty-six. The genetic variation already existing in each parent is thus further varied in the offspring by the random inheritance of 50 per cent of the offspring's genes from each parent. As a result, the potential number of different kinds of humans that can be produced, each with a unique genetic make-up, is so staggeringly large that is is almost beyond comprehension: a one followed by 3000 zeros. Clearly the possibility that any two individuals who have ever lived or ever will live could possess the same genetic make-up is infinitesimally remote (with the exception, of course, of identical twins).

Genetic recombination in an offspring is complicated by the existence of dominant and recessive genes. Whether or not an individual will have blue eyes or brown eyes depends largely upon this distinction. Genes at the same location on the same chromosome often exist in several different forms known as 'alleles'. Two alleles – one for blue eyes, another for brown eyes – determine eye colour. An offspring who receives from both parents alleles for brown eyes will have brown eyes, whereas one who receives two for blue eyes will have blue eyes. Many people, though, receive one allele for blue eyes from one parent and one allele for brown from the other. These people will be brown-eyed, because the allele for brown eyes is dominant over the allele for blue eyes and it therefore masks blueness. Each of these brown-eyed individuals nevertheless carries a gene for blue eyes. Two brown-eyed parents can thus produce a blue-eyed offspring if that offspring receives from each parent one of the masked alleles for blue eyes.

Whenever a particular trait such as eye colour is attributed to a particular gene, a very complex process is undoubtedly being over-simplified. Several, and perhaps many, genes are apparently involved in producing a trait. The gene that is identified for eye colour, or baldness, or some other trait may be merely the last gene to act in a sequence of steps involving other genes. Or, more likely still, each trait may be controlled by the interaction of several genes. Skin colour, for example, depends upon a number of variables, each of which in turn is probably determined by several genes: the amount of the dark pigment known as melanin, its distribution in the layers of the skin, the number of capillaries close to the skin surface, and the capacity to tan, among others.

Everyone carries recessive genes for various traits, and of these, probably an average of from eight to ten are lethal. Defects occur when both parents carry the recessive allele and pass it on to their offspring as a double dose. Almost 150 recessive diseases have so far been identified. The incidence of some of them is quite high: for severe mental defects, 800 for each one million births; for severe deafness, 500; for cystic fibrosis, 400; for blindness, 200; and for albinism, 100. Cystic fibrosis – which is characterized by the failure of a child to develop physically and by the accumulation of mucus in the lungs – is usually fatal at an early age, despite modern medical treatment. It is the most severe recessive disease among people of European ancestry, about five times as frequent as other genetic disorders, whether recessive or dominant. Almost 1500 individuals with cystic fibrosis are born every year in the United States, for example, thus posing a substantial health-care problem. Large numbers of other harmful genes undoubtedly exist which, if received in double dose from the parents, have significant effects on health, temperament, and the capacity to develop special skills. ♂♀

Dominant and recessive genes appear to have clear-cut effects in determining such traits as eye colour, but sometimes the interaction between the two is more complex because some genes are sex-linked. One of the human male's twenty-three pairs of chromosomes is distinctive in size and shape. This male chromosome (the Y) is much shorter than its equivalent in the female (the X). The normal human male thus possesses a twenty-third pair of chromosomes that consists of one short Y and one long X, whereas the twenty-third pair of a normal female has two long X chromosomes. The egg produced by the female, therefore, will always carry an X chromosome from her XX endowment, but in the sperm from the male it may be either X or Y. If a Y sperm fertilizes an egg, the result is XY and the fertilized egg thus begins its development as a male. But if an X-bearing sperm reaches the egg first, then the result is XX, the beginning of a female embryo. The presence of both X and Y chromosomes in the sperm, but of only X chromosomes in the egg, explains why the male parent is the sole determiner of the sex of his offspring.

The key to understanding sex-linked traits is the fact that alleles on the X chromosome have no counterpart on the Y. Males (who are XY) can thus have only one copy of their X chromosome alleles, whereas females (who are XX) have two copies, as is the case with all the other chromosomes. Numerous traits are known to be influenced by sex-linked genes on the X chromosome: baldness, red-green colour blindness, congenital cataract, glaucoma, near-sightedness, toothlessness, and a form of muscular dystrophy. One that has been closely studied is haemophilia, a condition that results in excessive bleeding from even the slightest scratch or cut. It is caused by an allele carried on the X chromosome but not on the Y, and it afflicts only males. Females are the carriers of the disease, but they almost never suffer from it. How is such a situation possible? The explanation is that females have the genetic make-up XX and that haemophilia is transmitted via the X chromosome. A female who inherits the haemophilia gene on the X chromosome from her mother will inherit also a counteracting gene on the X chromosome from her father. The genes will cancel each other out and she will show no signs of the disease, even though she can still transmit it to her offspring. On the other hand, a male might inherit the gene for haemophilia on the X chromosome from his mother – but he cannot inherit the counteracting gene because there is no room for it on the short Y chromosome he inherits from his father. The only way, therefore, in which a female can show signs of the disease is in the event of a haemophiliac male mating with a haemophilia-carrying female. Such an event is extremely unlikely, both because haemophilia is a rare disease and also because males who have it usually die before they reach the age of reproduction.

Each time a cell divides, it ordinarily forms new chromosomes, genes, and DNA that are exact reproductions of the originals. The remarkable perfection of this process maintains the continuity of our species, generation after generation, for each of the traits encoded in the genes. The process of self-copying, however, is not foolproof. On occasion, an imperfection, known as a 'mutation', will occur. Even if only a single bit of DNA in just one gene is involved, the copying process will reproduce that mutation each time the cell and its descendants divide. If such mutations were to occur very often, and if the individuals in whom they occurred were to survive and reproduce, enormous changes would take place in our species within a very few generations. Mutations, though, are rare. For most genes the chances are probably less than one in 100,000 in any one generation that it will mutate. Furthermore, most of those individuals in whom these mutations occur do not survive because of miscarriage, stillbirth, or death in infancy. Mutations are almost always eliminated from the evolutionary process because each represents a random alteration in the highly complex system of the human body. Virtually any change that occurs at random is likely to be harmful, in the same way that random changes in any part of an aeroplane's jet engines would probably be disastrous. A complex organism has evolved over a very long period of time, in delicate balance with its environment, and a mutation is likely to upset that balance.

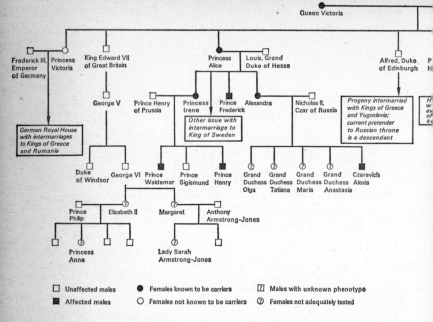

| Unaffected males | ● Females known to be carriers | ? Males with unknown phenotype |
| ■ Affected males | ○ Females not known to be carriers | ⊘ Females not adequately tested |

Haemophilia is a disease caused by the failure of the blood to clot. Before the modern availability of transfusions and drugs that promote clotting, an individual with haemophilia was subject to continuous bleeding and eventual death. The disease has been known since ancient times, and so has the fact that it appears only in the males of certain families. One of the second-century books of Jewish ritual that make up the Talmud exempts from circumcision a boy whose older brother had bled profusely following the rite, and even the sons of a female whose sisters had produced a male bleeder. That the exemption did not, on the other hand, extend to the father's sons by other females shows the clear under-

standing by the compilers of the Talmud about haemophilia's transmission through the female line but not the male line. In our own time, haemophilia has been prevalent in the royal houses of Europe, having apparently originated with Queen Victoria of Great Britain (1819–1901), whose descendants intermarried with European nobility. This diagram shows the relationships between the various royal houses and the path taken by the abnormal allele through subsequent generations. Note that all affected individuals were males (*shown by black squares*) because the trait is sex-linked and appears as a dominant in males. The unaffected females who nevertheless transmit the disease to their sons

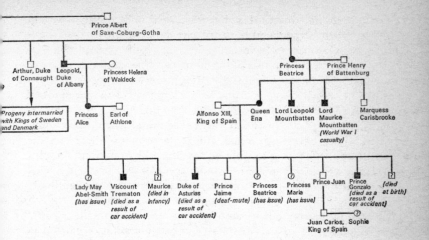

are known as 'carriers' (*shown by shaded circles*).

The disease was transmitted to the royalty and nobility of England, Spain, Russia, and Germany through at least two of Victoria's daughters (who were carriers) and also through one haemophiliac son of Victoria (who fathered a daughter who was a carrier). This son, Leopold, was an exception to the rule that haemophiliacs die before reaching reproductive age – but, being a member of royalty, Leopold naturally received constant preventive care and medical attention such as are rarely available to any commoners who suffer from haemophilia. The best known of Victoria's grandchildren to carry the disease was Alix, who became known as Alexandra after she married Tsar Nicholas II of Russia. She produced a single son, Alexis, who was a haemophiliac. Having no understanding of the genetic nature of the disease, Nicholas and Alexandra increasingly relied upon faith healers. The most notorious of these was Rasputin, who hastened the overthrow of the Tsar's government, which culminated in the murder of the entire family during the Russian Revolution. Among present-day royalty, Queen Elizabeth II of Great Britain may be a carrier (by way of her mother, who is descended from the German branch of the family), and so may Sophie, the consort of Juan Carlos, the present King of Spain.

Mutations do, though, become established in rare instances, and they are then perpetuated in the species. Some of the earliest hominids are presumed to have had DNA that mutated and changed instructions for the position of the large toe. Whereas the large toe of a monkey or ape can be moved so that it touches every other toe, a mutation caused changes in the bone or muscle of the large toe of humans so that it grows in line with the other toes. For a primate that still lived in the trees and used its feet for grasping, such a mutation would have been lethal. But for a primate already on the ground and attempting to walk on two legs, the mutation undoubtedly gave a great advantage over those primates that lacked it. Such a beneficial mutation would obviously have persisted and gradually have spread throughout the population. Another mutation, which occurred in the common ancestor of the anthropoids, led to a loss of the enzyme that acts as a catalyst in the conversion of glucose to vitamin C. The loss of the ability to synthesize vitamin C was not lethal because monkeys, apes, and hominids obtained all they needed of this vitamin directly from the plant foods they ate. In fact, the mutation was no doubt advantageous because it freed glucose for use as energy by the body. Only when the human diet changed over the past several thousand years as a consequence of agriculture did reduced consumption of food containing this vitamin lead to such nutritional diseases as scurvy.

Human variation also arises through new combinations of the genes received from each parent. Unlike mutation, though, recombination does not introduce new genetic material into the species. It merely reshuffles the existing genes so that individuals in the new generation will have gene combinations that differ from those of their parents. The most widespread cultural influence on recombination is the incest taboo, found in one form or another in all human societies. Incest taboos promote the flow of genes between populations, since people have to look farther afield than relatives for their marriage partners – and the result is an exchange of genes between different populations and the rise of new genetic combinations. In contrast, some cultural practices limit the number of possible new combinations. Human beings generally tend to marry those most like themselves. Most marriages take place between people who belong to the same social and economic class and who adhere to the same religion. Jews are most likely to marry one of their own religion, and Protestants least likely. Tall people marry one another much more frequently than mere chance would dictate, and the same is true of short people, fat people, thin people, deaf people, and people with the same skin colour.

Geography also can influence genetic recombination. When the only transportation available to most people was their own two legs, almost all marriages were between people in the same vicinity. Until a few centuries ago, most Europeans found a marriage partner within a third of a mile of their homes. With the invention of the bicycle, the average courtship distance increased to nearly a mile; the automobile, bus, and aeroplane have increased it even more. Nevertheless, most people – particularly those living in towns and cities – still find their marriage partners close by. A study of urban marriages made some years ago showed that about half took place between people who lived within fourteen city blocks of one another – and of these, almost half were within three blocks. Cupid's wings apparently do not have to sustain long-distance flights. ♂♀

The tendency for humans to vary at random through mutations and through new combinations of genes is severely limited by what is known as 'natural selection', which is the basis for Darwin's theory of evolution. Natural selection influences an individual's capacity to pass on genes to the next generation because of several facts clearly observable both in humans and in other animal species. The first is that each generation of adults is potentially capable of producing many more offspring than could possibly survive and reproduce. The second is that all of these offspring vary in their genetic make-up because of recombinations of genes from their parents and, rarely, because of favourable mutations. Third, those offspring that survive are the ones that possess the more 'fit' genetic make-up. These individuals will not only survive; they will also leave more offspring. In the long run, the more fit individuals and the descendants to whom they pass on their genes will replace those with a less favourable genetic make-up.

The sole criterion for fitness, therefore, is reproductive survival into future generations, and not any other strengths or weaknesses an individual might possess. Darwin's theory of natural selection was almost immediately misinterpreted. Tennyson had written of 'Nature, red in tooth and claw', ♂♀ but for Darwin, the process of evolution through natural selection did not imply aggression and violence. According to his theory, the individuals favoured by natural selection were simply those whose behaviour and biological equip-

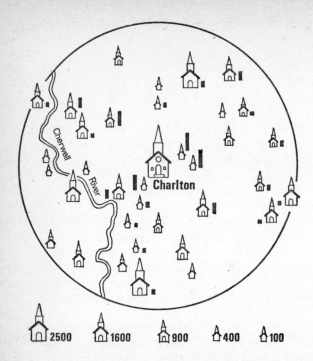

THE GENETIC ISOLATION OF MARRIAGE PARTNERS

Until the spread of modern transportation, almost everyone in North America and Europe found a marriage partner within the same village. This limitation on mobility has been documented by a study of marriage registers dating from the middle of the last century in the tiny village of Charlton, Oxfordshire, England. On the above map, Charlton at the centre and the surrounding villages are represented by symbols of churches (the larger the symbol, the larger the village). The bars indicate the relative contribution to Charlton's gene pool from each of the other villages. Clearly, almost all residents of Charlton found marriage partners either in Charlton itself or in the villages closest to it. The meandering line on the left shows the course of the river Cherwell, which evidently acted as a barrier to gene flow even though it was less than ten feet wide. ♂♀

ment enabled them to obtain more food and better shelter, made them less susceptible to disease and climatic changes, or were helpful in finding a mate and in producing many offspring. Thus, in terms of natural selection, an illiterate peasant who produces many surviving offspring is more fit than Leonardo da Vinci, George Washington, Beethoven, Emily Dickinson, the Brontë sisters, or Lenin, none of whom is known to have produced surviving offspring. By contrast to these, the Darwinian fitness of some individuals is awesome. Moulay Ismail, an emperor of Morocco in the eighteenth century, was said to have fathered 548 sons and 340 daughters. Even in monogamous societies, some people manage to pass on their genes to enormous numbers in succeeding generations. A Brazilian couple who had produced twenty-six living children as of 1976 already had seventy-two living grandchildren – and since all of the twenty-six children were still in the reproductive age or just entering it, many more grandchildren could be expected.

Natural selection operating on human populations is demonstrated with textbook clarity by the inheritance of sickle-cell anaemia. Anaemia is a condition which lessens the effectiveness of the haemoglobin in the blood in transporting oxygen and food. The particular kind known as sickle-cell anaemia causes the round red blood cells to collapse into the shape of a sickle, thereby reducing their oxygen-carrying capacity. In severe cases, the collapse of the red blood cells may cause heart, kidney, and spleen failure as well as paralysis. The sickle-cell trait and similar conditions are very prevalent across Central Africa, as well as in Morocco, Greece, Turkey, southern Arabia, and India. In some places, 30 per cent of the population may carry the abnormal allele that causes the disease. Before the spread of modern medical care, very few individuals born with this severe form of anaemia survived for long. The disease is still responsible for almost 100,000 deaths each year, mostly in Africa.

At first thought, natural selection might appear to have failed to operate, or such a harmful mutation would not have become geographically widespread and even, in certain areas, very common. Actually, just the opposite is true. Something in the collapsing cells apparently makes the haemoglobin they contain less susceptible to invasion by the malaria parasite. Indeed, the distribution of the sickling allele parallels very closely the distribution of falciparum malaria, the most deadly kind. Among populations in which malaria is prevalent, the frequency of the sickle-cell trait is also very great. In contrast, among nearby populations that inhabit higher and drier ground, where the malaria-bearing mosquito cannot live, the frequency of sickling is much lower.

In areas in which the sickle-cell trait occurs, individuals have one of three sorts of genetic make-up. Those in whom the trait is found have obtained one allele for abnormal haemoglobin (allele *S*) from one parent and an allele for normal haemoglobin (*A*) from the other parent. These *AS* individuals are buffered against malaria by a complex process. As soon as the malaria parasite attacks the red blood cells, oxygen tension is reduced and the cell collapses – thus encouraging the body's normal immunological defences to destroy both the abnormal cell and the parasite as well. People with the *AS* genetic make-up who do contract malaria therefore get it in a milder form – – and the penalty they pay for this advantage is a mild, non-lethal form of anaemia. Individuals with the other two genetic make-ups are much less fit, but in different ways. Those who receive two normal alleles from their parents (*AA*) do not suffer from anaemia, but neither do they receive any protection at all against the deadly form of malaria. Those with a double dose of the abnormal allele (*SS*) will be completely protected against malaria, but will also suffer from anaemia so severe as to mean almost certain death before they reach reproductive age.

In a malaria-infested environment, therefore, the individuals most fit to survive are those with the *AS* make-up – those who receive a high degree of protection in return for only mild anaemia. That fitness no longer operates, though, when *AS* individuals migrate to a malaria-free environment. They possess partial immunity to a disease that does not exist in their new environment and they pay a severe penalty by carrying a potentially lethal allele. Such a situation exists among those Africans who were transported as slaves to malaria-free areas of North America and Europe. Out of every four hundred North Americans of even partly African descent, one is born with severe anaemia (*SS*), and forty with one abnormal gene (*AS*), while the remainder (*AA*) are free from the sickling trait. Attempts have been made in recent years to locate the *AS* carriers and to inform them that mating with another carrier will result, on the average, in severe sickle-cell anaemia for one offspring out of every four, in mild anaemia for two, and in a normal haemoglobin for only one of the four. ♂♀

One thing should be emphasized about individuals with the sickle-cell trait who are nowadays kept alive by modern medical care (as well as about diabetics who now survive owing to insulin, and about haemophiliacs who now live to reproductive age because of transfusions and clotting drugs). These individuals are not less 'fit' in the Darwinian sense than are other members of the population – so long as their environment continues to include medical attention that keeps them alive and maintains their reproductive potential. Should the attention they receive suddenly end, then they would, of course, become less fit. Even before the rise of modern medicine, though, humans blunted the effects of natural selection by intruding their cultural behaviour between the occurrence of mutant genes and the weeding-out process of natural selection. Albinism, for example, is caused by a recessive gene which drastically reduces the pigments in the skin, eyes, and hair. An albino normally has a difficult time surviving because of extreme sensitivity to sunlight, reduced vision, and a proneness to skin cancer. In most societies, albinos are very rare: only one out of about every 20,000 people in Europe, for example. Albinos are nearly a hundred times more common than that, though, among such American Indian groups as the San Blas of Panama, the Jemez and Zuñi of New Mexico, and the Hopi of Arizona.

This extraordinary prevalence of albinism indicates that cultural selection has long counterbalanced the process of natural selection. Among the Aztecs, for example, numerous albinos lived in Moctezuma's royal household; they were considered wards of the state and were not forced to work in the sunlight. Albinos are a source of pride to the Hopi Indians, in contrast to the many other societies where they are the object of fear, superstition, and prejudice. Albinos perform in ceremonial dances along with other Hopi, and several have even served as influential chiefs and priests. Most Hopi albinos nevertheless remain unmarried, usually for economic reasons. A male albino is unable to work in the fields to produce food for his family; a female is similarly limited in the outdoor duties she can perform. How, then, do the Hopi albinos manage to pass on the allele for albinism to succeeding generations? Although an albino may not be a very good investment as a marriage partner, no such disadvantage attaches to an albino as a sexual partner. While the other men and boys spend the day in sunlit fields, the albino males remain in the villages, where they have ample opportunity to engage in sexual activity. Because of the Hopi's small population, just a few sexually active males can have an imposing effect on the frequency of albinism in the subsequent generation. ♂♀

*

The genetic characteristics of the human species can be understood more clearly by ignoring individual variations and looking instead at entire breeding populations (or gene pools, as they are sometimes called). A breeding population is a group of people who mate with one another much more often than they do with members of other breeding populations and that therefore differs from other populations in the frequency of certain genetic traits. The Basques who inhabit the western Pyrenees of Spain and France, for example, form a breeding population since for a variety of reasons – including cultural familiarity, common language, ethnic pride, and geographical isolation – they are very likely to mate with one another. No breeding population, though, is completely cut off from other populations. Some genes always flow into the gene pool from marriages with outsiders, and in the same way some genes are lost to other breeding populations.

Because we tend to think in terms of sociopolitical groups that inhabit defined national boundaries (like Great Britain or China), we usually overlook the immense variation that exists within such groups. What we call 'the Chinese', for example, actually comprise a great many breeding populations, each of which differs from others in the frequency of some genetic traits. At first thought, even such geographically small areas as cities might seem to form a single gene pool. And so they would if the inhabitants of urban areas married one another at random; but they do not. An urban centre in reality consists of many breeding populations, isolated from one another by social and economic class, religion, ethnic background, skin colour, and even physical stature. A study of one medium-sized French city showed a conglomeration of breeding populations, each of which numbered only about 2500 people.

Even though differences between breeding populations are perpetuated by cultural influences, such populations have usually been distinct from the outset. Imagine a town on the western frontier in nineteenth-century North America whose inhabitants include about a thousand males and females of reproductive age. News arrives that free land is available for homesteaders farther west, and so a small group of perhaps ten adults sets out to found a new farming community. The genes carried by these ten people could not possibly represent a cross-section of the entire gene pool composed of the thousand people in the town who are of reproductive age. The reason can be easily visualized in terms of a barrel containing a thousand marbles. Let us say, for simplicity's sake, that these marbles represent the entire genetic storehouse of the original population and that each of ten genetic traits is represented by a hundred marbles of a particular colour. A small splinter population can take along only ten of these genetic marbles when it migrates. To duplicate exactly the original breeding population, the splinter population would have to take a single marble of each colour. But extracting marbles at random from a barrel would almost never give a sample consisting of exactly one red, one green, one blue, and so on. In fact, the proportions are apt to deviate considerably from the proportions in the barrel, so as to give a total including perhaps three red marbles, two green, and no blue ones at all. The genetic make-up of the splinter colony would therefore be very different from the original gene pool.

Imagine also that in the next year, and in the year after that, similar small groups depart for other areas in the West to found new communities. Each one of these small groups must likewise differ from the parental population, as well as from all the other groups. Additional deviations in the frequency of genetic traits will occur in these new communities as they begin to produce offspring – not every one of whom will have an equal opportunity to reproduce. Individuals who are socially more influential or wealthier than others almost always have a greater fitness in the Darwinian sense. They will tend to produce more offspring that survive to maturity because these parents can usually obtain better living conditions for them. As a result, in a few generations the genes of the fit individuals will be over-represented in comparison to the genes of the less fit. Such differential reproductive fitness is usually more apparent in simple societies than in complex ones. Two headmen among the Xavante Indians of central Brazil, for example, sired approximately one-fourth of the entire population in their sizable village. ♂♀

The Amish of Pennsylvania represent a splinter group who differ both from the original gene pool in Switzerland and from the general population around them. The Amish are descended from fewer than two hundred founders who migrated to Pennsylvania from Europe largely during the period between 1720 and 1770. The descendants of these few founders now number about 45,000 people in Pennsylvania, Ohio, and Indiana. Because the Amish discourage marriage with outsiders, almost no new genes have flowed in from other populations. The extent of the inbreeding that has taken place is shown by the fact that only eight surnames account for 81 per cent of the Amish in just one county in Pennsylvania. One result of maintaining the original gene pool has been that certain genetic disorders occur among the Amish much more frequently than among other groups. A very rare kind of dwarfism is known to have affected about a hundred people in the entire world since it was first described medically in 1860. More than half of these cases occurred in a single group of Amish in Pennsylvania, and they have all been traced back to a pair of ancestors who arrived in the United States in 1744. ♂♀

New populations that are established in this way by a small sample of the original population are said to display the 'founder effect'. This effect accounts for the observation that populations of Jews around the globe – whose ancestors became dispersed from Palestine thousands of years ago – differ genetically from one another almost as much as they do from the populations in the nations where they now live. The Samaritans, for example, are strikingly different from every one of the varied populations, Jewish and non-Jewish, among whom they have lived over a period of several thousand years. They have always been treated as outcasts by other Jews because of their worship of pagan gods – a circumstance that explains the point of Jesus' parable of the 'Good Samaritan'. During the centuries just before the Christian Era, the Samaritans were a vigorous nation, with a population that probably exceeded a million. As a result of persecution by fellow Jews, Romans, Christians, Arabs, and others, the number of Samaritans has been reduced to a mere 500 who still survive in two communities in Israel. They represent an extreme of religious isolation in a people who apparently have changed little in culture for more than 2000 years and who have rarely permitted intermarriage. Down through the ages, their inbreeding has persisted – first-cousin marriages are preferred – to the extent that various genetic defects are extraordinarily frequent in certain families. Most members of the large Sadakah family, for example, suffer from colour blindness, and the incidence of deaf-mutism is high in the Alatif family. Whether or not today's Samaritans are the only true survivors of the ancient Hebrews, as they claim to be, genetic studies have shown that because of ostracism and consequent inbreeding they have an extremely high frequency of certain genetic traits.♂♀

Of the numerous attempts that have been made to sort out the breeding populations of the world by noting differences in physique and in colour of skin, eyes, and hair, nearly all have been largely fruitless. Skin colour is altered by tanning as well as by the long-term effects of climate; brown-eyed people may nevertheless carry recessive alleles for blue eyes and thus produce blue-eyed children; body size and shape are heavily influenced by diet, health, and other environmental variables. A much more precise way to arrive at differences between populations is to compare their blood types. Because of the widespread practice of giving blood transfusions, millions of people from breeding populations around the world have been identified by blood type. Details on the relative frequency of the several types of blood are now known for virtually every major population on earth. Also now known is that whether an individual inherits A, B, or O blood is determined entirely by different alleles at a single location on a chromosome. Here is a sampling of frequencies for the different blood types among some widely scattered populations:

| | O | A | B | AB |
|---|---|---|---|---|
| Toba Indians (Argentina) | 98·5% | 1·5% | 0% | 0% |
| Navajo Indians (New Mexico) | 77·7 | 22·3 | 0 | 0 |
| Blood Indians (Montana) | 17·4 | 81·2 | 0 | 1·4 |
| Aborigines (southern Australia) | 42·6 | 57·4 | 0 | 0 |
| Melanesians (New Guinea) | 37·6 | 44·4 | 13·2 | 4·8 |
| Siamese (Bangkok) | 37·1 | 17·8 | 35·2 | 9·9 |
| Asiatic Indians (Bengal) | 32·5 | 20·0 | 39·4 | 8·1 |
| Ukrainians (Kharkov) | 36·4 | 38·4 | 21·6 | 3·6 |
| Germans (Danzig) | 33·1 | 41·6 | 18·0 | 7·3 |
| Germans (Berlin) | 36·5 | 42·5 | 14·5 | 6·5 |
| Italians (Sicily) | 45·9 | 33·4 | 17·3 | 3·4 |
| English (London) | 47·9 | 42·4 | 8·3 | 1·4 |

Even a cursory glance at this table reveals the futility of generalizing about the breeding populations of the world. Some American Indians (the Toba) have a very high frequency of type O and a very low frequency of type A, whereas others (the Blood) have a low frequency of type O and a very high one of type A. The German popu-

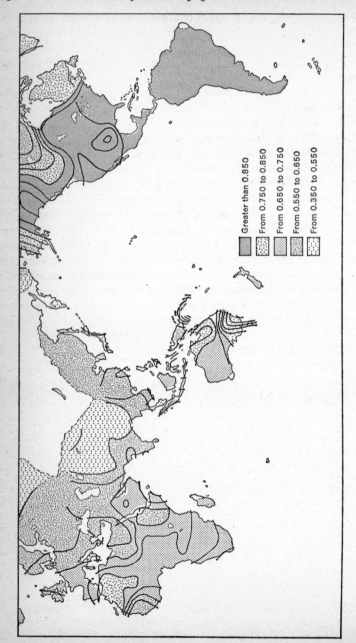

lation of Danzig obviously has a somewhat different inheritance from the German population of Berlin. Among the Berlin Germans, the frequency of blood types is similar to that among the Ukrainians – but, strangely enough, it is even closer to that of the Melanesians living halfway around the globe.

How is this patchwork distribution of alleles for blood types to be explained? The near absence of the B allele from among the American Indians has been particularly mystifying. After all, the ancestors of American Indians migrated to the New World from Asia, where the B allele reaches its highest frequency. Individuals with type B blood may have faced some environmental hazard (as yet unknown) in the New World that made the B allele a genetic liability, thus causing its virtual elimination through natural selection. Or, possibly, the populations that remained in Asia received some selective advantage from the B allele that caused an increase in its frequency there. In other instances, though, the effect of natural selection is more apparent, in that correlations have been discovered between particular blood types and certain diseases. A much higher frequency of duodenal and gastric ulcers has been demonstrated for people with type O blood, and they are also more likely to contract influenza and plague. Furthermore, recent studies indicate that those with type O blood are bitten more often by mosquitoes than are those with A or B, which means that people with O blood are more prone to malaria and other mosquito-borne diseases. Those with type A blood are

---

BREEDING POPULATIONS AND THE DISTRIBUTION OF ABO BLOOD TYPES

Skin colour is an unreliable guide to the classification of breeding populations because it is the result of a complex interaction among about six genes, and also because it is affected by the environment. Much less emotionally charged as a genetic basis for a classification of the major divisions of humankind is the distinction among blood types A, B, and O. The map shown here, based on data generated by new computer techniques, gives the frequency of the gene for blood type O in the indigenous populations of the world. O is the most widely distributed type, occurring on all continents and in all populations, and reaching its highest frequency among American Indians. Were a racial classification to be based on blood type O rather than on skin colour, the following peoples would be lumped into one race: French, Spaniards, most Sub-Saharan Africans, Aborigines of western Australia, and Eskimoes of Central Canada. And a different race would consist of Moroccans, Aborigines of northern Australia, and some Indian tribes in Canada. (The blank spaces for land portions of the map represent areas where full information is lacking.)

more susceptible than others to cancer of the intestines and salivary glands, and also to hepatitis, smallpox, pneumonia, staph infections, diabetes, and typhoid. Type B blood is mystifying because very few correlations have been discovered between it and diseases. Undoubtedly the relation between blood types and Darwinian fitness is a complicated one. The gene frequencies existing in populations today must be the result of numerous selective forces operating over a very long period of time. ♂♀

Adaptive advantage, though, only partly explains the present distribution of blood types. Another major influence has been the exchange of genes as a result of human migrations (either voluntary or forced). In Europe, for example, the B allele is most common in the areas that have been repeatedly invaded by Phrygians, Scythians, Huns, Vandals, Mongols, Ottomans, and other peoples from Central Asia, among whom the frequency of type B is the highest in the world. A succession of empires in the ancient world invaded other states, sacked their cities, and brought back slaves – who carried with them, of course, different sets of genes. In Athens during the fifth century B.C., somewhere between a quarter and a third of the population consisted of slaves who had been captured over a large area of the Mediterranean and the Near East. But this mixing of Greek genes with foreign ones was minor compared to the mixing that occurred as a result of Roman colonization. A single military expedition might bring back 50,000 slaves, most of whom (or their descendants) would eventually be incorporated into the Roman breeding population. So great was the shifting of people from one place to another under the Roman Empire – and the subsequent matings between individuals from different breeding populations – that at one point roughly 80 per cent of the inhabitants of Rome were of foreign ancestry.

With the advent of European exploration and colonization in the fifteenth century, populations began to move about on an unprecedented scale. About eleven million slaves were taken out of Africa, assuredly the greatest forced migration in history. The indentured labourers whom the British and Dutch eventually brought to their overseas colonies in place of slaves numbered in excess of four million Asiatic Indians, several million Chinese, and hundreds of thousands of Javanese. Voluntary migration was spurred by the development in the mid-1800s of the ocean-going steamship. In just ninety years, between 1840 and 1930, at least fifty-two million people left Europe for other continents. So great has been the geographic redistribution of the European breeding population that by 1970 about a third of all people of that ancestry were living outside Europe. The enormous human migrations that have occurred, particularly in the past several thousand years of history, go far towards accounting for the patchwork distribution of genetic traits on the face of the planet. ♂♀

The old geographical distinctions between people having become thus blurred, it is no longer possible to divide humankind into a few sharply defined 'races'. Among the larger and better known of these newer populations are the Black American (a mixture of West African and European populations plus a small component of American Indian genes), Cape Coloured (Bushman–Hottentot and Bantu, mixed with European, Malaysian, and Asiatic Indian genes), Latin American Ladino (South American Indian and southern European), and Neo-Hawaiian (Polynesian, Chinese, Japanese, Filipino, and European). The fact that new 'races' have arisen and old ones declined in the span of only several hundred years points to the futility of attempting to pigeonhole people into racial categories. Aside from being dubious biology, such pigeonholing is sociologically cruel. A mere difference in skin colour condemns large segments of populations in countries around the world, in generation after generation, to the injustice of inferior housing, nutrition, education, and employment.

Some populations with particular sorts of genetic make-up are better adapted to one climate, those with a different genetic make-up to another – but the hostility between people with different adaptations is not caused by their biology. Physical variation among human groups today has resulted in social divisions rather than in biological ones. Paradoxically, human beings arrived at their present domination of the world by developing from the outset cultures that emphasized mutual co-operation. The earliest hominids could not have survived on the African savanna without co-operation, any more than baboons can today. And at each stage of the evolution of human culture, co-operation was paramount. Yet humans today appear reluctant to share their humanity with those who differ slightly in such biological characteristics as skin colour and facial features, or in such sociological characteristics as language and religion. Both the biological and sociological aspects of what is often called 'race' are examined in the next chapter.

# 13

# The Chimera of Race

Carolus Linnaeus, the eighteenth-century Swedish biologist who developed the system still used today to classify animals and plants, examined the human species and found several distinct types within its diversity. He not only described the types physically, but also attributed to them certain behavioural and mental traits. Africans, for example, could be recognized by their dark skin colour, frizzled hair, and flat noses. In addition, declared Linnaeus, they were 'crafty, indolent, negligent . . . governed by caprice'. As for the fair-skinned Europeans, Linnaeus found them 'gentle, acute, inventive . . . governed by laws'.

Two things are wrong with Linnaeus' descriptions of what he conceived to be the main categories of humankind. First of all, skin colour, hair texture, and facial features have no genetic relation to personality, mental abilities, or behaviour – notwithstanding that such a belief has long been an intellectual assumption by people in Western societies. Films and popular fiction still portray Asiatics as sly and inscrutable, Africans as childlike, and American Indians as stolid. The traits of behaviour and personality that distinguish one group from another are not inherited but rather are learned. English yeomen, transplanted to the American colonies, were variously transformed into 'shrewd' Yankees, 'rambunctious' mountaineers, and 'courtly' Virginians. The second thing wrong with Linnaeus' classification is that whole segments of humankind cannot be categorized according to a few visible traits. Generalizations are futile about even the most obvious of such traits, skin colour. Some Sub-Saharan Africans are as light in colour as some Europeans. Some northern Europeans exhibit a high frequency of light-coloured hair, but so do some Australian Aborigines. And some Australian Aborigines have as dark a skin colour as many Central Africans halfway around the globe.

People of European ancestry often tend to think of the varieties of humankind as broad geographical categories based on skin colour: white Europeans, black Africans, yellow Asiatics, and red American Indians. Such categories, though, are inadequate because they fail to include numerous populations of the world, such as dark-skinned Asiatic Indians and light-skinned Pygmies and Bushmen of Africa. Furthermore, generalizations concerning skin colour are likely to differ from one society to another. Most people in the United States believe that Asiatic Indians, despite their swarthy complexions,

# MAMMALIA.

## ORDER I. PRIMATES.

*Fore-teeth cutting; upper 4, parallel; teats 2 pectoral.*

### 1. HOMO.

Sapiens.    Diurnal; varying by education and situation.

2. Four-footed, mute, hairy.    *Wild Man.*

3. Copper-coloured, choleric, erect.    *American.*
   *Hair* black, straight, thick; *nostrils* wide, *face* harsh; *beard* scanty; *obstinate*, content free. *Paints* himself with fine red lines. *Regulated* by customs.

4. Fair, sanguine, brawny.    *European.*
   *Hair* yellow, brown, flowing; *eyes* blue; *gentle*, acute, inventive. *Covered* with close vestments. *Governed* by laws.

5. Sooty, melancholy, rigid.    *Asiatic.*
   *Hair* black; *eyes* dark; *severe*, haughty, covetous. *Covered* with loose garments. *Governed* by opinions.

6. Black, phlegmatic, relaxed.    *African.*
   *Hair* black, frizzled; *skin* silky; *nose* flat; *lips* tumid; *crafty*, indolent, negligent. *Anoints* himself with grease. *Governed* by caprice.

LINNAEUS AND THE CLASSIFICATION OF RACES

This page from a translation of Linnaeus' *Systema Naturae* is typical of eighteenth-century thinking about the diversity of humankind. *Homo sapiens* is divided into feral humans (discussed in Chapter 1) and the four 'primary races' based on skin colour and geographical origin.

Note that each race is characterized not only physically but also by psychological–mental traits and by cultural practices. Linnaeus thus gave the stamp of scientific legitimacy to many folk beliefs about race.

belong to the 'white Caucasoid' race. In Britain, though, Asiatic Indians are lumped with Africans, Caribbeans, Chinese, Malaysians, and others into a category known as 'coloureds'. South Africans differ from people in both the United States and Britain in that they regard Asiatic Indians as forming a race distinct from other groups in their country: Europeans, Bantu, Bushmen–Hottentots, and Cape Coloured.

The most complex system for categorizing people is undoubtedly the one to be found in Brazil, where fine gradations of skin colour are combined with numerous social and economic distinctions. The official census in Brazil employs four categories of skin colour – white, yellow, brown, and black – but the ordinary Brazilians add a few hundred others. Thus someone with wavy hair and a ruddy skin colour is known as a *moreno*, whereas for one whose skin is somewhat darker the term is *mulato*. A person with the same skin colour as a *mulato*, but with curlier hair, is a *creolo*. Even these categories, narrow as they are, do not tell the whole story, since the way a Brazilian's skin colour is 'seen' often depends upon that person's social and economic status. A 'white' person is usually one with high prestige and a 'black' person one with low prestige, but a middle-prestige 'brown' who marries an upper-class 'white' will probably be listed as 'white' in the next census. If the same 'brown' were to marry a low-prestige 'black', then the colour change in the next census might instead be to 'black'. In one Amazonian town, everyone regarded a dark-skinned female as 'white' because of her wealth and education, but declined to recognize the town drunk as 'white' despite the very light colour of his skin. Brazilians claim to have done away with prejudice and discrimination based on skin-colour. In actual fact, Brazilians are among the most colour-conscious people on earth; their awareness of skin colour is merely complicated by a like concern with social status. ♂♀

In most of the world, though, skin colours are automatically associated with certain social stereotypes. 'Race' has become an ugly concept because *sociological* judgements have been made about the superiority or inferiority of certain *biological* traits. Biologically, a race is simply a breeding population in which distinctive inherited traits occur more frequently than in other breeding populations. The basis for defining a particular population as a race depends upon whatever biological criteria are being used. If the criterion is adaptation to varying amounts of sunlight, then skin colour is an important biological consideration in defining races. Equally valid as a criterion, though, is that of blood type – which, if applied, would provide a strikingly different set of categories. In neither instance is the biologist making a generalization about the superiority or inferiority of different races. On the other hand, the sociological phenomenon of racism defines whole groups sociologically, psychologically, and culturally on the basis of purely biological characteristics. Once groups of people are put into pigeonholes based on biological traits, these pigeonholes are then inevitably compared as sociologically superior or inferior, civilized or savage.

\*

Race does have an objective biological reality of its own, which can be separated from racist sociological considerations – as should be clear from the following brief account of race in a context free from overtones of prejudice. The common English or house sparrow provides a clear example of the biology of race in a single widespread species. A native of the Old World, this bird was deliberately introduced into the United States from England and Germany in 1852. Now, only 125 years later, it has spread throughout North America, and breeding populations occur all the way from southern Canada to below Mexico City. An examination of specimens from scattered locations throughout this range shows that distinct geographical races, which differ from each other particularly in body size, have already arisen. Those of the largest size are found in Canada, the smallest in the southwestern deserts, with birds in localities between these two regions tending to be intermediate in size – an adaptation to climate of the same sort as has been found in humans and in other warm-blooded animals. In other words, through no more than 125 generations, a single species has diversified into numerous local races that differ from one another and also from their ancestral populations in Europe. The house sparrows clearly fit the biological definition of races: populations which breed among themselves much more than they breed with individuals from other populations and thus differ in genetic make-up. ♂♀

Each of these races of the house sparrow, though, cannot be regarded as a 'pure', genetically uniform race. Pure races do not exist in the house sparrow or in any other sexually-reproducing animal, including humankind. Individuals of each race will interbreed with neighbouring races wherever their ranges overlap. No matter what the species, every race (except for certain laboratory-reared experimental animals) is 'mixed' because its members have exchanged genes with other races. The notion of the existence of pure races is an old one; but it is completely false. Before the science of genetics proved otherwise, inheritance was thought to be based on 'blood', which in each pure race was supposed to be uniform – thus giving rise to such now outmoded expressions as 'full-blooded Indian', 'a mixed blood', and 'bloodline'. 'Pure-blooded Nordics', for example, were supposed to have long heads, blond hair, blue eyes, and tall stature. Yet in Sweden, the very heart of Nordicdom, one study shows that only 10.1 per cent of army draftees fit this description. The concept of a Nordic race has now been completely discredited, as have attempts to identify such European races as the Alpine or the Mediterranean. The same thing holds true for other populations around the world. Even if each of the several thousand breeding populations ('tribes') known to anthropologists were to be regarded as pure races, the variations within each tribe would still be very great – and no single individual could be found who represented the 'pure type' of the entire tribe.

Far from being segmented into a number of pure races, all humankind shares the same basic storehouse of genes. Only a very small number of genes are significantly more frequent at certain places and times. If an individual from one geographical population (such as an African, an Asiatic, or a European) is chosen at random and then compared genetically with one from a different geographical population, a difference in about 35 to 40 per cent of the genes will be found to exist. This might seem to be a high percentage. But in a comparison of two individuals chosen at random from within the *same* geographical population the difference turns out to be nearly as great – close to 30 per cent. In fact, when analysed statistically, the genetic difference *between* two geographical populations is very much the same as the difference *within* a single population. In other words, Europeans differ genetically from one another almost as much as a European differs from an Asiatic or an African. The misery caused by racism therefore turns out to hinge on only a few percentage points of genetic differences.

In a new technique, called 'electrophoresis', precise measurement of differences between individuals is made possible by an analysis of the enormous variety of proteins in the human body. All of these proteins are genetically controlled and are therefore reliable indicators of human variation. Any two Europeans or two Africans or two Chinese selected at random will show approximately 200,000 differences in their proteins. Surprisingly, when a European is compared with an African or an Asiatic, the differences between the proteins of each increase only slightly over the basic difference of 200,000 between individuals of the same geographical population. The physical differences that seem so great to the naked eye between geographical populations are almost insignificant when body chemistry is studied. How can this be? The answer is that the differences between a European and an African are literally only skin deep, simply because the body's outer surface happens to be the locus of interaction between the individual and the environment. No wonder, then, that natural selection has produced greater variety in the genes that account for the exterior surface where the interaction takes place than it has in the other genes in the body. ♂♀

The problem with attempting to define races by a cluster of diagnostic traits is that most people supposedly belonging to those races lack these very traits. Thin lips, a thin nose, and straight hair are supposed to be diagnostic traits of a European race, and dark skin of an African one. Yet tens of millions of people living in India exhibit the 'European' traits of thin lips, thin nose, and straight hair, but also the 'African' trait of a dark skin. Are they 'European' or 'African'? Rather than searching for 'typical' traits, biologists have found it much more fruitful to emphasize the variation between populations in regard to specific traits.

Biologists have discovered that traits are not distributed at random but rather occur in patterns of gradually increasing or decreasing frequency, known as 'clines'. The existence of such gradients makes it virtually impossible to draw a line on a map to separate two distinct races. Such boundaries as do exist for particular traits will be exceedingly blurred. For example, the frequency of eyefolds increases gradually across the Eurasian continent from west to east, and the frequency of wavy hair increases in the opposite direction. In an examination of people from northern Europe southward across the Mediterranean, along the Nile, and into East Africa, the frequency of genes resulting in certain physical traits is seen to change gradually. At almost no point is it possible to draw a sharp line and say that this is where one kind of eye shape, hair form, or skin colour stops and another begins. Differences become obvious only when individuals from opposite extremes of the cline are compared: a light-skinned Scandinavian with a dark-skinned Sudanese, a thin-lipped northern German with a thick-lipped East African. Even the extremes of a cline do not indicate purity of race. Until the development of modern transportation several hundred years ago, no Swede had ever interbred with a Sudanese, yet genetic links existed between them because neighbouring populations all along the way had interbred.

Despite the obvious difficulties of racial classifications, some biologists and social scientists persist in attempting to make all of the world's human populations fit into one system or another. The classifiers, though, hardly ever agree exactly on their categories. One respected scientist, after a lifetime of study, has put forth a system of nine 'geographical races': American Indian, Polynesian, Micronesian, Melanesian–Papuan, Australian Aborigine, Asiatic, Asiatic Indian, European, and African. To account for the numerous populations that do not fit into his nine categories, he has been forced to recognize thirty-two additional 'local races' which are 'puzzling', 'marginal', 'isolated', 'hybrid', or 'of recent origin'. They include such well-known and sometimes numerically large groups as Eskimos, Pygmies, Bushmen, Ainu, Lapps, Black Americans, and Latin American Ladinos. Still other races intermediate between these local races can, of course, be identified, and yet others that are intermediate between those intermediates. One system of classification that attempts to account for such intermediate groups lists more than two hundred races of humankind. And some human biologists have recently estimated that a million races might be identified, the exact number depending upon the criteria used. At the other extreme, several systems of classification attempt to cram all of humankind into three basic races: European (or Caucasoid), African (or Negroid), and Asiatic (or Mongoloid). Such a limited system obviously reveals almost nothing about the remarkable biological diversity of the world's peoples. ♂♀

The visible traits that have been used to define races obviously arose as adaptations to the environment. Rapid changes in technology over the past several thousand years have increasingly isolated humans from the environment and have thus sometimes obscured the long-term adaptive advantages bestowed by certain physical traits. The nose, which serves to warm and to moisten the air taken into the lungs, is an example of an adaptation to climate that has nothing to do with geographical races. People living in the cold and dry regions of the world usually have long, narrow noses. This shape provides the greatest surface area of mucous membrane for moistening and is also effective in warming cold air. The distribution of nose shapes around the world shows a clear correlation with climatic stresses. Populations in Central Africa and in tropical Australia have the shortest, broadest noses, whereas many of the Europeans, Eskimoes, and American Indians who inhabit cold climates have narrow noses. Narrowness or breadth of nose is obviously not the mark of any particular geographical race. Populations occupying highland areas of East Africa have long, narrow noses, whereas those in the tropical rain forests nearby almost always have short, wide noses. ♂♀

Most attempts to identify races have focused on the adaptation of skin colour. All people inherit skin of a particular colour, which is, nevertheless, subject to environmental influences. The sun's rays stimulate the skin to tan – that is, to deposit additional pigment. (Africans also tan, although not as dramatically as northern Europeans do.) Even without direct exposure to sunlight, skin colour may vary with the seasons. Faulty metabolism often darkens the skin, and so does ageing. Despite such complications, a general distribution of skin colours may be observed in populations around the globe. The darkest-skinned peoples usually live near the Equator, and skin colour becomes progressively lighter in populations farther north or south. The savanna of East Africa is exposed to probably the most intense solar radiation in the world, and it is inhabited by populations with the heaviest pigmentation known. Peoples with skins approximately as dark are found elsewhere in the tropics, particularly in India, Melanesia, and northern Australia. Exceptions are usually due to one of two causes. The population may have migrated to these tropical areas no more than several thousand years ago, too recently for major changes in skin colour to have occurred – as is true of some American Indians, Polynesians, and Southeast Asians. Or a particular population may inhabit a tropical environment that is shaded by jungle growth, which would explain why the Pygmies of the African rain forest are much lighter in skin colour than the nearby Bantu, who herd cattle on the open savanna.

Skin colour is therefore related to the amount and intensity of sunlight, but it appears to be so related in a peculiar way. After all, since black absorbs sunlight and white reflects it, a dark skin would seem to be disadvantageous at the Equator. The sunlight it absorbs is converted into heat, adding to the already considerable burden of heat that the body must dissipate in the tropics. As a result, people with dark skins are much more prone to heat stroke than those with light skins. Just the opposite distribution of skin colour would therefore be expected: the lightest skin near the sunny Equator and the darkest in less sunny and colder latitudes. Dark skin must therefore offer selective advantages in the tropics that outweigh the selective disadvantages. One obvious advantage is protection against debilitating sunburn for those who must spend the daylight hours foraging for food. The sun's rays can also produce skin cancers, the most often fatal of which (the melanomas) occur early in life and thus in a Darwinian sense would weed out the unfit. So, on balance, the selective advantages of a dark skin in the tropics (protection against severe sunburn and skin cancer) must have outweighed the disadvantages (a greater heat load). Although direct evidence is obviously lacking, the skin colour of the hominids who evolved in the full sunlight of the tropics was most probably dark.

These facts and speculations, though, would still not explain why populations in the less sunny northern and southern regions of the globe usually have light-coloured skin. Quite the opposite would be expected, since a dark skin would absorb heat in these colder latitudes. A dark skin, though, is a disadvantage in less sunny environments in one particular way. Vitamin D can be manufactured by the human body only when ultraviolet radiation from the sun penetrates to deep layers of the skin. Vitamin D is essential for the conversion of calcium into bone, and a lack of it causes rickets, a crippling bone disease. Rickets is a selective force, in that any malformation of the bones of the pelvis is likely to reduce a female's chances of giving birth normally. She will probably produce fewer live children, and a shortening of her own life-span is likely because of the increased danger of death during delivery. In males, malformation of the pelvis or limbs is also selective because it would tend to decrease running speed in hunting or in battle.

People inhabiting northern latitudes, where the sun is weak and the sky is often clouded, thus need to absorb as much of the available sunlight as possible to avoid being crippled by rickets. They will be hampered in this if dark pigments in their skin block the ultraviolet rays that would promote the synthesis of vitamin D. Two things probably made possible the occupancy of cloudy northern Europe, particularly during the last Ice Age. One was the constant selection that favoured the survival of individuals with lighter skin. The second was a dietary change that included increased consumption of fish and thus of fish oils that are very high in vitamin D. In fact, a very light skin would not have been essential for northern Europeans so long as they maintained their hunting–gathering way of life – because they could have obtained sufficient vitamin D from wild food sources. Natural selection in favour of lighter skin colour, however, must have become a major force about 5000 years ago when the food-production adaptation spread to northern Europe, and grains low in vitamin D thus became the staple diet. Eskimos apparently confirm this hypothesis. They are much darker-skinned than most northern Europeans and so would seem to lack the selective advantage of a light skin for northern latitudes. But their subsistence for many thousands of years has been based on harvesting the sea and thus obtaining large amounts of the vitamin D that occurs naturally in fish.

Skin colour might appear to have become less of a selective force in recent centuries. After all, artificial lighting allows work to be done at night rather than in the sun (thus making the protection of a dark skin less important in the tropics) and supplemental sources of vitamin D are available as additives to milk and other foods (thus making a light skin unnecessary in northern latitudes). The selective advantages of light and dark skins nevertheless have continued to operate in technological environments. With the coming of the Industrial Revolution and its smog-obscured sun, rickets became widespread and particularly affected the growth and development of children. People with light skins possessed a selective advantage in cities where tall buildings, narrow streets, and smoke blotted out the light. (The disease eventually declined after the discovery that vitamin D could be obtained by adding fish oils to the diet – hence the 'cod liver oil' that was so widely used as a food supplement until a generation ago.) People with dark skins, on the other hand, are still gaining protection against the effects of strong sunlight. Dark-skinned individuals are much less susceptible to skin cancers than are people of European ancestry living in the same cities. ♂♀

*

During the past several centuries, light-skinned Europeans have been able to convince most of the world that a dark skin indicated inferiority in one way or another. The assumptions of superiority by western Europeans, though, is a recent development that is largely due to the colonial adventures of the industrialized nations. Certainly no such superiority could have been even claimed until the earliest beginnings of the Industrial Revolution. About 2000 years ago, for example, the Roman statesman and orator Cicero recommended against taking a Briton into one's house because, he said, more stupid slaves were not to be found in the entire Roman Empire. Ancient Greek art, literature, and mythology often portrayed dark-skinned peoples with respect. The Umayyad dynasty, which ruled the Moslem Empire in the seventh and eighth centuries, proudly referred to its members as 'the swarthy people' in contrast to 'the ruddy people', their Persian and Turkish subjects. Nor did Africans feel inferior because of their dark skins until after long contact with Europeans. Early European explorers in Africa reported that many Africans regarded light skin as repulsive – and, in fact, both Stanley and Livingstone felt a sense of shame at their own lightness in contrast to the richly dark-skinned people around them.

Almost all Europeans and North Americans of the nineteenth century unconsciously accepted what has been called 'scientific racism' – a belief that people in undeveloped countries are genetically deficient in the mental abilities needed to invent and to use a complex technology. Thomas Henry Huxley, one of the most noted biologists of the last century and the leading exponent of Darwinism, stated this faith in the hereditary superiority of people of European origins:

It may be quite true that some Negroes are better than some white men; but no rational man, cognizant of the facts, believes that the average Negro is the equal, still less the superior of the average white man. And if this be true, it is simply incredible that, when all his disabilities are removed, and [the Negro] has a fair field and no favour, as well as no oppressor, he will be able to compete successfully with his bigger-brained and smaller-jawed rival, in a contest which is to be carried on by thoughts and not by bites.

Huxley's scientific racism presumably appeared reasonable to Europeans and North Americans because they had become masters of the entire human species. Native populations in Africa, Asia, and the Americas had been unable to resist expansion by the European military, merchant, and missionary. ♂♀

If Huxley had lived for another half century or so, he would have seen these same native peoples successfully expel Europeans from their lands. And even in his own time, Huxley's knowledge of human history ought to have led him to a far different conclusion about the cultural superiority or inferiority of different peoples. No single population has ever had exclusive control over achievement. Any scientific racist who happened to be living about 10,000 years ago would have had to conclude that a superior race inhabited the Near East, where domestication, settled village life, trade, and advanced technology were already in existence. Clear evidence would also have been found of the inferiority of northern Europeans, who would not cross the threshold between hunting–gathering and village life for many more thousands of years. After the fall of Rome, China emerged as the greatest power and technologically the most sophisticated civilization in the world. As recently as 1793, the British sent a delegation to China to beg the mighty Emperor Ch'ien-lung for permission to open trade. But the emperor replied to King George III that China had no need to enter into trade with the 'red-faced barbarian' since, in his words, '. . . our dynasty's majestic virtue has penetrated into every country under heaven, and kings of all nations have offered their costly tribute by land and sea. As your Ambassador can see for himself, we possess all things.' ♂♀ In fact, any objective survey of the past 10,000 years of human history would show that during almost all of it, northern Europeans were an inferior barbarian race, living in squalor and ignorance, producing few cultural innovations.

Racism has traditionally shown two aspects: prejudice and discrimination. An understanding of how these two differ and how they are inter-related can go far towards explaining the attitudes of human groups towards outsiders. Prejudice is the emotional aspect of racism and discrimination the political and social one. Prejudice is what predisposes one to react unfavourably towards certain groups of people while totally ignoring contrary evidence that might alter that reaction. The group against whom prejudice is directed is usually perceived as a 'race' (such as the 'Jewish race' or the 'Gypsy race'), even though biologically it is no such thing. The prejudiced attitude usually lumps diverse groups into a single category, based on some trait that may be either real or imaginary; the groups themselves, though, may have little in common and may indeed have had scarcely any contact with one another. The Nazis, seeing little difference among Jews, Gypsies, Poles, and Ukrainians, regarded them all as belonging to an inferior race and marked them equally for extermination in death camps, even though these peoples differ in genetic inheritance, language, religion, culture, and nearly everything else.

Prejudices held by one group against others who are considered different have probably always existed. The names American Indian tribes gave themselves, for example, usually translate as 'Human Beings' or 'The People', thereby implying that other tribes must belong to a subhuman race. The people who live around the Arctic Circle are usually called 'Eskimos' – a contemptuous name, meaning 'eaters of raw meat', given them by neighbouring Indians – but their own name for themselves is *Inuit* or *Inupik*, which translates roughly as 'The Real People'. The Eskimos thereby separated themselves from the rest of humankind, which might qualify as 'people' but not as 'real' ones. Citizens of the United States of America do much the same thing when they identify themselves as 'Americans' – thereby effectively ignoring Canadians, Mexicans, Guatemalans, Peruvians, Brazilians, and other inhabitants of the Americas, all of whom are equally worthy to be so identified. The Eskimo and the citizen of the United States thus boastfully imply a bias in favour of their respective cultures in comparison with others.

The prejudices of the dominant group usually permeate the entire society, including the very people against whom such prejudices are directed. These prejudices almost always affect the prevailing standards for human beauty. Thus, although only 3 per cent of the inhabitants of the island of Jamaica are of European ancestry, an additional quarter of the population, as a result of interbreeding, have certain physical characteristics of the European type; they are set apart, as 'Coloured', from the darker-skinned 'Negroes'. Those born with the 'Coloured' physical traits that approach European ideals have a much greater Darwinian fitness than the 'Negroes' who lack them. 'Coloured' obtain superior housing, health care, and education, and, as a result, their rate of survival is high. They produce more children, who in turn have a better chance of surviving, than the darker-skinned members of the population. In this way, prejudice supplements natural selection.

Discrimination, on the other hand, is legal, economic, and social behaviour based on differences in attitude regarding various groups. Discrimination often takes the form of segregation based on physical characteristics, the prohibition of intermarriage between groups, and the separation of facilities for education and health care, to list just a few. Or it may take the subtler form of social behaviour in which members belonging to a subordinate group must display public respect – like using polite forms of address or giving way on the sidewalk – towards members of a dominant group.

The government of South Africa today represents the most extreme form of racial discrimination since the defeat of the Nazis. The official policy of apartheid has created a rigid caste system based on colour: white (European ancestry), yellow (Asiatics), brown (racially mixed populations), and black (native Africans). These colour castes have been segregated, both physically and legally, in a hierarchy of privilege, with the Europeans at the top and the native Africans at the bottom. Europeans are the only ones who may move freely about the country and participate fully as members of society. Laws specify the various rights of the other colour castes in owning land, marrying, obtaining an education, and moving from one neighbourhood to another. South African whites find it impossible to avoid being discriminatory, even though they may be personally opposed to the practice. They can publicly protest discrimination against the other colour castes, but this is a futile exercise, since they will be discriminated for in the favoured treatment they receive from the arresting officers. They will be brought to court under a more equitable system of justice than is applied to members of the other colour castes; and if judged guilty, they will be sent to a jail whose superior facilities are reserved for people of European ancestry.

Numerous attempts have been made to get at the causes of prejudice and discrimination. Personality traits, religion, economics, the balance of political power, and various social influences have all been pointed to, but none has provided a satisfactory explanation. A certain kind of authoritarian personality (characterized by contempt for weakness, aggressive tendencies, and a lack of self-awareness) has been shown in some studies of Anglo-Saxon cultures to be inclined towards prejudice. This is certainly not the whole explanation, since people in other cultures who have the very same personality traits do not always reveal an inclination towards prejudice. Another psychological explanation holds that social or economic frustration leads to prejudice against minorities, who thus serve as scapegoats. This interpretation, though, cannot account for the obvious fact that wealthy and privileged people are sometimes as bigoted as those who have suffered much frustration. Desire for economic gain has undoubtedly played a part, since clearly prejudice has often been used to justify economic imperialism. Yet this explanation fails to make clear why the economy based on slavery established by the Portuguese in Brazil was less blatantly racist than the slave society established by the English in the southern United States. Racial prejudice has occasionally been attributed to religion, as supposedly borne out by several ambiguous references in the Judaic-Christian Bible and the Islamic Koran. This reasoning, though, fails to explain why Protestant cultures have generally been more racist than Catholic ones, even though both follow essentially the same Christian tradition, or why racism is virulent in such societies as India and Japan, neither of which has been much influenced by the Bible or the Koran.

Whatever the exact explanation for prejudice and discrimination, their consequences are real enough. Both are destructive to victims and oppressors alike. The affected society not only sacrifices the potential contributions of the individuals who are discriminated against, but it always pays a severe penalty in conflict, violence, reduced productivity, and psychological damage. Black Americans in the United States have a significantly lower life expectancy than whites, owing to a wide variety of causes that include poor health care, malnutrition, unsanitary living conditions, employment at dangerous or taxing jobs, and those self-destructive reactions such as alcoholism and drug addiction that are common among victims of prejudice. United States census statistics analysed in 1976 showed that life expectancy for black males is 6 years shorter than for white males, and for black females it is 5.4 years shorter than for white females. For the Black American population as a whole, these figures add up to an aggregate loss – every year – of 130 million years of life as compared to white life expectancy. Even more appalling is the self-perpetuating system of lessened Darwinian fitness in which Black Americans are trapped by the social conditions that deprive them of those 130 million years of living, and that are keyed at birth to the colour of their skin. ♂♀

\*

A virulent new form of scientific racism declares that the social and economic conditions under which Black Americans live is genetically determined. In other words, their alleged inferior intelligence is supposed to prevent them from learning the skills that lead to better-paying jobs and thus to better housing, health care, and education. Such suppositions concerning the inferior mental abilities of blacks were given strong support with the publication in 1969 of an article by Arthur R. Jensen, a psychologist at the University of California (Berkeley). Jensen's starting-point is the fact that Black Americans on the average have scored fifteen points lower on IQ tests than have whites. He does not claim that the entire fifteen-point lag in IQ scores should be attributed solely to inheritance. Instead, relying upon dubious studies of identical twins (and white twins at that) as well as comparisons of blacks and whites in the 'same' environment (as if the two environments could possibly be the same), Jensen concluded that five points of the difference could be attributed to the blacks' unfavourable environment. That left a ten-point gap in IQ scores, which he attributed to blacks' genetically inferior mental abilities. (The scientific racist is nearly always concerned with the intelligence of Black Americans rather than with that of other North American minority populations. Chinese–Americans, for example, are almost never mentioned, perhaps because they surpass whites in average IQ scores and have an average cranial capacity somewhat larger than that of whites.)

Jensen seems to be saying that the intelligence of Black Americans was determined at birth, that they have difficulty in competing for jobs because it is lower, and that therefore it is a waste of governmental money and effort to provide programmes to do anything about the situation. This is a vicious argument because it subtly combines dubious science with judgements about superiority and inferiority – and then draws inferences concerning social policies. For example, Jensen asserts that efforts to improve black social conditions through educational and cultural enrichment programmes are fruitless. ♂♀

One difficulty in evaluating Jensen's argument is that of sifting out scientific fact from sociological opinion. Intelligence is a complex adaptive trait with many dimensions that have so far resisted explanation. Numerous genes appear to be involved, acting both singly and in combination with other genes. As yet, geneticists lack the knowledge to deal with the inheritance of such complex traits. Furthermore, as noted in Chapter 11, tests that have been devised for measuring intelligence are seriously flawed. One specialist believes that after correction has been made for all the biases in IQ tests, only about 45 per cent of the variation in scores can be attributed to heredity – a very different figure from the approximately 80 per cent claimed by Jensen. ♂♀

The genetic component in measurable intelligence is certainly important, but part of its effect resides in a distortion of environmental influences and consequently of IQ scores. Suppose that the United States were to force all females with large breasts to attend inferior high schools. As a result, females possessing genes for large breasts would not receive as good an education and would perform poorly on IQ tests, thereby reinforcing the stereotype that large-breasted females are dumb. In the same way, the genes that control skin colour may be said to affect the environment of these Black Americans for whom the opportunity and the incentive to do well on IQ tests are limited, which in turn excludes them from college and widens any small gap in childhood scores that might have existed.

From all that is known today about population genetics, inbreeding, migration, mutation, and natural selection, it would of course be foolish to deny that various populations of the world differ in intelligence. What does differ is the kind of intelligence that has proved adaptive for each population. In other words, it would not be adopting a racist stereotype to suppose that the hunter–gatherer Pygmies have been selected for a different kind of intelligence than, say, the urban Hausa of Nigeria – although it would be if a claim were made that either Pygmy or Hausa intelligence is inherently superior, and that one or the other should accordingly be relegated to an inferior social and economic status. Such a line of argument is intellectually insupportable so far as Pygmies and Hausa are concerned, and it is no less so concerning the intelligence of Black Americans.

The fifteen-point lag in IQ scores of black children can, of course, be explained by other than genetic arguments. Let me emphasize again a point I have already made: IQ tests are intrinsically unfair to minorities because they are devised by people belonging to the dominant culture, whose attitudes have developed in the course of their upbringing within that same culture. (White American readers who attempt the test on page 277 will find dramatic evidence of this.) Not only are the tests culture-bound; the testing procedures themselves are vulnerable to criticism. A proved psychological fact is that expectation of failure usually leads to failure. A white teacher who regards blacks as intellectually inferior will inevitably communicate to them this self-fulfilling prophecy. ♂♀ On the other hand, black children have been shown to score from two to three points higher when an IQ test is administered by a sympathetic black teacher than when the same test is given by a white teacher.

Nor are black children prepared to compete in IQ tests on an

Minority children compete with white children on IQ tests that have been prepared by members of the dominant culture. If, instead, the black culture were the dominant one in the United States, white children would undoubtedly find themselves at a similar disadvantage. IQ questions—keyed to nonwhite, lower-class experiences—were prepared for white, middle-class Air Force technicians and officers to test their verbal aptitude in such a reversed situation. These questions were easily answered by black servicemen, but most whites scored less than fifty per cent, and were thus rated as 'culturally deprived'. Here are some of the questions, with the answers given on page 278:

1. After a pair of dice is thrown, the dots showing on top add up to seven. What is the total number of the dots facing down ?
   (a) seven  (b) snake-eyes  (c) boxcars  (d) Little Jesus  (e) eleven

2. Cheap chitlins taste rubbery unless they are cooked long enough. What is the minimum amount of time they should be cooked ?
   (a) fifteen minutes  (b) one hour  (c) two hours  (d) a day  (e) a week

3. A 'handkerchief head' is
   (a) cool cat  (b) a porter  (c) an Uncle Tom  (d) a hood  (e) a preacher

4. 'I ain't got no dust' means I have no
   (a) money  (b) women  (c) clothes  (d) drugs  (e) wine

5. Another name for Al Hajj Malik Shabazz is
   (a) LeRoi Jones  (b) Malcolm X  (c) Muhammad Ali  (d) Bill Cosby  (e) none of these

6. A 'yard' is
   (a) a measuring stick  (b) a hundred dollars  (c) a playground  (d) some drugs  (e) a cigarette lighter

7. A 'set' is
   (a) a pair of new shoes  (b) a gig  (c) lights  (d) a movie  (e) none of these

8. 'Candied sweets' is/are
   (a) beautiful black sisters  (b) a dance  (c) reefers  (d) sugared yams  (e) comedians

9. 'The hawk' is
   (a) the wind  (b) the rain  (c) a knit cap  (d) pants  (e) shoes

10. January 15 is
    (a) Black Independence Day  (b) the anniversary of the founding of Liberia  (c) celebration of the Selma, Alabama, bus boycott  (d) Booker T. Washington's birthday  (e) Martin Luther King, Jr's birthday

11. In the famous blues legend, whom did 'Stagger Lee' kill ?
    (a) his brother  (b) Frankie  (c) Johnny  (d) his girl friend  (e) Billy

12. Which of the following words does not belong ?
    (a) grey  (b) shine  (c) blood  (d) spook  (e) black

**13.** Which has more meat ?
    (*a*) pig feet   (*b*) neck bone   (*c*) ox tail   (*d*) pig tail

**Answers:**

1 (a), 2 (d), 3 (c), 4 (a), 5 (b), 6 (b), 7 (b), 8 (d), 9 (a), 10 (e), 11 (e), 12 (a), 13 (b)

equal basis with white children. Both in the United States and in Britain, black children attend inferior schools where they are often taught by poorly trained teachers. Equal years of schooling for black and white children certainly do not mean equal educational opportunities. Furthermore, many black children come out of homes or neighbourhoods in which parents and friends do not place a high premium on scholastic achievement. And the language the ghetto-dwelling black child learns to speak is a radically different dialect from the Standard English used on IQ tests. (I emphasize that this dialect is different, not inferior. Black English has its own sound system, grammar, and vocabulary, all of which are linguistically as valid and elegant as the Standard English dialect.♂♀) In a more subtle way, Black American culture has made its own adaptation to prejudice by cautioning the younger generation against trying to excel – especially in the intellectual arena, which has long been treated as the preserve of whites. Given these and numerous other obstacles, black children have been severely penalized in taking IQ tests. In fact, Jensen's argument could be turned around and a case made for the remarkable 'inherited intelligence' of blacks, who have overcome so many environmental disadvantages with a mere fifteen-point lag on IQ scores.

The Genetics Society of America spent two years discussing the controversy of a possible genetic basis of IQ and in 1976 adopted a resolution – which was supported by 94 per cent of the members (a total of 1488 specialists in genetics). Among the statements in the resolution were these:

It is particularly important to note that a genetic component for IQ score differences *within* a racial group does not necessarily imply the existence of a significant component in IQ differences *between* racial groups; an average difference can be generated solely by differences in their environments ... In our views, there is no convincing evidence as to whether there is or is not an appreciable genetic difference in intelligence between races. ♂♀

No excuse whatever exists for justifying the whites' harsh treatment of people with darker skins by claims of either biological or mental inferiority. Almost all anthropologists who have had close contact with peoples around the world believe deeply that they are generally similar in innate mental abilities. Nevertheless, at the end of the last century, the British justified their exploitation of Africans and Asians as a mission, in the words of Kipling, to 'take up the White Man's burden'. But the British Empire is no more, and there is little reason to suppose that several hundred years from now other white-skinned peoples will still dominate the world. By that time, perhaps the lessons about the biology and sociology of race will have been learned – and the future world leaders (whoever they may be: Asiatics, Africans, or Latin Americans) will not attribute the inferior social and economic status of people with white skins to an inferior biology.

# IV: The Mind and the Environment

# 14

# The Intelligent Senses

All healthy human beings are born with the same complex brain and the same sensory organs for looking out upon the world, for detecting sounds and touching objects, for delighting in odours and tastes – yet the ways in which different individuals react to the same or similar events are not the same. People differ in perception, learning ability, memory, thinking, and creativity (subjects which are discussed in this chapter and the next). The result of all this is that human beings have remarkably different views of the world. To some people, a thunderclap is a manifestation of complex physical and meteorological forces; to others, it may be a communication from the gods; to a few others, it is above all reminiscent of a fiery passage in the music of Wagner. People looking into a cave may variously consider it a potential habitation, a sanctuary in which to hold religious rites, a place of danger and mystery, a symbol of female sexuality, or (as in Plato's *Republic*) a metaphor for reality. Some people possess heightened sensory awareness. Wine-tasters, for example, can identify not only the region in which a certain wine was produced but sometimes the actual vineyard as well. Males are usually better than females at discriminating between coins of different sizes by the sense of touch. The explanation is that most males carry coins in a pocket and select them without looking, whereas females carry coins in a purse and choose the appropriate one by sight.

Humans inhabit a world surrounded by objects and events which they must perceive, identify, classify, and judge. Yet they tend to underrate their sensory abilities in comparison to those of one animal species or another. Although hawks may see farther than humans, although dogs detect odours more acutely, and although bats have superior hearing, human sensory equipment on the whole does an excellent job of alerting us to what is happening. Humans can see a burning candle at a distance of thirty miles on a dark but clear night, and also detect objects ten billion times as bright as that. They can smell just one drop of perfume after it has diffused throughout a three-room apartment, hear the tick of a watch at twenty feet, and detect the taste of sugar when a mere teaspoonful of it has been dissolved in two gallons of water. Ever since Aristotle, humans have traditionally thought in terms of five senses: vision, hearing, smell, taste, and touch. They do, though, possess still other senses. Kinaesthesis is the awareness of the position of the limbs, of muscle tension, and of the workings of more than a hundred body joints. This sense is essential to the human ability to stand, to walk, to hold objects, and to move about in the environment. The vestibular sense of gravity and of balance depends upon tiny receptor cells deep in the inner ear. In addition to that of touch, at least three other senses are located in the skin: those that detect pain, warmth, and cold.

Because humans live primarily in a world of sight, this chapter emphasizes that particular sense. The common folk wisdom that 'seeing is believing' is rarely questioned, even though it makes assumptions that are untrue about the way in which humans perceive the world. When you place a heavy typewriter on a desk, you fully expect that the desk will support it because you have been trained since infancy to see it as a desk, not as the six-sided, walnut-coloured object your senses tell you it is. Because you have been taught that desks are sturdy, you glance at this particular desk and assume that it will support the weight of the typewriter – a belief that goes far beyond any evidence that is conveyed by the sense of sight. The human senses afford only scant clues to the world of objects; yet people do not behave in accordance with even this small amount of sensory information. Such wariness about sensory information is fortunate, because the senses are not completely reliable guides to the external world.

In general, people assume that their eyes convey the external world as an accurate copy, which is sent over nerve pathways to the brain and then displayed there as on a screen. The entire process is sometimes compared to the operation of a camera. Everyday experience nevertheless demonstrates that the visual system is easily tricked. Place a straight stick in water and the eyes clearly see that the portion below the water line is bent. Intelligence, of course, will correct this sensory impression by telling us that it is the rays of light, not the stick, that are refracted as they pass from thin air to the dense medium of water. The eyes can be tricked easily in many ways. Close them and press down on the eyeballs, and you will 'see' a flash of light. You have thus fooled the entire eye–nerve–brain system by enabling a visual experience to be created in the absence of light. Nor do people always see with the eyes. Rich and complex visual experiences, such as dreams and hallucinations, totally bypass the eyes, activating certain cells in the brain instead.

So it becomes obvious that humans cannot regard the senses as invariably accurate mirrors of the world. The situation is further complicated because of the unique experiences, personality, needs, motivations, and cultural expectations that every person brings to sensory events. A youthful Plains Indian warrior who isolated himself on a 'vision quest' usually returned with his vision, simply because he had worked himself into an intense emotional state that made him receptive to the experience he and his society expected. Others who have sought visions of the supernatural in this way are the hermits of Buddhism, ascetic orders of Christian monks, the Jewish Essenes (whose membership may have included Jesus), and the Whirling Dervishes of Islam. Clearly, the various ways in which humans interpret the impressions with which their senses continually bombard them are geared both to cultural expectations and to the individual personality. Humans think of objects in terms of the data brought by the senses – but these data are deeply affected by what they know, or think they know, about those objects. In a well-known story by Edgar Allan Poe, a purloined letter was not 'seen' even though it was in plain sight, owing simply to the expectation of most people that a stolen object will be hidden. We not only believe what we see; we also see what we believe.

A vast difference clearly exists between the real world (as defined and measured by the instruments of physical science) and the world as perceived by individuals (who employ only their unaided senses). This difference is based on three obvious facts. First of all, events may be fully capable of affecting the senses, but they are not noticed for some reason or other. Second, numerous events are out of the range of the unaided senses. Many of the sound vibrations that are continually occurring are either too faint in volume or too high in pitch for human ears to detect. Unaided sight cannot detect extremely small objects, such as the teeming micro-organisms on the surface of every object in the visible universe. Nor do humans possess sensory organs capable of detecting a wide range of electromagnetic phenomena that includes gamma rays, X-rays, radio waves, and infra-red rays. Third, people almost never perceive exactly the event that is presented to the senses. Features of any object presented to the vision may be ignored, added to, or distorted – thereby creating optical illusions. ♂♀

The assurance that human beings display while moving about their environment is truly remarkable in view of the scanty information delivered to the brain by the senses. People look at the front of a house and instantaneously 'know' that rooms will be found behind that façade. They see the rear bumper of an automobile protruding from a carport, and from that single clue their minds summon up a picture of an entire automobile. Young children possess the same senses that adults do and these senses are nearly as efficient – yet no young child could make accurate judgements about a house just from seeing the façade or about a car merely from its bumper. It is not that children fail to receive the same sensations that are received by adults; rather, they have not yet learned to interpret the information those sensations bring to them. Older children and adults have learned to translate sensory stimuli, by the process known as 'perception', into organized experiences ('percepts').

Most psychologists make a basic distinction between sensing and perceiving. Sensations are relatively simple, such as a high-pitched sound caused by a vibrating motor. Percepts, on the other hand, are complex associations of many sensations – as when a high-pitched sound is interpreted as a cry for help, and is then combined with the sensations of an odour of smoke, the sight of flames, and an acrid burning in the nostrils to cause the complex behaviour of a person dashing into a building to rescue someone from a fire. The same sensations are always produced by the same stimuli: no matter where or when a red traffic light flashes, it is always seen as a red light. But percepts about such things as a flashing red light may vary considerably, depending upon what has been learned since this sensation was last encountered (such as having received an officer's summons for not bringing an automobile to a full stop). Perception, therefore, is a psychological process whereby humans organize and interpret the evidence about the environment that is gathered by the senses. Perception is usually thought of as automatic and effortless and as taking place without deliberate thought. Experiments indicate, though, that percepts take time to be formed, sometimes no more than a few thousandths of a second, or sometimes as much as several seconds for even a simple geometrical shape. And, as pictures in which the sensations are ambiguous or incomplete can demonstrate, percepts may take a very long time to be formed.

A remarkable thing about perception is that people organize the information offered by the senses as rapidly as they do, and then go on continually reinterpreting it in light of new information. A person looking out upon a landscape will slowly shift the gaze from one side of a spreading tree to the other. As far as the light-sensitive nerve endings in the eye 'know', it is the image of the tree that has moved rather than the gaze that takes it in. Our perceptual organization of the world, however, tells us that trees do not move (which is why Macbeth is so reassured by the witches' prediction that he will be vanquished only when Birnam wood moves to Dunsinane hill). That trees are stationary objects is a percept about the environment that people learn at an early age, and that they persist in believing despite what the images detected by the eyes communicate. Another commonplace experience is to perceive images as remaining constant although they are in fact undergoing marked changes – a phenomenon known as 'object constancy'. A dinnerware plate is continually perceived as round even though it is usually viewed at an angle from which it is really seen as an ellipse. A door is always perceived as rectangular, even though the image it forms in the eye consists of various trapezoidal shapes that change as it swings open and shut. Humans continue to perceive the world as orderly and constant although the information gathered by the senses is disorganized and changing. The mind rejects the clear evidence of the senses because experience has taught that dishes are round and doors are rectangular.

\*

Although most people tend to organize visual stimuli in a limited number of similar ways, some perception depends to a large extent upon the individuality of the perceivers. One of the most obvious influences on perception is that people usually see what they expect to see, and those expectations are the direct result of previous experiences, learning, and motivations. One classic experiment divided volunteers into six groups whose members had a common interest in a particular subject, such as religion or economics. Various images and words were then flashed upon a screen. Those whose interest was religion were the quickest to perceive the word *sacred* and those interested in economics were quickest to perceive *income*. Hungry people are likely to perceive food and food-related objects in meaningless inkblots. Children often see candy in designs that show none, and tests indicate that poor children often overestimate the size of coins.

Clear differences in perception occur not only between individuals but even in the same individual at different times. The common belief that people perceive the world differently at every stage, from childhood to old age, has been confirmed by various experiments, and these have also shown that increasing age brings with it a hardening of expectancies. As children mature, they rely increasingly upon perceptual constancies (like the shape of a dish or a door, referred to on the previous page). And as perceptual learning and experience increase over the years, people become more prone to certain kinds of optical illusions. If they are accustomed to seeing right angles in their environment, then an illusion that depends upon the perception of right angles will deceive them. Differences in perception according to sex also appear to occur, but it is uncertain whether these are related to biological differences between the sexes or to the sex roles that various societies have imposed. North American males, for example, are said to be more 'field independent' than females – that is, more resistant to influence by the context in which sensations occur. Field-independent people, placed in a specially designed room in which no visual clues exist about vertical and horizontal planes, can adjust a rod to true vertical. The explanation for male superiority in such tests might very well lie in North American child-rearing practices, which encourage males to be venturesome, rather than in any biological or physical differences in perception between the sexes. ♂♀

Claims are often made that certain people possess the capacity to go beyond the normal limits of perception. These abilities include in particular three forms of extrasensory perception (ESP): telepathy ('mind reading'), clairvoyance (the perception of an object out of the normal range of human senses), and precognition (the ability to perceive something that has not yet occurred). Belief in such unusual abilities is obviously very old – as witness the oracles, witchcraft, and divination of the ancient world – but scientific interest in the subject is quite recent. Most scientists have held aloof from the study of ESP simply because it has long attracted charlatans. A few distinguished scientists, though, have believed in it; the seventeenth-century astronomer and mathematician Johannes Kepler, for example, even made his living by casting horoscopes.

Numerous claims for ESP have later been explained by new

scientific knowledge or have been exposed as hoaxes. Yet some cases continue to defy explanation by any known scientific method. A few decades ago a middle-aged Englishwoman announced that such noted musicians as Beethoven and Brahms were dictating musical compositions to her. These works were examined by leading musicologists, almost all of whom agreed that they bore an uncanny resemblance to the musical styles of the composers in question and did not simply mimic stylistic quirks. Highly trained musicians declared that counterfeiting such works would be extremely difficult, yet it was assumed that the woman had done exactly that. A thorough investigation nevertheless showed that she came from a simple working-class background, had studied piano only for a brief period as a child, had never been taught composition, and was not known by her friends to have displayed any particular interest in music. Her case so far defies solution. An uneducated woman could not by any normal means produce compositions with all the earmarks of those by some of the greatest composers who ever lived. On the other hand, we can hardly suppose that the ghosts of German musicians would have waited their turn to dictate in English new works to an uneducated woman who had no interest in music.

A problem presented by ESP is that scientific procedures do not now exist for evaluating such baffling cases as this Englishwoman's. Nevertheless, attempts have been made to put research into ESP on a scientific basis. A common experimental procedure employs a special deck of twenty-five cards, made up of sets of five cards, each displaying one of five different symbols (a star, a cross, a square, a circle, and a series of wavy lines). In a typical experiment, the cards are shuffled and then put on a table, out of sight of the person being tested. The individual is then asked to guess the order of the cards (a test of clairvoyance) or to name the card which the experimenter is concentrating on (a test of telepathy). If the individual possessed no special ESP powers and merely guessed, the rules of chance would dictate that the correct card would be named five times during an experiment with an entire deck of twenty-five. Some people do considerably better than that. Over a period of four years, in test after test, one woman correctly identified an average of 6.8 cards. This score may not appear to be overwhelmingly better than the score of five that would be achieved by merely guessing, but statistically it is remarkable. Some other individuals have scored quite low in this test, though in an unusual way – by identifying not the card the

experimenter was looking at, but often the very next one in the deck
– which suggests the possibility of precognition.

No examples of cheating, either by the scientists conducting such
tests or by the people being tested, have been disclosed. Nevertheless,
because ESP violates all known scientific rules, the very large majority of psychologists remain unconvinced. Mental telepathy, for
example, can be explained only in terms of brain waves somehow
transmitted from one person to another. But this is an unacceptable
explanation because brain waves are an extraordinarily weak form of
energy that could not conceivably travel from one brain to another
and, in fact, can be detected only by very sensitive instruments.
Furthermore, any proof for the existence of ESP would necessarily
have to be based on the exceptional individual's possession of sensory
equipment that differs strikingly from that of the population at large
– something that ESP researchers have so far been unable to show.
And finally, if some exceptional individuals do indeed possess extrasensory powers of precognition, then why have they not bankrupted
the gambling casinos of the world by foretelling the cards in black-
jack or the next number on the roulette wheel? An answer to this
question can in fact be given. Psychologists have taken subjects who
scored high in ESP tests to Las Vegas. They failed to break the bank.

No simple statement can at present be made about whether or not
ESP truly exists, either in the human species generally or in a very
few gifted individuals. A number of very baffling cases demonstrate
that certain people do have powers that cannot be explained at
present in terms of known physical laws. Yet it has been impossible to
design foolproof experiments to test these individuals, to compare the
results with unexceptional people, and to find alternative explanations that can be fitted into any of the known principles of science
governing the universe. ESP obviously must be regarded as a possibility in the human species, but one that so far remains unproved.
This situation is not at all unusual in science. Copernicus' theory
that the earth revolved around the sun was predicated upon the
parallax of the stars, yet the existence of parallax was not proved by
astronomers until two centuries later. And, of course, the existence
of atoms has been postulated for well over 2000 years, but the fact
that they could be split was not dramatically demonstrated until the
appearance of a mushroom cloud over Alamogordo, New Mexico, in
1945.♂♀

*

Social scientists have long known that the way people perceive the world is influenced by the culture in which they are brought up. It has been noted, for example, that cultures give varying emphasis to round objects as distinct from rectangular ones. In Western cultures, rectangular objects tend to predominate, as witness the shapes of houses, furniture, television and movie screens, books, doorways, and numerous things constructed with carpenter's tools. Circular objects are much more common in many other cultures; thus the Zulus of South Africa live in circular houses inside circular compounds, keep their cattle in circular pens, and use circles in the

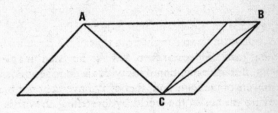

SANDER PARALLELOGRAM

imagery of their religious ceremonies. The way these traditional shapes affect perception has been formulated into what is known as the carpentered-world hypothesis, and has been tested by means of the optical illusion known as the Sander Parallelogram, shown on this page.

A person brought up in a Western culture who looks at this parallelogram tends to suppose that the diagonal line *AC* is longer than the diagonal *CB*. Measurement with a ruler, though, proves that *AC* is actually about 15 per cent shorter than *CB*. A moment's thought explains why a Westerner is likely to make this error. The carpentered world in which we live exposes us to rectangular surfaces, but these are rarely seen as right angles because objects are usually viewed from one side or another. We almost never see the rectangular top of a coffee table from directly overhead. Rather, we usually view it from one side and at an acute angle, which distorts it into the form of a parallelogram. Our everyday experience thus tells us that diagonal *AC* on a coffee table or any other three-dimensional rectangular object would be longer than diagonal *CB*, and so in a two-dimensional parallelogram we also automatically perceive *AC* as though it were longer. But people in rural Africa, who live in a circular world, are not hampered by any such preconception concerning rectangular forms. To them, that *CB* is longer is thus obvious. On the other hand, people in rural Africa are much more likely to be susceptible to various optical illusions involving circles.♂♀

One major attempt to explain cultural differences in perception is based on language. The case was made by the linguist Edward Sapir, who wrote in 1929:

Human beings do not live in the objective world alone, nor alone in the world of social activity as ordinarily understood, but are very much at the mercy of the particular language which has become the medium for their society.

Several years later Benjamin Lee Whorf, one of Sapir's students at Yale, began a painstaking comparison of the Hopi Indian language with European languages, and also of the different ways in which Hopis and people in Western cultures perceive the world. He concluded that humans are prisoners of the language learned in childhood. Language, Whorf stated, becomes 'not merely a reproducing instrument for voicing ideas but rather is itself a shaper of ideas . . . We dissect nature along lines laid down by our native languages.'♂♀

The Sapir–Whorf hypothesis would seem at first glance to be reasonable. Common sense tells us that an object is more easily perceived, talked about, and remembered if an everyday word in the language exists to describe it. The Eskimo language, with its numerous words for different kinds of snow, should therefore make Eskimos more alert to the subtle differences in snow conditions that speakers of other languages would overlook. This is possibly true, but it is true also that when a need exists to express something, speakers of a language have no difficulty inventing new words – as indeed skiers have done to distinguish among different kinds of snow. Whorf was, however, more interested in differences in the basic structure of language than in commonsense notions about vocabulary. Some experiments seem to confirm the validity of this approach. Navajo-speaking children and English-speaking Navajo children on the same reservation were compared in the ways they sorted certain objects. The Navajo-speakers generally sorted the objects on the basis of shape, whereas the children who spoke English sorted them on the basis of colour. One explanation for the difference is based on certain features of the Navajo language. The Navajo verb that speakers of English translate as 'to pick up' has different forms which depend on the qualities of the object being picked up. One form of the verb is used if the object is round and thin, a different form if it is long and flexible. The same emphasis on the shape of objects is found in other Navajo verbs for actions, such as 'to drop' and 'to hold'. The Navajo language seemingly forces that attention be paid to shapes and therefore makes its speakers more likely to categorize objects on that basis. Yet the force of this apparent confirmation of the Sapir–Whorf hypothesis was diluted considerably by the discovery that native speakers of English in Boston schools also sorted objects on the basis of shape. ♂♀

Most linguists and psychologists are wary of the Sapir–Whorf hypothesis. For every experiment that has seemed to confirm that a language inevitably forces those who speak it into certain perceptual pathways, others have been made that failed to support the hypothesis. Language does not, it would appear, so much *determine* cultural differences as *reflect* cultural concerns that already exist. Nor has substantial evidence been found that any language seriously limits what its speakers can say. Isolated Melanesian hunter–gatherers and food-producers who encountered sophisticated technology during World War II quickly adapted their language to things and ideas they had not previously conceived could possibly exist. The history of language is not so much the story of people in different cultures misled by their languages as it is the story of a successful overcoming of the limitations built into all language systems.

\*

Early in this century an influential United States psychologist, Edward B. Titchener, became convinced that his science should concern itself with the elements of experience that formed a kind of 'consciousness' and that were based on such sensory experiences as colours, tastes, and smells. From such a concern, he argued, a definitive statement about the mind of our species would eventually emerge. He set as his first task, therefore, to analyse the familiar perceived world and isolate the elements of sensation. In regard to colour, he claimed to have isolated about 35,000 sensations; for tones, about 11,000; for tastes, a mere four (sweet, sour, bitter, and salty). Eventually he arrived at a grand total of 46,708 elementary sensations, plus an undetermined number of smells, all of which he believed to be the components of human consciousness. He later elaborated his theory by adding to sensation such other things as pleasant and unpleasant emotions, and by mixing sensations to form perceptions. His work was influential for a time, but nowadays no one sets store by it – and psychologists remain as confused as before about what 'consciousness' really is.

The notion of consciousness has long been a subject for dispute among philosophers and psychologists, who have alike fretted endlessly over the differences between mind and matter or between body and soul. Probably no subject has evoked so many metaphors. In the nineteenth century, when geologists began to uncover the record of the past by excavating layers of the earth's crust, consciousness came to be pictured as consisting of layers that could be peeled back one by one to reveal the nature of an individual's mind. Somewhat later, when remarkable discoveries in chemistry were being made, consciousness came to be regarded as a compound structure such as could be analysed in the laboratory. With the expansion of the industrial age, a new metaphor likened consciousness to the boiler of a steam engine, whose energy had to be released, either in behaviour or in dreams, to forestall the danger of an explosion. Everyday language is filled with metaphors that contain assumptions about consciousness. We 'grapple' with a problem or 'approach' it from a different 'standpoint' until we 'grasp' it. We can be 'broad-minded' or 'narrow-minded' in approaching a problem; our consciousness may be 'agitated' or 'altered'; we can 'hold' something in our mind, let it 'penetrate', or 'get it off' our mind.

The paradox of consciousness is that although we can be conscious that there is a problem in defining it, the definition continues to elude the consciousness. Psychologists have often found it easier to agree on what consciousness is not than on what it is. The notion of having 'lost consciousness' is commonly used for a particular state in which perception is absent. Various injuries to the brain and other parts of the body, as well as severe emotional stress, alcohol, drugs, and hypnosis, can all produce this state. Although a loss of consciousness does not reveal what consciousness is, it nevertheless does emphasize the existence of an experiencing self, a mind that is aware and that can reflect upon its own actions. Most people indeed regard themselves as possessing some kind of conscious mind that is separate from the rest of the body. Evidence has been gathered that people carry in the brain an image of their own bodies. An amputee, for example, is still conscious of sensations in a limb that has been removed. From studies of the growth of consciousness in children, it appears that until they are several years of age they do not develop the ideas about space, size, and direction that enable them to describe the relation of objects to each other and to the children themselves. ♂♀

All humans periodically lose consciousness in sleep. We are so accustomed to the normal rhythm of sleep and wakefulness that we do not consider how strange it is that the consciousness on which we pride ourselves, and which we regard as the very essence of individual personality, should be suspended altogether for about a third of our lives. Of all human behaviours, sleep is one of the most mystifying and least understood. Until the past few decades, most people supposed that sleep was the time when the brain rested. Scientists now know that the sleeping brain is as active as the waking one, and that at certain times during the sleep period it is furiously at work in the processing of information. The belief that sleep is the consequence of fatigue has been found to be, at best, an oversimplification. Nor is it the function of sleep to give relief from an overload of sensory stimulation during the waking day. Volunteers who submitted to experiments isolating them from all sensory stimulation have been placed in separate rooms that were completely darkened and soundproofed; they were even supplied with gloves to eliminate tactile sensations. The first day, with sensory stimulation completely absent, they slept for an average of between twelve and fourteen hours. The explanation for this probably lies in the fact that the volunteers had nothing to do except to sleep; certainly it could not have been the result of any need for relief from sensory stimulation.

Scientists do not even know how much sleep people need. A generation ago, most hygiene books stated that adults require eight hours of sleep each night. Sleep researchers are now discovering, though, that the amount of sleep needed is very much an individual matter. Cases are known of extremely active people who for half a century never slept more than four hours a night. On the other hand, even a healthy person may need as much as seventeen hours on occasion. Claims have been made from time to time concerning people who supposedly went for extremely long periods with no sleep at all, but most such cases never survived scientific scrutiny. The longest verified case on record is that of a high-school youth who was kept under constant observation by researchers from the Stanford University Sleep Laboratory, and who stayed awake for 264 consecutive hours – exactly eleven days – without exhibiting any serious emotional changes. In fact, he remained so alert that on the last night of his vigil he beat one of the researchers in every game they played in a penny arcade. Nor did he exhibit any exceptional need to make up sleep afterwards. Following a first sleep lasting only about fourteen hours, he stayed up for twenty-four hours before going to sleep again, this time for a mere eight hours. ♂♀

Sleep researchers have so far failed to answer fully the obvious question: What lures us every night from our work, our leisure activities, our family and friends into the solitary world of sleep? It is difficult to believe that human beings spend about a third of their lives in a state that has no function. Yet one researcher became so pessimistic about the failure to pinpoint the functions of sleep that he came to wonder whether it had any function at all:

If sleep does not serve an absolutely vital function, then it is the biggest mistake the evolutionary process ever made. Sleep precludes hunting for and consuming food. It is incompatible with procreation. It produces vulnerability to attack from enemies. Sleep interferes with every voluntary motor act in the repertoire of coping mechanisms. How could natural selection with its irrevocable logic have 'permitted' the animal kingdom to pay the price of sleep for no good reason? In fact, the behaviour of sleep is so apparently maladaptive that one can only wonder why some other condition did not evolve to satisfy whatever need it is that sleep satisfies.

Almost no scientists, however, believe that natural selection plays such tantalizing games with human behaviour. ♂♀ Before going into some possible functions that can be postulated for sleep, I want to explain in more detail what sleep is.

The modern understanding of sleep began quite by accident in 1952, when a graduate student was assigned to observe the eyelids of sleeping volunteers to see whether any movement occurred. He observed that at certain times during the night the eyeballs of sleepers darted about furiously beneath the closed lids. (Eye movements are very easy to detect, even when the lids are closed; ask someone to perform these movements and see for yourself.) Such activity was totally unexpected, since sleep had long been thought to be a time of quiescence, not one in which the brain was actively generating eye movements that were often faster than could be produced by a waking person. Since then, much more has been learned about rapid eye movement (technically known as 'REM') during certain stages of sleep. REM sleep is always accompanied by very distinctive brain-wave patterns, a marked increase in blood flow and in the temperature of the brain, irregular breathing, convulsive twitches of the face and fingertips, and the erection of the penis and clitoris. REM sleep is active sleep, even though the large muscles of the body are completely relaxed. The other kind of sleep is known as 'NREM' (that is, non-REM). During this state, breathing is regular, body movement is generally absent, and brain activity is low. Perception shuts down because the senses are no longer gathering information and communicating it to the brain. NREM sleep is sometimes called 'quiet sleep' but in one respect that is not so; snoring occurs during this state.

A number of curious experiences occur at the onset of sleep. A person just about to go to sleep may experience an electric shock, a flash of light, or a crash of thunder – but the most common sensation is that of floating or falling, which is why 'falling asleep' is a scientifically valid description. A nearly universal occurrence at the beginning of sleep (although not everyone recalls it) is a sudden, unco-ordinated jerk of the head, the limbs, or even the entire body. Most people tend to think of going to sleep as a slow slippage into oblivion, but the onset of sleep is not gradual at all. It happens in an instant. One moment the individual is awake, the next moment not.

The first period of sleep is always NREM. It consists of four stages, during each of which the sleeper becomes more remote from the sensory environment. Children in particular are virtually unwakenable at the fourth stage. Even if they can finally be roused, it may be several minutes before they return to awareness. This deepest fourth stage is the period during which most of the talking in one's sleep, sleep-walking, night terrors, and bed-wetting by children take place. After the fourth stage, the sleeper retraces all the stages back to lighter sleep. The downward progression into the first deep sleep is smooth, but the upward progression is marked by irregular jumps from one stage to the other. The first REM period begins about seventy or eighty minutes after a person has fallen asleep and usually lasts for only about ten minutes. The entire NREM–REM cycle averages about ninety minutes, but with some individuals it is as short as seventy minutes and with others as long as 110. The two kinds of sleep – as different from each other as sleep is from wakefulness – continue to alternate throughout the night. With each cycle,

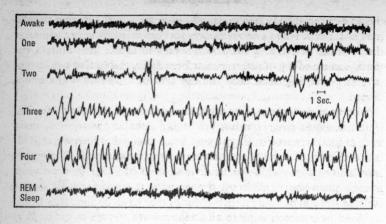

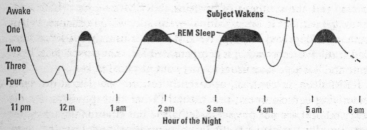

THE PATTERNS OF SLEEP

---

The electroencephalograph (EEG) is a device for recording the electrical activity of the brain by means of electrodes placed on various parts of the scalp. The typical EEG patterns shown here make plain that the activity in an individual's brain changes in consistent ways from wakefulness to NREM sleep and then to REM sleep. A person who is fully awake but lying down with the eyes closed shows the pattern at top, one of high frequency but low amplitude. As the sleeper enters the first stage of NREM sleep, brain waves of lower frequency begin to be recorded. When the deepest sleep of the fourth stage is reached, the waves have low frequency and high amplitude. Note that the brain waves of REM sleep are quite different.

In fact, they are much more similar than the others to those of the wakeful state – even though in other ways REM sleep is very deep. During REM sleep, people are very difficult to waken, they do not respond to sensory stimuli, and they have lost the use of virtually all of the body's major muscles. Since REM sleep is the stage during which dreaming occurs, the loss of muscle tone is probably an evolutionary adaptation that prevents the body from acting out dream activities.

The chart at the bottom plots the frequency with which the different stages of sleep typically occur throughout the night, as revealed through continuous monitoring with an EEG. The chart makes clear that a person does not the amount of REM sleep gradually increases, to the degree that it may become as long as sixty minutes just before awakening, whereas the amount of NREM sleep decreases markedly. An adult who sleeps seven and a half hours spends from one and a half to two hours of that period in REM sleep, mostly towards the end of the sleep period.

The new view of sleep that has emerged in the past few decades from numerous laboratories is not one of sleep as 'death's counterfeit', as Shakespeare put it. ♂♀ Sleep is not passive in the sense that it is the absence of something characteristic of wakefulness. Rather, it is an active state in which the brain is never at rest. One theory about human sleep assigns different functions to the two kinds of sleep. NREM sleep apparently does the things that have traditionally been assigned by common sense to all sleep: growth, repair to the body's tissues, and the synthesis of proteins. NREM sleep is a biological necessity; without it, an individual eventually would collapse. When someone is deprived of sleep, NREM sleep is usually made up first. And until the deprivation is compensated for, that person feels lethargic and less able than usual to carry out physical tasks.

REM sleep, in contrast, apparently restores the neural processes underlying consciousness; it is mental rather than physical. People deprived of it are not physically lethargic but emotionally irritable; they usually perform poorly in concentration and learning tests. REM sleep appears to be essential to integrate recently learned material into long-term memory. Students who stay up all night cramming for an examination the next day usually do not do as well as those who have had some sleep. The explanation is that the students have momentarily learned a lot of new facts, but these facts cannot be remembered unless they have been processed during sleep for incorporation into the memory. REM sleep also seems to help people cope with day-to-day stress. Experiments have shown that volunteers who were exposed to stressful situations had a sharply in-

simply descend gradually into sleep and then gradually wake up. Rather, the various stages of sleep are passed through again and again. With each cycle, the amount of REM sleep increases, until at the end of the sleep period it may last for a full hour. The fourth stage of NREM, when sleep is deepest, is the most puzzling. This stage does not appear to occur in other mammals, and even in humans it occurs only during the early part of the sleep period. Although it is extremely difficult to awaken a sleeper during this stage, this is also the one during which sleepwalking occurs.

creased need for REM sleep, during which time they apparently made peace with the traumatic experiences. Such experiments offer fresh evidence that sleep is one of the most active parts of a person's day. ♂♀

Another explanation of why we need to sleep is related to the biological rhythms that influence the behaviour of all living things. Every animal must adapt to fluctuations in the environment: the ebb and flow of the tides, night alternating with day, the phases of the moon, and the change of seasons. All living things have evolved biological rhythms that match these environmental cycles. Even though humans can nowadays turn night into day by flicking on electric lights, and can race the rising sun in supersonic aircraft, most of human history has been spent in adapting to the rhythms of the environment. Such responses, built into the human body throughout millions of years, cannot quickly be lost. Indeed, more than a hundred physiological functions in humans oscillate between maximal and minimal efficiency once a day. These daily rhythms have been reported for body temperature, blood sugar, liver glycogen, white corpuscle count, adrenal gland activity, DNA synthesis, cell division, and mental performance. Body temperature, for example, peaks during the middle of the day and falls to its lowest point during the early morning hours. People who stay up during the night usually feel chilly around 4 a.m., even though they are in a well-heated room. Individual scores on various tests that measure mental performance are usually much lower if the tests are taken at night than if they are taken at midday. Nor are such poor performances due to the loss of sleep caused by waiting up to take the test during the night. Those who have gone for twenty-four hours without sleep still score higher at midday than they do at night.

An evolutionary explanation for sleep might exist after all: people sleep during the depressed phase of their daily rhythm, the hours when they are least efficient. Although each person follows daily rhythms, the exact timing of those rhythms is an individual matter. Some people awaken in the morning in a highly active state, ready to meet the day; others are lethargic during the daylight hours and do not reach a peak of attentiveness until evening. Such individual differences between day and night activity appear around the sixth week after birth, showing up first in changes in the heartbeat and in body temperature. By the end of the first year of life, a child has all of the clearly defined rhythms found in adults. As in adults also, great differences exist between individual infants in the precise timing of the many rhythms in each twenty-four-hour period. In fact, so different are the rhythms for each person that here might be a good starting-point for the biological definition of individuality. ♂♀

*

Researchers have awakened large numbers of people during REM sleep, and 74 per cent of these recalled their dreams – whereas only 7 per cent of those awakened from NREM sleep could do so. Furthermore, a dramatic difference in the kind of dreams was reported for each sleep stage. Those rare people who had dreamed during NREM sleep reported brief and rather unexciting dreams. The events were generally realistic, with few persons or objects depicted and with little visual imagery. In contrast, the dreams of those awakened from REM sleep were complex, exciting, and often so vividly distorted that they frightened the dreamer. The vivid dreams of REM sleep are undoubtedly one of the most striking examples known of dissociation – that is, the separation of consciousness into two seemingly independent entities. Most people who remember their dreams do indeed report two levels of consciousness: one at which the dream is observed and the other at which the dreamer participates. EEGs indicate that human infants and many species of mammals also dream during REM sleep, but this kind of dreaming must assuredly be different from that of mature humans. Once hominids reached a new behavioural plateau, characterized by language and by fully developed culture, dreams must have assumed a new significance. They could be talked about, interpreted by the individual and the social group, and be given a meaning. What in hominid evolution had previously been private and unconscious now gave *Homo sapiens* a new capacity for self-awareness and for knowledge of the inner life of other members of the group.

All people dream, but those in different societies differ greatly in the way they evaluate and interpret dreams. People in some societies hold dreams to be identical with reality. In Borneo, for instance, a man who dreams that his wife has committed adultery has the right to ask her father to take her back. A Jesuit missionary in the seventeenth century complained that the Iroquois Indians 'have, properly speaking, only a single Divinity – the dream. To it they render their submission, and follow all its orders with the utmost exactness.' The Iroquois felt obliged to carry out in their waking hours whatever they thought they had done in their dreams. 'This people,' the Jesuit continued, 'would think itself guilty of a great crime if it failed in its observance of a single dream.' Individuals in other cultures regard dreams as prophetic signs – as in the *Iliad*, where Agamemnon is visited in a dream by a messenger of Zeus who tells him what actions to take. The Old Testament also contains numerous prophetic dreams, such as those of the pharaohs and of Jacob and Joseph.

Aristotle did not accept the view of dreams as divination that was current in the Greece of his time. Instead, he anticipated the theories of Freud by regarding dreams as reflections of waking experiences and emotional needs. According to Freud, it is in dreams that personal fears, hopes, and anxieties which have been repressed are later released. Recent research has confirmed portions of his theory and contradicted others. As Freud noted, most dreams are very personal. Dreamers usually perceive themselves as participants and about two-thirds of the time they dream of close acquaintances and family members. On the other hand, the dreams of most people are less bizarre than Freud supposed. Thought of in terms of art, dreams are usually representational (that is, more or less faithful to visible objects) or impressionistic rather than abstract or surreal. ♂♀

The vast body of information that exists concerning dreams in various societies has shown that certain aspects of dreaming appear to be the same for humans everywhere, but that others are very much influenced by the particular society and by the personality of the individual who is dreaming. One universal, for example, is that males and females have different dreams. Males dream about other males more often than they do about females, whereas females dream about both sexes equally. Almost every dream also shows cultural influences. Dreams collected from the Yir Yoront tribe of Australia, for example, show with remarkable consistency a subject-matter that could apply to few other groups of people than this one. The male Yir Yoront is likely to dream about having sexual intercourse with a female whom the marriage rules of his society deem an appropriate partner. If the female is not an appropriate mate, something in the dream interferes with intercourse – and the greater the society's prohibition against sexual relations with this female, the more stringent the interference becomes. ♂♀

Dreams belong to a category of phenomena known as 'altered states of consciousness', which have attracted increasing attention in

Western societies during the past few decades as a result of the use of hallucinogenic drugs and meditation, along with the spread of esoteric religious movements and various 'consciousness-expanding' cults. The notion of an altered state of consciousness implies that certain states are modifications of the 'normal' consciousness in which human beings carry on their everyday lives. The altered state of consciousness thus represents a broad category of human experience and behaviour that is difficult to define precisely. It is easier to give examples: alcoholic intoxication, the hypnotizing effect of driving along a monotonous stretch of superhighway, the state just prior to falling asleep, hypnotic trance, the trance that occurs in response to rhythmic drumming, day-dreaming, intense absorption in a single task, the complete muscular relaxation that may occur during sunbathing, and various religious experiences – to list only a few of the more than sixty that have been identified.

Certain drugs – termed 'psychedelic', which means 'mind-manifesting' – have been used for thousands of years and in many different cultures to alter consciousness. Perhaps the mildest of these is marijuana, which is obtained from the common weed known as Indian hemp. It has long been used as an intoxicant in some Asiatic societies, where it is regarded as legally and morally acceptable – even though many of these same societies condemn the use of alcohol. It has been known at least since 2737 B.C., when a Chinese emperor mentioned it in a work on drugs. The effects of marijuana vary from person to person and also from one setting to another. The most common effect is the enhancement of sensory stimuli. Colours appear brighter, food tastes better, music sounds more resonant, and sexual experiences become more intense – all of which may lead to a sense that the world has somehow been given more meaning. A danger in the use of marijuana is that it can heighten unpleasant as well as pleasant experiences. People who are distressed, frightened, or anxiety-ridden may find these feelings exaggerated by marijuana. Much more potent drugs are LSD, the amphetamines, and peyote (which has long been part of the religious rituals of certain American Indian groups). As with marijuana, the effects of these drugs vary with the user's prior experience or expectations, the setting, and even with the persons in whose presence the experience takes place. The altered state may last from several hours to more than half a day; the emotional effects range from euphoria to uncontrollable panic, either of which may be accompanied by hallucinations. The world suddenly seems to be beyond the individual's control and the self becomes dissociated into two parts, an observer and a participant.

Not all altered states, of course, depend upon drugs. Yoga, meditation, and similar practices have long been a way of life in Asiatic cultures, where many people believe that a heightened consciousness follows the relaxation of body and mind. In fact, the vocabulary of Sanskrit, an ancient language of India, contains about twenty nouns that correspond to the English word *consciousness* – evidence of the importance attached to such matters among certain peoples in Asia. Until recently the nature of meditation, for all its antiquity, had not come under scientific scrutiny, supposedly because as a mystical experience the phenomenon could not be examined objectively. But research begun in Japan during the 1950s showed that meditating Zen Buddhist monks undergo measurable physical changes. Striking alterations in the electrical activity of the brain were observed. Meditating monks whose eyes remained open showed a predominance of the alpha waves that ordinarily do not become prominent until the pre-sleep period when the eyes are closed and the individual is completely at rest. In addition to other changes in brain activity, a significant reduction was observed in the body's rate of metabolism.

A dispute has arisen over whether similar results can also be attributed to 'transcendental meditation' – which, unlike Zen or yoga, does not require many years of rigorous training in physical and mental control. One recent study failed to detect any significant biochemical changes during meditation, or any major biochemical differences between meditators and others who were merely relaxed. Another study, however, did show striking metabolic changes that differed from those produced either by sleep or by hypnosis. The highly relaxed state of the meditators was the exact opposite of one that has probably always been characteristic of the hominids – the 'fight-or-flight' reaction, which can mobilize the entire body by sudden increases in blood pressure, heart rate, flow of blood to the muscles, and consumption of oxygen. This reaction is still deeply entrenched in our genetic make-up even though it is an anachronism in a crowded, complex world to which people must learn to accommodate, since to fight would be futile and to flee is virtually impossible. Many scientists believe that the constant stimulation of our nervous systems in this way, accompanied by the lack of opportunity to respond physically to stress, is responsible for the high incidence of hypertension and similar diseases now prevalent. If this is so, then meditation – which amounts to a relaxation rather than an activation of the nervous system – may be a worthwhile adaptation to life in the modern world. ♂♀

Altered states of consciousness have, until recently, been quite rare in Western cultures. The few Western evidences of concern with these states come primarily from ancient Greece (for example, the Dionysian cult and Plato's belief in divine madness) and from the Judaeo-Christian tradition (David dancing in ecstasy before the Ark of the Covenant, the visions of Ezekiel, and possession by the Holy Ghost at Pentecost). All of these, however, appear to have been influenced greatly by Asiatic religions. The tradition of altered states is probably indigenous to Europe only in a form of witchcraft that employed hallucinogenic plants, and in the dancing manias that spread throughout Europe several hundred years ago. The cult of the tarantella, named after the city of Taranto in southern Italy where it flourished, is one of the best known of these. (The city also gave its name to the tarantula, a large spider whose bite was erroneously supposed to have brought on the mania.)

Western countries, and in particular the United States, have seen numerous experiments in recent years with ways to alter consciousness; LSD and other psychedelic drugs were declared to expand the mind so effectively as to provide a basis for solving humanity's problems. The drug cult has largely run its course, only to be replaced by others concerned with the search for altered states: alpha waves, the revived interest in primitive Christianity, various kinds of meditation, even sky-diving. Despite the diverse beliefs and techniques employed, all of these have in common a turning away from the world in favour of exploring the inner self. Clearly, large numbers of people, bewildered by complex modern societies to which they cannot adapt, are in a headlong retreat from reason, if not indeed from the rich world of the mind that has characterized hominid history.

# 15

# A World in the Mind

The sensory impressions that bombard us, the fruits of our per-ceptions, the unending accumulation of experiences – all these must be put into some sort of storage if they are to be remembered quickly when the need arises. For memory is not simply one of the most intriguing aspects of human mental activity. As a prerequisite to reasoning, it is demanded by intelligent behaviour. The ability to solve a problem – or even to recognize that a problem exists – de-pends upon it. Without memory, humans would have to react to each event in life as though no such thing had ever previously occurred. Deprived of memory, a person at the wheel of a car would have to ponder anew every red traffic light, analysing the conduct of other drivers, taking note of pedestrians crossing the street, and drawing the conclusion that appropriate behaviour demanded a full stop. In fact, in the total absence of memory, the very perception of each traffic light would be an entirely new experience.

William James, the first psychologist in the United States, was especially intrigued with memory. Once, in an effort to discover whether it could be improved through exercise, he spent eight suc-cessive days memorizing a 158-line passage from the works of Victor Hugo, noting the time it took. He then devoted more than five weeks to memorizing the poetry of Milton. He now considered himself ready for the crucial part of the experiment: was his memory suffi-ciently honed by the latter exercise so that he could memorize passages from Victor Hugo faster than before? The first time, memorizing the 158 lines had required an average of fifty seconds per line. But when he tried committing a different 158-line passage by the same author to memory, the process went more slowly than it had before the practice with the Milton – an average of seven seconds longer for each line of Hugo. James thus concluded that exercises of the memory did not improve it in the same way that physical exer-cise improves physical performance. He also concluded that the somewhat reduced speed in memorizing the second set of lines from Hugo was due to mental fatigue. More recent research, based on studies of a large number of people, has shown both of his conclusions to be correct. ♂♀

Memory depends upon three processes: encoding, storage, and retrieval. The way in which each of us encodes information – that is, gives organization to what is received from the environment – will clearly affect our capacity later to retrieve that information from storage. In fact, individual differences in memory are usually due to varying principles of encoding, as is clear from a simple experiment. Compile a list of words from several categories – such as the names of animals, plants, and articles of clothing – but be sure to scramble the words. Such a list might go, 'Cat, hat, rose, rat, redbud, raincoat', and so on. Read the list to a few of your friends, telling them that they will later be asked to recall as many words as possible. Some will recall more words than others, but from the order in which the words are recalled it will be clear that each has imposed a particular pattern of organization on the scrambled list. Some people will lump the animals into one category, the plants into another, and the articles of clothing into still another. Some people will disregard such categories and instead organize on the basis of rhyme ('cat', 'hat', 'rat'). And still others will have remembered by some other process such as alliteration, encoding together 'rose', 'rat', 'redbud', and 'raincoat'. Whatever method is used, each person will clearly attempt to cluster words, even those with no apparent relationship, according to their own personal ideas, interests, or motivations. Freud was aware of such tendencies, and an important result of his psychotherapeutic method was its revelation of the unconscious categories we all use.

After encoding, the information must be stored – perhaps for only a few seconds, as in dialling a phone number, or perhaps for a lifetime when the information consists of someone's name. The encoded and stored information must then be made available for retrieval. Since the processing capacity of the human memory is limited, it would be a waste of time to process for retrieval in the distant future those memories that must be retained only briefly. A zip code that will probably not be used again will need to be remembered for only the few seconds required to write it down. Other information, on the other hand, must be stored in the memory for as long a time as possible without distortion. The ideal memory system would have several kinds of storage – and indeed all scientific evidence does point to the existence in the human memory of more than one retention system.

Many psychologists believe that memory consists basically of two different systems, which can be understood if you imagine that you are calling someone and have to look up the phone number in the directory. You find the number – which is, let us say, 739–1984 – and dial it, but get a busy signal. You wait a few moments and then decide to try the number again. If the time elapsed since your first attempt is more than thirty seconds, the chances are that you cannot recall the number correctly for the second call. This kind of memory is identified as short-term and it deteriorates fairly soon – a good thing, for otherwise our minds would be cluttered with trivia. Imagine now that you are frustrated by having had to look up the number again and again. So this time, studying it more closely, you discover in it some associations with knowledge you already possess. The 739 happens to be one digit less than your street address, 740 Pleasant Avenue, and 1984 is also the title of the futurist novel by George Orwell. Now you will have no trouble remembering the number, not just for the next few minutes but possibly for decades, because it has been stored in the long-term memory system. The process of forming associations is, by the way, one of the prime techniques used in 'memory-training' courses.

Everyone apparently possesses both short- and long-term memory, and the total quantity of things remembered is about equal in most people. What differs from one person to another is the kind of things that are remembered. Individual personality, interests, biases, and experiences in life explain why one person possesses an uncanny ability to recall chemical formulas, and another to remember exactly where a particular painting hangs in the Louvre. Certain rare individuals have access to an astounding quantity of things that have been encoded, stored, and retrieved. One of the most remarkable memories known to science is that of a man who recalled almost everything he experienced. When he was shown fifty-two digits, arranged in four columns and thirteen rows, he would examine them for several minutes, after which he would repeat them without an error – and he could do so column by column, row by row, diagonally, or even as a sequence of fifty-two digits. He was tested in verbal recall by being shown a long list of words, which he repeated perfectly. Fifteen years after being given that word test, he was asked to repeat the words in their correct order, and did so without error. Most of us tend to envy a person with such an extraordinary memory, but in fact he paid a severe penalty for it. He utterly lacked the ability to forget. Once an image was stored in his memory, he could not erase it, even though it was of no conceivable use to him later in life (as was true of the word lists and the number sequences given him as tests). More distressing, his uncanny memory interfered with his understanding of written materials and made abstract thinking extremely difficult for him. ♂♀

This man did not have what is commonly called a 'photographic memory' (technically known as 'eidetic imagery'); rather, his extraordinary ability was due to a different phenomenon known as 'synesthesia'. People who possess it can intermingle different sensory perceptions – so as, for example, to experience numbers and words in terms of colours and sounds. In the case just described, synesthesia provided additional environmental cues which helped the man re-create the entire original situation many years afterwards. The Russian composer Rimsky-Korsakov apparently possessed synesthesia also, for he associated the major keys of C, D, A, F, and F-sharp with the colours, respectively, of white, yellow, rose, green, and greyish-green. A photographic memory is similarly very rare, but it differs from synesthesia in three major respects. It is usually found only in children; it is concerned solely with visual images and seems to have no link with other sensations; and the image persists for a few minutes only, rather than for years.

The exact nature of both short- and long-term memory is little understood. Two explanations have been offered for short-term memory, and both of them use the metaphor of a half-filled but leaking bucket. According to one, known as the passive hypothesis, memories simply fade away through disuse, much as water would leak from such a bucket. The other, known as the active hypothesis, suggests that short-term memories encounter interference from incoming new memories, just as water added to the bucket forces out droplets of the water already in it. Various tests have been devised to study short-term memory. In one of these, lists of consonants were read to volunteers, who were then asked to write them down in the same order. The result showed that lists of five consonants were usually remembered perfectly and that most people can accurately recall seven items; beyond that number, however, the ability to remember dropped precipitously. The items recalled most accurately were those at the beginning of the list and those at the very end. The same effect has been noted in the misspelling of long words; most errors are made in the middle of words. No one has adequately explained this effect, but it may be that the very effort of remembering produces a certain amount of forgetting. The first few items thus would be readily recalled, but the effort made to remember them might cause subsequent ones to be forgotten. The recall of the very last items probably has a different explanation. These are remembered simply because they are the most recent and thus are freshest in the memory.

Short-term memory is a very temporary repository for information, and therefore psychologists have speculated about the importance of a system so apparently inefficient. At least three functions have been pinpointed. One is that short-term memory is needed to recall the beginning of a sentence until the end has been reached and the meaning grasped. A second is that short-term memory allows information no longer needed to be disposed of so that attention can be focused on new information. Anyone who mentally performs a series of arithmetical steps (such as adding digits, subtracting from them, and then dividing) has no need to retain each of the steps since the aim is to arrive at the final number that is the solution of the problem. A third function of short-term storage is to allow time for certain memories to be selected for long-term storage and then encoded, while those not needed for the future are simply forgotten.

Short-term memory lasts a maximum of thirty seconds, but it can be extended by repetition. Mentally repeating a phone number or other information keeps it in the short-term system. After the repetition stops, it will fade quickly unless some associations are made that serve to transfer it to long-term memory. The amount of information that can be retained by repetition, though, is quite small – as anyone will discover in trying to remember by repetition three new phone numbers at once. If new information is to be stored more or less permanently, then it must be transferred from short-term to long-term memory by the process of associating it with information that already exists in the long-term system. An example of this is the previously mentioned device of recalling a phone number in terms of a street address and the title of a novel by George Orwell. An unconscious decision about what to do with new information is made within less than thirty seconds after it has been received – whereupon it is either allowed to fade from the short-term memory system or given further processing so that it can be stored in long-term memory.

Very little is known about long-term memory, but among the things known is that the common notion of it is incorrect. Remembered material is not placed on some kind of videotape or recording device in the brain, from which it is simply played back when information has to be retrieved. That no such thing occurs will become obvious to anyone who tries to recall an event that occurred several years ago. Suppose you arrived in Rome in July 1973. Long-term memory will not furnish you with a coherent script of this event, but rather with a large number of seemingly unrelated associations which are then reorganized. First you might recall some trivial aspect of the arrival, such as the expression on the face of a hotel clerk. Then you might remember that the weather was unusually hot, and after that you might find yourself recalling the experience of passing through customs at the airport. Two people travelling together to the same foreign city will each recall a different sequence of events, even though they have been exposed to exactly the same circumstances. Long-term memory, therefore, is not simply a process of fishing out a coherent, sequential recording from a memory tank. It is, rather, an active process of reconstructing past events, piece by piece, as is demonstrated by those 'tip-of-the-tongue' memories in which something is almost, but not quite, recalled. In trying to recall a name, the way it begins or ends is usually the first thing remembered, followed by the number of syllables; the next step is often a recollection of other words that it rhymes with; after that come memories and allusions that the name conjures up. Then, suddenly, all of the bits and pieces of information associated with it come together and the name is finally remembered.

Long-term memory not only stores specific information; it also uses new information to reorganize the old. People do not store facts solely as facts but rather as general rules, which can be related either to other facts already in storage or to those that may be added in the future. For example, people do not usually remember the populations of the cities of the world. Instead, they remember a general rule: an encyclopaedia, gazetteer, or world almanac will provide those facts. Such general rules are obviously not indelibly imprinted in the long-term memory system. The memory of these rules is constantly being changed because of the acquisition of new information and the consequent revision of previous information, just as the information in an encyclopaedia, gazetteer, or almanac must be periodically updated in a new edition. Otherwise we would be forever locked into old memories and find it impossible to learn from experience or to acquire new skills.

The way in which information is encoded for long-term storage is influenced by the culture in which one's ideas about the world have been moulded. People in Western cultures enter a dwelling and see various kinds of couches, chairs, beds, tables, and lamps. These items are easily remembered because they are automatically encoded into such familiar categories as 'living-room furniture', or 'bedroom furniture'. But show the same objects to natives of interior New Guinea, for example, and they will have great difficulty remembering them, simply because they lack convenient categories into which to encode what they have seen. North Americans and Europeans would be in the same position if they tried to encode the strange tools and ceremonial objects that are familiar to New Guineans. Differences in the method of encoding account for those explorers' tales about the remarkable memories supposedly possessed by the inhabitants of exotic places. Their memories are usually not remarkable at all; they merely possess categories that outsiders lack for encoding familiar items in their environment. ♂♀

Common-sense opinion has long held that alcohol interferes with the memory because of the observation that people in a sober state often cannot remember what occurred when they were drunk. Actually, a person's memory when sober is not necessarily better. Rather, one's memory will be better when one is in the same state, either drunk or sober, as at the time the original events occurred. This important truth about memory lies behind the Charlie Chaplin film *City Lights* (1931). Part of the plot concerns an alcoholic millionaire whom Charlie saves from suicide. When sober, the millionaire has no recollection of Charlie or of the event; drunk once again, the millionaire greets Charlie as his long-lost friend. In an experiment with this phenomenon, volunteers were asked to learn a list of words while they were either drunk or sober. Those who learned the list while drunk were able to remember it better when they were again drunk than when they were sober. Those who learned the words while sober, on the other hand, had better recall while they were in a sober state than while they were drunk. In other words, anything that alters the state of consciousness – whether it be alcohol, meditation, drugs, or strong emotions – can affect the memory. Memories stored during a totally relaxing vacation quickly fade into forgetfulness during a frantic working day, but can be recalled when one's state is again totally relaxed. Such everyday experiences indicate that memory is usually tied to a particular state of consciousness, and that it is usually most vivid when the state in which it was experienced is reproduced. The explanation for this appears to be that the brain processes the information received through the senses at different speeds, depending upon whether one is relaxed or aroused. The same material is more easily retrieved at the same level of arousal as when it was organized. The full recollection of an experience can be triggered by duplicating the original level of arousal or by evoking a symbol of it (just as in Proust's *Remembrance of Things Past* the taste of a tea-soaked madeleine unleashed a flood of memories that was eventually to fill seven volumes). ♂♀

Because humans are such visual animals, they tend to emphasize the role of vision in memory. But in addition most people possess rather remarkable memories based on the other senses. That humans have an excellent capacity to encode sounds is demonstrated by the ability to identify an unseen speaker by the quality of his or her voice even when it comes through the limited transmitting capacity of the telephone and is further affected by a head cold. A distinctive taste or odour may be recalled for decades. Nevertheless, these capacities for remembering sensations seem insignificant when compared to the visual memory. In one experiment, 2560 photographic slides showing various scenes were projected on a screen at the rate of one every ten seconds over a period of several consecutive days. One hour after the last of the slides had been projected, each of the viewers was shown 280 pairs of pictures. One of each pair was a picture selected at random from the 2560 already seen; the other was one roughly similar in content that had not been among those projected. The viewers were then asked which of the two pictures they had seen previously. If they had merely guessed, their scores would have averaged around 50 per cent, but they were in fact correct approximately 90 per cent of the time. The results of subsequent experiments with picture memory have been even more remarkable. Volunteers who had been shown a total of 10,000 pictures were able to remember them with about 85 per cent accuracy even after a couple of days had passed. ♂♀

*

The memory process does not always work efficiently. When it fails, the phenomenon known as forgetting takes place. This failure poses an intriguing problem. Why, after an event has surmounted the many impediments to its successful storage in long-term memory, should it not then be retained? Numerous explanations have been offered, and all of them can be put into three basic categories that employ the metaphor of a house. According to the psychoanalytic explanation, memories do not disappear but may simply be blocked by the unconscious from retrieval at the moment, quite as effectively as though a room in a house had been walled off. The second explanation, the physiological, claims that memory decays with disuse, just as a room in a house will deteriorate if not cared for. Finally, the behavioural explanation states that other events stored in the memory may interfere, much as the clutter in an attic interferes with retrieving a particular object that has been stored there.

The psychoanalytic explanation has been demonstrated by psychiatrists to be true for some supposedly forgotten memories, generally unpleasant ones, which patients have been enabled to recall. And hypnotists have likewise enabled people to recover memories that seemed lost forever. Such memories obviously had not been erased but had merely been walled off. Further supporting the hypothesis of walled-off memory is the evidence that repression never shuts off memory entirely. People who have been reminded of a subject involving memories they have repressed and supposedly forgotten are still likely to show physical signs that something about the unremembered experience is causing them pain: stumbling over certain words, blushing, sweating, or suddenly jerking the head.

The second explanation – of a deterioration from disuse, as proposed by the physiologists – also has much to recommend it. According to this hypothesis, each time a person learns or experiences something a physical trace of it is left in the brain or in the neural pathways. This memory trace, though, must be maintained through use or else it will deteriorate. Evidence does exist that at least some forgetting is due to such disuse. One who had normal vision for the first few years of childhood, but who then suddenly became blind, by adulthood will have lost all visual memories and in this respect will be indistinguishable from one who has been blind from birth. And, as many people know from personal experience, subjects that have been studied in high school or college but not used later in life – such as trigonometry, calculus, or chemistry – are usually forgotten almost completely. A major problem with this explanation of forgetting, though, is that no precise locations for memory traces have been identified in the brain or the nervous system. Furthermore, it fails to account for the everyday experience that memories based on the senses decay much more rapidly than do memories involving physical skills. Anyone who roller-skated as a child has no difficulty in doing so again, even after many decades of not putting on skates. Yet this same person will find it virtually impossible to recall many sensory experiences dating from these same childhood years. ♂♀

Finally, the cluttered-attic hypothesis points to an important cause of forgetting: conflict among the many different learning experiences to which a person is exposed. When humans learn something new, their ability to remember it is indeed hampered by things learned previously, as it will also be by things they may learn in the future. Suppose, for example, that you are given a list of eight or ten nouns to memorize. You certainly will have no difficulty in memorizing them after a short time. Then you are asked to memorize a second list with the same number of nouns, which are related in some way to those on the first list, such as synonyms or antonyms. You similarly memorize this second list without difficulty. The next day you are asked to repeat the first list. Almost no one can do so perfectly, and most people will make the mistake of substituting some nouns from the second list. The closer in association the nouns in the two lists are, the greater the interference. If you are given a third list of nouns to memorize the next day, a fourth list on the following day, and so on, recall will decline precipitously. In short, the more you learn, the more your mind becomes cluttered like a disorderly attic and the more rapidly you forget.

The cluttered-attic hypothesis unquestionably accounts for some aspects of forgetting, primarily those that are verbal, but not for memories concerning events or the visual appearance of objects. The psychoanalytic and the physiological explanations similarly have received support from some experiments, but valid objections have also been raised about them. Each explanation is probably correct at least in part. But it would appear that forgetting is a process so complex as to occur in different ways under different circumstances.

\*

Throughout life, humans learn physical skills (bicycling), symbolic systems (language), facts (the date of the Norman conquest of

England), and also bodies of knowledge (human biology). Most important, they learn what behaviour is considered appropriate for members of a particular society. This great variety in the process of learning is a hallmark of our humanity. Such activities as eating are, of course, a built-in biological necessity and do not need to be learned. But the utensils that are used, the question of whether the meal is eaten while sitting or reclining, the preference for certain foods, and the rules of etiquette that are observed – all these stem from an individual's experience and from the culture in which one has been brought up. All animals eat, but only humans learn to dine.

A newborn infant learns almost immediately that when it cries a nipple will be offered. Soon afterwards, learning combined with maturation leads to the development of many physical skills, like crawling and standing up. By the beginning of the second year of life, verbal learning begins. At a very early age, a child also begins to make percepts and to solve problems. Somehow, over a period of from fifteen to twenty years, the individual accumulates the complex repertory of skills that allow survival outside the family. Much of this learned behaviour is very simple, such as that an automobile must stop at a red light; some of it is far more complex, such as playing a musical instrument. Most complex of all is the kind of learning that goes into integrating numerous skills so that the individual is equipped to interact constantly with a great variety of humans. No other species even approaches humankind in the vital role played by learning. Nor does any other species extend learning through the lifetime of the individual. Only humans are still learning – about death – as they breathe their last.

No wonder that a subject of such importance should be a source of considerable dispute. Exactly how do people learn? A partial answer was given early in this century by the Russian scientist Ivan Pavlov. He based many of his experiments on the existence of reflexes – that is, automatic reactions to stimuli. These are not learned but rather depend on inherited characteristics of the nervous system, as when people automatically draw a hand away from a painful object. The best known of Pavlov's experiments was concerned with the reflex action that causes dogs to salivate in the presence of food. Dogs do not ordinarily salivate in response to other stimuli, such as the sound produced by a metronome. But Pavlov set about to connect the reflex action of salivation with just such a stimulus, one that was totally meaningless so far as food is concerned. Again and again, he offered food to a dog while a metronome was clicking, until eventually the dog learned to associate the particular sound with food. Finally, when he turned on the metronome but offered no food, the dog produced quantities of saliva anyway.

Pavlov had, in other words, succeeded in modifying a reflex so thoroughly that a stimulus having nothing whatever to do with food produced the reflex reaction of salivation. The dog had learned – or, in more technical language, had become 'conditioned'. After Pavlov had repeatedly turned on the metronome but withheld food, the flow of saliva decreased and eventually stopped altogether. The conditioned response had now suffered what is known as 'extinction'. But so long as he did from time to time combine the sound of the metronome with food, the conditioned response of salivation was maintained. Through a process known as 'reinforcement', the occasional pairing of food with the sound was sufficient to keep the conditioned response alive.

The experiments Pavlov performed, and the vocabulary he used, are still very much a part of the way psychologists view the learning process in humans. The scope of his work, however, was limited, since he was concerned primarily with responses that occurred whenever a specific stimulus was presented; much of human behaviour is more complex than that. What exactly is the stimulus that causes a feeling of anxiety while one is waiting outside a restaurant for some tardy person? In most examples of behaviour, no specific stimuli can be identified. Instead, an individual actually influences the environment to generate consequences, doing something to get something – as when a child is on good behaviour so that permission to go to the circus will be granted. If the generated consequences are pleasurable or rewarding, then the response will be repeated and grow in strength. If they are unpleasant, then they will tend to be avoided.

This different approach to conditioning has been developed by B. F. Skinner of Harvard University. Skinner believes that the individual operates on the environment to obtain rewards – hence the term 'operant' that is applied to this kind of conditioning. Whereas Pavlov's animals were deliberately conditioned to learn specific stimuli, Skinner's are made to teach themselves through reward and reinforcement. A laboratory rat placed in a specially designed cage will explore it at random. Eventually the rat will touch by accident a metal bar which causes a food pellet to drop into a feeding dish. At first the rat probably makes no connection between the bar and the delivery of food. But after it has pressed the bar several times, and has each time been rewarded with food, it begins to learn the connection between the two events. Soon it is pressing the bar as rapidly as it can to maintain the flow of pellets. So long as this action continues to produce food, the specific behaviour is being reinforced. ♂♀

The success with animals in such experiments has led some psychologists, those known as 'behaviourists', to believe that human behaviour is similarly no more than a matter of conditioning. Common sense tells us that many human feelings and attitudes have been shaped by experience. A person who has met with a painful accident just after hearing a certain sound may for a long time become fearful whenever that sound is heard again, although eventually, in the absence of further reinforcement, the response will undergo extinction. Conditioning as an idea actually is not new, although demonstrating it scientifically by means of controlled experimentation is. In fact, the seventeenth-century English philosopher John Locke wrote:

Many children imputing the pain they endured at school to their books they were corrected for, so join these ideas together, that a book becomes their aversion, and they are never reconciled to the study and use of them all their lives after . . . There are rooms convenient enough that some men cannot study in, and fashions of vessels ever so clean and commodious, they cannot drink out of, and that by reason of some ideas which are annexed to them, and make them offensive. ♂♀

Behaviourists, though, have gone much beyond such occasional experiences to visualize a world in which all human feelings and activities have been shaped by conditioned responses. Humans supposedly behave the way they do because they are repeating actions that have been rewarded by parents, teachers, and friends, and avoiding actions for which they have been punished. To behaviourists, the sum total of human personality is simply the result of prior conditioning and shaping. Human beings have been stripped of their individual motives, emotions, and thoughts – in fact, of virtually any capacity to control their own destiny.

Nowadays many psychologists believe that the behaviourist view of human actions is incomplete and distorted. It is also a dangerous view, in that it denies the freedom of humans to live as diverse individuals – the very freedom, in fact, that has enabled us to become human. Even the idea that learning is the product of stimulus followed by a response has come under attack as being much too simple an explanation for a complex process. Imagine that a dog is to be conditioned to lift its paw every time it hears a certain tone. According to conditioning theory, this can be accomplished merely by sending a mild electric shock through the dog's leg while the tone is being sounded. The dog will soon be conditioned to pull its paw away whenever it hears the tone, even in the absence of the shock. Now imagine the same experiment, but with a single change: the dog's leg has been completely paralysed by a local anaesthetic which prevents the dog from responding to the shock. The tone sounds, the shock passes through the leg, but the dog does not pull it away. In other words, a stimulus has been received but the response has been completely eliminated by the anaesthetic. Yet once the drug has worn off, the dog will pull away its paw when it hears the tone, showing that it has learned to do so even in the absence of a response.

A further objection to behaviourist theory is that animals are limited in what they can be taught by conditioning. Every species has a repertory of behaviours that are genetically programmed; an animal's behaviour can almost never be altered so as to conflict with its programme. A laboratory rat can easily be conditioned to flee when it associates a noise with danger, simply because flight is the rat's inborn reaction to danger. A rabbit, though, does not hop away from danger; instead, it freezes. The rabbit cannot be made to behave otherwise, no matter how much its behaviour is conditioned. What holds true for animals apparently holds true for humans as well. People often behave in a certain way because that form of behaviour has been adaptive during the hominids' evolutionary history. Most people today experience fears that probably were experienced also by our hominid ancestors, such as the fear of falling from a height and a fear of the dark. These fears are assumed to be inborn – as the result of natural selection – simply because those who experienced them, and behaved accordingly, were much less likely than others to be killed by a fall from a tree or by predators in venturing from the safety of camp at night.

Conditioning is certainly not the only kind of learning experienced by humans; some psychologists distinguish from five to seven additional ones. ♂♀ Learning consists of the constant integration of small particles of information into larger units, and these units into still larger ones. People unconsciously do this every time they hear a sentence. A succession of seemingly unrelated words is very quickly organized into larger and larger units, until eventually the meaning of the entire sentence has been absorbed. Here, in slow motion, is the way we unconsciously discover the meaning of a sentence as simple as *The girl jumped the hurdles*. The first word provides almost no information, but it is already something on which a larger unit can be built. Native speakers of English know that *the* is an article to be followed by a noun (or, sometimes, by an adjective that precedes a noun). The next word, *girl*, sets the first level of organization. It is a noun, which combines with *the* to form a noun phrase. Furthermore, it is singular, and this will affect the verb – which is the next word, *jump*, with the auxiliary *-ed* that places it in the past tense. *The hurdles* constitutes another noun phrase, but this one is the object of the verb. This second noun phrase is grouped with the verb at a higher level of organization, the verb phrase *jumped the hurdles*. We now have an initial noun phrase, *the girl*, and a verb phrase, *jumped the hurdles* – two units which we combine into a sentence that conveys meaning. Once we have mastered the organization of this extremely simple sentence, we have learned a way to construct an almost endless number of sentences with a similar structure, such as *The man washed the dishes*, *The girl fired the gun*, and *The woman flew the aeroplane*. No theory of stimulus–response conditioning can explain the way we as children, even before we enter 'grammar school', learn these grammatical rules of our native tongue.

Humans are apparently born with a capacity to acquire language, just as they are born with a blueprint for learning to walk. The growing child learns to walk and to talk without being consciously aware of the way either feat was accomplished. This innate capacity endows speakers with the general structure that is common to all languages, but that structure does not go so far as to dictate the precise tongue each child will speak – otherwise everyone in the world would speak the same language. Thus, no one acquires a language by learning every one of the possible sentences to be constructed from it – which would be literally impossible because theoretically the number of sentences that could be formed is infinite. Instead of learning billions upon billions of such sentences, humans unconsciously acquire rules (such as the simple one just described) that can generate a near-infinite number of sentences in their respective tongues. ♂♀

Most learning situations for humans are similar to that involving language in that they offer a wide range of potential responses, not just a simple conditioned one. Instead of saying *The girl jumped the hurdles*, the speaker might have said *The hurdles were jumped by the girl* or *She jumped them*. And, of course, the speaker had as well the option to remain silent. Complex human behaviour obviously cannot be explained in terms of conditioning alone. People remember many things that they seemingly have no reason to remember. And the fact that these things are remembered must mean that they have been learned at some time – even though no response was then made and no reinforcement has since been received. Stimulus–response cannot explain why we remember an inconsequential item read in a newspaper weeks ago. As an alternative to conditioning, many psychologists now consider learning to be a part of what are known as 'cognitive processes'. Instead of the behaviourist's concept of a passive mind that is a mere reflection of the stimuli encountered throughout life, cognitive psychologists view human mental processes as being extraordinarily active.

According to cognitive psychologists, human sense organs are constantly besieged by simultaneous stimuli, yet the individual actively selects only those sensations that are regarded as the most important at the moment. These sensations are then organized into perceptual patterns. For example, an approaching man is perceived as an entity and not as a collection of such data as worn clothing, scuffed shoes, unkempt hair, a shopping bag held in the hand, and so on. This information is compared with what has been previously learned about people with this general appearance. The old and the new information are both weighed, and associations between them are rapidly formed. The active mind might arrive at the conclusion that one is being approached by a panhandler and decide upon the behaviour of avoidance. If, however, the man were to reach into the shopping bag and offer a Bible, explaining in cultivated tones that he has taken a vow of poverty while doing missionary work, a totally new association will be made between the old and new information. What has in fact taken place is far beyond a mere response to the stimulus of this man's appearance. What has been acquired is knowledge itself – a view of human behaviour that may require immediate revision of much of what has been learned in the past. Cognitive psychologists, therefore, do not believe that learning can be separated from all of those closely related and complex mental processes that are characteristic of the human mind: perception, thinking, language, and problem-solving. Once solved, a problem no longer represents a problem but rather amounts to new knowledge itself.

*

Each object or event in the world is unique because some difference – no matter how slight – can be found to separate it from all others. Humans tend to ignore this uniqueness and instead to assign objects and events to categories based on shared attributes. Such categories are known as 'concepts', and they are the basic way in which humans impose order and meaning on the environment. Concepts simplify the complex stimuli that constantly assault the senses by first sorting them out and then lumping them together into categories based on common attributes. Whenever two or more objects, people, or events have been placed in the same category, a decision has been made that they are in some way similar. Even a child about three years of age can categorize – to the extent of placing shoes, socks, and sweaters into the higher category of *clothes*. Although the world seems to offer our perceptions a virtually infinite number of objects, we do not inhabit a completely unstructured universe. Certain attributes of objects are more likely to occur in association with one another than not. Creatures with feathers, for example, are much more likely to have wings than are creatures with fur. Conceptual thinking is the very essence of human mental life, and no one could get through a single day without continually relying upon it.

Human existence would be intolerable if each of the thousands of objects and events encountered hourly were to be regarded as unique. If we looked at a forest and saw elms, hickories, birches, pines, and so on as unique objects rather than as forming the single category *trees*, our mental processes would almost immediately become crippled. Concepts also relieve us of continually learning about every new object or event. Each person we meet is an individual, yet we tend to classify individuals conceptually – and then to behave accordingly. When I walk into a museum, I am aware of my individuality and so is the person who is keeping an eye on me. We nevertheless ignore distinctive personal traits, classify each other as *visitor* and *guard*, and behave in ways appropriate to those roles. ♂♀

Out of the multitudes of attributes in the world around us, we first discover which are relevant and then we classify them according to the way they are relevant. *Mare*, for example, is a category for all horses sharing the attributes of being adult and female. Any breed of horse with these attributes would be included. Colour is not regarded as a relevant attribute, and so an adult female appaloosa is regarded as a mare. Nor is size a consideration; the adult female of the miniature Shetland breed is also a mare. Many concepts are based on their shared consequences, as when automobile, bus, train, and bicycle are placed in the category *vehicle*. This emphasis on utilitarian value probably stems from an important fact in human evolution. Survival has depended upon the ability to understand objects and events in terms of their consequences of providing food or for warding off danger. No one will ever know for sure, but it seems probable that the first concepts humans formed were *dangerous* and *not dangerous*.

Adults automatically use conceptual thinking almost every moment of their lives, but this ability develops gradually from infancy onward. The most impressive study of the development of conceptual thinking in children is the one that has been carried on during more than half a century by Jean Piaget and his colleagues in Geneva, Switzerland. ♂♀ In recent decades, Piaget's theory of four stages in mental development has become extremely influential. According to this theory, the first stage is the sensory–motor one, spanning approximately the first eighteen months of life and antedating the use of language. During this stage, children begin to know their environment through perception and motor responses, which seem similar in many ways to those of an intelligent animal. Already, however, children display mental abilities far beyond those of most adult animals. A child one year of age who wants a toy that is resting out of reach on a blanket will pull the blanket towards itself to obtain the toy.

During the second or pre-operational stage (from the age of about eighteen months to seven years), children symbolically represent the objects and events in their environment through language. Cognitive development now takes a great leap forward in ways that are uniquely human. Children use the symbols of language both to communicate thoughts to others and to think about objects. They are no longer restricted to the present but can recall the past and look ahead to the future. Nevertheless, children in this pre-operational stage are severely limited conceptually. They are unable to carry out mental operations that go beyond their immediate perceptions. Show a child in this stage two drinking glasses – one glass low and wide, the other tall and narrow – containing equal amounts of milk. Because the level of the milk in the tall, narrow glass is higher, a child at the pre-operational stage will believe that this one contains more milk. Such children are unable to perform the mental operation necessary to visualize the milk in the tall, narrow glass being poured into the low, wide one.

A somewhat older child, about age seven and just entering the third stage of concrete operations, will usually understand that the volume of milk does not depend upon the shape of the glass. Children in this stage have advanced mentally to a point where they can assign objects to appropriate categories and then put these into even more inclusive categories. All breeds of dogs are thus assigned to a single category based on what the children perceive as shared attributes. This category, *dog*, is then combined with other categories, such as *birds* and *snakes*, to form the higher category *animals*. By the end of this stage, or at about the age of eleven, children have mastered virtually all problems that require them to go beyond their immediate perceptions. Their thoughts, though, are still limited. Operations are directed primarily towards objects and events that are occurring in the present or that have occurred in the recent past. Although children in this stage do understand the existence of the distant past and the far future, they are not greatly concerned with enormous time spans. In other words, most cognitive acts deal with concrete reality rather than with the exploration of possibilities.

Between the ages of eleven and fifteen, according to Piaget, children finally move forward into the stage of logical operations, which is the culmination of all previous developmental trends. Adolescents become liberated from the tight grip of immediate reality; they can think about the possible as well as the actual present. In solving a problem, they can consider all variables, then change each of the variables one at a time while either excluding the others or holding them constant. They can do this in sequence until all possibilities in a given problem have been exhausted. The earlier stages of childhood mental development, though, do not disappear, and an adolescent might draw upon the learning of previous stages in solving a problem. The adolescent might first deal with objects and events of reality, a process characteristic of the first sensory–motor stage. This information might then be organized along the lines that have developed in the pre-operational and concrete-operations stages. Such organized information may then be transformed by the cognitive acts of the fourth stage to form hypotheses and to test them against reality. This sequence of cognitive acts is often referred to as 'scientific thinking', but all adults unconsciously think in this way during much of their waking day.

Critics of Piaget's theory have particularly objected to his belief that cognitive development proceeds at approximately the same rate for all children – in other words, that it is a universal and invariant characteristic of the human species. Psychologists now know that the ages at which children pass through each stage differ from one individual to another and also from culture to culture. Psychologists know, too, that special training can sometimes greatly accelerate the development of cognitive operations, and that being brought up in an environment unfavourable to that development can retard it. Another insufficiency in Piaget's theory is that he has dealt exclusively with pre-adult thought processes and has ignored cognitive ability during the many decades of adulthood. This oversight is particularly serious because conceptual abilities usually change considerably between adolescence and adulthood. An exception is to be found in very gifted children, who retain into their later years a superior ability in grasping abstractions – possibly because gifted persons are offered challenges and opportunities that maintain their skills in abstract thinking. Most adults, though, experience a slight decrease in the ability to form new concepts – which often becomes a rapid deterioration in the elderly. Such deterioration might well be due to illnesses, injuries to the nervous system, medication, and alcohol rather than to increased age itself.

But the major objection to Piaget's theory concerns the most crucial stage of all, the first or sensory–motor one. Piaget emphasizes the complex motor co-ordination of the infant – the accurate reach for an object by the age of six months, crawling by ten months, walking by fifteen months – but ignores early cognitive abilities that are yoked to the maturing nervous system. Infants cannot, of course, tell psychologists when they are thinking, but it is possible to infer that they are by noting changes in heart rate, eye direction, vocalization, and general level of excitement or attention. As early as the second month of life, infants seem to form mental representations of events (technically known as 'schemata') from their encounters with the environment. The stimuli that evoke the greatest duration of attention are, surprisingly, those only moderately different from the schemata rather than those that are totally novel. This reaction explains an observation that is made by most parents: infants are more enthusiastic about a new toy that is somewhat like one they already have than they are about a toy that for them represents something completely new.

A typical experiment consists of showing infants an orange-coloured cube repeatedly, until it becomes familiar. They are then shown both a moderately different object (such as another orange-coloured cube, but one that is much smaller) and a totally different object (such as a yellow cylinder). Infants become visibly excited by the moderately different smaller cube; the totally new yellow cylinder, on the other hand, produces no vocalizations or other signs of excitement. The attention that infants give to slightly unfamiliar objects indicates the development in the first year of life of a new cognitive structure. This structure is the hypothesis, which reaches extraordinary complexity in adults but which exists also in children, although at a much simpler level. Infants apparently form hypotheses when they attempt to reconcile a slightly different object with their familiar schemata. Such experiments seem to demonstrate that infants less than a year old are thinking beings who attempt to reconcile discrepancies in their environment. This view goes counter to the belief of Piaget that infants less than eighteen months old know the world only in terms of sensory impressions and motor activities, with no signs of cognitive development until after this stage has been completed. ♂♀

*

The topics discussed so far in this chapter have been, in one way or another, related to what is usually called 'thinking'. Everyone knows that thinking involves the brain. Not so well known is that thinking also involves muscular activities in the eyes, limbs, heart, and speech organs. Professional gamblers often wear dark glasses because they know that the size of the pupils of the eyes can reveal their thought processes. Anyone trying to solve a mental problem will show a steady increase in the size of the pupils until the solution has been arrived at, after which the pupils contract rapidly. A person asked merely to think about lifting a weight with the right arm shows changes in the right biceps that can be measured by sensitive instruments as electrical impulses. A significant increase in heart rate occurs in subjects asked to solve problems, with the greatest increase taking place at the moment when the solution is arrived at. Apparently all of us talk silently to ourselves while thinking. Electrodes placed on the tongue and lips of people who are then asked to recall the lines of a poem show muscular activity very similar to that involved in reciting the lines aloud.

Thinking about problems is sometimes made unnecessarily difficult by mental habits that restrict people to well-worn channels of thought. Here is an example. A large truck had become solidly wedged under a low bridge in Kentucky. Experts on the construction of bridges were consulted about ways to dislodge it, and they offered various suggestions. Because these people were totally involved with bridges, they approached the problem in a conventional way: jack up the bridge to release the truck. But a young newsboy, who had not yet been trapped into habitual patterns of thought, had a much better idea. He suggested that the truck should be lowered – as was easily accomplished by letting air out of the tyres. The newsboy displayed what psychologists call 'creative thinking', even though they are not quite certain what it is. Creative thinking is obviously similar to conventional reasoning in that both are controlled, rational, and directly related to some problem or event. Creative thinking differs from straightforward reasoning, though, in that the problem is not handled in a conventional manner.

Psychologists as yet have little understanding of what causes creative people to select only certain items from all the information available to everyone, and then to combine elements of these in ways that produce a novel idea. All healthy people inhabit a familiar world of sights and sounds, yet some creative painters, musicians, and poets can break the codes by which others see and hear, thereby revealing the world in a new way. This ability has sometimes been referred to as a 'natural gift', and probably it is true that some aspects of creativity are inherited. Other aspects of it, though, apparently are not inherited. Psychologists have searched for ways to measure creativity and have devised several methods, one of which is the Remote Associates Test. The person taking it is asked to find a word related to other words – like *blue*, *cottage*, and *cake* – that are not normally associated with one another. A creative answer, of course, might be *cheese*. The three given words, which ordinarily do not fit into any familiar category, share a common attribute when they are thought of in terms of blue cheese, cottage cheese, and cheesecake.

Most psychologists agree upon four aspects of creative thinking that appear to be interrelated. One of them is sometimes referred to as 'the prepared mind'; for example, Einstein's concept of relativity could not possibly have occurred to him if he had not already possessed a deep knowledge of physics and mathematics. Second, creative thinking involves a period of incubation, either long or short, during which a problem is being worked on unconsciously while attention is focused on other matters. Third, creativity involves a sudden illumination in which the solution to a problem appears as if from nowhere. This is the 'Eureka!' phenomenon (Greek for 'I have found it!') – an exclamation supposedly uttered by the mathematician Archimedes. The king had presented him with the problem of determining the amount of gold in an intricately carved crown. While taking a bath, Archimedes noted that his body displaced an equal volume of water – and thus arrived at a solution to the problem. Archimedes had presumably bathed many times before, but in this instance a prepared mind, knowledge of the elements of the problem, and an incubation period during which the problem had been thought about all came together. A connection was made between bathwater and a king's crown, two items not normally linked. Finally, creative thinking usually requires evaluation and testing of the solution to determine whether it is workable, followed by refinement and possible revision. Archimedes could immediately test his illumination by putting an object of known value, such as a cube, into a filled tub of water and then noting that the volume of the overflowing water was the same.

More is known about individual differences in creativity than is known about the creative process itself. Some people excel at the kind of creativity that involves staring out the window, others in the kind that demands the use of the hands in manipulating tools and instruments. Some people are creative in libraries, others in laboratories, and still others in interpersonal relations. A creative person whose age is in the thirties or early forties is likely to be more successfully creative than a person still under thirty, presumably because the older person has had more time to accumulate the knowledge on which creativity can be built. That still does not explain, though, why creativity should decrease after the late forties – and no agreement exists about the cause. By this age, a vast store of knowledge exists, the brain is finely tuned, problems have been mulled over for decades, skills have been perfected – yet, mystifyingly, in field after field, creative accomplishments go into a decline. (Exceptions do, of course, occur at both ends of the range of years. Mozart and Schubert, among other musicians, were extraordinarily creative at very early ages. In contrast, Handel was still composing operas and oratorios in his late sixties, and Verdi wrote a masterpiece, *Falstaff*, when he was eighty.)

### AGE AND CREATIVITY

The age of greatest creativity varies from one profession to another. It is, of course, also influenced by physical and mental health. A survey some years ago of unique contributions in fields ranging from the physical sciences to creative writing reveals a peak in creative accomplishments in the group between the ages of 30 and 39. This table, based on studies covering thousands of individual careers, shows the percentage of important contributions made in each decade of those careers. ♂♀

| Field | Under 20 | 20s | 30s | 40s | 50s | 60s | 70s |
|---|---|---|---|---|---|---|---|
| | | | | Age | | | |
| Chemistry | 1 | 23 | 39 | 23 | 11 | 3 | 0 |
| Physics | 0 | 21 | 35 | 27 | 11 | 5 | 1 |
| Psychology | 0 | 21 | 36 | 21 | 15 | 5 | 2 |
| Practical inventions | 3 | 27 | 38 | 20 | 8 | 3 | 1 |
| Chess championships | 0 | 29 | 47 | 19 | 5 | 0 | 0 |
| Short-story writing | 0 | 18 | 37 | 24 | 13 | 6 | 2 |

Further complicating the understanding of creativity have been studies that compare individuals who are very similar in IQ, experience, and training. One person will be creative in new situations and the other will not be. In the example given from the Remote Associates Test, many apparently intelligent people never arrive at the answer *cheese* – although once they hear it, they understand why it is a creative response. Such people possess the knowledge and experience needed for a creative answer, as well as the intelligence to apply these to the problem. Yet they fail to do so.

Creativity and intelligence apparently are two different mental abilities. Only 17 per cent of the people who score high on IQ tests also score high on creativity tests. A minimum amount of intelligence is obviously necessary for creativity, but beyond that the influence of intelligence appears to be negligible. One explanation, of course, is that IQ tests are not designed to assess creativity but rather to measure the extent to which an individual follows accepted patterns of thought. An IQ question has only one correct answer, such as the response to 'What is the capital of the state of South Dakota?' In contrast, a creativity test measures thinking that diverges from customary patterns and that has many possible answers – such as the question, 'What uses can you think of for both a yardstick and a book?'

A distinguishing characteristic of creative individuals is a pre-occupation with complexity and novelty. Creative people prefer complex paintings, musical works, and games over simple ones. When asked to tell what images are evoked by meaningless inkblots, they are likely to give complex and unusual answers. In the case of one particular inkblot, people who had been shown by previous tests to be non-creative were reminded of such things as 'smudges' or 'dark clouds'. One creative individual, on the other hand, identified the blot as 'magnetized iron filings', and another as 'a small boy and his mother hurrying along on a dark windy day, trying to get home before it rains'. Creative people have been shown to put themselves into situations that increase their opportunities to do novel things, like becoming an architect instead of a bookkeeper. People who test low on creativity do just the opposite. The preoccupation with novelty explains the paradoxical gullibility of many creative people in fields other than their own. Johann Sebastian Bach firmly believed in the mystical properties of numbers and Mozart strongly subscribed to the symbolic trappings of Freemasonry; Charles Dickens always aligned his bed on a north–south axis to benefit from the magnetic currents given off by the earth's poles. Even Benjamin Franklin, the very symbol of practicality, belonged to a mystic sect that believed in transmigration of the soul.

*

All of the chapters so far in this book have dealt in one way or another with those distinctive hallmarks that set humans apart from other living things. One more can now be added. Humans are the only members of the animal kingdom who continually invent new problems for themselves. Even a primate species as close to humans in evolutionary history as the chimpanzee generally faces the same problems, generation after generation: finding food, water, and a mate, and interacting with other members of the group. Changes in chimpanzee behaviour do not result from causes within them but rather from outside influences – as, for example, when primatol-ogists camp nearby and thus introduce new objects and events into the chimpanzee's environment. Only humans continually act in ways that are intended, both deliberately and consciously, to solve problems that thus alter their physical and social environment. And once they have done so, they have created situations that demand the solving of new problems. One category of such problems has so far been touched upon only occasionally in this book. That is the interaction of individuals with one another inside the social network – the subject of the next section.

# V: Humankind in the Social Network

# 16

# The Social Bond

Human beings are highly social animals who cannot survive outside a society until they have first learned numerous skills. Organized and long-lasting societies are rare among mammals (the wolf pack, the prairie-dog town, and the baboon troop are notable exceptions), and societies are by no means the rule even among the non-human primates. Society, though, is universal among humans, obviously because it has performed major adaptive functions that increase the chances for survival. Society is the counterpart of adaptive mechanisms built into the bodies of other mammals, such as speed, brute strength, powerful teeth and jaws, and instinctive reactions. 'Society', of course, is a convenient label that has no existence of its own outside the living members who compose it. Society does not act; people do. Expressions such as 'society must' or 'society controls' are not literally true but are metaphors or reifications. The English language is, unfortunately, unwieldy in making this distinction without sometimes awkward circumlocutions. So when I occasionally resort to the metaphorical use of 'society', I hope this distinction will be kept in mind.

Some of the characteristics of human society are implicit in the way the word has been used so far in this book. It is composed of members of a single species; the dogs and cats we bring into our homes are not members of our society. A society is also a territorially distinct organization, occupying a well-defined space which is often defended against members from other societies. Furthermore, a society involves sustained ties of interaction among its members. These things are true also of many kinds of animal societies (such as those of the ants, bees, certain birds, and wolves), but two additional characteristics make human society unique. First of all, the members of a particular society are mutually interdependent to an extent unequalled in any non-human society. The well-being and often the very survival of each member of a human society depends largely upon the behaviour of the other members. Second, a human society is characterized by a high degree of autonomy – that is, it is not subject to control by any other organization that may be one of its constituent parts. The population of the United States thus constitutes a society, whereas individual families, communities, business and fraternal organizations, the 'high society' of the *Social Register*, and scholarly 'societies' do not. Society is, basically, the largest group with which most people can identify; and its influence on the individual is much greater than that of any smaller group.

Above all, every society is organized in such a way that codes, rules, habits, expectations, customs, and etiquette ensure appropriate behaviour by its members. These social controls begin in infancy – through a process technically known as 'socialization' – and they continue throughout the life of every individual. Even so, not all people act appropriately all of the time in any society. Inappropriate behaviour is usually forgiven so long as it does not breach a serious code or value. (Of course, a few members of every society are judged to be 'crazy', a label that usually is applied because they behave unpredictably or fail to do what is expected of them by other members.) Any society's standards for appropriate behaviour are likely to bewilder outsiders. Singing a traditional song incorrectly might be a serious breach of everything one society stands for. In other societies, a mistake in the formalities of greeting may relegate a person to low status as surely as if that individual had the reputation of being a fool. In Western societies, rebels against what is expected of them are often imprisoned or – as in the Soviet Union – treated as mental deviants. In either event, these individuals remain unwilling members of the society against which they have rebelled in the first place. Rebels may leave their own society, but if so they must become members of some other society and submit to its standards, traditions, and ideals.

As a member of a society, each individual acquires a vast repertory of ways of doing things and even of thinking and feeling. A Japanese, for example, possesses certain standards for achievement, ideas about appropriate behaviour for males and females of various ages, and convictions about the supernatural. Although some features of Japanese life can be found in other societies as well, the entire array of them is exclusively Japanese and it makes up the Japanese culture – a word used in referring to the totality of learned behaviours in the context of a social system. Such things as how often people bathe, and whether they prefer to eat grasshoppers or beefsteak, belong as much to culture as do avant-garde painting and literary debates. Culture is so much a part of the behaviour of the members of a society that individuals usually take it for granted – which explains 'culture shock', the sudden realization, on arriving in a foreign place, that the assumptions of the people around you are quite different from yours. Your arrival similarly causes culture shock to the people whom you visit, simply because an outsider is likely to bring into question aspects of behaviour that have always been regarded as customary. When Captain Cook asked the chiefs of Tahiti why the men ate apart from the women, they looked at him in wonder and disbelief at such a foolish question. They thought and thought, and finally one offered the only explanation they had: 'Because it is right.'

Culture is essential to the survival of human beings because they lack the instincts that enable other animals to survive and reproduce. Animals have inherited complex forms of instinctual behaviour which appear at the appropriate times without having been learned from other members of their species. A pronghorn antelope is born with the instinct to flee, at the same time raising a patch of white hairs on the rump that warns the rest of the herd of danger. Human beings exhibit few such automatic reactions to stimuli. The pupils of the eye widen in the dark; a sneeze expels irritants from the nose; a yawn draws oxygen into the lungs; a limb jerks away from the source of sudden pain. Otherwise, humans survive as a result of the things they are able to learn, not the things they are born with. And because of their complex brains and their possession of language, humans can learn more things more rapidly than other animals, and they can respond with a greater flexibility of behaviour. Instead of inheriting habits and skills, they must learn these from other members of their society during the course of their lives. In short, culture is what is learned from the cumulative experience of past generations, shared among contemporaries, and preserved beyond the individual life-span of a society's members.

Culture can exist only within the context of human society – and in the absence of culture, conversely, human society is impossible. The two are inseparable. Culture, therefore, is the society's blueprint for behaviour: what must be done, what ought to be done, what may be done, and what must not be done. Social scientists have fully enumerated the bizarre ways in which human behaviour can vary from one society to another. Hindus do not eat beef; Moslems and Jews are forbidden pork; and whereas North American and European Christians eat both, they avoid eating rats, lizards, and grasshoppers. The Todas of southern India thumb their noses at another person as a sign of respect, but North Americans and Europeans regard such behaviour as highly disrespectful. Examples of such culture-linked differences in behaviour have been documented almost endlessly from societies around the world, whose respective members display apparent Darwinian fitness. Their very fitness calls into doubt assertions that North Americans, Europeans, or members of any other society possess any sort of absolute cultural truth. Most social scientists, therefore, think in terms of 'cultural relativity' – that is, with the assumption that each practice or belief of a society must be understood in relation to the cultural and social context in which it occurs. ♂♀

Failure to understand the phenomenon of cultural relativity, combined with the North American and European tendency to meddle in other societies, usually produces disastrous results. That is what happened in 1830 when the British exploring vessel *Beagle* reached Tierra del Fuego, at the southern tip of South America. The crew of the *Beagle* represented the most highly developed industrial society of the time, and the Fuegian Indians were possibly the simplest of New World societies. The well-intentioned captain of the *Beagle* decided to take back with him four Fuegians, in the hope of educating them and then returning them to their homeland, where they could introduce 'civilized' ways. The four (who were soon reduced to three as a result of smallpox contracted from the British) lived for a year with a minister near London, who taught them English and the 'civilized arts'. King William IV granted them an audience and presented them with numerous gifts, the baubles and trinkets of the industrial age. At the end of 1831, the *Beagle* sailed back to South America, carrying the three Anglicized Fuegians and also Charles Darwin as the naturalist for the expedition. Darwin reported being impressed by the apparent success of the experiment in supplanting one set of cultural values with another. To him, the three Fuegians appeared to display the English virtues of merriness, modesty, and pride in personal appearance.

Upon reaching Tierra del Fuego, the three were deposited in the area where they wished to settle, and where the mother and brothers of one of them soon arrived. Darwin wrote of the reunion after a separation of three years: 'The meeting was less interesting than that between a horse, turned out into a field, when he joins an old companion. There was no demonstration of affection; they simply stared for a short time at each other; and the mother immediately went to look after her canoe.' Nearly a year passed before the *Beagle* again returned to that vicinity. Soon a canoe approached, bearing the Indian Jemmy whom Darwin, on the voyage back from England, had admired for his good nature and careful attention to personal appearance. But now Darwin observed that Jemmy was

. . . a thin haggard savage, with long disordered hair, and naked, except a bit of blanket around his waist. We did not recognize him till he was close to us; for he was ashamed of himself, and turned his back to the ship. We had left him plump, fat, clean, and well dressed; – I never saw so complete and grievous a change. ♂♀

Jemmy related that York and Fuegia Basket, the other two Fuegians, had married and that York had stolen the gifts Jemmy had brought back from England. That was the last the *Beagle* crew saw of the people who represented the experiment in cultural change. Further information was provided by the crews of other ships that visited the area several years afterwards. Jemmy instigated the massacre of six missionaries who had set up a station there; York was murdered after he killed another man; Fuegia Basket returned completely to her native ways. The three Fuegians, who had seemingly progressed in a few years from the 'primitive' to the 'civilized' state, had acquired only the veneer of British culture. They obviously had retained the beliefs and customs with which they had been inculcated since birth as members of their society.

\*

Every society has its own standards and goals, which are sometimes explicitly stated but often are unconsciously assimilated as part of the process of growing up within that society. Some of the goals of the United States are explicitly enumerated in the preamble to the Constitution: '. . . to form a more perfect Union, establish Justice, insure domestic Tranquility, provide for the common defence, promote the general Welfare, and secure the Blessings of Liberty to ourselves and our Posterity.' Other goals of United States society can be inferred from the behaviour of its citizens: to respect ownership of property, to make a profit, to obtain a formal education, to hold a permanent job, and to defer immediate gratification for the future benefit of one's children. People in the United States rarely question these goals, even though at least some goals undoubtedly would appear strange to members of a different society. Whatever the goals of a society may be, they shape its basic institutions. The goal in the United States of placing a high premium on individual freedom and achievement is expressed in the nation's political institutions (such as democracy and the Bill of Rights), its economic institutions (capitalism and accumulation of wealth), and its religious institutions (religious freedom and the separation of church and state).

Even the wealthiest societies lack the inexhaustible resources necessary to achieve all of their goals. The goals given high priority are those considered so important that the society is willing to divert considerable resources to achieve them, at the expense of other goals with lower priority. Eskimo society, for example, places a high value upon the enduring partnership between two males who, living in an environment of scarce resources, agree to act as if they were close kin, to support each other in all things, and to share when one of them is in need. This economic partnership has a higher value than marital fidelity, which explains why one Eskimo will lend his wife to a partner whose own wife is unavailable at the time. Values in the United States are quite the opposite. A man who exchanges his wife's favours for his own enrichment or advancement is regarded as at best a panderer.

A society as a whole observes long-term goals, but the day-to-day interactions between groups and individuals are influenced by guides to conduct known as 'norms'. Norms set boundaries for what people must or should do to be acceptable to other members of the society. Norms exert their influence by inspiring in each member of society a matrix of 'oughts': negative ones, which forbid certain conduct, and positive ones to encourage conduct of a different kind. Some norms are so deeply ingrained from infancy that people mistakenly think of them as inborn and attribute the behaviour arising from them to 'human nature'. At one time or another, people in the United States have attributed hard work, pride, envy, good, and evil to human nature rather than to the norms of their society. Possession of a conscience simply means the assimilation by an individual of society's norms to such an extent that these norms unconsciously govern behaviour in a specific situation. Everyone admires the person who forthrightly stands up and declares, 'My conscience compels me to take this action' – but more admiration should really go to the society for its success in inculcating this individual with its norms. Such people are not even aware that norms are influencing their behaviour; instead, they attribute their actions to the vague thing they call 'conscience'.

The norms that encourage or enjoin certain behaviours are never exactly the same from one society to another. No matter how repugnant certain conduct is in one society, at other times and places it may very well have constituted a norm. Cannibalism, incest, infanticide, murder, torture, and theft have all been normatively proper in one society or another. What has sometimes been dramatically termed 'the clash of civilizations' is merely the difference in the interpretation given by different societies to the same acts. None of the major religions today practises human sacrifice, but numerous religions at one time or another have regarded it as not only an acceptable practice but indeed a sacred one. In the previous century, people in the United States declared their abhorrence of the torture practised by some American Indian tribes; yet every 'civilized' nation (including the United States) has used torture to obtain information or to force changes of belief.

The idea that a society's norms determine the behaviour of its members is one that arose during the nineteenth century when anthropologists were studying very simple societies. The idea came to be uncritically accepted that people are born into a world in which society's norms have already been set, and that early education makes these norms an integral part of every member's personality. The way we act does, of course, sometimes depend upon the norms we have internalized since childhood. Robinson Crusoe was influenced by norms in showing revulsion when Friday declared his intention to devour the body of an invader of their island. This norm is further bolstered when children nowadays read about Crusoe's revulsion. Nevertheless, more recent sociological thinking, particularly in regard to complex societies, tends to regard few of a person's day-to-day activities as determined by norms. In fact, almost all of everyday life is experienced as negotiable behaviour in interactions with other members of the society. Humans are not normatively programmed robots; nor are they cultural dupes who will always behave in predictable ways regarded as the norms of their societies.

In the endless flow of situations that constitute experience for members of a complex modern society, much happens that is strange or even nonsensical. Meanings are often unclear, seemingly inexplicable events take place, and situations do not seem to follow expectations. One norm of North American culture is a horror of physical cruelty – yet such a norm is irrelevant to most of our daily conduct. We allow television to display hours each day of scenes of physical cruelty; we are lax in prosecuting people who physically abuse their children and wives; we bestow decorations on soldiers and police who employ cruelty as part of their lawful duties. Norms have not provided us with an astronomically large number of keys to behaviour in all daily situations, and so we must deal creatively with them, negotiating the social environment within the general constraints of our society's norms. The irrelevance of most norms to daily behaviour is probably an inevitable consequence of modernization. The world has become so complex, and the possibilities for action so numerous, that norms could never equip the individual to deal with every situation. In modern societies, norms stake out the boundaries of behaviour and attract attention only when an individual's behaviour oversteps those boundaries. ♂♀

People who violate the norms that are held (or asserted to be held) sacred by their society are said to exhibit 'deviant behaviour'. Until recently, most members of United States society regarded premarital sex as deviant behaviour; yet among some societies in Polynesia, the refusal to participate in premarital sexual relations is considered deviant. The study of peoples around the world has clearly shown that one society's sin may be another society's virtue. No single way of acting at all times and all places has been regarded as deviant. The claim has been made for the universal prohibition of incest, but incest was practised among the ruling families and wealthier classes in ancient Egypt, Peru, and aboriginal Hawaii. And, as social workers in the United States have attested, father–daughter and brother–sister incest are considerably more common than is generally realized. Certainly we might think that a father who murders his own child would be condemned in every society, but that is not so either. After all, Abraham was fully willing to sacrifice his son Isaac at the bidding of Jehovah. In some societies, the normative duty of a father is to put to death a son whose aggressiveness constitutes a threat to the general well-being. The ancient Greeks and Romans both believed that each family should execute its own deviants because that method was more humane and also less likely to cause tension between different kin groups.

The alacrity with which a society's members label acts as deviant is truly remarkable. The early French sociologist Émile Durkheim once used the metaphor of a society composed of saints as a striking example:

Imagine a society of saints, a perfect cloister of exemplary individuals. Crimes, properly so called, will there be unknown; but faults which appear venial to the layman will create there the same scandal that the ordinary offence does in ordinary consciousness. If, then, this society has the power to judge and punish, it will define these acts as criminal and will treat them as such. ♂♀

Durkheim is saying that the distinction between the good citizen and the criminal in a society will show up even among saints – simply because people will tend to label certain behaviours as deviant even though the deviance amounts to only the slightest fall from perfect sainthood. Saying what is deviant behaviour thus becomes extremely difficult, not only because deviance varies from one society to another but also because it varies within the same society at different times and among different groups of people. Theft, shoplifting, grand larceny, fraud, assault, homicide, suicide, homosexuality, prostitution, child molestation, juvenile delinquency, use of heroin, treason, and mental illness are just a few of the behaviours that have been labelled as deviant in North American society. What could possibly be their common denominator? Some people might say that they share a violation of the law and a conflict with society's norms of right and wrong. This explanation is inadequate because violations are almost never clear-cut; if they were, then no need would exist for law courts. Most otherwise upright citizens are at one time or another deviants, in violation both of the legal code and of the norms of society. Scarcely a citizen of the United States has not committed theft (such as taking home stamps and supplies from the office for personal use), fraud (inflating deductions to outwit the tax collector), or infraction of traffic laws (exceeding the speed limit) – yet these people certainly do not consider themselves to be thieves, perjurers, or violators of the traffic codes.

Defining deviance is further complicated by the different standards applied to socio-economic classes. Most people in North America and Europe believe that the crime of stealing is much more commonly committed by the poor than by the wealthy, but that is not so. Prison, not crime, more commonly characterizes the poor, the unemployed, and the non-white. Many poor people currently imprisoned in the United States are not there because they were convicted of any crime but because they are awaiting trial and cannot afford meanwhile to post bond. A study made about a decade ago showed that white-collar crimes in the United States totalled $1.7 billion while the lower-class crimes of burglary and theft totalled only a third as much. Furthermore, considerably fewer white-collar criminals are arrested, indicted, or convicted – but if they are, their sentences are much lighter than those meted out to lawbreakers among the poor. In one recent year, United States courts convicted more than 500 individuals of tax frauds that averaged $190,000 each. A mere ninety-five of these received jail sentences, which averaged only nine and a half months. By contrast, these same courts convicted about 4250 people of such crimes as car theft and burglary, which involved considerably less money and were rarely more violent than crimes of tax fraud. Yet some 60 per cent of these car thieves and burglars were sentenced to prison – and their terms averaged twice as long as those of the relatively few people who were sentenced for massive tax frauds.

Most people suppose that the violation of norms leads to social controls, and they regard the legal system as an organized social response to the fact of deviance. But deviance may in fact be caused by social control. If a certain behaviour is labelled deviant and stringent laws are passed to prohibit it, then obviously a great deal of this kind of deviant behaviour will occur. During the time that the manufacture of liquor was prohibited in the United States, a great many people became deviants either by selling it or by consuming it. When the prohibition was repealed, this kind of deviance disappeared. Situations similar to prohibiting the sale of liquor exist today in regard to the possession of marijuana and to homosexuality. Members of society actually create deviance by making rules forbidding such behaviour. In other words, deviance is not so much a quality of character as it is a label that has been successfully applied to someone.

An important question nevertheless remains. Why do people label certain kinds of behaviour as deviant rather than other kinds? No society has ever regarded as deviant the love of children, respect for the aged, charity, co-operation, bravery, sharing, or self-sacrifice, to mention just a few. Yet sometimes even trivial behaviours are labelled deviant, as was the case with the wearing of long hair by males during the 1960s. One explanation places deviance at the opposite pole from charisma. Charisma is a quality that sets apart an individual from others in the society because that individual appears to be endowed with superhuman capabilities. According to this explanation, whereas some members of society are superhuman and far above the average, then others – the deviants – will be viewed as being much worse than the average. In actual fact, they are regarded as subhuman.

Mental illness is a clear example. People in Western societies have held very different views about mental illness at one time or another – regarding sufferers as possessed by demonic forces, as wonder-workers or soothsayers, as beyond salvation, as criminals, or as a Bedlam sideshow. The mentally ill are nowadays treated with compassion in modern societies, even though they are still regarded as strange, possibly dangerous, and certainly unreliable deviants. They are regarded as less than fully human and are thought to represent a potential threat to the activities of the vast numbers of average people. In other words, deviance is a variable phenomenon that changes from place to place and from time to time; it represents a departure from the group's normative expectations at the moment; and it produces sanctions that attempt to punish, isolate, or correct the individual whose behaviour has been labelled as deviant. ♂♀

Social scientists have identified two types of norms: folkways and mores. Folkways are the patterns of behaviour that a society regards as 'right' or 'natural' in such routine matters as attire, etiquette, or speech. Folkways constitute the general expectations of the entire society, not simply the norms of a particular group, such as the Parent–Teacher Association or the American Legion. Violation of a folkway carries no legal sanction and, in fact, usually results in little more punishment than temporary social avoidance. The worst thing that will happen to a North American who violates the norms of dining behaviour by attacking a steak with the fingers and jaws will be a sharp decrease in the number of dinner invitations.

Each folkway at one time must have had adaptive significance, but in most cases the folkway has endured long after the need for the adaptation has passed. No one knows for sure just how most folkways arose or what causes them to spread throughout the society until eventually they became institutionalized. Handshaking and raising the palms as a greeting, for example, may have originated as ways to show that no weapons were being held; as folkways, they survive in a time when weapons are supposed to be carried only by designated officers of the law. New folkways constantly arise as technological innovations are introduced, but no one has yet adequately explained why new ones related to the same invention should differ from one society to another. Folkways in answering the telephone are an example. In North America, people say *Hello*; in Britain, the form is *Smith here*; in France, it is *Allô, allô, allô*; and in Spain, it is ¡*Habla!* ('Speak!').

Mores constitute a special category of norms, and they differ from folkways in the intensity of the feelings they arouse. Mores are almost always regarded as essential to the well-being of society, and thus severe punishments are inflicted upon violators. Sexual conduct, in particular, is governed by a great number of mores in all societies – as is perfectly understandable, since it affects the family, the foundation upon which society itself is built. Folkways and mores thus represent two extremes of a continuum of norms, with most social behaviour falling somewhere between them. In the United States, for example, welshing on a bet is strongly disapproved of, but it rarely brings sanctions beyond a reputation for untrustworthiness. Somewhat more serious violations are sexual promiscuity, compulsive gambling, and association with known criminals. The United States system of laws recognizes the existence of this continuum. Some laws are simply codified folkways – such as those against littering, jaywalking, or smoking in an elevator – whose infraction may be penalized by court fines but almost never by a jail term or a serious decline in prestige. On the other hand, a large body of laws – those against homicide, robbery, assault, and rape – apply full legal force to some of the most sacred mores in United States society.

*

When the history of any society is examined, a number of trends can usually be observed – among them, changes in goals and norms, an increased complexity of institutions, and differing forms of political organization. Whether or not such changes are regarded as 'progress' is beside the point. The important thing is that changes in societies do not occur haphazardly. No society, of course, is destined to proceed inevitably through a fixed sequence of stages, such as the stages of 'savagery', 'barbarism', and 'civilization' postulated in the nineteenth century. On the other hand, the possible directions a society may take are very limited. Every known society can be fitted into one of a small number of categories, such as band, tribe, chiefdom, state, or empire. Each of these categories is marked by the prevalence of certain social and political institutions and by differences in subsistence patterns, density of population, economic relations, and family organization. When the history of a particular society is known over a long stretch of time, its passage from one category to another can be seen clearly. The written records of the Hebrews, Mesopotamians, Greeks, Romans, and others clearly document evolution from simple hunting–gathering bands to complex empires. Such evolution, of course, is by no means a Mediterranean phenomenon. The Zulus of southeastern Africa, for example, during the past five hundred years have evolved from small chiefdoms, often warring with one another, to unification into a large chiefdom and then into a powerful state.

Most theories of socio-cultural evolution do not claim that all societies must inevitably become more complex. Some societies have remained at about the same level for thousands of years: those of Eskimos, Australian Aborigines, Bushmen, and Paiute Indians, among others. Some have even regressed to simpler levels – notably Imperial Rome, which broke up into clusters of primitive agrarian societies about 1500 years ago. Beginning in A.D. 410 and continuing through the year 536, Rome was repeatedly sacked by Visigoths and other northern tribes. The empire crumbled into petty states and its once complex economy was reduced to local self-sufficiency. Many industries throughout the former empire disappeared altogether. The copper mines shut down for four hundred years, and brass was not manufactured again for nearly a thousand. Trade withered because a strong central government could no longer protect the merchants. With the curtailment of trade, the skilled artisans who had contributed to the grandeur of Rome abandoned their craft traditions and turned to agriculture. The depopulation of urban centres caused Rome eventually to revert to a simple agrarian society, a state out of which it had evolved eight centuries before.

The regression of that empire, however, was exceptional, and equally exceptional are those other societies that have changed little over thousands of years. Most societies do change, and almost always the change is in the direction of increased complexity. For this kind of evolution, three explanations have traditionally been offered: racial abilities, environmental pressures, and the influence of great leaders. All three explanations have serious shortcomings. Least upportable is the racial one, which ascribes superior mental and physical abilities to one population over others. It was in vogue during the 1800s and early in the 1900s, while people of European ancestry were successfully colonizing much of the world. From previous chapters of this book, though, it should be plain that European military and technological superiority goes back only a few hundred years. And since the geographical populations ('races') that inhabit Europe had evolved many thousands of years before, any genetic superiority to other populations of the world should have made its appearance much earlier.

Nor do environmental pressures adequately account for the course taken by social evolution. The notion that the environment, particularly the climate, determines which societies will flourish was popularized by Ellsworth Huntington, a professor at Yale, in a series of books written between 1915 (*Civilization and Climate*) and 1945 (*Mainsprings of Civilization*). Among other things, he asserted that the human intellect works at maximum efficiency in a variable, temperate climate with numerous storms. According to his theory, these optimal climatic conditions were responsible for the superior human health and energy and the high civilization found in the northern United States and in western Europe. Environmental determinism such as this has been thoroughly discredited. The high civilizations of the Maya and the Khmer and of Sub-Saharan Africa flourished in climates that were not temperate and variable, but tropical and wet; the climate in which the civilizations of Mesopotamia, Egypt, and the Indus valley arose was hot and arid. At an obvious level, of course, climate sets the outer limits of socio-cultural possibility. The Eskimoes of the Arctic could no more become food producers than the Aztec Indians of Mexico could have based their subsistence upon walrus hunting. Climate, however, cannot determine the specific kind of society that will develop in any given region – as is demonstrated by those environments that have been inhabited by notably different kinds of societies. The same arid regions of Mexico, for example, were inhabited both by simple hunter–gatherers and by the high civilization of the Mixtecs, who had largely liberated themselves from their environment by the construction of irrigation works.

Finally, major changes in society have often been attributed to the accomplishments of great leaders. Ever since the discovery of writing, humankind has been encouraged to think of history in terms of Hammurabi, Moses, Pericles, Julius Caesar, Charlemagne, Elizabeth I, and other leaders – simply because the leaders, who have always controlled communications, wanted it that way. They made certain that their exploits were celebrated and that the world looked upon them as the prime movers in cultural achievements. Great leaders, though, are not society's prime movers; they are its manifestation. The glories for which the Elizabethan Age is noted actually were emerging before Elizabeth ascended the throne. The same thing can be said of technological innovations. We can be fairly certain that if James Watt had spent his time at the University of Glasgow writing poetry rather than tinkering with machines, someone else would have perfected the steam engine and the Industrial Revolution would have proceeded in Britain in much the same way. The foundations for the technology of the steam engine had already been laid by others (such as Newcomen) and the cultural basis for making use of such a discovery already existed.

In fact, several hundred of the most important technological discoveries and inventions of the past several centuries were made simultaneously by two or more individuals working in complete ignorance of the others' efforts. Some of these are:

OXYGEN: Priestly and Scheele, 1774
TELEGRAPH: Morse, Henry, Steinheil, and Wheatstone and Cooke, about 1837
PHOTOGRAPHY: Daguerre and Talbot, 1839
TELEPHONE: Bell and Gray, 1876
AEROPLANE: Wright brothers and Dumont, 1903

Even though the actual inventions are the work of particular individuals of genius, the adoption of them – and the social and cultural changes they bring – must ultimately depend upon the desire for change among the masses of anonymous people who make up a society. One of the greatest geniuses ever known, Leonardo da Vinci, conceived of the aeroplane in the fifteenth century, but nothing came of his conception because the societies of the time had no need for aircraft, nor did they possess the technology necessary to manufacture them.

A more compelling explanation than race, environment, or great leaders for the way societies have evolved is to be found in technological innovation and its consequences. Technology is important for the way it extends the human being's basic physical equipment: eyes, ears, brain, and muscular energy. The microscope and telescope are extensions of human vision, the radio of hearing, just as automobiles and aeroplanes are extensions of the ground it is possible to cover on foot, and as computers are of the storage capacity of human memory. Such technological changes, the outgrowth of culture, are equivalent to the biological changes brought about in an animal species by genetic alteration. In either instance, new levels of adaptation become possible. Even a seemingly minor cultural change can produce reverberations throughout the entire society. Thus the internal-combustion engine has meant not only a new automotive industry, but also marked changes in the economy, a landscape drastically refashioned by highways, and something of a revolution in social relations as a result of increased mobility.

Such technological innovations as automobiles, tractors, electric power plants, and computers have produced rapid evolutionary changes because they speed up the flow of energy through a society. In the simplest human society, the muscular energy of its members will be employed to harvest the energy from the sun that is locked in plant and animal tissues. This simple society can endure so long as the harvest of energy exceeds the muscular energy expended. Any innovation that supplements human muscle (even one as relatively uncomplicated as a hunting bow) provides additional energy – and consequently makes for a more reliable food supply, produces more goods, increases populations, encourages new social relations, and thus acts as a stimulus to the entire society. A society which through technology unlocks great amounts of energy beyond that of which human muscles are capable has a potential for evolving into one of great complexity, such as would not be possible to a band of hunter–gatherers. The energy-rich society can support a large and dense population, can divert labour into specialized occupations (like government bureaucracies that in themselves produce no energy directly), can support complex institutions and build libraries and other information-storing systems – all of which open the way to still further technological innovations. ♂♀

*

Socio-cultural evolution has so far been discussed at the level of extremely broad trends, such as the transition from an agricultural society to a modern one. Evolution does, of course, occur at less dramatic levels. Radical changes that have taken place in the structure of a society often become obvious only at hindsight. When the aeroplane was invented, for example, few people could visualize the way it would shrink the globe and produce new human visions – of global unity and also of mass destruction. The social changes brought by technological innovations, particularly those that have occurred during the past few centuries, have been studied in detail by several researchers. ♂♀ One major conclusion to be drawn from their work is that the number of cultural items in a society (all the way from objects as trivial as the paper clip to structures as complex as political parties) has a direct relation to the rate of social change. When the number of such items is few, innovations will also tend to be few; but as their number grows, and with it the sum total of innovations, so does the rate of social change. For example, an inventory of cultural items – from tools to religious practices – in the society of the hunting–gathering Shoshone Indians, who inhabit the Great Basin between the Rocky Mountains and the Sierra Nevada, totalled a mere 3000. No estimate has been made of the number of cultural items to be found among the modern agriculturists who inhabit the same Great Basin states of Nevada and Utah, but the total would no doubt be in the millions. Social change in modern United States society is obviously proceeding rapidly in the area that was once occupied by the Shoshone – bands whose culture, as revealed by archaeological excavations, appears to have changed scarcely at all for thousands of years.

Because the rate of social change is always slower than that of technological change – an effect known as 'culture lag' – social institutions tend to be under continual strain. In its turn, paradoxically, that strain itself has served to breed further social change. This may be seen in the replacement of human labour by machines over the past few centuries. As a result, vast numbers of skilled craftspeople lost their jobs. Females became wage earners because the muscular energy required was no longer so great as before. And that change resulted in still others, notably in family life. Machines brought, in the short term, dislocation, bewilderment, and misery for huge numbers of people. Ultimately the disruption was so great as to call for further adaptations, like those seen in modern societies today – social welfare programmes, minimum wages, child-labour laws, safer working conditions, release from back-breaking labour, and universal literacy.

Societies, however, do not always accept innovations simply because there is a need for them. A major cultural innovation in the United States in recent years has been a shift in the responsibility of caring for the aged. The change that has relegated elderly persons to nursing homes and retirement communities came about because the new mobility in transportation and communication has virtually eliminated the traditional pattern of living near one's parents after marriage, and has thus loosened generational ties. This is a cultural innovation that is unlikely to be accepted at the present time by the Japanese because one of the norms of their society is that the aged are to be venerated. To take another example: most of the American Indian tribes of the Plains and the Great Basin adopted the new technology of the horse and the gun, around which they built the flamboyant Plains Indian culture of the last century. Some of the Shoshonean tribes, though, lived in societies that were not prepared for these innovations. Whenever these Indians obtained a horse, they ate it.

The archaeological record of technology can thus often indicate changes that have taken place in societies. The earliest tools of the hominids, for example, were extremely simple, made with little more effort than that of knocking one stone against another to produce an edge. It is important for understanding social evolution to note that these tools were extraordinarily similar over a wide geographic range, and remained so for well over a million years. Hominids obviously were behaving very much the same everywhere. They possessed roughly the same abilities to communicate with one another, to search out game animals and plant foods, and to organize themselves into social units. But very slowly at first, and then at an accelerating rate, a number of different tool traditions emerged, to be followed by wholly different technologies. A worldwide examination of archaeological sites dating from about 10,000 years ago reveals a remarkable diversity of technologies, and of societies as well.

Then with the Bronze Age, beginning several thousand years ago, the evolution of technology slowly veered in the opposite direction, towards a single, worldwide body of knowledge. This has been achieved by the modern nations and is now on the way to being achieved by developing countries as well. Television sets, cameras, and automobiles manufactured by corporations based in the United States, Germany, and Japan (and with factories in places like Singapore, Indonesia, Taiwan, and São Paolo) are the same except for minor stylistic differences. The Phantom, Mirage, and MIG jet fighters produced by the United States, France, and the Soviet Union differ in detail but are basically alike. And in the realm of popular culture – rock music, film-making, clothes, soft drinks, and so on – there is scarcely any difference at all from one modern society to another. The technological sameness that is settling over the world obscures, however, a basic fact about societies. Not only are they socially and economically unequal in comparison to one another; gaping inequalities exist within them as well.

# The Lowly and the Mighty

The history of humankind makes it plain that at no time did members of our species ever construct an enduring society in which all members – male and female, young and old, skilled and unskilled, rich and poor – were equal in the benefits they received. Even the simplest of hunting–gathering bands is divided along the lines of sex, age, and the eminence of particular families. In an examination of any society, past or present, a critical issue is the unequal distribution of rewards; 'stratification' is the gauge for measuring who is really who. As originally used, the word referred to the geological layers in the earth's crust: topsoil, subsoil, rocks, and so on. But perhaps inevitably, it was soon being applied to the strata or class structure of human society – as the phrase 'upper crust' makes plain.

Every known society has been stratified, even those so small and simply organized as to appear virtually classless. In the societies of the Eskimos, the Pygmies, and the Australian Aborigines, for example, distinctions are to be found between males and females, between the revered elderly and the uninitiated young, between the married and the unmarried, and between one kin group and another. Hunter–gatherers often do not reveal clear-cut stratification, but social inequalities nevertheless do exist. A survey some years ago of approximately a hundred hunting–gathering societies showed that twenty-seven kept slaves and twenty displayed significant distinctions based upon wealth. Even those that some anthropologists have described as egalitarian make subtle distinctions based upon prestige, power, or property. For example, explorers who knew the supposedly egalitarian societies of the Plains Indians in their heyday observed definite class distinctions. George Bird Grinnell, the naturalist and explorer, wrote of the Cheyenne:

Family rank, which existed among the Cheyennes as among other Indians, depended upon the estimation in which the family was held by the best people. A good family was one that produced brave men and good sensible women, and that possessed more or less property. A brave and successful man has raised his family from low to very high rank; or a generation of inefficient men might cause a family to retrograde. ♂♀

As societies become increasingly complex, the number of classes within them increases. In addition to distinctions regarding sex, age, marital status, and kinship, others are made on the basis of possession of herds or land, political influence, and the ability to intercede with the supernatural. All the known written records left by the societies of antiquity confirm not only the existence of social stratification – rich and poor, powerful and powerless, free citizen and slave – but also such inequalities were regarded as 'natural' rather than as of human doing. Social inequality became even more marked with the rise of the urban state and still later with industrialization. Every individual belonged to a specific category that was defined as occupying a particular status in the society. Numerous new distinctions were added: between middle class and working class, educated and non-educated, poet and peasant. The judgement was made that certain categories were better than others and that each category implied a restricted choice of opportunity.

All social primates form hierarchies based on both power (the ability of a dominant animal to make a subordinate one do its bidding) and status (access to food and females). Because both power and status hierarchies also occur in human societies, the temptation exists to regard human systems of inequality as merely another aspect of the primate heritage. To do so, though, would be to regard inequality as a biological given – and thus to imply that nothing can be done about it but to await whatever slow changes may be brought about by evolution. No evidence has been found to support the view that human hierarchies are a direct outgrowth of those in non-human societies, notwithstanding the similarities between the two. And in fact they differ in at least one major respect: human hierarchies operate within a context of moral awareness and cultural values that is utterly lacking in non-human primates. Humans know that hierarchies exist, and they can talk about, praise, deplore, or justify them – things that non-human primates certainly cannot do. Humans can see both the good and the evil functions of hierarchies and act to minimize the latter, whereas non-human primates are forced by their inheritance to respond to status and power in stereotyped ways.

The terms 'social stratification', 'social inequality', and 'class' are basically synonymous, and may refer to any hierarchy of positions that tends to interfere with the satisfaction attached to being a member of a society. The most visible of such inequalities is wealth. The folk saying that 'money isn't everything' is patently untrue. A person who has wealth can purchase goods and services denied to those who do not. Mere access to these confers a degree of power that is visible to all and thus becomes a clear sign that deference is due. Surveys have shown, for example, that drivers of Mercedes-Benzes or other prestigious cars are much less likely to be stopped by police in the United States for exceeding the speed limit than are drivers of low-prestige cars travelling at the same speed. Nor can truth be found in the saying that 'you can't buy health'. In the United States, the death rate of people who earn more than $10,000 a year is only half that of people who earn under $2000. Wealth, power, prestige, and honour combine to lengthen the life-span and to add to a general sense of well-being.

Wealth in the United States is concentrated in the hands of about 4 per cent of the population, who own more than a quarter of the nation's real estate, three-fifths of all privately held corporate stock, a third of the nation's cash, and a very large proportion of United States Treasury notes. Even after the debts of these people are subtracted, they are left with a net worth of more than a trillion dollars – enough to purchase the entire national output of the United States plus that of Switzerland and the Scandinavian countries. Furthermore, because ownership of only a relatively small percentage of the total stock of a corporation is necessary for control, owning three-fifths of the nation's stock investments gives these people power over most of the nation's industries and businesses. ♂♀

To attribute social stratification to unequal wealth alone, though, is to oversimplify the problem in the same way that Karl Marx did. An individual's social position really is determined by the interaction of numerous variables. Each society will project its own version of the positions that bring with them the greatest privilege and respect – the monarch, the warrior, the priest, the merchant, the yeoman, the poet, and so on – and such prestige often has little to do directly with wealth. Each society, of course, will define the ideal in its own terms. To a Pygmy, the male with the highest prestige is not likely to be the strongest, most aggressive, wealthiest, or shrewdest, but rather the one who shares most generously. Even among modern societies, considerable differences are to be found in the criteria used for establishing rank in the social hierarchy. Studies show that family connections, for example, are much more important in Great Britain and in Japan than in the United States. Citizens of the United States place a higher premium on education than do those of the Netherlands and Sweden. Biological variables – such as sex, age, skin colour, and physical or mental abilities – of course play their part in establishing status. So also do social and cultural variables: ancestry, occupation, and noteworthy accomplishments.

People somehow unconsciously put all these variables together and emerge with a cumulative assessment. Usually they are not aware of the weight given to each variable, or of the reason why certain variables are included in the assessment but not others. Studies have shown that when such variables are presented one at a time, most people have no difficulty in making choices between them. In the United States, higher status is generally accorded to those who are white rather than black, Protestant rather than Catholic or Jewish, rich rather than poor, white-collar worker rather than blue-collar, and married rather than divorced. Assessments of status become difficult when all these criteria are applied to a particular person. What will be the social status, for example, of a wealthy, married male who is nevertheless uneducated, of blue-collar origins, and Jewish? Sociologists are still trying to account exactly for the way more weight is given to one or another of a cluster of traits in determining status.

Most people in the United States are in remarkable agreement concerning which are high-prestige and which are low-prestige occupations. This uniformity is thought to be a byproduct of the values encouraged by industrialization, although the evidence is somewhat ambiguous. The prestige accorded various occupations has in general been similar in both modern and developing nations, in Western and Eastern societies, under communist and non-communist governments – whose only common denominator is in fact industrialization. In all these societies, people rate highest the occupations that involve power, material rewards, the authority to deal with crises, and service to the social group. On the other hand, studies of simple, non-industrial societies have shown that occupations with these characteristics are likewise given the highest prestige. A justice of the Supreme Court of the United States is given a

Social status is often directly related to livelihood. Certain occupations are unmistakably higher in prestige than others. A large-scale study of the prestige ratings accorded various occupations, made in the United States in 1963, was similar to other such studies that have been made since 1925 – and one striking thing to be noted is the general consistency of the ratings over four decades. One reason for this is simply that certain things about the favoured occupations do not change very much: the relative level of income, the associated glamour and publicity, the power that can be wielded, and the importance of the contribution to the society at large. Each occupation in the survey was rated on a scale up to 100. Since the average of these ratings was 71, occupations were considered to have high prestige if their rating was above that and correspondingly less prestige if their rating was below 71. Here are some of the occupations that were ranked in the survey. ♂♀

| Occupation | Score |
|---|---|
| Justice of the US Supreme Court | 94 |
| Physician | 93 |
| Scientist | 92 |
| State governor | 91 |
| College professor | 90 |
| US Congressman | 90 |
| Member of President's cabinet | 90 |
| Chemist | 89 |
| Diplomat | 89 |
| Lawyer | 89 |
| Dentist | 88 |
| County judge | 88 |
| Architect | 88 |
| Minister, priest | 87 |
| Psychologist | 87 |
| Mayor of a large city | 87 |
| Airline pilot | 86 |
| Banker | 85 |
| Biologist | 85 |
| Sociologist | 83 |
| Public-school teacher | 81 |
| Owner of small factory | 80 |
| Building contractor | 80 |
| Musician in symphony orchestra | 78 |
| Novelist | 78 |
| Economist | 78 |
| Artist | 78 |
| Electrician | 76 |
| Railroad engineer | 76 |
| County agricultural agent | 76 |
| Government welfare-worker | 74 |
| Farm owner | 74 |

| Occupation | Score |
|---|---|
| Undertaker | 74 |
| Newspaper columnist | 73 |
| Policeman | 72 |
| Reporter on daily newspaper | 71 |
| **Average** | **71** |
| Radio announcer | 70 |
| Bookkeeper | 70 |
| Insurance agent | 69 |
| Carpenter | 69 |
| Mail carrier | 67 |
| Local official of labour union | 67 |
| Railroad conductor | 66 |
| Travelling salesman | 66 |
| Plumber | 65 |
| Automobile repairman | 65 |
| Barber | 63 |
| Machine operator in factory | 63 |
| Owner of lunch stand | 63 |
| Truck driver | 59 |
| Clerk in store | 56 |
| Lumberjack | 55 |
| Restaurant cook | 55 |
| Nightclub singer | 54 |
| Filling-station attendant | 51 |
| Dockworker | 50 |
| Coal miner | 50 |
| Restaurant waiter | 49 |
| Taxi driver | 49 |
| Bartender | 48 |
| Janitor | 48 |
| Garbage collector | 39 |
| Shoe shiner | 34 |

very high rating, but so is the peacemaker in a simple society that lacks judges, courts, police, or other legal mechanisms.

*

Stratification systems are generally of two kinds: open systems in which people can move from one rank to another (classes), and closed systems in which such movement is extremely limited (castes). The most extreme and complex example of social stratification known is the caste system of India. The entire Indian society is divided first into five major strata: the topmost Brahman (priest), the Kshatriya (warrior), Vaishya (merchant), Shudra (servant, labourer, peasant), and finally, below all of these, the 'Untouchables' who in India nowadays are usually referred to by the name Mohandas Gandhi gave them – Harijans, or 'children of God'. Numbering upward of eighty-five million people, the Harijans have traditionally filled the society's most menial occupations: street sweepers, latrine cleaners, and scavengers. ♂♀

The five strata are further divided into subcastes, known as *jatis*, which are usually marked by numerous differences in marriage customs, diet, religious practice, attire, and dialect – about as many differences, in fact, as would be found between a white resident of Brooklyn and a Navajo Indian. No one knows for sure just how many *jatis* exist today, but the number exceeded 2300 when an attempt to count them was made in 1901. The *jatis*, in turn, are further subdivided into local units whose members share a particular way of life. Each local unit governs the behaviour of its members by enforcing certain regulations – making sure that they engage in the occupations assigned to the caste, eat only the foods that are deemed proper, marry a person of the same caste, and avoid 'contamination' through contact with members of lower castes. Although each caste is supposed to have a hereditary vocation, fewer than half of the people of India actually do the work prescribed for their castes. The reason for this is the obvious one: the castes do not reproduce themselves at exactly the same rate, so at any particular time some caste-occupations will have too many workers and others too few.

Probably no group of people in history has ever been socially so degraded as the Harijans. In some parts of India, a member of these lowest castes may not come within about twenty feet of a Brahman. And until recently in many areas, a Harijan was not permitted to build a brick house or to wear clothes or jewellery resembling that worn by members of the higher castes. Harijans still are forbidden to enter religious shrines and temples; they are denied the right to use certain streets, sidewalks, bridges, or transportation lest they contaminate the higher castes. The British were appalled by the lot of the Harijans and about a century ago made some small efforts to alleviate it. Gandhi, although himself a Brahman, fought to raise the position of the lowest castes. When India became independent, the new constitution offered hope of relief, and indeed the political status of the Harijans has changed somewhat for the better. Yet in most of village India, the degradation of the lowest castes remains very much as it was a century ago. Even major political changes seem not to affect their position materially. When the Communist Party took control of the Indian state of Kerala about two decades ago, all the leaders of the new government were members of high castes, most of them Brahmans. Caste is so intimately intertwined with village life – with law, custom, religion, the economy, and in fact the entire social fabric – that it seems impossible to extirpate.

Many attempts have been made to explain how such a system could have come about. Some scholars see it as simply the survival into the present of regulations established by rulers in ancient times. Others consider it a clever plot by the high-ranking castes to maintain power. Neither of these explanations alone is sufficient. The caste system apparently developed over a period of about 3000 years out of an ideological, religious, social, and economic matrix peculiar to Southeast Asia. Basic to the caste system is the ancient Indian idea that every human group possesses a particular 'substance' that has both physical reality and legal–moral force. The members of each *jati* are believed to transmit particles of that caste's unique substance from one generation to another. An individual's bodily substances (such as hair, blood, faeces, and semen) are thus related to those produced by other members of the same caste. The uniqueness of the caste substance is further maintained by the members' eating certain foods together and by refusing to eat in the company of members of different castes. The lower castes are therefore prohibited from touching not only the persons of those belonging to higher castes, but also the water, food, kitchen utensils, or clothing used by them. To do so, it is believed, might cause the 'pollution' of the higher-caste individual concerned, and therefore such transgressions are severely punished.

Hindu worship has codified these beliefs. Priests are believed to have inherited the ability to endow an image of a god with living substance. Worship at a Hindu temple is sponsored by a ruler or a wealthy man, who provides the offerings which the priest will transform into divine substances. The worship cannot proceed without specialists belonging to various occupational castes – cooks, singers, dancers, and temple servants, among others – who feed, entertain, and generally attend to the god. Members of still other castes – those whose occupations are barbers, launderers, and bathing attendants – also participate to make sure that each worshipper is ritually clean and free from any defiling substances. Ultimately, nearly all the castes in a community will be incorporated into the worship, in hierarchical order. The Brahman as priest is at the top, followed by those belonging to the ruling and merchant castes who sponsor the worship. Below them are those who attend to the details of the worship and, finally, at the very bottom are the Harijans who clear away wastes and remove polluting bodily substances. The act of worship also serves to reaffirm the positions of the castes, in that a portion of the offerings made to the god is distributed to each in a set order, from high to low. In the process, the lowliness of the lowest castes is further reinforced by their being permitted to receive only what is left over by those of higher castes, who have been given their portions directly.

But no account of the religious – ideological base upon which the caste system is built is a complete answer to one crucial question. How can a system that makes the lives of scores of millions of people so utterly hopeless have been perpetuated century after century? Obviously the caste system must perform adaptive functions in Indian society such as are filled by no other institution. Various social and political scientists have pointed to the security, solidarity, and preferential access to certain jobs that membership in a caste affords. Each caste represents its own little world with its specific traditions, authority, control over certain resources and occupations, and mutual aid among its members. The ability of those in need to call upon fellow members thus makes the caste a haven for even the lowliest Indian. Another practical reason for the persistence of the caste system must be that it offers status superiority to all Hindus except those belonging to the bottommost caste. Even among the Harijans there are sharp distinctions of status. The higher of these lowest castes regard the lower as polluted, in much the same way that they themselves are regarded by the high castes as being polluted. In other words, all of the castes, except the bottommost of the Harijans, are superior to at least some castes. Abolition of the entire system would, of course, give caste members the freedom to mingle as equals with higher castes – but it would also allow the inferior castes to mingle with themselves.

These explanations, nevertheless, are still insufficient. The caste system supposedly provides security for members because of the monopoly held over certain occupations, but in fact it rarely does so. Although certain of the lower castes are in theory metal-workers, potters, weavers, and so on, in practice they merely provide cheap farm labour for landlords and form a pool of menial labourers in towns and cities. No account of the caste system can possibly ignore the economic function of an exploited labour force. The Harijans in particular have traditionally been serfs of the dominant castes, forced to supply free labour whenever it was demanded of them. The British colonial administrators abolished the slavery of the Harijans in the last century, but the change did little to improve their economic position. To this day, very few Harijans own any land, and the holdings of those few who do are so small that they remain exploited peasants. Not only do the Harijans serve as India's basic agricultural force, but they also perform services regarded as distasteful. Neither the nation's economy nor the social structure of village India could be maintained without the cheap labour of the lowest castes. ♂♀

The Hindu caste system has sometimes been regarded as an isolated phenomenon in human history. The specific details of its workings in India are, of course, too complex and too extraordinary to have been duplicated exactly in any other society. Even so, somewhat similar caste systems have existed elsewhere – not only in the Buddhist cultures of Sri Lanka, Tibet, Korea, and Japan, but also in several of the Moslem societies of Asia and in some African tribal kingdoms that flourished before European colonization. Moreover, in the Mesopotamian states of about 5000 years ago a vast number of specialized hereditary occupations were ranked and given moral force, in much the same way as castes are, by the religious–ideological system that prevailed. In the New World, the most complex such system was found among the Natchez Indians of the lower Mississippi valley, who ranked people in hereditary castes: the Great Sun followed by the Little Sun, and those by Suns, Nobles, Honoured People, and finally Stinkards. The Natchez castes, though, differed from those of India in an important respect. Whereas the Asiatic Indian caste system rigidly maintains the barriers between castes, certain complex features of the Natchez system forced individuals in each generation to move up or down in rank.

Most North Americans pride themselves on belonging to a free society that is at the opposite pole from the Indian caste system. They believe that every citizen earns a position in life, rather than being born into it – that individuals can become more or less what they want to be so long as they have the ability and the ambition. Such a view is occasionally bolstered by the success story of some person who has risen from poverty to riches. The sociological fact that the standing of most people in North America is much the same as their parents' is usually dismissed with some statement along the lines of 'at least they had the opportunity'. The truth is that equality of opportunity is rare in North American society. A child of white, Protestant parents, belonging to a high-prestige family, with kin who are established leaders in many occupations, who has been educated at a boarding school and a college whose admission policies are highly selective, will enjoy enormous advantages in wealth, in style of living, in access to desirable marriage partners, and in health such as are denied to a child born into a family of a different kind. Low-status North Americans who have somehow managed to acquire wealth usually find themselves in very much the same position as the occasional low-caste Hindu who breaks through the caste barrier: they learn the brutal fact that wealth can rarely be converted into power. Prejudice against blacks, ethnic Catholics, Jews, people with Spanish surnames, and American Indians is analogous to the ideas held by Asiatic Indians about ritual pollution; in either instance, limits are set on what the new wealth can purchase. In India and in North America alike, a Harijan or a member of a minority is excluded from many social situations and especially from marriage into the elite, even though the life-style of the elite is financially possible.

Some social scientists have argued that whatever caste system exists in the United States is not comparable to that of India because it does not offer a religious justification for discrimination and prejudice, as does the Hindu system. That is hardly correct. The United States is predominantly a Christian nation, and Christianity – beginning with the teachings of Jesus, through the Apostle Paul and the Church Fathers, into modern times – has acknowledged the existence in human society of sharp gradations in power and prestige. Furthermore, in the view of St Augustine, since such a hierarchy is the 'natural' state of humankind, the misery of the lower classses is accordingly justified: 'Inasmuch as they are deservedly and justly miserable, they are by their very misery connected with order . . . They would be more wretched if they had not that peace which arises from being in harmony with the natural order of things.' ♂♀

In the United States, the dominant whites often act as though they shared the Hindus' notions of pollution and defilement by keeping blacks out of their front parlours and away from their daughters. Much as in India, a hierarchy thus exists in which membership is hereditary, and in which one's position is easily identified according to the colour of one's skin. In the southern United States as in India, members of the higher castes maintain their superior position by promptly punishing lack of deference from those of a lower caste. In both societies, the topmost groups find it in their interest to perpetuate a system that confers upon them economic and sexual advantages along with social prestige. The economic advantage is the most obvious; in both societies a ready supply of cheap labour from the low castes is guaranteed. In sexual relations, high-caste males have access both to females of their own caste and also to those belonging to low castes – a freedom that is denied to low-caste males, as well as to the sheltered high-caste females. The prestige that goes with belonging to the high castes is obvious in almost every area of life.

The caste system that prevails in the United States is also sometimes said to differ from that of India in the important respect that the latter have no 'markers' comparable to skin colour in the United States. That is true, if only to a limited extent. Indians of low caste can leave their native villages and claim a higher caste in the cities, where they will be unknown. But markers do exist that are every bit as visible as the skin of United States blacks. In the first place, members of the lowest castes in India generally do have a darker skin. Second, other markers of caste are prevalent, such as diet and attire (which can of course be changed), and also dialect and cultural behaviour (which are much more difficult to alter or disguise). The question of markers is really only a quibble. Much more important is the undeniable fact that in the United States and India alike, caste is determined by the accident of birth. Individuals born into a low caste are considered inherently inferior and are relegated to a disadvantaged position, regardless of how faithfully they adhere to the norms and values of those in the castes above them. ♂♀

*

One consequence of stratification is that people belonging to various classes and castes differ in their 'life chances' – that is, of remaining healthy, of obtaining desirable things and positions, and indeed of surviving. Being born into a wealthy family provides superior chances of survival as an infant, or receiving a superior education as a child and adolescent, and later of entering an occupation with opportunities for amassing wealth. In its turn, wealth enhances one's standard of living and thus the length of time the individual can expect to remain vigorous and capable of amassing yet additional wealth. The superior life chances enjoyed by the upper class become especially prominent during crisis situations. When the *Titanic* struck an iceberg in 1912 and sank with the loss of more than 1500 lives, not all classes were equal in their chances of surviving. A mere 3 per cent of the female passengers in first class drowned (and most of those remained voluntarily on the sinking ship), as compared with 16 per cent of those in second class and 45 per cent of those in third class. This differential mortality by classes was partly due to their location in relatively more or less vulnerable areas of the ship. It was also due to the protection that superior life chances can buy. Many third-class passengers were held at gunpoint below deck while the passengers from first and second class were abandoning ship.

A consequence of life chances is 'life style', which refers to the patterns of behaviour and thinking characteristic of a particular class. Numerous studies have confirmed a common-sense observation: members of different strata in society do have differing life-styles, covering a wide range of cultural behaviours. Life-styles and life chances reinforce each other. Individuals with unfavourable life chances tend to follow life-styles characterized, for example, by a low value placed on education, by unstable family ties, and by proneness to drug use. This perpetuates unfavourable life chances for their children. The life-styles of the upper and lower classes in the United States may be contrasted in almost every way: work habits, attire, diet, residence, family relations, sexual customs, leisure activities, even the very fibre of thought. In comparison to upper-class families, working-class families watch more television, read fewer books and magazines, and join fewer clubs and organizations.

Working-class males are more likely to drink beer than Scotch, to smoke cigarettes rather than pipes, to go bowling or fishing rather than to play tennis or golf. Working-class adults have sexual relations less frequently, less experimentally, and apparently with less satisfaction than members of the upper class; they are also more likely to be separated or divorced. The lower classes have developed a lifestyle that reduces insecurity by forging a network of personal relationships with kin and with other members of their own class. This network extends also to religious affiliation. Working-class people are much more likely to be Roman Catholics, Baptists, Mormons, or members of fundamentalist Protestant sects, whereas those with a college education are much more likely to belong to the Congregationalist, Episcopalian, or Presbyterian denominations. Clearly, churches in the United States tend to follow class lines. ♂♀

The universal inequality of life chances has led some scholars to conclude that stratification must fill some vital need in human society – as indeed it does, for it allocates roles. Every society is built around roles, and because its members are continually dying off, new members must constantly be recruited who have been motivated to fill those roles. But the roles in a society are far from equal. Some are more dangerous than others; some demand more physical or mental stamina; many demand special skills and long training; and certain of them are essential for the survival of the society. Every society must, therefore, develop ways of motivating people to undertake the more dangerous, arduous, or essential roles – and to reward them for doing so. The three most common rewards are prestige, power, and property, and they make stratification inevitable. The role of a brain surgeon, for example, is one that few members of society will ordinarily be able to fill. The potential brain surgeon must train for at least thirteen years after graduation from high school, and at tremendous expense. The work is extremely stressful, requiring precise co-ordination between eye and hand, plus a willingness to be responsible for the lives of others. In light of such drawbacks, almost no one would want to be a brain surgeon unless society offered rewards. In the United States, society does just that: the incomes earned by brain surgeons are consistently among the highest.

The opposite can, of course, be argued. Some roles in society are so disagreeable, so dirty, and so monotonous that people should rightly demand high rewards for performing them. Garbage collectors render essential services, performing back-breaking labour under very unpleasant conditions that are sometimes a threat to their health. They could justifiably consider their role as deserving of high reward as that of the brain surgeon. Garbage collectors, nevertheless, are not so rewarded – showing that the importance and the arduousness of certain roles in society only partly explain why they are better rewarded than others.

One obvious explanation for the difference lies in the sheer power of certain occupational groups to demand high rewards from society. Of all the life-preserving occupations (such as the Coast Guard, police, and fire-protection), only doctors dictate where they want to serve, the hours they will work, and the payment they will demand. A police officer does not negotiate to work on one case rather than another, or base remuneration on the number of arrests made. Yet doctors in the United States are allowed to set their own fees, basing them on whatever the market will bear. They can do this because they thoroughly control medical-care services – a vast industry which is second only to housing in its size and proportion of the gross national product – and also because they have engineered scarcity in their profession by controlling access to medical schools. Neophyte doctors learn their trade by practising on ward patients, who are powerless to protest without possibly forgoing any medical help whatever. Throughout their careers, doctors force us to pay them while they continue to educate themselves by the 'practice' of medicine on our bodies. We pay for X-rays and diagnostic tests, but the doctors retain control over these, and will release them only to another member of the medical freemasonry. Inequality obviously is related not only to rewards but also to the capacity of certain groups to control their sector of society.

Some social scientists and political philosophers have argued that inequality is not built into societies and that a truly egalitarian society is possible. At the centre of this argument is the belief that the removal of environmental inequalities would make all human beings equal. In other words, any intelligent and healthy child would possess the potential to become a brain surgeon. Furthermore, a child properly brought up in a utopian society supposedly would not be concerned about differences in the cleanliness, safety, or physical hardship of various roles. Each child would be willing to make whatever contribution was necessary.

No utopian group has ever survived long enough to put these arguments to the test, and indeed most such groups have been extremely short-lived. In 1841 some of the leading intellectuals of the time – Nathaniel Hawthorne, Ralph Waldo Emerson, Margaret Fuller, and Charles Dana, among others – established at Brook Farm near Boston a communal group dedicated to plain living and high thinking. Each member was expected to share equally in the manual labour needed to make the group self-sufficient. The community survived for six years, but long before then most of the founders had departed. A disillusioned Hawthorne concluded that 'a man's soul may be buried and perish under a dung-heap or in a furrow of the field, just as well as under a pile of money'. ♂♀ Nor have the prophetic visions that inspired many Marxists at the time of the Russian Revolution come to pass. More than a half century later, members of certain classes in the Soviet Union live little better than the nineteenth-century serfs while leaders in government, industry, and science are rewarded with chauffeur-driven limousines, large city apartments, country houses, a superior diet, and preferential health care. For example, Leonid Brezhnev, first secretary of the Communist Party, at the time of writing owned an international assortment of expensive automobiles: a Cadillac, a Lincoln, a Rolls-Royce Silver Cloud, a Citroën-Maserati sports car, and a Mercedes 450 SLC, not to mention a Russian-made Zil.

Far from having faded away, social inequality actually increased as human adaptations became more complex. Beginning with the hunting–gathering adaptation and continuing through those of food production, urbanization, and industrialization, each change in adaptation has led to increasingly greater social inequality. During the early stages of modernization, it appeared that once again a penalty would be paid in increased social inequality. Instead, the trend towards ever-widening differences in life chances has faltered, and some social scientists believe that a reversal may now be under way. Although enormous inequalities in wealth and prestige still exist in modern societies, they are far less than those to be found, for example, in France under Louis XIV or in Russia under the tsars. More people in Europe now own land, or have access to it through governmental co-operatives, than ever did in the past. Voting rights for all citizens – male and female, rich and poor – have increased the political power of the great masses of the population. Individuals have won the right to join together in political parties, labour unions, and associations to protect their interests. Most important, modernization has entailed a general broadening of the conception of who is a full member of the society, entitled to its protection, to equal treatment under the laws, and to at least a minimum of life chances. Not only equality itself but the *idea* that one can achieve it has become a pervasive aspiration in modern societies, regardless of the form of government and regardless of whether it is in actuality true.

Why should the trend towards increasing inequality have been reversed in modern societies? One obvious answer is that the modern complexity of social, political, and economic systems has forced those individuals at the top levels to depend upon the skills of those at lower levels. A modern society could not survive for more than a few months were all members of a union that controls a specific occupation – such as the teamsters in the United States or the dockworkers in Britain – to cease working. The special skills upon which modern societies have been built give the possessors of those skills tremendous bargaining power. This may be part of the explanation. An even simpler one may lie in the enormous wealth produced by modern societies. The upper classes can easily share some of their wealth with those less fortunate while suffering no significant reduction in their own enjoyment of luxuries.

What has been said here of social stratification may have given the erroneous impression that the strata are unyieldingly rigid. In actual fact, even the most caste-ridden societies afford both individuals and entire groups the opportunity to move up or down the social ladder. In North American and European societies, a rise in status is occasionally due to the virtues of hard work, thrift, and a willingness to take chances – whereas a descent is due to the vices of prodigality, laziness, and timidity. Physical attractiveness and unusual mental abilities are important also, but so are trivial things. One study revealed that the males selected to advance in corporate training programmes in the United States were considerably taller than the average. In nearly all modern societies, 'marrying up' is an important way of rising in the hierarchy. Almost always, though, it is females who improve their social status through marriage. The reason is that a family's status is usually gauged by that of the husband. A high-status male can thus marry down without a loss of prestige, but a high-status female cannot because she will have to assume the lower status of her husband. Marrying down by males partly explains why modern societies have such a relatively high percentage of unmarried upper-class females. Each upper-class male who marries 'beneath himself' means one less marriage partner for an upper-class female.♂♀

An individual's change of status in society is also connected with the changes experienced by the group as a whole. Those in India who traditionally worked at certain jobs in mining or trade found their entire caste suddenly elevated after British colonialism and, still later, industrialization had placed a high premium on these activities. On the other hand, the Brahmans as a group have generally been drifting downward because modern India is no longer willing to support large numbers of non-productive priests. Nor can the Brahmans easily adapt to changed conditions by moving into other occupations, since they would then become polluted by contact with lesser castes. Whenever Black Americans as a group achieve increasingly greater access to desirable jobs and professions, the social position of each black as an individual will rise as a matter of course through identification with the group. An unexpected byproduct of the youth counterculture in the United States in the 1960s and 1970s has been the opening up of positions in the higher strata of society. Most of the youths who formed that counterculture came from privileged backgrounds and would have found it easy to enter selective colleges and occupations affording high prestige. For each privileged youth who rejected the opportunities offered by birth, a place was left vacant to be filled by youths from lower classes and from minority groups.

*

As an aggregation of numerous individuals in organized and constant interaction, human society has sometimes been compared to the insect societies of bees, wasps, ants, and termites. Some social insects do indeed display characteristics of human society: mutual aid, territoriality, sustained interactions among members, and distinct roles and activities based upon caste. Insect aggregations, however, constitute an altogether different category from human societies. Their social organization is based solely upon the capacity to react automatically to certain events. A honeybee larva that is destined to become a queen will always be a queen, and a worker will always remain a worker (with certain very unusual exceptions). A queen bee cannot rise or fall in status during her life; she belongs to no family or other subgroup within the organization of the hive; and she will never try to change the social system into which she was born. She does not recognize different kinds of kin, or select males with high prestige as potential marriage partners, or change her role during her lifetime, or instruct her offspring in the expectations, aspirations, and mutual obligations of the hive society. Human society obviously differs from all other aggregations of animal species, no matter how large or complex these may be or how intelligent their members may appear. The next two chapters will dwell at length on some of these uniquely human aspects of society: marriage and the family, and the growth and development of the individual within the social network.

# 18

# The Family as an Institution

The severing of the umbilical cord at birth separates the child from the mother, but the cord is at once symbolically reconnected in a new context. Replacing the cord as a conduit is the family, which feeds the developing child with ideas about the society it has entered and about the multitude of things that will qualify it for full-fledged membership. Later, marriage will sever this conduit between the individual and the parental family, but a new tie is created as the couple founds its own family and produces a future generation that will pass through the same cycle of birth, severing, and rebirth. In all societies, marriage is a passage from one status and role to another. No matter how private the actual ceremony may be, it remains a social event because two people affirm their commitment to the values of their society. In return, society rewards them by declaring that theirs is a socially sanctioned union, in which any children to be born are deemed legitimate – that is, accorded the full status and rights common to all members of the society.

Marriage has several features that make it a highly unusual relationship. For one thing, it establishes a set of reciprocal rights and obligations between the parties that affects every area of life: ownership of property, roles of male and female, rearing of children, relations with the supernatural and with society's institutions, as well as numerous seemingly trivial details of day-to-day living. Second, marriage is presumed at the outset to be permanent, 'until death do us part', even though in actual practice it often is not so. A third important feature is that marriage involves both a sexual and an economic relationship. Finally, and most important, marriage is the foundation on which all the other institutions in society are erected. The behaviour that is learned within the family becomes the model for behaviour in other sectors of society. By passing on the cultural traditions of the society to the next generation, the family helps to keep the culture itself alive.

The family is a uniquely human invention, which could have developed only because of the kind of species we are. It has evolved as the best solution to the hominids' twin needs of prolonged child care and obtaining food through division of labour. It provides the framework for the construction of the complex social institutions that are a hallmark of hominid life. The family could not have developed in the absence of still another uniquely human trait: the conscious control by the brain of sexual desire, selfishness, and aggression. With this control must have developed an increased capacity for the love which promotes enduring relationships, both within the immediate family and with the larger network of kin.

Because the family is such a crucial human invention, no society is without it, even though customs concerning marriage and family differ greatly in societies around the world. People in Western societies are so used to having a marriage commence with a wedding ceremony that they sometimes find it difficult to visualize marriage beginning in any other way. And indeed every society requires the performance of some ritual act, however simple, in order for the tie to be considered a marriage. Among Pygmies, the specific public act that proclaims the new relationship to the society at large is the groom's depositing of a killed antelope at the entrance to his in-laws' hut. ♂♀ Among the Winnebago Indians of the upper Great Lakes, the female merely accompanies the male to his parents' house, where she gives her finery to her mother-in-law in exchange for plain clothes – and that is that. This seemingly minor exchange is as valid a wedding ceremony as those that in some Mediterranean societies may go on for a week. For the Winnebago society similarly recognizes that two people have formed a union, that they must honour obligations to one another, that they have established an economic partnership, that their offspring will at birth be recognized as members of the society, and that the pair has rights in, and responsibilities to, the society at large.

Because the family is so central to the way the human pattern of life has evolved, the prophecies of recent years about its decline and its anachronistic status cannot be taken seriously. The family could never disappear without having the human way of life as we know it disappear also. In the absence of the family, the other social networks and institutions that have been built upon it would disintegrate, because the social cement that holds society together would dissolve. Yet is it not theoretically conceivable that a human society might survive without the family? Imagine, for example, that total control of a society were to be lodged in some great, revered leader. She issues an edict, which is scrupulously obeyed, that all females are to be inseminated artificially with semen from males selected for compatibility of genetic traits. The resulting offspring are taken from the mother at birth and reared in communal nurseries, and later in communal schools, where they are inculcated with the values of the society. All of these children will be regarded as equally legitimate. When the children mature, they become either breeders or semen-donors for producing the next generation. Sexual relations take place solely for pleasure; any offspring accidentally conceived are to be regarded as illegitimate and are thus aborted. The economic partnership of the family will have become unnecessary because all private property, production, and distribution of goods have been placed in the hands of the bureaucracy established by the wise leader. The family as we know it will have been abolished, but the society would continue to exist.

Although such a situation is by no means a theoretical impossibility, attempts to abolish the family have never succeeded, either because of the intrinsic strength of the institution or because of the difficulty of changing social behaviours that have evolved over tremendous periods of time. The Israeli kibbutz represents an attempt to curtail the influence of the family, but even here the family unit has coalesced. Particular males and females have become preferred partners, and offspring reared communally have been brought back into the family setting. No matter how unusual a society's marriage customs might be, every society has had some kind of family organization. How can this persistence of the family be explained? Of the many explanations that have been offered, a particularly compelling one is that based upon natural selection. In all animal species, individuals act as if they were attempting to increase their Darwinian fitness – that is, to produce the greatest number of offspring in the next generation. Through family organization, humans achieve this in two ways. First, males can be certain that particular offspring are theirs. And then they can do everything possible to see that these children have a greater chance than other children to survive.

No wonder that so human an institution should have given rise to speculations about its origins. Some scholars have sought its roots in the behaviour of social mammals – such as the pride of lions, the wolf pack, or the baboon troop – but the differences between a human family and a group of mammals are so far-reaching that any link between them is tenuous at best. Most attempts to explain the origins of the family can be placed in one of three categories: original promiscuity, the mother–infant bond, and original-pair marriage. Promiscuity can easily be dismissed. Several nineteenth-century political philosophers put forward the idea of a promiscuous horde which placed no regulations on sexual intercourse until eventually permanent male–female relationships developed. As proof, supporters of this explanation have pointed to certain simple societies, in which sexual customs appear to be promiscuous, as survivors into the present of the original state of affairs. Among the societies often cited are those Polynesian ones in which premarital sex is an approved behaviour, and that of the Eskimos, in which the custom of wife-lending is common. Behaviour that might appear promiscuous to North American or European sensibilities, though, is not so to the people concerned. Polynesians and Eskimos have very strict concepts of the family and of the behaviour that is proper for its members, even though these concepts may differ from our own. And, of course, original promiscuity fails to explain the precise way in which the transition was made from the horde to the family.

Another proposed explanation is that the family began with the bond between the mother and her offspring because the identity of their biological fathers was usually not known. Supporters of this view find evidence for it in the occasional societies that trace descent and kinship through the mother's side rather than through both sides or through the father's. In these societies inheritance is through the female, and the newly married couple lives with the wife's mother. This kind of family, though, can almost always be linked with environmental conditions and the kind of adaptation the society has made rather than to any bond between mother and child. A society that obtains most of its food through the raising of garden crops by females, as do the Hopi Indians of Arizona, is likely to be of this kind – but one in which hunting by males is important almost never is.

The third explanation asserts that the family arose from a bonded male–female pair at the beginning of hominid history, just as Adam and Eve were the archetypal family in the Garden of Eden. According to this view, even among the earliest hominids the need existed for females to bring up the children and for males to protect them – which is true. This explanation further contends that the original pairs arose because humans have an instinct for monogamous union – which is assuredly not true. An instinct is an automatic behavioural pattern common to all members of a species. Despite such common phrases as 'the instinct for self-preservation', humans are not believed to possess any instincts, either for monogamous mating or for anything else. If a monogamous instinct did in fact exist, then it would be present in all humans. How would it then be possible to explain the polygamous marriages that exist around the world? The conclusion emerges that one hypothesis or another to explain the origins of the family might be put forth, but that the full explanation may never be known. Most probably, the family developed along with symboling, tool use, co-operation, division of labour, sharing, and an emphasis on social behaviour as yet another part of the adaptive complex that went into becoming human.

Second only to the question of origins has been speculation about the specific functions of the family. What does the family do for the individual and for society as a whole? The answer is that it does a great deal. In 1933, the President's Research Committee on Social Trends described the activities traditionally performed by the family in the United States: procreational, economic, educational, religious, protective, status-giving, and recreational, as well as affording companionship. Now, little more than four decades later, some of these functions are no longer performed in an important way by the family and some are so changed that they can scarcely be recognized as traditional family behaviour.

Such changes in the modern family do not indicate a decline in its importance, or any rending of the social fabric. Rather, the modern family in the United States is doing what families have always done: adapting itself to the changing society of which it is a part. In all societies in the past, the family was both a producing and a consuming unit. The entire family either foraged for food or produced it co-operatively; clothes and tools were often manufactured at home. In other words, the family earned its own living and consumed the fruits of its own labours. In modern societies, and in many developing ones as well, the family is now primarily a consuming unit that leaves production to factories. This change does not indicate a breakdown in the family but rather a shift in emphasis in its functions. For the United States family that in an earlier time lived on the frontier, the emphasis was on production. The emphasis now is on consumption. Previously the family members laboured to produce food together; now they shop together.

Similarly, the function of companionship performed by the family has expanded, at the same time that other functions are becoming less important. In previous centuries, the family in Western societies was ruled by an aloof and often tyrannical father–husband whose edicts could not be questioned by either wife or children. That has changed, so much so that the ideal function of the family nowadays is the provision of an atmosphere of intimacy and warmth: affection freely given and received, equality between husband and wife assumed, major family decisions made after open discussion in which the children often participate, and freedom of self-expression encouraged. ♂♀

Of the many functions that the family still performs in modern society, four are particularly important and I will discuss each briefly. The most critical is that of providing a social structure whereby the society can be perpetuated. This involves, first of all, the production of offspring and their care during the long period of childhood dependency. The actual biological parents do not necessarily have to be the ones who provide this care. It is sometimes provided by others, but these are usually members of the family network, such as siblings, aunts and uncles, or grandparents. Children must not only be cared for; they must grow up in such a way that they become full participants in the society. The child must learn not only skills necessary for survival but also the way the entire culture operates. Such things are, of course, taught by friends, schoolmates, neighbours, and teachers as well as by parents. Institutions outside the family share in this socialization process: formal schools impart the accumulated knowledge of the society, religious organizations teach moral behaviour, and political institutions instruct in rights and obligations. The supplanting of the family by other institutions, though, is often largely a matter of appearance. The voice of the family is still a loud one in the way these institutions are allowed to socialize children. Moreover, the family's influence has already left its mark before the institutions have their turn at influencing the child. Most children still learn the difference between right and wrong in a family context, and their ideas about the world as well are shaped there first.

The second crucial function of the family is to provide a means by which society can recognize offspring as legitimate and competent to carry on its traditions. Rules about legitimacy are really the licensing of parenthood by society. Every society defines who has the right to procreate and to bring up a fully accepted member of that society. In a small and simple society, the infant born to unlicensed parents has no clearly defined position in the group and no one to ensure that this child will grow up mindful of the group's cherished traditions. The problem of illegitimacy must be solved, either by infanticide or by adoption into a legitimate family. Western societies have generally cast out mothers who defied the rules of legitimacy and have branded the offspring as bastards, thus automatically relegating them at birth to low social status.

Both simple and complex societies are concerned about legitimacy because the infant is the focus of many important relationships involving the roles played by the biological parents and the networks of kin to which they belong. These relationships cannot be established if the infant has no acknowledged father or at least a male willing to assume that role. Furthermore, the already-married father cannot take care of illegitimate offspring without failing in at least some of his obligations to his own legitimate family. The unmarried father of an illegitimate child might be limited in his future options when it comes to establishing a family of his own. The rules of legitimacy are enforced because of the consequences for parents and for society in general, but the punishment is inflicted upon the innocent illegitimate child. Sophisticated modern people may declare that they no longer set great store by legitimacy, but in this they are out of the mainstream so far as most of the world's societies are concerned. People in about 60 per cent of all societies take a very permissive attitude towards premarital sexual relations, but even these societies do not approve of the birth of a child outside the bounds of what each defines as legitimacy. ♂♀

Yet another major function of the family is the regulation of sexual behaviour. Human societies vary tremendously in permissiveness or restrictiveness concerning sexual relations, but even the most permissive establish at least some norms, to which the preponderance of their members conform. These rules are enforced for the good of society, in that they ensure a reduction in sexual conflict between families and the production of legitimate children to perpetuate the society. Adultery is permitted in some societies, particularly for males, but the conditions under which it may take place, and with whom, are nevertheless regulated. In this, Western societies for about the last 1500 years have been among the most restrictive in the world. Many of their sanctions concerning adultery and premarital sex seem to be breaking down, but whether they really are may be illusory. The sanctions sometimes are perhaps not so much breaking down as undergoing redefinition. The change in attitude towards adultery during the past few decades, for example, apparently does not indicate a breakdown of the family, but rather a transition to a clearer definition of the circumstances under which extramarital relations are permitted.

In addition to the functions of perpetuating a society, legitimating offspring, and regulating sexual behaviour, a fourth major function of the family is the economic one. Up until the Industrial Revolution began, the family was the basic production unit. Marriage entailed the merging of production abilities more than the merging of hearts. 'It's not man that marries maid, but field marries field, vineyard marries vineyard, cattle marry cattle' goes a German peasant saying that sets forth the economic aspect of marriage. The economic importance of marriage is often recognized explicitly by a transfer of wealth from the family of one member of the couple to the family of the other. A sampling of the world's societies has shown that a majority require the groom or his kin to pay money or goods (known technically as 'bridewealth') to the bride's family to compensate for the loss of her economic services and to affirm his right to any children produced by the union. In about 13 per cent of these societies, the payment is in the form of free labour by the groom for the bride's family – labour that is sometimes performed before the marriage can take place, as happened with Jacob and Rachel in the Old Testament. The tradition in Europe and India of a dowry paid by the bride's family to the groom's family or to the married couple is quite rare; it appears in only about 4 per cent of the world's societies. In contrast to bridewealth, dowry is not considered compensation for the loss of the groom's productive labour in his father's household. Rather, it is intended to cover the cost of maintaining a female who, in those societies in which dowry is common, is usually considered to be an economic burden. Among the British upper classes in the previous century, for example, females produced virtually nothing at all except an heir (and in the process of so doing also produced additional children who were expensive to maintain and educate). Under such conditions, it was almost inconceivable that an upper-

class male would marry in the absence of a large marriage settlement. ♂♀

Bridewealth is prevalent in China, Japan, many Arab nations, and
most of Sub-Saharan Africa. Missionaries have deplored the system,
regarding it as the enslavement of females who in their eyes are being
sold as chattels. Nothing could be further from the truth. The groom
who hands over cattle or iron tools for a female is not purchasing
her. He is recompensing her family for her lost services, and he is
also promising to take good care of her. If he mistreats her, he has to
return her to her family, thereby losing both economic services and
his bridewealth. A family that produces numerous offspring, equally
balanced between sons and daughters, is therefore in an enviable
economic position. In exchange for its daughters it receives cattle or
tools, which can then be used as bridewealth to obtain fecund wives
for the sons in the family. These daughters-in-law represent both a
labour force and a potential for producing additional females, who
will bring even more bridewealth into the family. A family that continues to produce many offspring could thus grow powerful and
wealthy in only a few generations. This economic aspect of marriage
is sufficient to explain why, in some parts of the world, family vies
with family to produce as many children as possible.

*

With so many of society's functions assigned to the family, the widespread practice of divorce seems perplexing. The divorce rate has
risen astronomically in the United States during this century – by
more than twelve times between 1860 and 1970 – and some people
have therefore concluded that a high divorce rate is an inevitable
consequence of modernization. But the explanation for divorce is not
as simple and clear-cut as that. Actually, the rate of divorce varies
greatly from one modern nation to another. The United States
currently has the highest rate in the world – more than fifteen
divorces each year for every 1000 existing marriages – but in equally
modern and much more permissive Sweden the rate is less than half
as high. Nor is a high divorce rate a characteristic solely of modern
societies; the rate among some hunter–gatherers is about equal to
that of the United States. Further complicating the understanding of
divorce is that various countries at one time or another have had
higher rates than the United States does now. Westerners tend to
think of Japan as a stable society, but in 1887 – before it became

industrialized – it probably had a higher divorce rate than any other country. Not until the 1920s, after Japan had become industrialized, did the rate there begin to fall below that of the United States.

Divorce is a problem inherent in marriage itself. Two people (or three or more in polygamous unions) – each with individual values, needs, and aspirations – must live together with a minimum of tension and unhappiness. Some societies have developed ways to lessen marital strains, such as through lowered expectations about what the individual can expect from marriage. The Chinese, for example, extol family life but warn their children not to expect romance or happiness from it. Another common way to prevent marital strains, one that is widespread in pre-industrial societies, is to place a higher value on the network of kin than on the relationship between husband and wife. Elders arrange the marriage, direct the affairs of the couple, and act as peacemakers when disputes arise.

Preventive measures, though, are not always sufficient and unhappy marriages do still occur. What is done in such cases varies from society to society. In Spain and Ireland, legal separations are permitted, but not divorce. In some societies with extensive networks of kin, the marriage may be preserved in name only, with the husband and wife confining their contacts to the absolute minimum. Such methods of easing the burden of an unhappy marriage show that the members of society generally do everything possible to avoid divorce and to seek alternative solutions to marital unhappiness. The importance of preserving marriages is obvious. Divorce threatens societies, particularly small ones, by breaking agreements between the couple's kin groups, by stirring up dissension over repayment of bridewealth or dowry, and by raising problems about the custody of children.

Despite the drawbacks of divorce, some societies have adopted it as the ultimate solution. Far from being condemned, however, divorce should really be praised. Of all the alternatives for societies to put an end to marital conflict, divorce is the one most fair to both parties. It is the only alternative that permits the wife as well as the husband to make a fresh start through remarriage. (In societies that have traditionally made no provision for divorce, like those of India and Japan, a husband might take a concubine but no such freedom was accorded to the wife.) Nor does divorce indicate any contempt for the institution of marriage. In fact, people who obtain divorces would appear to be the most enthusiastic supporters of the institu-

tion. In the United States most divorced people – about two-thirds
of the females and three-fourths of the males – remarry. And they
do so rather promptly, usually within less than three years after
divorce. Approximately a quarter of all marriages currently existing
in the United States are unions in which at least one of the parties
had been married previously.

Divorce statistics present a distorted picture of marital dissolution
in the United States. In 1860, an average of only 1.2 out of each 1000
existing marriages were dissolved by divorce, whereas by 1970 the
figure had risen to 15.2. The important point, though, is often overlooked that in 1860 an additional 32.1 marriages were dissolved by
the death of one of the spouses. The combined rate of dissolution in
1860, therefore, was 33.3 per 1000 marriages – almost exactly what it
is today. Because the life-span of people in the United States has so
increased that both husbands and wives are living to much greater
ages, the probability of escaping from an intolerable marriage by
death has greatly diminished. A compensatory response has apparently arisen: to dissolve by divorce many marriages that would
under earlier conditions have been dissolved by the death of one of
the partners. In summary, the overall rate of marital dissolution in
the United States has changed scarcely at all in more than a century,
although the cause for these dissolutions has increasingly shifted
from death to divorce. Even so, death still continues to terminate
more marriages in the United States than does divorce. ♂♀

Perhaps the reason that North Americans and Europeans are so
concerned with divorce is that it negates all they have been led to
expect about romantic love. Love has long been celebrated in story
and song; it is one of the most pervasive themes in advertising; it is
the most common subject of gossip. Individuals in the thrall of
romantic love behave in distinctive ways that easily set them apart
from the individuals who are not in love. North American society in
particular teaches the young that falling in love is proper, and it
even subtly suggests the etiquette and the procedures for doing so.
Much of children's literature consists of stories and poems about
love, and children are promised that they will one day grow up to
love someone in particular. People in love, though, usually do not
realize that they have been prepared for the experience since childhood. They believe that their love is unique, but also that such an
event can strike at almost any time and place, and that when it does

the parties concerned are helpless victims of a force more powerful than themselves.

Studies of romantic love have often produced findings that run counter to everyday beliefs. Females supposedly fall in love oftener and more deeply than males – an impression that probably stems from the stereotype of the female as the more emotional sex. Various studies, though, have shown that males are generally more romantic and are more likely to develop feelings of love early in the relationship. And studies of the attitudes of college students have led to the surprising conclusion that the head rules considerably more often than the heart does. The conclusion of one such study, ♂♀ based on more than a thousand college students, states:

Contrary to rather strong popular impression, the female is not pushed hither and yon by her romantic compulsions. On the contrary, her romanticism seems to be more adaptive and directive than that of the male. Apparently she is able to exercise a greater measure of control over her romantic inclinations, adapting them to the exigencies of marital selection.

Neither males nor females usually become infatuated in the way celebrated in song, story, and movie romances. Nor does their infatuation totally disregard the flaws in the character and personality of the loved one (the 'love is blind' motif). Contrary to a widely held belief, young North Americans rarely fall in love with people unworthy of them. In fact, correlations of personality tests with questionnaires about romantic experiences reveal that most young people make choices that are rather sound from the standpoint of compatibility. They are usually sound economically and socially as well.

Some social scientists have looked beyond the apparent irrationality of romantic love to discover the benefits it might offer in North American society. A major benefit is that the high value placed on romantic love enables the newly married couple to remain blind to one another's foibles while adjusting in the early stages of marriage. This is particularly important in North American society, which lacks large networks of kin who might otherwise smooth out marital difficulties. Disillusion, though, is inevitably the result when the couple discovers that the promises of romantic love can never be fulfilled and that they will have to settle for a relationship that emphasizes companionship and reciprocity. One study has confirmed this disillusion by measuring the attitudes towards love by people who have been married for different lengths of time. Individuals married fewer than five years were observed to have a *less* romantic conception of love than those married more than twenty years. Indeed, disillusion shortly after marriage explains why the divorce rate is highest for those who have been married less than two years. Despite such disillusion, North American society in general benefits from the pervasive influence of romantic love. Love reinforces the tendency to marry and to produce children, which is obviously essential for the perpetuation of the society. Further, it eases the transition to the roles of husband–father and wife–mother that the society has established as its norms. And finally, romantic love validates the couple's belief that they have 'done the right thing' in making 'a proper marriage'.

The societies of the world can be placed along a continuum which ranges from the very major to the very minor influence of romantic love upon the selection of mates. North America is at one extreme in its exaltation of romantic love. North Americans who state that they are marrying without love are under suspicion, and usually feel obliged to offer some overriding explanation, such as 'We're too old for that sort of thing', or 'My last marriage was such a disaster, this time I want someone reliable.' At the opposite extreme were the upper classes of China under the Manchus and previous dynasties. They viewed love as a tragedy that might upset the elders' plans to unite two kin groups. This is not to say that romantic love did not occur, but only that it was regarded as irrelevant. Love is a recurrent theme in Chinese literature, one of whose conventions is that unrequited lovers are transformed into doves – but these tales were upper-class phenomena that did not interfere with marital arrangements. Most of the world's societies can be placed at various points between the extremes of North America and China. These other societies usually regard romantic love as a phase of youth that will someday be outgrown. In any event, little attention is paid to it and it does not interfere unduly with the marital arrangements made by kin. Perhaps at the very centre of the continuum is India, where the ideal relationship is thought to be one in which love eventually appears following betrothal or the marriage itself.

Because romantic love can crop up in any society, those in which it is regarded as a threat obviously must find ways to control it. A number of solutions have been arrived at. The simplest is child marriage, a strategy of contracting betrothal or marriage at an age so young that the parties have no opportunity to interact with other adolescent children. In India until recently, a child bride went to live with her husband in his father's household, but the marriage was not physically consummated until both reached puberty. Another common strategy is for the society to limit severely the number of partners eligible for marriage, as occurred in China, where villagers could not marry one another because supposedly they were all related. A third strategy is to isolate young people, either physically or socially, as in the harems of Islam or the duenna (chaperone) system found in southern Europe and Latin America. Variations on these three basic methods of control have been tried, but all share the aim of preventing an outbreak of romantic love – or at least of harnessing it as a marketable commodity.

\*

The societies of the world present a confusing diversity of family arrangements. The arrangement regarded as ideal in most modern

---

THE MYTHS AND THE REALITY OF MARRIAGE IN THE UNITED STATES

---

Most people in the United States hold beliefs and assumptions about marriage that will be revealed in their answers to the following true–false questions:

|  | True | False |
|---|---|---|
| 1. The longer a couple has been married, the more accurately each will perceive how the other thinks and feels. | ( ) | ( ) |
| 2. The greater the involvement of the husband in his work and in the community, the greater the marital satisfaction of both spouses. | ( ) | ( ) |
| 3. The happiest marriages are those in which the personalities of the husband and wife change very little – or if they do change, it is in the same direction and to the same degree. | ( ) | ( ) |
| 4. Husband and wife should each accurately perceive the other's role for the greatest satisfaction and adjustment. | ( ) | ( ) |
| 5. Husband – wife consensus on such matters as religion, recreation, finances, and philosophy of life will increase with the length of marriage. | ( ) | ( ) |

The answer to each statement is 'false' – at least according to studies of white, middle-class couples. Many common-sense notions about married life obviously have not been supported by research. ♂♀

societies, one which accounts for more than half of the households in the United States, is the 'nuclear' – that is, a married couple living in its own home with unmarried children but without any other relatives. Because the nuclear family is so familiar to people in Western societies, they often assume that it is the elementary building block for all societies. Such a view is ethnocentric. The nuclear family actually is quite rare, occurring only in industrialized nations and in certain hunting–gathering societies. It apparently represents an adaptation to particular economic conditions – a shortage of food at certain seasons of the year in the case of hunter–gatherers, and in an industrial economy the need to be geographically mobile to find a new job if necessary. Nor is the nuclear family as isolated from kin as is sometimes supposed. All studies of family life in the industrialized nations reveal that nuclear families continue to maintain contact with a wide range of kin, and that the most common use of leisure time is visiting relatives.

The emphasis that the nuclear family places upon the married pair rather than upon the network of kin produces a particular kind of social behaviour. Because in-laws and blood relatives have little influence upon the couple, the nuclear family cannot ask for very much support from kin. Nor, on the other hand, does the nuclear family usually recognize claims upon it from kin more distant than parents or siblings. Because of the weakness of these reciprocal exchanges, fewer pressures are brought to bear upon the nuclear family to settle near relatives. And because kin groups have little to gain from arranging a marriage between two people who will be independent, societies in which nuclear families are common generally allow more freedom in the choice of a mate. One result of all these behaviours is an intensifying of emotion within the nuclear family unit, beginning with the mutual attraction of two people and continuing throughout the marriage in their interactions both with each other and with their children. This interaction accounts for both the intimacy and the fragility of the nuclear family. If the husband and the wife do not obtain love and companionship within the family, they will have little incentive to maintain the union. As might be expected, the divorce rate is very high in societies where the nuclear family is paramount, whether it be a modern society or such hunter–gatherers as Bushmen and Australian Aborigines. The nuclear family is thus basically impermanent. It endures only so long as parents and their children live together. When the parents are divorced or die, or when the children move away, the nuclear family dissolves.

At the opposite pole from the nuclear family is what has been called the 'extended family' – that is, members of several generations living under one roof. In China, a man and wife live with their unmarried sons and daughters, their married sons and the sons' wives and younger children, and the grandchildren or great-grandchildren in the paternal line. In families that emphasize the female line, such as the Zuñi Indians of New Mexico, the extended family may consist of an aged woman, who heads the household, her married daughters with their husbands and children, and the unmarried daughters and sons as well. In many African and Arabian societies, an extended family may also be composed of two or more brothers, each with his several wives, together with their adult sons, who may also have wives and children, all living close together in a compound or in tents.

Whatever its exact make-up, the extended family is a social invention that offers many advantages. People in modern societies can turn for aid to organized charities and welfare agencies, but people who live in the non-urban, pre-industrial societies where extended families are most common must turn to their many kin. An aged or infirm relative would represent a crushing financial burden to a nuclear family, but the burden on an extended family is much less since it can be shared by many more members. Another advantage is that the extended family is more durable than the nuclear one. Members come and go but the unit maintains its identity because of its sheer size and its interlocking relationships. The extended family also serves as a loan agency, which amasses wealth and then disburses it to members for purposes that will further increase the family's standing – such as paying bridewealth for a favourable marriage, buying land, or financing the education of a promising youth. Furthermore, the extended family offers protection to its members in those societies that lack an adequate police system.

Since the extended family can do so many things, why is it not the prevailing form in all societies? Part of the answer is that it represents a specific adaptation in those societies that have no established institutions for enforcing laws, for caring for the poor and aged, for loaning money, or for embarking upon co-operative community projects. Another part is that the extended family is intrinsically fragile and unwieldy, which explains its rarity even in those societies where it is regarded as the norm. To be truly effective, a large extended family needs the managerial skills of strong leaders, usually both a male to direct its external relations with other families and a female to manage the internal affairs of the household. Such strong leaders are rarely available in each generation. A second weakness stems from the extended family's very ability to provide social services. Since it lends itself so easily to caring for its poor, infirm, and aged, it has no way of ridding itself of such persistent drains on its resources. Finally, the extended family usually increases in size at each generation, with the result that the only way it can stay together is by continuing to amass additional wealth or lands. Few extended families can survive generation after generation, without suffering some economic setback, owing perhaps to drought, to price changes on world commodity markets, to political changes in the society, or even to dissipation by the head of the family. Whenever an extended family suffers such a reversal, members break away and establish new families on their own. ♂♀

An experimental variant of the extended family is found today in communes that have been formed by young people who are attempting to turn away from the nuclear families in which they grew up. These variants do not consist of people related by blood or by marriage. Rather, they are an aggregation of independent nuclear families, together with some unmarried males and females, who own property in common and who have chosen to live together physically and economically. The life-style of these communes is also reminiscent of the extended families of pioneer North America, which provided a pool of co-operative labour for the many tasks required for economic survival. If these non-related extended families are to survive from generation to generation, they must answer a basic question with which the traditional extended families are also confronted. How can they ensure that they will not break up into several nuclear families? To date, no mechanism has appeared in the communes that would guarantee their survival from one generation to the next.

\*

Perhaps the strangest known family arrangement is one that exists in a few places in Africa: the marriage of two females. It takes place when a father who has only daughters calls one of them a 'male' and arranges for her to take a bride. The bride is then encouraged to have sexual relations with numerous biological males until she becomes pregnant. Her offspring are then recognized as the legitimate offspring of her female 'husband' and the line of descent does not die out. This kind of family tie occurs rarely in societies that stress to an exaggerated degree the importance of male heirs in continuing the father's line of descent. Aside from such isolated curiosities as the one just described, the possible family arrangements are fairly limited. We can visualize the possibilities as ranging from promiscuity at one extreme to celibacy at the other.

Total promiscuity is accepted in no society, since even the most permissive nevertheless have incest taboos and rules concerning the age or kin affiliations of potential marriage partners. The explanation for this, of course, is that no society could survive if it did not offer protection, care, and security for the young – and these aims are incompatible with unbridled sexual relations. Celibate marriages do occur in a few societies, although they are very rare for the obvious reason that such an arrangement would mean the eventual elimination of the society itself. In India, a devout Hindu male, married or unmarried, may take a vow of celibacy as a certain way of finding the deity or of arriving at sanctity. Mohandas Gandhi took such a vow at the age of thirty-six, when he had already been married for twenty-four years. He followed the various rules of Hindu celibacy, which include not looking at females, not sitting on the same mat with them, and not taking hot baths, which might cause sexual stimulation. Gandhi added to these prohibitions the complete elimination from the diet of milk, butter, or other animal products that might feed his animal passions. Despite his vow and his observance of the rules, Gandhi found that he had to struggle constantly to remain celibate – and he even 'tested' himself by sleeping unclothed with young females.

Between the poles of promiscuity and celibacy, remarkably few combinations of males and females within the family are possible, and all have been tried. These other possibilities are group marriage, polyandry (one female married to several males), polygyny (one male married to several females), and monogamy. Of these few possible forms of marriage, only two – polygyny and monogamy – are common. A closer look at the possibilities will demonstrate why that is so.

Social theorists in previous centuries often assumed that group marriage was prevalent when humans existed in a state of savagery.

As I have already mentioned, that is highly unlikely, both on theoretical grounds and also for the reason that group marriage is found in no society today, regardless of how 'savage' it might appear to be. Group marriage has been claimed for one society or another, but closer examination reveals either that it did not exist or that it was not the preferred form. Spouse-exchange among the Eskimos is not group marriage, since the union of a single male and a single female endures beyond the temporary partnership that encourages two males to exchange wives. The Toda of India have engaged in group marriage, but they did so in response to a temporary situation. The Toda once practised female infanticide, which of course led to a shortage of females, with resulting fraternal polyandry (several brothers sharing a single wife). When the British colonial government outlawed infanticide, the proportion of females increased suddenly. The Toda brothers adapted to the situation by adding wives to the household containing the one they already shared.

A moment's thought reveals why group marriage arises only in special situations and is not the norm in any society. For one thing, it offers no advantages over any other form of marriage. A society that encourages sexual variety for males would find polygyny superior to group marriage; a society that provides such variety for females could better do so by polyandry. Second, group marriage lacks the exclusive rights to services, both economic and sexual, that aggressive males have demanded from females in practically all societies. Finally, group marriage would cause a number of problems for any society that adopted it. How could incest taboos be enforced in group families with numerous offspring of unknown paternity? How would property and inheritances be apportioned? How could networks of kin be maintained?

Although no society has institutionalized group marriage, the idea persists and attempts are made from time to time to establish it. The most ambitious and long-lasting attempt even at its height numbered only 306 people. This was the Oneida Community in central New York State, established in 1848 by fifty-eight adults with their children. Their utopian venture was a self-sustaining commune, and possibly the most radical social experiment ever attempted in the United States. The Oneidans built their own living quarters, produced all of their own food, made their clothes and shoes, and provided an excellent education for their young. The members practised economic communism, holding all property jointly, with the aim of eliminating competition for material things. Their economic survival was assured when one of the members invented a steel trap that was vastly superior to all others on the market. By 1860 it had become the largest-selling trap in the United States and for seventy years it was the only one used by the Hudson's Bay Company. Later, the community began manufacturing the Oneida silverware that is still highly valued today. The community was notable as well for its accomplishments in architecture, in communal living, in a novel system of social control based on mutual criticism, and in economic planning. But it is best remembered for its experiment with group marriage.

A central belief of the Oneida Community was that romantic love produced selfishness, jealousy, and hypocrisy, thus making spiritual love impossible to attain. In its place, the members put forward the idea of 'free love' – a term they in fact coined – by which all adults were considered married to all adults of the opposite sex. Every male thus had sexual privileges with every female, although the rules of the community stated that permission first had to be requested through intermediaries. For about the first two decades after its founding, the members refrained from producing children. They used a method of birth control which they called *coitus reservatus* (that is, sexual intercourse up to but not including ejaculation by the male). The method obviously demanded extraordinary control, attainable only after long training. Younger males were required to develop their skills with older, experienced females who were past menopause and thus would not conceive when accidental ejaculation occurred. Similarly, the experienced males trained the young females. A byproduct of this arrangement was that it ensured a continual supply of sexual partners for the older members, both male and female, who otherwise would not have fared well in competition with younger members. *Coitus reservatus* obviously succeeded. During the first twenty years of the community's existence, only about thirty children were conceived by accident. Eventually the community decided that it must propagate a new generation. In 1869 scientific methods were applied to determine who would mate with whom, and the Oneida Community thus became the world's first large-scale experiment in eugenics. Between then and the break-up of the community ten years later, fifty-eight children were born, at least a dozen of them sired by John Humphrey Noyes, the minister from Putney, Vermont, who had founded the community.

The Oneida Community survived for only three decades. One naturally wonders why a social experiment that was also a phenomenal economic success was not more enduring. Some scholars have attributed its decline to the intrinsic weaknesses of group marriage in comparison to monogamy, but this would seem to be true only to a limited extent. Tension in the community did increase because of demands for a revision of the rules of group marriage. Young males often objected to being denied sexual relations with females of their own age; some of the young females felt that they were being sexually exploited by aged males; and some mothers were unhappy about being separated from their children. More important causes for the break-up, though, had nothing to do with any intrinsic weaknesses of group marriage. Members of the clergy in the United States attacked the 'free love' practised by the community, and in its virulence the pressure campaign was second only to that waged against the Mormons. Still more important is that John Humphrey Noyes retired as leader in 1877 without having adequately trained new leaders. And a contributing influence was the great financial success of the Oneida silverware. This business enterprise eventually assumed more importance than the social and religious doctrines that had led to the community's founding in the first place. In 1879 the community formally disbanded – and many of the members immediately entered into monogamous marriages. ♂♀

Whereas no society has institutionalized group marriage, a small number of societies are known to have practised polyandry: the Tibetans, the Marquesans of the South Pacific, and several local groups in India and Ceylon. A polyandrous marriage usually involves the union of a single female with several brothers, although the actual wedding ceremony unites the female with only the eldest of them. No brother can claim exclusive rights to such a wife, any more than one brother can claim exclusive rights to the common property of land, dwelling, and animals. All of the known instances of polyandry appear to be adaptations to very specific local conditions. Sometimes the economy demands that males travel a great deal, usually to engage in trade. The marriage of several males to a single wife ensures that at least one is at home to care for her and the offspring. Or a group of brothers who have inherited a small parcel of land may pool their resources in a polyandrous household. The cost of maintaining several wives is thus reduced, and so is the number of heirs who will compete for their small parcel of land after the brothers are dead.

Polyandry thus solves a number of the problems specific to group marriage. Inheritance, for example, poses no problem because land can be bequeathed intact to all male offspring, who will then enter into their own polyandrous marriage. Sexual jealousy is minimized because the husbands are usually brothers in economic partnership. Polyandry, though, offers only a single advantage over other forms of marriage: an increased ability to survive economically by pooling resources. Should their economic situation improve markedly, the brothers then begin to accumulate as many wives as they can afford – and some of them even leave the group to establish their own monogamous or polygynous families. ♂♀

Group marriage and polyandry are very rare, but the same thing cannot be said about the remaining two forms, polygyny and monogamy. A sampling of 565 societies made about two decades ago revealed that polygyny was practised in about 75 per cent of them. ♂♀ Not all the males in these societies do so, though; that would obviously be impossible because of the limited availability of females. Males may extol polygyny and desire many wives, but the fulfilment of that desire will be limited by the high cost of maintaining a large household. If two cannot live as cheaply as one, then obviously neither can three or four. Not only the several females must be supported, but also the many children resulting from the unions, along with the kin of several wives. Even though every male in a polygynous society might aspire to marry many wives, only the very wealthy can afford the practice. The Koran allows a Moslem male to take four wives, but a study in the Moslem city of Karachi, Pakistan, showed that less than 1 per cent of married males had more than one wife and none had the four that are permitted.

Claims have been made that polygyny offers a number of advantages absent from other forms of marriage. If the society has more females than males, then polygyny supposedly represents an excellent method of providing for the surplus. The possession of several wives is a visible symbol of male prestige, and one that is said to be less wasteful of resources than other ways of flaunting wealth and power. Further, the entire society supposedly benefits because polygyny allows superior males to contribute disproportionate numbers of offspring to the population. Not one of these supposed

advantages, though, has any basis in fact. First of all, very few polygynous societies have a significant excess of marriageable females.
Second, those males who do acquire additional wives for the sake of
their own prestige do so at the expense both of other males, who are
condemned to bachelorhood, and also of the exploited first wife,
whose situation is one plagued by jealousy, bickering, and competition. Finally, the males in the society who are physically most fit are
not the ones likely to have many wives; rather it is the old males
who have had time to accumulate the wealth necessary to support
them.

Of all forms of marriage, the most common and the most widespread is monogamy – even though, paradoxically, it is the preferred form for a mere quarter of the societies in the sample of 565.
Indeed, it is the only form of marriage that is to be found in every
society in the world. Humans obviously are monogamists, if only reluctantly so. In such monogamous societies as the United States,
where numerous divorces are followed by remarriage, the prevailing
form might more accurately be described as 'serial polygamy' – that
is, marriage to several spouses, but to only one of them at a time. The
important thing about monogamy, though, is not the number of
times people have been married but the fact that each is legally
bound to one person at a time. That so many societies are overwhelmingly monogamous, even though people in them often do not
regard this form of marriage as the ideal one, indicates that it must
provide benefits lacking in the others. One sociologist who specializes
in studies of the family has enumerated eight such benefits, of which
four seem paramount: relatively few members of society are excluded
from marriage, as they would have been by either polygyny or
polyandry; sexual jealousy on the part of several wives or several
husbands sharing a single spouse is avoided; inheritance, property
rights, and the treatment of kin present far fewer problems; and
children can establish close emotional ties with both parents. For
the pattern of life that humans have developed, monogamy clearly
provides more advantages than do other forms of marriage.♂♀

*

Every society promulgates rules about who can marry whom. Certain
kinds of marriage partners are preferred and rules are enforced
against unions of certain other kinds. Such prohibitions are often
referred to as 'incest taboos'. An examination of incest taboos in the

United States (as of 1969) revealed that every state had passed laws prohibiting certain kinds of marriage, although the prohibitions often differed from one state to another. Thirty of the states prohibit marriage between first cousins, but such marriages are permissible in Wisconsin if the female is older than fifty-five – that is, beyond child-bearing age. Even though marriage between first cousins is permitted in seventeen states, this kind accounts for only a fraction of I per cent of all marriages in the United States. Maryland is unusual in that it allows a male to marry either his great-great-grandmother or his great-great-granddaughter. A glance at societies around the world shows that they similarly vary a great deal in the degree of interbreeding that is allowed. In the province of Andra Pradesh on the eastern coast of India, as many as 25 per cent of all marriages are between uncles and nieces. In Japanese feudal families, about 20 per cent of marriages were between first cousins. All societies prohibit two kinds of marriage – father–daughter and mother–son – and often the prohibition is extended to the brothers of the father and the sisters of the mother. In addition, almost every society has prohibited brother–sister marriage.

Such incest rules represent a basic paradox in the way that humans find mates. Instead of simply marrying the females readily available in their households – sisters, daughters, aunts, and nieces – males force their related females to marry into other households, thereby imposing upon themselves the task of finding females to replace the ones they have married off. A second seemingly inexplicable thing about incest rules is that many societies further prohibit marriages between people who are socially linked but not genetically related. The Koran, for example, prohibits a man from marrying his foster mother, foster sisters, mother-in-law, stepdaughters, or sisters-in-law. Yet another paradox is that incest taboos do not make economic sense because they require a family's property to be divided among offspring in each generation. Recognizing this, the ruling and wealthy classes in a few societies – the Incas and the ancient Hawaiians and Egyptians – encouraged brother–sister marriage. One examination of the genealogies of chiefs and their male descendants in Bechuanaland revealed that 70 per cent had married close relatives, most often first cousins; but uncles had also married nieces, aunts had married nephews, and half-brothers had married half-sisters. Such marriages forge social links between branches of the ruling line and therefore are of obvious economic value, as is clear from a native proverb:

'Child of my father's youngest brother, marry me, so that the cattle may return to our kraal.' ♂♀

How can the seeming irrationality of incest taboos be explained? Considerable ink has been shed to bolster one explanation or another, but social scientists are far from agreeing about any of these. Some explanations can be dismissed easily, such as the assertion that humans possess an 'instinctive' horror of mating with blood relatives. The mere fact that a cultural behaviour is universal does not mean that it is an inherited instinct. Fire-making also is a cultural universal, but the ability to make a fire is not transmitted through the genes. Humans have replaced the instincts of lower animals with social inhibitors, and so adult humans are not under the control of any instincts whatever. Furthermore, if there were an instinct against incest, could not societies simply rely upon natural inclination instead of placing taboos upon it? Actually this would not be a valid objection, since avoidance of any behaviour is never complete. Relatively few murders are committed each year in North America and Europe, yet all Western nations enforce severe penalties against murder. Similarly, most people do not commit incest, but nevertheless societies institute sanctions in an effort to keep the minority in line.

The psychoanalytic explanation for the incest taboo attempts to compensate for the weaknesses of the one based on instinct. According to Freud, parents discourage any sexual interest in their own persons on the part of their children. A son who is sexually attracted to his mother, or a daughter who is attracted to her father, learns that these feelings must be repressed because the parent of the opposite sex might inflict punishment. According to the explanation, these feelings persist in the unconscious, where, through being repressed, they often produce exactly the opposite behaviour – hence an exaggerated horror of incest when actually that is what is desired. The psychoanalytic explanation does not explain, though, why incest prohibitions are extended far beyond the immediate family to include persons only distantly related or not related at all.

Various biological explanations have also been proposed, the most widely accepted being that inbreeding produces harmful effects in the offspring. These harmful effects are supposedly observed by the members of society, who then try to prevent them from occurring again by a prohibition of incest. This explanation appears to be supported by the existence of large numbers of harmful recessive genes in modern populations. If two close relatives were to marry, then the chances would be very high that their offspring would get a double dose of certain recessive genes. One study in the United States of father–daughter and brother–sister incest showed that only seven of the eighteen resulting offspring were normal and thus deemed fit for adoption. The remaining infants either died or showed severe birth defects. ♂♀

Some social scientists, who doubt that inbreeding is the explanation, point out that thirteen generations of incest by the Ptolemaic dynasty of Egypt produced the charms of a Cleopatra. The amount of brother–sister incest in the ruling families of ancient Egypt, though, has been greatly exaggerated. The second Ptolemy had indeed married his sister, but the couple produced no living offspring. Since both partners had been fertile in previous marriages, this failure to reproduce might have been due to the harmful effects of inbreeding. The first product of a brother–sister union was the fifth Ptolemy to hold the throne. Such marriages occurred again in the sixth and seventh generations, and these gave rise to several offspring who survived to adulthood without apparent abnormalities. These were the only examples of incest in Cleopatra's ancestry. She herself was married at different times to her two younger brothers. Both unions were childless and probably were not consummated, since the husbands were still children at the time of the weddings and the spouses did not live together during almost all of their married lives. Thus it is not generally true that Egyptian dynasties reproduced by brother–sister incest. And when they did, the effects were not free from the risk of infertility. ♂♀

The fact is clear that inbreeding in modern populations gives rise to a much higher transmission of undesirable genetic traits. Probably the most detailed study of the effects of inbreeding has been made in Japan, where first-cousin marriage is encouraged. Not only did the researchers find a higher frequency of infant death and malformations, but they also discovered that children born of related parents suffered from numerous handicaps. These included smaller stature and lower weight, a delay in the age at which children walked, a weaker hand grip, and lower performance in verbal tests and in virtually every subject taught in school. ♂♀ Inbreeding will not, of course, have deleterious effects if the related parents do not carry harmful recessive genes. Charles Darwin's ancestors and descendants provide a striking example. His ancestry included a number of first-cousin marriages. His wife, Emma Wedgwood, was also his first cousin and she similarly was descended from a number of first-cousin marriages. Considering this long tradition of inbreeding in two lines, remarkably few serious genetic defects show up, although some minor ones would appear to.

Too many objections stand in the way of accepting the harmful effects of inbreeding as the origin of the prohibition against incest. Simpler societies, both present-day and of antiquity, most probably did not carry a heavy load of lethal recessive alleles. Once offspring with genetic defects have been produced in a small band, the recessive alleles are likely to be weeded out. Suppose, for example, that some members of a small band carry a harmful recessive allele but that the band prohibits interbreeding. Thus no offspring is likely to receive a double dose, and the recessive genes will therefore remain in the population. On the other hand, if inbreeding did take place, numerous offspring would inherit one recessive allele from each parent and thus receive a double dose. The particular disease caused by the recessive gene would then appear – and natural selection could act against these alleles, eventually eliminating them from the population. Furthermore, in simple societies offspring born with obvious defects are usually killed at birth. Only a few generations of such selective infanticide would eliminate almost all the harmful recessive genes from the small population.

A second objection to inbreeding as an explanation of the incest taboo is that it fails to account for why many societies encourage or prohibit marriage with certain kinds of cousins. The North American kinship system does not distinguish between the different kinds of first cousins – known technically as 'parallel' and 'cross' cousins – although the distinction is a major one in much of the world. The offspring of siblings of the same sex are parallel cousins; the children of your mother's sister, for example, are your parallel cousins. Offspring of siblings of the opposite sex are cross cousins, such as the children of your mother's brother. Various societies place great importance upon marriage with one or the other of these kind of cousins – but genetically the two kinds represent the same degree of inbreeding.

Despite such objections, the biological explanation could conceivably account for the universality of incest taboos. Inbreeding would have been particularly damaging when the early hominids lived in small bands. These bands could not have withstood the high rate of death and disability resulting from double doses of harmful mutations. Those groups that happened to have cultural restrictions against inbreeding would have been favoured by natural selection over those that did not enforce the taboo. Eventually the bands without incest taboos would either have died out or have become so reduced in numbers that they could not compete with those that did have them.

Societal explanations have also been offered. At an obvious level, incest produces confusion about a person's role in the family and status in society. A male child resulting from the union of a father and a daughter would thus be the half-brother of his mother, the son of his half-sister, and a grandson of his father. This objection is really not a valid one because it confuses role with the biology of reproduction. If a father were to inseminate his daughter and she had a son, then the infant would simply be her offspring. Whether the biological father was her own father, the iceman, or an anonymous donor from a sperm bank would be beside the point. And if the biological father were to marry her as well as impregnate her, then she would simply exchange the role of daughter for that of wife. A situation somewhat like this actually occurs in Tibet and in several other societies, where a man may enter into a polygynous marriage with a mother and her daughter. The younger of the two females is thus the stepdaughter of the male and at the same time his wife, two roles which she has little difficulty in filling.

Another societal explanation emphasizes the importance of the incest taboo in promoting co-operation between family groups through the process known as 'exogamy' (that is, marrying outside the group). The founder of modern anthropology, Edward B. Tylor, in 1881 described the importance of marrying-out:

Exogamy, enabling a growing tribe to keep itself compact by constant unions between its spreading clans, enables it to overmatch any number of small intermarrying groups, isolated and helpless. Again and again in the world's history, savage tribes must have had plainly before their minds the simple practical alternative between marrying-out and being killed-out.

Tylor followed this statement with a quotation from Genesis (34:16): 'Then will we give our daughters unto you, and we will take your daughters to us, and we will dwell with you, and we will become one people.' ♂♀

Too many objections would appear to stand in the way of this

explanation. For one thing, intermarriage does not ensure the pre-
servation of an alliance with another group. After all, Britain and
Germany fought two world wars despite intermarriage between their
royal houses – and the passage from Genesis quoted by Tylor actually
refers to an alliance that was broken almost immediately. Furthermore, alliances can be forged with outside groups in the absence of
intermarriage. As a matter of fact, many societies co-operate over
long periods of time not because of intermarriage but because it is in
their mutual interest to do so for the sake of trade, access to each
other's resources, or military assistance. A more formidable objection, though, is that this explanation confuses exogamy with incest. Exogamy prohibits certain kinds of marriage in the interest of
forcing society's members to marry-out. But the very people prohibited as marriage partners in some societies are acceptable sexual
partners.

In fact, it is not the incest taboo that is universal; rather it is the
rules of exogamy. Many societies have severe penalties against
marrying a close relative (thus breaking the rules of exogamy), but
these same societies may be indifferent to sexual relations with close
relatives (thus breaking the rules against incest). Among the Belcher
Island Eskimos of Canada, for example, the only marriage rule that
exists is one barring marriage between members of the same nuclear
family. Sexual relationships are nevertheless known to occur fairly
often between fathers and daughters and between siblings and half-
siblings, but the members of the community choose to ignore them.
Such unions usually result from situations in which a female who fills
the role of female household head eventually comes to fill the role of
sexual partner of the male household head as well, even though she is
his daughter or sister. For example, an unmarried daughter might
become head of the domestic unit when her mother dies, in which
case she would also fill the sexual role of consort to her father. ♂♀ Nor
is incest absent in modern societies. In the wealthiest county in
California, and also one whose population is the best educated, at
least one person in every 1000 – each year – is reported to have been
involved in father–daughter incest.

An explanation for the origins of the incest taboo that separates
incest from exogamy, and that deals with the known facts, is based on
the realities of social life among the early hominids. Fossils show that
most hominids died young, certainly by age forty. As mentioned in
Chapter 2, the age of the onset of menstruation has been dropping

steadily. Among the early hominids, it very likely occurred later than at present, say by the age of sixteen. Furthermore, as the discussion in Chapter 6 of lactation among the Bushmen as an inhibition to pregnancy indicates, offspring may have been born only every four years. To all these limitations on population increase, add the high infant mortality, perhaps 40 per cent, and the custom of female infanticide. So, with less than twenty-five years of potential fertility, a wide spacing between offspring, and high mortality at birth and during the childhood years, a female hominid in her lifetime probably produced no more than an average of two or three surviving offspring.

The possibilities for incest among the early hominids would therefore have been virtually non-existent. By the time a boy reached puberty, his mother would be aged or dead, and the same thing would have been true for daughters and fathers. Because of the small numbers of hominids and the need of a male hunter to form a bond with a female gatherer, females would have been spoken for as soon as they reached puberty. Opportunities for siblings to mate must therefore have been severely limited. A boy's elder sister would no doubt have been married by the time he reached puberty, just as he himself would have been married by the time his younger sister reached puberty. One additional bar to brother–sister incest must have been the small size of hominid families, thus increasing the chances that all the offspring in a family belonged to one sex. In short, the early hominids would have found it extremely difficult to commit incest, even if they had wanted to. Most of them must have married-out, not because of the harmful genetic effects of inbreeding or the social disruption that might be caused by incest, but simply because they had no other choice if they were to mate at all.

The population structure of the early hominid bands could thus account for the origins of incest avoidance and explain the consequences as well. Incest avoidance bestowed obvious adaptational advantages, some of which have already been mentioned: prevention of harmful inbreeding, clarification of social roles, and the formation of alliances. (Note that these advantages are offered as consequences of incest avoidance, not as the causes of it, as they were in those explanations previously discussed.) Because humans since the early hominids have married-out, their social structures must have incorporated outbreeding from the beginning. In other words, the forms of the family that developed over a period of several million years, the rules of kinship, and the ways of reckoning descent – all of these would have been predicated on the assumption that immediate relatives do not interbreed. Only in the past few thousand years, and especially the past few centuries, has the structure of the human population changed markedly. Instead of hunter–gatherers who produced few surviving offspring, now agriculturists and peasants produced many, and these were closely spaced. This change was due to the shorter period of lactation because of the availability of milk and mush, earlier puberty, and a longer reproductive span for most people. It thus became much easier to commit incest, since potential partners were available inside the family, as they had not been when hominid parents died young and produced few surviving offspring. Most people, though, did not commit incest – simply because the societies into which they were born had already been erected on the premise that it is not done. The taboos that were built into the hominid pattern of life by necessity would eventually have served to prevent incest when the opportunity did become available. ♂♀

*

Social thinkers have always, it seems, foreseen the decline of the family. Plato feared that the Hellenic world might collapse because of a weakened family system. The early sociologist Auguste Comte believed that the anarchy stemming from the French Revolution had crept into the family and was insidiously destroying it. To survive, Comte declared, the family had to maintain its monogamous and patriarchal structure. John B. Watson, the major exponent in the United States of behavioural psychology, predicted in 1927 that by 1977 marriage would no longer exist in the United States, owing primarily to the automobile and the life-style it encouraged. The year 1977 has come and gone, the family survives – and other social thinkers today continue to express fears for the family half a century hence.

Such dire predictions notwithstanding, a reading of the sociological literature would lead any fair-minded person to conclude that although the family is changing in major ways, it is also likely to endure. The family is woven into the social fabric and it could hardly become extinct without unravelling nearly everything of which it is a part. Further supporting the belief that the family will endure is its demonstrated ability to adapt to unique conditions in a diversity of cultures. Nevertheless, prophets continue to decry the breakdown in the traditional family and to point to danger signs. They particularly concentrate upon the dramatic acceleration in divorce in every Western nation. Divorce, though, is not putting an end to marriage; as has been noted, most people who obtain divorces remarry. The aspect of marriage that is ending is the idea of strict monogamy, that a person has to stay with a single partner for a lifetime. The decline of the extended family in both Western and developing nations is similarly viewed with foreboding, but often overlooked is the compensatory strengthening of the nuclear family. Pessimists point out that the family is rapidly losing its traditional functions, particularly the economic and educational ones – but they often fail to recognize that at the same time it is expanding its psychological functions (companionship, intimacy, and emotional support).

Many of those who declare that the family has no future are disturbed by the alternatives to traditional family patterns that they see arising: trial marriage, cohabitation without legal union, group marriage, and communes. These alternatives have been widely publicized, but they apparently are not very prevalent. Two sociologists recently estimated that no more than 8 per cent of the population of the United States live in non-traditional family arrangements. ♂♀ Nor are these alternative arrangements as threatening to the traditional family as is sometimes believed. Not only do the rural communes that have been founded by young people in the United States, for example, usually pattern themselves on the traditional family, but their members indeed often refer to themselves as 'the family'. The Israeli kibbutzim suggest that the family structure is not easily changed or eradicated. One aim of these co-operatives was to liberate females from their bondage to the family. In the kibbutzim today, though, most females remain child-centred during their reproductive years and fill the traditional roles of housewives and mothers – although before and after these years they continue to work more or less equally with males. ♂♀

Instead of debating whether the family will survive, a different question should be asked: Will the family survive in its present form? The answer, of course, is No – simply because the long history of the hominids has shown that no adaptation, no institution, no social invention has remained unchanged for very long. Change represents one of the major components of the human equation.

# 19

# The Human Ages

The first chapter of this book, in discussing feral children, emphasized a point that has been a main theme throughout: that humans must learn to be human. The infant is born with the capacity to develop in almost infinite human ways, but this development is never random. Through constant interaction with parents, peers, and other members of society, the developing child acquires a pattern of behaviour that mirrors the world it inhabits. The child learns who and what it is through interaction with others – an interaction that has been described as 'the buzz of implication'. The developing child, often without realizing it, assimilates the unstated values of the society. A boy who is reprimanded by his father for punching another boy might also sense his father's disguised approval of such 'masculine' behaviour. A lower-class black child who senses that an upper-class white child is being given more attention by the teacher is unlikely to place much credence in that teacher's statements about social equality. So completely does an individual assimilate the organized patterns of the particular society, that a sailor cast upon a deserted island does not revert to unsocial behaviour. Even though no other human being is present, the sailor continues to bathe and to dispose of bodily wastes. Nor is the sailor likely to abandon the morality, fears, hopes, and channels of thought that have been part of the personality since infancy.

'Socialization' is the process whereby a child becomes a full member of the society and the culture into which it is born. Socialization is also a process whereby an individual is guided into feeling inclined to do what that society regards as having to be done. In fact, one way to assess the intrinsic strength of a society and to predict whether it will prosper is to examine the concern that one generation shows for the succeeding generation. A society that offers its children and youths opportunities to develop their capacities to the fullest, that instills the knowledge that will help in understanding the world and the wisdom that will help in dealing with changes is a strong society. Contrary to what many people believe, though, to become socialized is not the same thing as to become 'civilized'. After all, the Nazis who operated the death camps and torture chambers were outstanding products of the socialization process that prevailed in Germany during their time. Children receive from the family their earliest instruction in the rules that prevail in the society. Through the family, they are subtly implanted with modes of thinking and of acting that will remain with them long after they have become adults. Because these complex and delicate tasks have been entrusted to the family, societies will permit threats to their many institutions, but not to the family itself.

A basic paradox about society is this: everything in society depends upon the actions of individuals, yet individuals act only because they have acquired the ability to do so as members of society. And, to compound the paradox, the society that comes into existence because of the actions of individuals in it is the very source of the skills, motives, and other capacities those individuals possess. Society and culture already exist before the individual is born, but they are also incorporated within the individual. In other words, social life makes people what they are, yet the continuity of social life depends upon human activities. Only from a society already in existence, composed of people interacting with one another, can the new members born into the society acquire the symbols and concepts of self that equip them to be members of society.

It would be misleading, though, to regard socialization as simply a process of indoctrination. Socialization does not turn out individuals who are indistinguishable from one another, as though they had emerged from a mould. Nor does the personality that results from socialization represent merely the overlay of culture upon a biological core. Rather, the individual personality emerges as a complex interaction between society and inherited biology. Society can shape a person's inherited temperament, but it cannot transform that temperament into a complete reversal of its own nature. Socialization, in fact, helps to explain the differences as well as the similarities among the members of a society. An individual emerges with a distinctive way of behaving despite the pressures of socialization because basic physical and mental traits are influenced by a wide range of socializing agents: family, peers, school, religious and occupational groups, the mass media, and various other formal and informal teachers. All individuals could not possibly absorb all of the experiences in precisely the same way. The specific events in an individual's life and the subtle interactions that take place during the various stages of the socialization process result in a virtually unlimited number of at least slightly different personalities.

Most of an individual's development as a social being occurs during the childhood years within the family. At the same time, these are the years of major physical and mental development. Contrary to what many people believe, physical growth does not proceed in fits and starts as children pop up one year and then scarcely grow the next. Human growth is a steady process, which increases in velocity during the early teens, with the start of adolescence. The average boy is slightly taller than the average girl until the girl's spurt of adolescent growth begins, between the ages of eleven and thirteen. She becomes not only taller but also heavier, equally as strong, and sexually a good deal more mature. Only when the boy's adolescent spurt begins, about two years later than a girl's, does he finally become the larger and more muscular of the two. The reproductive system of both boys and girls matures at about the same time as the adolescent spurt of growth. The penis begins to enlarge at some time between the eleventh and the fifteenth years, and this growth is completed within two years after it begins. In both sexes, the appearance of pubic hair is the earliest sign of the onset of sexual maturity. The first menstruation is a late event in female puberty and almost always comes after the peak of the growth spurt. ♂♀

The age of the onset of menstruation (known as 'menarche') has decreased to little more than twelve years in well-fed modern populations, whereas in populations that are inadequately fed it may take more than eighteen years for girls to build up the necessary reserve of fat for menstruation to begin – which explains why overweight girls begin to menstruate earlier than thin ones. The trend towards early menarche, though, seems to have halted, at least among middle-class United States females. A study of girls in a Boston suburb showed that the average age of first menstruation remains the same, 12.8 years, as it was for their mothers. Previous studies had indicated that in each decade girls experienced their first menstrual period about four months earlier than those in the preceding decade – but apparently that trend has come to a halt, presumably because the effects of an improved diet have now about reached their maximum. (The age of 12.8 years for first menstruation is merely an average, and should present no cause for alarm about early or late onset. The girls in the study showed an enormous variability, ranging from 9.1 to 17.7 years, usually depending upon whether they were stout or thin.) ♂♀

In a satisfactory environment that includes adequate nutrition and freedom from disease and stress, physical growth proceeds in an orderly manner. The same thing cannot be said for psychological growth, which is affected by numerous variables: the presence or absence of the mother, the role of the father, society's attitudes about child-rearing, the influence of peers, and the age at which separation from the mother occurs, among other things. In all societies, the role of the mother, either the biological or the sociological one, is central. Radical experimentation with human mothers and their infants is obviously out of the question, so psychologists have studied the non-human primates. Infant monkeys grasp the mother's fur in a reflex action, then continue to hold on until they locate a nipple. Psychologists several decades ago became intrigued by the question of whether the fur or the milk was more important to the infant monkey – and experiments to answer this question have provided much information about mother–infant relations.

The psychologists constructed two pseudomothers with which infant monkeys were placed from the moment of birth. One, made from bare wire and equipped with bottles from which the infants could suck milk, emphasized the importance of food. The other, made from soft terry cloth, offered no milk but did provide a furry, maternal warmth. In other words, the satisfaction of hunger was separated from the physical comfort provided by the mother's presence. The infants constantly remained clasped to the soft mother – unless they were hungry, at which time they went to the milk-mother. When they were scared or felt unwell, they would stay with the soft mother even though they were hungry. Infant monkeys obviously cannot live without food, but neither can they do without something soft that touches their skin and gives them a feeling of protection and security.

When these experimental monkeys matured, they revealed that even fur and food are not enough. They exhibited no sexual behaviour. When female monkeys who had been raised with pseudomothers were placed with males who had had a normal infancy, the males wanted to copulate – but the females refused, running away, threatening, and striking at the males. Eventually, sexually experienced males – through persistence, skill, and sheer physical power – managed to impregnate four of these females. The females bore living young, but they did not want to care for them. The infants grasped their mothers, only to be pushed away and given no maternal affection. In fact, the mothers treated their own offspring as they would any unknown animal that intruded into their cage, hitting it and stepping on it.

Obviously, the absence of a real mother had deprived these females of something vital to their development. One thing certainly was physical interaction between mother and child. Another was that real mothers encourage their infants to play with other young monkeys. Subsequent experiments have shown that the effects of maternal deprivation on young monkeys can in part be obliterated by offering the infants even one hour a day of contact with monkeys their own age. Visual contact alone, though, is not sufficient. The young need the opportunity to touch, groom, and play if they are to grow up as adults capable of mating and of caring for their own offspring. These experiments demonstrated clearly that social isolation, both from mother and from peers, produces irreversible effects that can prevent the normal development of many essential behaviours. ♂♀

An intriguing thing about these experiments was the absence of what humans call 'mother love' in the treatment the deprived females gave to their infants. Most North Americans and Europeans nowadays assume that mothers 'naturally' love their infants, and that mother love is rooted in our primate heritage. Experiments with nonhuman primates cast doubts on this, suggesting that mother love is in part a socially learned behaviour. And in recent years, some social historians have shown that previous to modernization, European mothers usually viewed with indifference the survival, development, and happiness of their young children.

Such a statement must inevitably be greeted with incredulity by modern parents. Recent sociological and historical research, though, points not only to a lack of maternal sentiment on the part of mothers but also to a coldheartedness that subordinated infant welfare to the needs of daily living. This heartlessness was not so much a matter of deliberate cruelty towards infants, although that was certainly common enough, as of unfeeling neglect. Several hundred years ago, doctors often complained that parents allowed infants to stew in their excrement for half a day, left them unattended in front of the hearth until their garments caught fire, and placed them unguarded in the barnyard where they were eaten by hogs. Little more than a century and a half ago, an observer at Montpellier, France, stated that filth and lack of care were responsible for more infant deaths than epidemic diseases. Such observations were made repeatedly in other European countries and in other centuries.

Mothers displayed little of the affection and concern for helping their infants develop as individuals that characterize the modern mother (and which the experiments with monkeys just mentioned have shown to be so essential to infant development). One doctor in the previous century noted the behaviour of mothers in the town of Laval, France: '[The mothers] don't sing; they don't talk to the infant; they don't try to awaken its senses; they make no effort to develop the child's sensations through merriment or through the little coquetries of maternal tenderness.' ♂♀ Such behaviour was not untypical. French mothers often referred to their babies as *les créatures*, did not know their offsprings' ages, and even forgot the number of children they had. In England, one patron of a hospital for foundlings complained that mothers left their infants 'lying in the gutters and rotting on the dung heaps of London'. Legitimate infants as well as illegitimate ones were deposited at the doors of charitable institutions – which, given the dismal conditions prevailing there, was tantamount to infanticide. About 15 per cent of all foundlings deposited at the Paris General Hospital in 1760 were legitimate, and the proportion still had not lessened a century later. Desperate poverty, of course, accounted for much of the abandonment – but so did indifference.

Such neglect was not an aberration of maternal behaviour in the previous few centuries. Rather, it was a condition that had long prevailed in Europe, despite our romantic notions to the contrary. During the Middle Ages, the world of childhood within the family did not exist. This was true for all classes, and for the lower classes it was true until well into the nineteenth century. As soon as children demonstrated that they could get along without their mothers, usually by about the age of six, they went directly into the adult working community. The European family of centuries past served to transmit life, property, and surnames, but it did not play a very great role in caring for the child – in striking contrast to the modern family's awareness of the importance of that function. Nowadays, the sciences of paediatrics and psychology devote themselves to the problems of childhood, and their findings are transmitted to families by mass communications. As a result, people in modern societies are deeply concerned with the physical, moral, and sexual problems of childhood – a concern that did not exist at all in the Middle Ages and for centuries thereafter. ♂♀

A remarkable example of the failure of mother love was the common practice of European mothers of sending their infants long distances to be cared for by mercenary wet nurses. This custom of boarding out legitimate infants should not be confused with abandonment of illegitimates nor with bringing a wet nurse into the home to feed the infant under the supervision of the mother. Instead, immediately after baptism, the infant was sent to a peasant cottage where, if it survived the long journey, it would spend the next two years. In France, mercenary wet-nursing became a highly organized industry. Unmarried females intentionally became pregnant so that they would have milk and thus be able to work as wet nurses. Peasant females sent their own newborns to inexpensive wet nurses so they could take in better-paying nurslings from the cities. The poverty that motivated mothers to become wet nurses certainly did not foster an environment that was hospitable to good mothering, or even to physical survival itself. By all contemporary accounts, the conditions of sanitation and care were appalling. The mortality of foundlings sent to the rural wet nurses around Rouen, France, in the eighteenth century was an astounding 90 per cent. Even more astounding is the fact that the mothers knew this was a certain sentence of death for their infants.

How can we, living in a century in which a mother is assumed to feel an inborn surge of love for her infant, account for such indifference? The explanation usually offered is based on the high infant mortality that prevailed in past centuries. A mother would be psychologically foolish, this argument states, to invest her affection in an infant who had one chance in four of dying by the age of two. Even if the infant survived the first few years of life, there would be one chance out of four that it would die as a juvenile. Because of the enormous odds against a child's surviving to maturity, mothers supposedly withdrew emotionally from their infants in order to better deal with the heartbreaking loss if it occurred. Such an explanation appears to be self-evident, yet it contains a basic flaw. The truth is that the absence of maternal care was largely responsible for the high infant mortality in the first place. Mortality would have been much lower had mothers breast-fed their infants at home, provided sanitary conditions, and given comfort and security. All these things were beginning to happen in the nineteenth century and the result was a sharply reduced rate of infant mortality – long before modern medicine had much of an effect. Only when cultural attitudes towards children changed with modernization, and mothers started to care about the welfare of their infants, did the slaughter of the innocents gradually end.

Significantly enough, the maternal tenderness known so well today began early in the previous century among the factory workers who were the vanguard of modernization. During the centuries when mercenary wet-nursing was widely practised, the factory workers were the only ones who never participated on a large scale. Infants of factory mothers were almost never boarded out for longer than the working hours of each day. When an enlightened mill owner in the last century offered maternity leave at full pay, working mothers rushed to take advantage of it, thereby reducing infant mortality by one-fourth. The factory workers often suffered a poverty as dire as that of others belonging to the European lower classes, and they laboured at least as long in order to survive. Nevertheless, they never succumbed to the temptation of allowing their infants to die needlessly, presumably because their cultural attitudes were already being moulded by the new values and beliefs that accompanied modernization.

\*

Important events in the human life-cycle – birth, maturity, marriage, death – are observed by all societies in special ways that call attention to them as life crises. These rituals have two things in common. They mark the transition from one kind of life to another; and they are stressful situations in which new adjustments to other individuals must be made. Even those individuals who display no visible reaction whatever to the stress of interacting with others, and indeed may feel none, cannot escape being influenced by the attainment of adulthood, by marriage, or by bereavement – simply because it becomes necessary for them to adjust to new relationships. The death of someone in the immediate family removes with finality an interacting individual, and usually a substitute must be found with whom there will be a new relationship to approximate the old. If the death is that of one aged parent, then the relationship to the remaining parent can never be quite the same. The birth of a child is similarly an occasion of stress. The addition of an infant changes the inter-actions that already exist between parents. If it is the first child, the mother must significantly reduce her attentions to her husband. If the family already includes other children, their relations with each other, with the new infant, and with their parents will change markedly.

An attempt was made in 1908 by Arnold van Gennep to classify these life crises, which he labelled 'rites of passage' and defined as 'rites which accompany every change of place, state, social position and age'. He observed that the passage from one state to another is marked by three phases: separation, transition, and incorporation. During the first phase, interactions are reduced. At the time of death, the participants are of course literally separated; during an illness, the separation from other family members is partial; when an initia-tion takes place, the separation is only temporary. The second stage – the transitional (or 'liminal', a word derived from the Latin for 'threshold') – is ambiguous because a phase is being traversed that does not entail the interactions of the previous state or of the coming one. Initiation ceremonies in simple societies may include a transi-tional phase lasting for several years and involving numerous rituals, such as ordeals, physical mutilation, and disclosure of the secrets of the tribe. The transitional phase of mourning also is drawn out and involves numerous rites, among them wearing distinctive dress, repetition of stock phrases and prayers, emotional and physical self-punishment, and the acting out of grief in the presence of others. Finally, during the third phase, incorporation, the passage is con-cluded and the individual has arrived at a new state, with all of its rights and obligations. The resumption of normal activities is usually symbolized by a specific way of participating in the society, whether it be taking communion, setting up housekeeping, or going to war.

Of all rites of passage, the most complex are usually those asso-ciated with initiation (erroneously referred to as 'puberty rites' be-cause they often occur around the time of sexual maturity). These emphasize the transitional nature of the passage because the liminal phase is very much drawn out. They also emphasize the ambiguous status of the initiate, who is between two phases of life. The initiate is conceptually dead, and may indeed be treated the way a corpse is usually treated in the same society. The initiate may be covered with earth, forced to lie motionless in the position of burial, or made to live for a while in the company of masked monsters who represent the spirits of the dead. Often initiates' names are taken from them. Although part of the initiate is dying, a new part is being born – which accounts for many of the ambiguous symbols employed during this liminal phase. These include huts and tunnels (symbolic of both tombs and wombs), the moon (which waxes and wanes), the snake (which appears to die when it sheds its old skin, only to re-emerge in a new one), the bear (which apparently dies when it hibernates in the fall, yet reawakens in the spring), and nakedness (the mark both of a corpse prepared for burial and of a newborn infant).

An important fact about the liminal passage is that the journey is a social rather than a solitary one. The initiation is undertaken with comrades among whom bonds are forged that transcend any previous distinctions of status, age, or kinship. In many African and Australian societies that practise adolescent circumcision, the initiates are secluded together in a hut, and food brought them by their mothers is shared equally. No special treatment is afforded the son of a chief or a headman. Friendship between initiates is encouraged, and they are considered to be linked by special ties which persist long after the rites have been concluded.

Rites of passage are often thought to be merely some primitive ritual which modern societies have outgrown. That is not so; indeed, such rites appear again and again in some of the most obvious ceremonies and rituals of modern societies. Witness, as just a few examples, baptism and circumcision at birth; confirmation and Bar Mitzvah at puberty; the numerous ceremonies and rituals connected with marriage, including the bachelor's party, the bride's shower, and the wedding itself; initiation into a fraternal organization or club; and the mortuary rites that mark the final passage.

Even the training of a United States paratrooper incorporates aspects of the initiation rite. The training is officially a non-religious affair, but it is accompanied throughout by numerous rituals and superstitious practices. In one training unit, for example, the jump-master draws a line on the ground at the entrance to the plane. Each prospective jumper then steps on the line before entering the plane – a ritual that is supposed to ensure a safe landing. The trainees also carry numerous charms which are said to possess magical powers, such as a pair of socks worn on a previous successful jump. The initiate learns the secret gestures, songs, prayers, and jokes of this elite brotherhood of soldiers. As in other initiation rites, the primary emphasis is upon the transitional or liminal phase. The trainee makes five practice jumps, each of which marks a step towards final acceptance in the society of paratroopers. The successful completion of the last jump is marked by a reversal of roles. The sergeant relaxes military discipline by shaking the trainee's hand, inviting the use of first names, and even rolling the trainee's parachute for him. The liminal period ends in a ceremonial climax, a symbolic birth as a new man. A party is held, at which enormous amounts of alcohol must be quaffed in a single gulp during the time required for a parachute to open.

The final phase of incorporation takes place on the day after the last jump. It consists of an elaborate military ritual to mark the end of rigorous training and the final acceptance of the initiate. Although the military unit of organization is the platoon, on this one day the men assemble in alphabetical order, thereby effectively erasing platoon distinctions and uniting all the successful initiates into a single paratrooper brotherhood. The post chaplain reads from the Bible, thus giving religious sanction to the initiates' accomplishment. The division commandant pins a pair of metal wings to each man's chest, a symbol of his emergence as a new person. This altered status is dramatized when the superior officers go against military protocol and salute the new paratroopers. The rite of passage is now complete. The initiates have been wholly separated from their past lives and are now reborn into a new brotherhood. ♂♀

Statements are sometimes made that adults mishandle the transition from adolescence to adulthood, and that the result is the problem of the 'generation gap'. Modern adolescents and their parents do appear to differ in regard to life-style, politics, religion, sexual behaviour, and almost everything else. These differences, though, may not be due so much to a gap between generations as to an 'information gap' – the varying amounts of information available to young people and to their elders. Today's young people have been exposed to vastly more information than have their parents, just as these parents were exposed to more information than the generation preceding them. About two-thirds of today's college students, for example, come from families in which neither parent went to college. Numerous studies have shown that college-educated people think and act differently from the non-college-trained. In other words, as much of an information gap exists between college-educated and non-college-educated in the same generation as exists between parent and child. Furthermore, the gap between generations is much less than the publicity about it would indicate. Surveys of the 'youth culture' in the United States in the late 1960s revealed that a mere 2 per cent of students were engaged in protests concerned with major issues.♂♀

The true generational problem is the marked increase in the duration of adolescence, which in modern societies now usually covers a span of years longer than childhood. Adolescence used to be a brief interlude between puberty and adulthood, during which the status, rights, and obligations of the mature member of society were gradually assumed. In the previous century, adolescence usually ended when the first apprenticeship was concluded; a few generations ago, it was extended to the time of graduation from high school; a generation ago, it usually concluded with college graduation. Nowadays it often continues until the late twenties, through graduate or professional school, as a consequence of the increasing length of time necessary to accumulate information in a technological society. In other words, an increasing proportion of the population remains socially adolescent, in the sense of maintaining dependent relations with parents, until the late twenties – in a time when superior nutrition and health care are making for earlier physical and sexual maturity.

\*

All societies have ways of initiating the next generation into their particular systems of value. They do it by extolling culture heroes and mythical beings, paying reverence to distinguished ancestors, telling stories, teaching songs, and setting up symbolic displays such as totems. Britain, for example, has its stories of Robert Bruce and the spider and of Dick Whittington and his cat. The United States perpetuates tales of George Washington and the cherry tree, of Johnny Appleseed and Casey Jones, among others. A major way in which United States parents communicate the value system of their society to growing children is through the fiction of Santa Claus. Like much else in the culture of the United States, Santa Claus has European antecedents, but naturalization has turned him into something quite different from those forebears. The original Santa Claus was the fourth-century bishop Nicholas, whom Dutch merchants and sailors of Amsterdam made the patron saint of their city. ('Santa Claus' is an approximation of the Dutch *Sinterklaus*, which is a variation of *Sint Nikolaas*.) Almost everything about Santa Claus is a creation of the United States culture during a fifty-year period in the nineteenth century. Santa Claus was first mentioned in the 1812 edition of Washington Irving's popular *A History of New York . . . by Diedrich Knickerbocker*. Clement Moore's 'An Account of a Visit from St Nicholas' (known also as ''Twas the Night Before Christmas') appeared in book form in 1837 and became increasingly popular in succeeding decades. Finally, a teacher at the U.S. Military Academy at West Point did a painting of Santa Claus in the now familiar act of disappearing down the chimney. These were the basic ingredients that went into the evolution of Santa Claus, who emerged in his present form during the corrupt period, known as the Gilded Age, that followed the War Between the States, and who after 1870 began increasingly to appear on Christmas cards.

Many things would seem wrong with Santa Claus as a true symbol of the United States value system. In a nation that takes pride in forthrightness and honesty, here is a figure who every year puts on false whiskers and counterfeits jollity. In a nation that has achieved efficient mass production, here is a myth about toys being hand-crafted by non-union dwarfs in a workshop at the North Pole. In a nation that has extended rapid transportation all the way across a once primeval continent, Christmas presents are delivered by rein-deer power. As if these things were not enough to raise strong sus-picions about Santa Claus, other questions come to mind. Why did the myth require decades to develop, finally to emerge during the Gilded Age, when merchant princes were despoiling a continent? And why is it that the people concerned with the creation of the myth turn out to represent the vested interests? After all, Washing-ton Irving was a publicist paid by John Jacob Astor to write favour-ably about his activities, including maltreatment of Indians; the West Point artist can be assumed to represent the military establish-ment; and Clement Moore was a religious conservative who wrote tracts attacking Thomas Jefferson for having subverted the Christian faith. Santa Claus's jollity is no accident. It reflects his contentment with the existing social order.

Nor is this all. Something else, something even more basic, seems amiss in Santa Claus. Economic rewards in the United States have not gone to the good, the meek, and the pure in heart but to the shrewd, the exploitive, and the ruthless. The well-behaved rich child will receive a roomful of expensive toys, but the equally well-be-haved poor one will have to make do with shoddy merchandise from the dime store on the corner. A reality of the adult world is unrelenting competition in an economic arena, where those who succeed wrest status, power, and property from those who fail. This assuredly is not the economic world inhabited by Santa Claus. Children are told that Santa Claus rewards all children who are good, and that wealth or poverty makes no difference – as is patently not so.

The Santa Claus myth clearly raises a paradox, which a few scholars have attempted to explain. Some have interpreted the myth as an unconscious attempt by people in the United States to ease a bad conscience about their materialistic values. This is an inadequate explanation, since Santa Claus is bound up with one of the most materialistic and least spiritual manifestations of culture in the United States, the ballyhoo of Christmas shopping. Others have stated that giving expensive gifts at Christmas is a way for parents to ease their guilt about neglecting their children during the rest of the year. If this were so, why would parents insist that the gifts are brought by some unrelated old gentleman rather than by themselves? Still others have stated that Santa Claus represents a wish by adults to return to the golden age of childhood, in which the limits of good and bad behaviour are clearly defined. Why then have the parents not concocted a superchild rather than the image of a counterfeit grandfather?

None of these proposed rationales is adequate because none examines the myth in terms of its influence in socializing children to the realities, particularly the economic ones, of United States society. Two clues are particularly important. The first is that although Santa Claus is descended from certain demonic agents of chaos in Europe who noisily emerge during the Christmas season – the Lord of Misrule, the Boy Bishop, and the Saint Nicholas who consigns bad children to a devilish companion – in the United States he is no rebel, no overturner of institutions. He is typically a United States creation, displaying the capitalistic virtues of hard work, hope for better things, endurance in the harsh environment of the North Pole, and punctuality in meeting his Christmas deadline. A second clue is that Santa Claus is the invention of adults, who then foisted it on their children. Most children become suspicious of the reality of Santa Claus at a very early age – through hints from older children, television, or even seeing many Santa Clauses on street corners. Nevertheless, their parents encourage them to write letters to Saint Nick under the implied threat of not receiving gifts. In short, children are set up by their parents for the inevitability of a disillusioning revelation. They are led to believe that they exist in some magical economy in which a mere letter will produce an abundance of gifts. These gifts need not be laboured for and saved for, but rather will flow naturally to those who are good.

Why should parents be so cruel as to mislead their children? No clear-cut conspiracy, of course, goes on among parents to foist Santa Claus upon their offspring; yet cultural patterns often have consequences that the participants are not consciously aware of. Parents no doubt guess that the revelation about the non-existence of Santa Claus may be traumatic. They are undoubtedly aware also that the revelation will teach the children something of lasting value, something that is essential to economic survival in the United States. The child's reaction to the news that Santa Claus is a fiction is almost invariably one of having been swindled, cheated, lied to by parents. Many parents try to ease the blow by making the Christmas of revelation one in which they bestow particularly extravagant gifts. But the parents know in their hearts that they are giving their child a gift much more valuable than any that can be bought: the gift of an unmasked Santa. They are telling the child that Santa Claus's world has no counterpart in the real world that the child will be entering. Out there, valuable things will have to be purchased with real money, which will have to be earned in an economic environment where hard work and cunning, not simple goodness, are rewarded. The valuable things of this world are not distributed to those who wish the most but to those who are able to pay the most. The disillusioned child has thus been given a dramatic lesson in the capitalistic economy of Adam Smith, at the cost of only a few heartaches and a few tears that will soon dry. Real life is like that, the parents seem to be saying – and at the same time they demonstrate what growing up as part of society is all about. ♂♀

\*

The end result of the childhood socialization process is that each society generally produces individuals who behave like one another more than they behave like members of other societies. Leo Tolstoy, writing in *War and Peace*, characterized people from different parts of Europe:

A Frenchman is self-assured because he regards himself personally, both in mind and body, as irresistibly attractive to men and women. An Englishman is self-assured, as being a citizen of the best-organized state in the world . . .

An Italian is self-assured because he is excitable and easily forgets himself and other people. A Russian is self-assured just because he knows nothing and does not want to know anything, since he does not believe that anything can be known. The German's self-assurance is worst of all, stronger and more repulsive than any other, because he imagines that he knows the truth – science – which he himself has invented but which is for him the absolute truth. ♂♀

Tolstoy's generalizations about national character can be challenged as biased, but they emphasize an inclination among many people. People do see members of other societies as having been socialized in unique ways. Most North Americans have been taught in school that ethnic stereotypes are unreliable, and furthermore most know intellectually that such stereotypes are often unjust. Obviously not all Italians are carefree, nor all Latins passionate, nor all Poles stolid, nor all Germans rigid. Yet we often think of members of various national groups as displaying 'typical' traits.

The tendency to perceive members of national groups as stereotypes was studied in three generations of undergraduates at the same United States university in the years 1932, 1950, and 1967. Students were asked to select from a list of eighty-four traits the ones they considered most applicable to various nationalities. Members of each generation displayed remarkable agreement about the first five traits they selected, but the traits changed somewhat from one generation to another. Here, for example, are the five traits most commonly attributed to the Chinese by the three generations:

| 1932 | 1950 | 1967 |
|---|---|---|
| 1. Superstitious | 1. Loyal to family | 1. Loyal to family |
| 2. Sly | 2. Tradition-loving | 2. Tradition-loving |
| 3. Conservative | 3. Quiet | 3. Industrious |
| 4. Tradition-loving | 4. Superstitious | 4. Quiet |
| 5. Loyal to family | 5. Industrious | 5. Meditative |

Even though the current generation of students rarely perceive Chinese as superstitious and sly, they have replaced these stereotypes with others.

A change has taken place in the way the most recent of the three generations assign national characteristics. Students of the present generation tend to emphasize favourable traits – except where their own national character is concerned. Within each succeeding generation, the adjectives applied to citizens of the United States have become less flattering. In 1932, only 33 per cent of the students considered the people of the United States to be 'materialistic', but by 1967 the percentage had risen to sixty-seven. 'Conventional' and 'ostentatious' did not even appear in the list of eighty-four traits assigned by the previous two generations, but the present generation rated them as tied for sixth and seventh places. One explanation, of course, might be that today's college students are more analytical of themselves and their society. Also, people in the United States have been shown in one recent study to deprecate themselves more than do other national groups – which, if accurate, would be yet another United States national characteristic. ♂♀

Social scientists are divided about whether or not such stereotypes have any basis in fact, whether national character is really the end product of socialization. Despite the great range of variation in individual behaviour within any large and complex society, people in the United States, Russia, China, and Japan obviously differ greatly from one another. These differences are seen not only in language, attire, and food preferences but especially in psychological attitudes: ideas about self, feelings of guilt or shame, definitions of masculinity and femininity, and beliefs about sexual behaviour, to list only a few. Modern studies of national character attempt to isolate such behaviours and to explain them in cultural rather than biological terms. Whereas earlier researchers were sometimes vague about what 'national character' meant, modern researchers generally agree that it refers to enduring personality traits and patterns that are more common among adult members of one society than they are among those of other societies. ♂♀

Perhaps no people have been scrutinized as thoroughly as the Japanese in an effort to discover their national characteristics. Social scientists have been intrigued by the remarkable speed with which Japan transformed itself from a feudal state into a modern power, and by its astoundingly rapid recovery after the losses of World War II. Is there something in the Japanese national character that has made these things possible? The question can, of course, be answered in economic terms by reference to the supply of cheap labour, or in political terms by referring to the tradition of authoritarian governments. But it can also be answered in terms of the drive to achieve and of the central position of the family in Japanese culture.

Japanese families differ from those in the United States in many respects, one of the most important of which is that children sleep with their parents at least until puberty. Several years are then spent in making the transition to sleeping with older brothers and sisters, with the result that some children who are sixteen years of age may still be sleeping part of the time with their parents. Such an arrangement obviously blurs the distinction between the generations; it emphasizes the interdependence of individuals in the family; it places obstacles in the way of intimacy, sexual and otherwise, between husband and wife. Perhaps the major consequence is devotion to the parents and an especially strong tie to the mother that persists in an almost infantile form. And since almost no one lives alone in Japan, children develop a strong sense that the family is of central importance.

Child-rearing as practised by Japanese mothers encourages certain traits, such as striving for success, that become very pronounced later in life. Japanese children are generally treated with much permissiveness and indulgence. Physical punishment appears to be considerably less common than in the United States, and in its stead children are threatened and made fearful. The most effective punishment is inflicted when the mother assumes an air of quiet suffering in response to her child's misbehaviour, so that the child is made to feel guilty. The mother acts as though she had taken upon herself the burden of responsibility for having caused the child to misbehave. She publicly reproaches herself if her children conduct themselves badly or if they fail to meet the standards she has set for their success. Any child who fails to succeed has, therefore, visibly hurt the mother, with the result that the child suffers feelings of guilt. A child also feels obliged to succeed as a way of repayment for the self-sacrifice that the parents constantly remind the child they have made. Those Japanese who grow up feeling guilty because of not having behaved properly to their parents usually try to make amends by displays of hard work.

Japanese child-rearing is believed to have produced other behaviours commonly noted in adults. Sexual inhibition, due largely to the family's close sleeping arrangements, is particularly characteristic of most Japanese. Married couples engage in sexual relations as quickly as possible, virtually without foreplay. They also have intercourse much less frequently than do married couples in the United States. Sexual inhibition is matched by inhibition in personality development. The Japanese language possesses several words that are equivalent to the English 'happiness', but no words that refer to extreme degrees of it (like 'exuberance', 'exhilaration', 'ecstasy', and 'gaiety'). Neither do the Japanese often give exuberant expression to their emotions. The strong sense of obligation to family, combined with the need to achieve, produces an underlying tension which the Japanese appear to hold in check by compulsive orderliness and attention to small points. Although authorities on the Japanese disagree about details, they do agree that the Japanese have a national character that is distinguished from others in its suppression of emotional display, avoidance of extremes, sexual inhibition, need for achievement, and attention to the fine points of a problem. ♂♀

\*

Experiences in childhood and in adolescence are particularly important in moulding personality, but the socialization process does not end there. The sequence of roles continues after adolescence: employment, marriage, parenthood, grandparenthood, and retirement. And the final role must ultimately be faced – that of a dying person. Socialization is a continuing process of adjustment in which the individual is supported by society but at the same time informed of society's demands and expectations. The passage through each new role subjects the individuals to stress, making it impossible for them to be the same afterwards. An advance in income and status, a move from a rented apartment to a suburban house of one's own, a change in residence from one city or one country to another – all demand resocialization. The adjustment to new life-styles may require adults to change their style of dress, taste in foods, manner of speech, political beliefs, and possibly their moral sense as well, several times during their mature lives.

In our own day, growing old has become increasingly stressful. The pre-modern society did not retire its elders but instead increased their responsibilities. After all, in societies in which few people usually lived to old age, elders had a scarcity value, and for this reason alone they were accorded status. Because they had lived longer than others, they knew more and thus filled an important role as a repository of the society's knowledge. Modernization has forced a change in the status of the elderly. Retirement usually represents a sudden loss of occupational role. The role of elder counsellor no longer exists because rapid technological changes have made the knowledge, manners, and even morals of the elderly obsolete. Not only are the elderly unneeded in the labour market, but they are treated as intruders into the rest of society as well. Often consigned to loneliness, boredom, and poverty, the elderly in modern society find little dignity remaining in their role.

The cult of youth is sometimes thought to be a twentieth-century phenomenon, but 3600 years ago an Egyptian papyrus prescribed treatments to transform an old man into a youth. The ancient Greeks and the Germanic tribes attributed to their gods magical ways of postponing old age. And in the sixteenth century, Ponce de León went in search of the Fountain of Youth. This very ancient concern is more pressing today because the proportion of the population over sixty-five in modern nations is increasing rapidly. In the United States it is already 11 per cent and is expected to approach 20 per cent soon after the year 2000. The life-span for most people in modern societies fluctuates between seventy and eighty years, after which it decreases rapidly. The number of those reaching a century averages about two or three per 100,000 population. Only one person in a million can expect to reach the age of 105 – and only one in about forty million the age of 110.

Little is known for certain about the ageing process, even though it has been a major preoccupation of medicine since ancient times. In fact, the theories of ageing current today differ little from those commonly recognized at the beginning of this century. Some can be dismissed readily, such as the once common belief that ageing is due to intestinal toxins, which can be neutralized by eating such foods as yoghurt. Another belief was that the male hormone has a rejuvenating effect; at one time, numerous ageing people (including the poet William Butler Yeats) underwent operations that grafted glands from young non-human primates. If a supply of the male hormone were indeed necessary to prevent ageing, then those who have a much decreased supply would be expected to die earlier. Actually, the opposite is true. Eunuchs tend to live to slightly more advanced ages than intact males. Finally, some scientists have stated that the best way of ensuring long life is to be descended from long-lived grandparents. The evidence, though, is ambiguous. The children and grandchildren of people who have lived to old age generally do tend to live somewhat longer than average. On the other hand, a recent study reveals little correlation between people who lived into their nineties and the ages reached by their descendants. Genetic factors obviously play a part, but so do disease, environmental conditions, and other influences not yet well understood. Rather than inheriting longevity itself, people seem to inherit more or less susceptibility to such major killers as cancer and heart disease. ♂♀

Explanations for human ageing have not progressed much beyond the images that have come down to us from antiquity and from medieval medicine. One view is of the human body as a vessel containing a vital substance that eventually is depleted or destroyed – which has led to such well-known symbols of age as the burning candle, the withered leaf, and the nearly empty glass. In its modern form, this 'wear-and-tear' hypothesis proposes that the very act of living causes the accumulation of mutations or the breakdown of the body's immunological defences. This hypothesis also assumes that people, like machines, simply wear out with age. But human bodies differ from machines in having the capacity to repair themselves. A continual turnover takes place in most human tissues, and cells are regularly replaced. Fingernails grow and skin heals over a wound; new bone growth repairs a broken limb; the liver can be abused to the extent that much of its tissue is lost, but it can regenerate itself practically to its previous mass.

Another ancient view is that humankind has been given, either through the gods or through biology, an allotted span of years of life – which has produced the symbols of the emptying hourglass, the lengthening shadows of sunset, and the progression of the seasons towards winter. The modern version of this hypothesis states that the life-span of a cell or of an organism is programmed genetically and that not much can be done to prolong its existence. Among mammals, life-span does seem to be correlated with metabolism (that is, the pace of living). The point used to be made that a shrew can live for a year and a half, a dog for eighteen years, a chimpanzee thirty-five, a horse forty, and an elephant seventy – and that the life-span of each of these animals is about as long as it takes the heart to beat roughly a billion times. Were humans to fit this pattern, their maximum life-span would be between thirty-five and forty years. Grandma Moses, though, lived to be 101, a period during which her heart beat about three and a half billion times. Nor have animal experiments revealed that every species has its own clock of life which runs down at an appointed time. Studies of some forty strains of laboratory mice have shown that longevity is genetically determined to an extent of no more than 20 or 30 per cent, the remainder apparently due to environmental influences. Whatever the exact explanation, human ageing is a reality and the organs of the body do decline with age.

Compared to a human aged thirty, a seventy-five-year-old person has only 70 per cent of the heart output, 55 per cent of the strength of hand grip, 40 per cent of the maximum oxygen intake during exercise, and 36 per cent of the taste buds.

Some students of the ageing process have wondered why humans should live so long after their reproductive powers have waned. Natural selection would, of course, favour parents who remained alive to care for offspring that were still dependent. But that selective advantage certainly does not explain why a female need live for some thirty years beyond menopause, after her last child could possibly be born. An explanation for the ageing process may simply be that natural selection has never operated upon it. Those diverse manifestations of ageing – like the decreased density of bone in the skeleton, the loss of elasticity in the skin and muscles, and the hardening of the arteries – may occur simply because no reason exists for them not to occur. We may possibly grow old by default rather than by design. Genetic causes for these manifestations of ageing could have arisen early in evolution – and never have been weeded out because they affected humans only after the reproductive years had long passed. In fact, humans may never have been selected either for or against a long life, and so longevity may never have been an issue until cultural selection in modern societies favoured certain individuals who were able to purchase the health care that assured longevity.

When death finally comes, no animals except humans and chimpanzees appear to display signs of mourning. The chimpanzee's display is trivial compared to the great emphasis placed on death in human societies. Death to a human is not the simple passing from one state to another. An elderly person who is isolated from friends and family and without interests or activity might be considered psychologically dead, even though the body is still functioning well. Biological death might be thought to be clear-cut, but actually it too is ambiguous. Various medical criteria exist to determine the moment of death, although none is really adequate. Cessation of breathing, loss of heartbeat, or disappearance of electrical activity in the brain might seem clearly to indicate it – yet the parts of the body do not all die at the same time. Some organs remain alive after official death; these are the ones used in transplant operations.

The social moment of death cannot be defined precisely either. The death of even the loneliest person has repercussions for the society. At the very least, every society has rules and regulations about the treatment of the dead and the redistribution of possessions. Such social rituals as the funeral, mourning, and acts of commemoration all serve to acknowledge the event, to sustain the living, and to express the concern of society. Most societies maintain in one way or another the fiction that death is not final. They continue to revere invisible agents or spirits, to worship ancestors, to appeal to the dead in time of need, and to placate them with offerings. 'There is no death!' proclaim the funeral rites – but at the same time, the members of society know that death is indeed a reality. They work quickly to mend the hole that death has made in the social fabric. Accumulated wealth, property, and power are redistributed; new interactions are entered into to replace those formerly engaged in with the departed. The story of one human life ends, but society has taken as a symbol of it the fresh green seed that waits inside the shrivelled husk. The ultimate rite for the life-passenger is concluded, but the members of the next generation have already been produced and indoctrinated in the ongoing process of socialization.

# Epilogue

# The Future of the Species

As A.D. 1000 approached, portents that the world was coming to an end spread throughout Europe. Necromancers pointed to mysterious signs that graves were about to open and yield up their dead; sorcerers attempted to influence the future by practising devilish arts. Evidence for the imminent destruction of Europe was seen in the incessant raids by the barbarian Norse and the Saracens. Even if Europeans survived these invading hordes, many people believed, their way of life would be forever destroyed. Nothing of the sort occurred. The Saracens became a link that transmitted the learning of ancient Greece to the Western world, where it soon stimulated an intellectual revival. The savage Norse became Christianized and built cathedrals, monasteries, and town halls; they were responsible for the spread of Norman, and later of Gothic, architecture throughout western Europe; the atmosphere in the courts of their rulers was one in which scholarship, poetry, and music flourished.

Now, as the year 2000 approaches, sinister portents are once again being described. In place of the threat from the Saracens and the Norse, people in Western societies look with apprehension upon the growing might of the Soviet Union and of China. The possibility of nuclear annihilation, the population explosion, famine, pollution, the exhaustion of the earth's supply of raw materials – a litany of dire predictions that can be extended almost indefinitely – all appear to signal an ominous breakdown in the human adaptation. Suddenly we are faced with a complex of interrelated crises that some pessimists have labelled 'terminal civilization' – that final obliteration of all the glorious things that humans have achieved. Indeed, something in our species' stewardship of the planet seems to have gone very much awry. Urgent new crises erupt while earlier ones recur in every corner of the globe. We despair of finding real solutions because the solution of one problem so often creates new ones. To reduce air pollution, we switch to low-sulphur coal; but to obtain it we must deface the land with strip mines, which cause further deterioration in the environment. The human equation, as we approach the year 2000, no longer seems to balance. The biological and cultural adaptations that have evolved over millions of years appear no longer to equal survival and well-being. Whereas several hundred years ago people regarded the future as more certain and knowable than the past, today scientists have uncovered much that had long remained unknown concerning human origins – with the result that almost all of the unknowns now seem to lie in the future.

Many humans feel a vague anxiety about the possible melting of the ice caps or the fizzling out of the sun; but the problems facing our species are much more urgent than these. Some must in fact be solved before the year 2000. Although, paradoxically, this book began with the broad sweep of tens of millions of years of primate and hominid history, as I conclude the story of our species I find myself concerned with developments that will occur within a mere few decades. Some people have concluded in despair that we are soon to become the victims of our own evolutionary success. For them, the question to be answered is not 'What is the future of our species?' – but rather 'Does our species have a future?'

Readers will undoubtedly have detected in these pages my personal, and seemingly contradictory, bias: an exaltation of the values of the hunting–gathering adaptation but at the same time a faith in the future benefits of modernization. Admittedly, little cause for rejoicing can be found in the recitation of the litany of ills that now beset our planet – but these ills are the result of breakdowns in technology, not in the modern adaptation itself. Modernization is more than technology alone; what it entails is technology interacting with biological and social systems. As the new adaptation of modernization is being forged, it is understandable that one of its component parts – which happens to be technology – should go temporarily out of balance.

I thus find myself in the position of being an advocate for both the earliest and the most recent of human adaptations, a position roughly equivalent to attempting to pull oneself up by one's own bootstraps and reach for the stars at the same time. Yet, of what wonders our species, with its almost infinite capacity for adaptation, has shown itself capable! Little in the human fossils of a million years ago indicates that their descendants would some day dominate the planet in a totally unprecedented way. As recently as perhaps 20,000 years ago, there were still more baboons than humans in the world. Only through the privilege of hindsight can we see that our species was evolving in a way that allowed it to fill a unique role, to escape from the restraints of the environment, and to replace much of organic evolution with socio-cultural evolution. Can such a creature be so mindless as to cause its own destruction? I do not think so. I do not claim prophetic powers, but I do believe that some predictions can safely be made about what lies ahead. First, though, we must confront the near-term hazards. Of these, three are paramount: a global environment too befouled for human survival, the threat of nuclear war, and the spectre of mass starvation in a burgeoning population.

*

Will we so remake the living environment that has nurtured our species that we are unable to survive? This threat is a real one because of the unprecedented power our species now wields over the globe and all its inhabitants. We are today more than the dominant form of life; we are capable of abolishing all forms of life, including our own. The mere presence of even a single human in any remote part of the world inevitably brings about extensive modifications of the environment. Every species does, of course, alter its environment by the very fact of living in it. When the leaves and growing twigs of certain trees are fed upon by monkeys, for example, the trees are stimulated to sprout more branches than they would do ordinarily. The human habitat, though, is not simply the tips of the trees; it is everywhere across the globe.

Among the numerous examples of mindless tampering with the environment by humans, a particularly striking one is the Aswan High Dam in Egypt. This barrier across the Nile, two miles wide, backs up water into Lake Nasser, an immense human-made reservoir. When completed in 1967, it was the biggest and the most expensive dam in the world. The Egyptians anticipated that the dam would produce major benefits: it would prevent the annual flooding by the Nile, provide water for irrigation, and generate hydro-electric power. What the Egyptian planners failed to take into account was the intricate web of relationships that had long existed between the river, the valley lands, certain forms of animal life, and the human population. And so the anticipated benefits have largely been annulled by disastrous side-effects.

Before the construction of the dam, the annual flooding of the Nile regularly deposited rich silt along the banks, thereby at once fertilizing the land and carrying away the salts that abound in desert soil. Now, however, the enriching sediments are trapped in the reservoir behind the dam, and as a result the land downstream has lost much of its former fertility. To make up for the nutrients that the river once provided without cost, millions of tons of chemical fertilizer must now be applied each year. The fertilizer factories built to meet this new need require enormous amounts of electricity, thus consuming a large percentage of the hydro-electric power that the dam was built to supply in the first place. Furthermore, the newly dug irrigation canals have added to the salt content of the soil, with the result that the construction of drains and pumps to desalinate the land will eventually cost as much as the dam itself. The effect upon fish, an important food source in the Nile and in the eastern Mediterranean as well, has likewise been disastrous. In the absence of the nutrients that were formerly swept downstream by the river, the sardine catch alone dropped by 97 per cent within three years after the dam was completed.

Indirectly, the dam has also had severe effects upon the health of Egypt's population, most of whom are concentrated along the banks of the Nile and around its mouth. Schistosomiasis, a debilitating parasitic disease, had long been endemic in Egypt, attacking a very small proportion of the population. The parasite is carried by snails that inhabit shallow waters, such as those of irrigation canals. Previous to the construction of the Aswan High Dam, the canals dried out each year, thus killing most of the snails and greatly lessening the number of parasites. Now that the canals are filled the year round with irrigation water from Lake Nasser, the snails have multiplied astronomically. As a result, about half of the entire population of Egypt today suffers from schistosomiasis – and the increase in productivity that had been anticipated as one benefit from the dam has been counterbalanced by the severely debilitating effects of the disease upon human workers. Infected individuals lose up to half of their former strength and vitality, and the weakness persists even after the body no longer harbours the parasite. The consequent reduction in the ability to work suffered by the people currently or previously infected has meant an annual economic loss to Egypt estimated at about $550 million.

The human capacity to dominate the environment of the Nile valley has brought ruinous consequences instead of the promised blessings. The anticipated increase in total food production did not occur because of the loss of nutrients once carried by flood waters, the sharp decrease in catches of fish, and the loss of arable land owing to the accumulation of salts. A large part of the electricity generated at the dam is now diverted into manufacturing chemical fertilizers and into operating drainage systems to remove salts from the soil. Instead of contributing to human well-being, the dam has spread disease throughout the Nile region, thus greatly decreasing the ability of farmers to capitalize upon the waters brought by the irrigation canals. In short, the dam has been an ecological calamity. ♂♀

The Aswan disaster suggests just one way in which the human species has made life difficult, and even precarious, for itself. To cite a few of the more alarming prospects: many scientists believe that pollutants accumulating in the atmosphere may build up into a greenhouse effect and thus make the planet too warm to be habitable; that the water vapours released by supersonic aircraft could blanket the planet permanently with clouds and thus shut out the sun's energy; that the pollution of the seas could destroy its plankton and thus the higher forms of life that depend upon it; or that mass poisoning might result from accumulations of mercury, lead, and other industrial wastes. I do not believe, however, that such catastrophes will occur, or even that pollutants will continue to be a major problem once modernization has become the major human adaptation. Although built in modern times, the Aswan High Dam lacks several hallmarks of the modernization adaptation. One of the distinguishing features of modernization, as described in Chapter 9, is planning – the assessment in advance of the social and biological consequences of a new technology. This did not take place at Aswan, but that such thinking ahead is becoming a policy of modern nations may be witnessed in the current debates over questions like those of nuclear energy, supersonic aircraft, and food additives. Ecological damage due to pollutants is being lessened by new conservation practices, which can be expected to become routine as resources grow scarcer or more expensive. Already about 35 per cent of the copper and 40 per cent of the lead used in the United States are recycled. Coal will become too precious a source of organic compounds to be burned. The products of nuclear energy will no longer be disposed of in underground caverns but will be used instead as sources of heat and metals. Humans will find it both technologically feasible and in their economic interest no longer to make a dungheap of their environment. ♂♀

The second major hazard facing our species is a nuclear holocaust. Regardless of the severity of a nuclear war, some human beings could be expected to survive, either because they were sufficiently distant from the sources of radiation or because they possessed the selective advantage of a high tolerance for radiation. Those who survived the immediate impact of the nuclear explosions would nevertheless be exposed to radiation from fall-out. These survivors would, in many cases, produce egg and sperm cells containing mutations that would result in abnormal offspring. Tragically high though the toll of malformed offspring would be, large numbers of functioning offspring could also be expected to survive. Would they find themselves on an otherwise lifeless planet? Most probably not. Plant and animal species vary widely in their sensitivity to radiation. Many familiar foods would no longer be available, but inventive human survivors would undoubtedly exploit new food sources out of necessity.

Although *Homo sapiens* would endure as a species, the survivors would find it virtually impossible to reconstruct the kinds of societies to which they had previously belonged. Modern societies are the result of billions of small changes – biological, psychological, social, political, economic, and technological – that have occurred since hunting and gathering. Such changes in their exact sequence could never again be reproduced. Our ancestors were able to take the path towards modern technology because of the huge resources of metals and fuels that were available for them to exploit by means of a very primitive technology. Much of the earth was once covered by towering forests that provided wood for energy and for building; copper lay on the surface of the earth; iron was easily mined. Such accessible resources were long ago depleted. Now, oil wells must be drilled thousands of feet deep, often under the seas; seams of coal must be followed through tortuous underground caverns; a sophisticated new technology has grown out of the necessity for extracting metals from low-grade ores. Today's resources can be obtained only through a complex modern technology – one that depended originally upon the easy availability of inexpensive resources such as will never be obtainable again. If modern technology were suddenly to end through a nuclear holocaust, the survivors would find it impossible to resume sophisticated processes with the capacities still available to them. The adaptations that the survivors would make, and the societies that would emerge, would undoubtedly represent a new kind of world, one whose exact nature would be nearly impossible to predict.

In addition to the threats of an uninhabitable environment and of nuclear holocaust, a third major challenge immediately facing our species is whether it will be able to feed its own burgeoning numbers. The first sixteen centuries of the Christian Era saw a doubling of the human population, from a quarter of a billion to half a billion. From this number, it doubled once again in the space of only another two hundred years, and by 1930, a mere century or so afterwards, that one billion had become two billion. In 1975 the figure reached four billion. All reliable projections indicate that it will pass the six billion mark before the year 2000. To give some idea of the magnitude of this growth, the current population of Tokyo alone is believed to exceed the population of the entire world no more than 20,000 years ago. In southern Asia alone, the increase in the potential labour force is currently taking place at a rate of more than 350,000 people every week.

Concern about overpopulation stems from simple arithmetic. Imagine that in the same year that the *Mayflower* reached the New World, a healthy young couple settled on some other newly discovered continent. Imagine also that this couple produced eight living offspring, four male and four female – not an unreasonable figure for those times – and that these interbred and likewise produced eight offspring per couple. When the founding couple died, they would thus have left behind them a total of forty living descendants. If the tradition of eight children per couple were maintained, and if all the offspring survived, the original couple would thus become the ancestors of a total progeny alive today that numbered 134,217,728. Such hypothetical examples are supported by figures on the growth of specific populations. The French-speaking population of Canada totalled about 7000 in 1759, when the British defeated the French and further migration from France to Canada came to an end. The number of French-Canadians has now increased to approximately six and a half million. The British won the Battle of Quebec, but the French-Canadians won the battle of the cradle.

Some visionaries have suggested that the problem of overpopulation will eventually be solved by colonizing the moon and planets, to which excess populations could then be exported. Such efforts would solve nothing. Assume that it were somehow possible to start immediately exporting all increases in population to Venus, Mercury, Mars, and the moon, and that the practice continued. If the present rate of population increase both on earth and on these solar bodies continued, in a mere fifty years the density of the population on all of them would be the same as on the earth today. The costs of colonization on such a scale would, of course, be prohibitive. The United States would have to spend about twenty times its gross national product to export just the people being added to its population every year. ♂♀

If exporting excess populations to other planets will not solve the problem of overpopulation, what will? Modernization will – for the reason that people in modern societies tend to produce far fewer children than do those in undeveloped or developing countries. Parents in a modern nation must decide whether or not an additional offspring is worth the huge financial investment that is now necessary to prepare a child for full participation in society. The cost of raising one middle-class child in the United States, from conception through post-graduate education, is now approaching $200,000. Potential parents in modern societies thus find themselves in much the same situation as potential parents in a society of hunters and gatherers. The hunter–gatherers must ask themselves whether a new infant is worth the extra labour involved in carrying it about and in finding additional food, and also whether the new infant is worth the risk of depriving an older child of food. The cost, in money or in risk, is very high for both the modern and the hunting–gathering adaptations. In both, some families will always be larger than average because a few parents willingly accept the added burden – but in general the number of offspring is considerably fewer than in peasant, agricultural, or early-industrial societies. For these latter, the cost of maintaining each child is low, since the child begins productive labour at a very early age; mobility is not a factor; and no large outlays must be made for education. The declining birth rate in modern societies is not a new development in human history, but rather a return to the behaviours of the earliest human adaptation.

Nevertheless, the rapid rise in world populations can be expected to continue until modernization has spread around the globe. How are all of these people to be fed? In Brazil, to take just one example, food production will have to be doubled in the next eighteen years to prevent famine. In the world as a whole, the amount of cultivated land available by the year 2000 to sustain each person, and thus the number of available calories *per capita*, will have been reduced by about half. Increased population densities will mean not only vast numbers of deaths from famine, but also stunted bodies and minds among the survivors. Making room for more people and bringing marginal lands into production are certain to degrade the environment still further.

But modernization has already developed the technology to feed a vastly increased population – according to some estimates, fifty or even possibly a hundred billion people. One reason why the four billion people alive today are not themselves being adequately fed is that the technological component of modernization has outrun the political, social, and economic ones. Poor countries cannot afford to modernize their agriculture rapidly and the affluent countries have not been willing to pay the bill enabling them to do so. The oil-rich Arabs are investing in armaments, foreign corporations, and tourist hotels rather than in a modernized agriculture for undeveloped nations. As just one example, a shortage of fresh water for irrigation places a limitation upon food production. The technology already exists for desalting the sea; all that is needed further is money, but at present the nations that have it do not appear willing to share what they have with the have-nots. Most people in North America and western Europe also consume many more calories than they need, whereas most people in southern Asia, Africa, and Latin America have to make do with far fewer.

The world food supply could be increased dramatically if wiser use were made of the ecological food chain. The first link in all food chains is the ability of plants to convert solar energy, air, and water into food energy by the process of photosynthesis. These plants are then fed upon by animals, which are in turn fed upon by still other animals, and so on until the animals become food for humans – or, in the words of Isaiah (40:6), 'All flesh is grass.' Each link in the food chain involves the loss of more than 80 per cent of the energy stored in the previous link. The longest such chain known to sustain any human group is found in the diet of some Eskimoes. To gain a pound in weight, an Eskimo must consume 5 pounds of seal meat. These 5 pounds are the product of 25 pounds of fish, which in turn had consumed 125 pounds of shrimp and other sea invertebrates. These invertebrates, finally, had been sustained by feeding upon 625 pounds of algae – all to add a single pound to the weight of one Eskimo. In other words, about 99.8 per cent of the energy originally synthesized from the sun by the algae had been lost, so far as human consumption is concerned, by the time it reached the Eskimo. The situation is very much the same in many other societies whose people live mainly on meat from domesticated animals or on predatory fish that are the end of long food chains. It is thus not visionary to predict that humans will increasingly cultivate the plants and small animals at the beginning of food chains in place of the large animals at the end.

The technology already exists for a very high-yield agriculture, for intensive farming of the sea to produce algae and shellfish, for developing varieties of plants with high protein content, and for cultivating major new crops. In the space of a few years, new varieties of rice – plus, of course, large amounts of fertilizer and machinery – converted the Philippines from an importer to an exporter of this major food source. Experimental varieties of wheat increased the harvest in Pakistan by about 70 per cent in only three years. Although the technology for vastly increasing food production is ready, the social and cultural systems have not kept pace. Nor has a world-wide human ethic as yet emerged that takes account of modernization. If every citizen throughout the world were to contribute just $10 a year to the manufacture of fertilizer, world food production would rise immediately by about 50 per cent. If the sophisticated agriculture now practised in Holland were extended to the world's three and a half billion acres of cultivated land, the planet could support a population of sixty billion people – and their diet would be nutritionally as satisfactory as that of the well-fed Dutch. If the same amount of land were managed as efficiently as the Japanese manage theirs, the world could support a population of about ninety billion people on a typical Japanese diet. Production could be further increased if the modern nations were willing to invest in techniques for growing new synthetic foods. Even the efficient techniques of modern agriculture require nearly one acre to feed one human – yet a single tank a cubic yard in volume can produce from algae virtually all of a human's protein, vitamin, and caloric needs.

Dire predictions about a human population unable to feed itself obviously have little basis in fact for the foreseeable future. Many of these predictions stem from the 'Principle of Population' announced in 1798 by Thomas Malthus: that human populations are limited by their food supply because they increase geometrically (that is, 1, 2, 4, 8, and so on), whereas food production can be increased only arithmetically (1, 2, 3, 4). The resources available for agriculture that Malthus knew about were land, water, and the muscle power of humans and animals. These are still the basic resources for much of the world. But for the modern nations, agricultural production has soared owing to two resources of which Malthus could not have been aware: mechanical energy from fossil fuels and the application of a new technology. Mechanical energy is used to operate farm equipment, to manufacture fertilizers and pesticides, to pump irrigation water, and to transport raw materials to and from the farm. The application of technology has similarly been on a scale that Malthus could never have anticipated. The physical properties and the chemistry of soils are now tested precisely; strains of plants resistant to diseases are bred; the genetic improvement of breeds has increased milk and egg production; new engineering designs for irrigation and drainage systems have reduced the loss of water. For us in the modern world, the agricultural modernization of the undeveloped countries is in our interest, not only because of our obligations as members of the human family but also because economically it makes good sense. The emerging modern ethic no longer accepts disease, starvation, and war as 'natural' controls of population. An improvement in the conditions under which the rest of the world lives is the only sure way to slow down the growth of populations – and eventually to reduce the cost of our own commitment to the rest of humankind. ♂♀

Although cleaning up the environment, preventing nuclear war, and feeding the world's growing population are the most urgent matters that face humankind, questions of a different sort are being asked about the biological future of our species. Have we stopped evolving? Are we at long last reaching the outermost twig on our evolutionary branch? So complete is human mastery of the global environment that we have difficulty in thinking of humans nowadays as being forced to adapt. Other organisms adapt to their environment through changes in their genes as a result of selective pressures from the environment. Humans alone can also adapt by changing the environment to fit their genes.

Some scientists believe that anatomical and physiological evolution began to slow down once human culture had evolved, to a degree that nowadays most of the possibilities for biological evolution seem to have been exhausted and only the evolution of culture itself is still significant. Such beliefs are based on erroneous assumptions about human evolution. First of all, no one alive today can possibly foretell what may be the significance of seemingly trivial biological changes that are taking place in our bodies. Only by hindsight can anthropologists now understand the significance for a primate, born millions of years ago, of a pelvis so distorted in shape that the creature found it easier to stand erect than to travel on all fours. Second, human evolution is demonstrably an ongoing process. Major changes in allele frequency are known to have taken place in a matter of only several hundred years – as, for example, in the sickle-cell trait, the ability of adults to digest milk, and the distribution of blood groups.

Biological evolution did not come to a halt when culture appeared, nor is it likely to do so when cultures have become even more complex than now. As is true for all other living things, human genes continue to mutate. Every one of the tens of thousands of genes inherited by an individual has a tiny probability – perhaps one chance in 100,000 or 200,000 – of changing in some way during that individual's reproductive years. In fact, the mutation rate among modern humans is undoubtedly greater than in the past, as a result of increased radiation and of new chemical substances introduced into the environment. An extremely small number of these mutations would, according to the law of probability, be beneficial, but all of the others would be harmful because they would disrupt an already functioning human system.

Harmful mutations in the past have been eliminated by natural selection, and undoubtedly it will continue to operate in keeping humans fit to inhabit the environments they have created. Consider, for example, the condition known as 'achondroplastic dwarfism', a mutation that produces people with a normal head and trunk but with abnormally short arms and legs. (Most of those who served as court jesters in Europe suffered from this condition.) Such dwarfs usually have good general health and average intelligence, yet the mortality at birth and in childhood of their offspring is five times that of non-dwarfs. For some reason, the selection against this kind of dwarfism is severe indeed. Natural selection obviously still serves to make achondroplasts much less efficient in transmitting their genes to future generations, as compared to people who do not suffer from this condition.

Modern medical procedures have, though, allowed people with certain lethal mutations to survive. Retinoblastoma, for example, is an eye cancer of children that until recent decades almost always proved fatal before the mutant gene could be passed on to the next generation. Medical treatment now enables about 70 per cent of the carriers of this mutant gene to survive, reproduce, and thus transmit the defect to their offspring. Medical science has similarly been successful in keeping alive people with haemophilia, diabetes, and other formerly lethal genetic diseases. Are these people living proof that the laws of natural selection are in the process of being repealed through human intervention? Not at all. As any species changes in relation to its environment, selective pressures are redirected rather than reduced. Several million years ago, selective pressures on the ability of the hand to grasp branches lessened, but the ability of these same hands to manufacture tools nevertheless increased.

Many diseases that in previous adaptations resulted in early death or otherwise interfered with the ability to produce surviving offspring are no longer, in the modern environment, eliminated by natural selection. People suffering from these diseases are as fit in a Darwinian sense as any other members of the population – so long as they can depend upon receiving medical attention. The spectre has been raised of a future population composed largely of people with genetic diseases, kept alive at tremendous public expense by medical intervention. At present, approximately 100,000 haemophiliacs in the United States are kept alive by globulin therapy that costs $22,000 per year for each one. Nevertheless, a fear such as has been expressed is unrealistic. Phenylketonuria (PKU) is an inherited disease that causes severe mental retardation. Reliable tests now exist for detecting PKU in newborns; nearly forty of the fifty states make such tests compulsory. Once detected, the disease can be treated easily by use of a particular kind of diet, with the result that almost all treated children develop normally. The total cost of the screening programme is significantly less than the cost of caring for a single patient with PKU during a lifetime of institutionalization. ♂♀

Are doctors acting in the best interests of the species, though, in allowing such children to survive, to marry, and to pass on the gene for PKU to future generations? Many people are indeed concerned that the physically weaker members of the population, as well as the less intelligent and less successful ones, are outbreeding 'superior' individuals in the society. A shift is obviously taking place in the genetic contribution to the United States population being made by various socio-economic classes. On an average, an educated, upper-class female nowadays will give birth to two children during the entire span of her reproductive years, whereas an uneducated, lower-class female, on an average, will produce about four. To convert this statistical fact into a general conclusion that the United States population is becoming less healthy or less intelligent would, however, be to engage in faulty reasoning. No proof whatever has been offered that the upper classes in the United States owe their privileged position to superior genetic endowment. A more likely explanation for that privilege is that descendants of white immigrants who arrived early in the United States have had a much greater opportunity to accumulate wealth than later immigrants and their offspring. And in regard to Black Americans, no conclusions whatever can be drawn, since until very recently they had almost no opportunity to acquire wealth, education, or power.

A further concern is that our species as a whole is declining in braininess, that hallmark of hominid success. Around the world, those portions of the population usually considered to be most intelligent are indeed producing fewer offspring than the mass of the population. What is often overlooked, on the other hand, is that those with the lowest intelligence similarly produce few or no offspring. The United States population probably includes as many feeble-minded people as it does persons of genius. Geniuses are given the opportunity to reproduce, even though they do not always exercise it to the fullest – whereas the feeble-minded, many of whom are institutionalized, usually have no such opportunity at all. Furthermore, mental disability is often accompanied by, and is probably linked with, various physical disabilities. The reproductive success of people who suffer such combined misfortunes is far below the average. In short, whatever unknown alleles result in either extremely intelligent people or very stupid ones are being eliminated constantly, and at about the same rate. The average intelligence of populations, both in the United States and elsewhere, will no doubt remain very much the same – until environmental changes in the future exert new selective pressures.

Cannot positive steps, then, be taken to ensure a larger proportion of intellectually more gifted and physically more healthy humans? A few influential geneticists have proposed that sperm from donors for artificial insemination be preserved by freezing until, later in life, those donors' genetic make-up has been demonstrated by achievement and by mental and physical health. Guidelines for determining the relative superiority of that make-up would, though, undoubtedly be a continual source of dispute. Nor does any way exist to determine whether the traits preferred today – intelligence, mental stability, energy, courage, and so on – are determined genetically (in which event they might be passed on to offspring) or environmentally (in which event they would not be). Another potential problem was emphasized when, in 1975, the British Royal Society recommended to Parliament that rock-music stars be prohibited from selling semen to commercial sperm banks. The Society pointed out that the popularity of certain rock stars could result in having thousands of offspring from the commercially available semen of a single such donor. Problems of inbreeding might then be the result, since these offspring could intermarry without knowing that they were half-siblings. Further, a rock star might carry a deleterious gene that would unwittingly be passed on to an unprecedented number of offspring.

In 1932, Aldous Huxley's *Brave New World* described a future society in which new individuals were bred artificially in test tubes. Geneticists have already solved many of the scientific problems that Huxley treated with grim satire, and apparently they will soon be able to influence greatly the course of human evolution. The foetus can already be examined in the uterus for the detection not only of sex but also of numerous possible genetic defects, thereby giving the mother the option of aborting the foetus if the diagnosis is unfavourable. Geneticists also now have the ability to clone – that is, to remove cells from a parent so as to produce artificially as many identical offspring as desired – not only plants but certain animals as well, and probably will in the future be able to do the same with humans. Supporters of large-scale cloning have envisioned a world populated by millions of equivalents of Jesus, Socrates, Shakespeare, Leonardo, and Einstein. Cloning could, though, be just as effective in producing numberless counterparts of Ivan the Terrible, Attila the Hun, or Adolf Hitler. An even greater problem is that any individual judged to have some superior trait (the goodness

of Jesus, the creative brilliance of Socrates and Shakespeare, the
scientific originality of Leonardo and Einstein) inevitably carries
numerous genes for other traits that might be genetically harmful.

Genetic engineering – the direct manipulation of the DNA
genetic code by changing, subtracting from, or adding to the
message received by the cell – has been said to hold great potential
for bettering our species. The liver of a foetus carrying the PKU
trait, for example, could be signalled to correct itself and to synthesize the missing enzyme. The potentialities of such genetic engineering become insignificant, though, when compared to the
possible manipulation of the cultural environment. Let us imagine
that the citizens of the United States decide to increase IQ by genetic
methods. They might, for example, urge married couples to have
their children by artificial insemination of sperm from donors who
score high on IQ tests. No one can predict exactly what would
happen, but probably no more than 1 per cent of all couples would
agree. These volunteers would, though, be likely to have fairly high
IQs already, and thus be quick to recognize the benefits to their
species in genetic engineering. Now assume further, for the sake of
this example, that half of an individual's IQ is determined by inheritance and the remaining half by environment. Calculations
reveal that this sort of genetic intervention would change the overall
IQ of the United States population by less than one tenth of a single
point in a generation – and that some 1500 years would be required
to raise the national IQ by a mere four points. In contrast, a study in
Philadelphia showed that after six years of improved schooling the
IQ scores of the children tested had risen by an average of 5.1
points. In other words, six years spent in a superior school environment may be more effective than 1500 years of genetic engineering.♂♀

Obviously, no serious scientific obstacles prevent maintaining, and
even improving upon, the biological inheritance that has brought
humans to a position of unprecedented dominance. Can the same
thing be said concerning the cultural implications of biological and
technological change? Innovations formerly occurred so slowly that
they were scarcely perceptible to anyone at the time, and cultural
institutions were thus able to make a gradual adjustment. Now,
though, crucial decisions regarding human welfare must often be
made at a frenetic pace. Many of today's familiar innovations –
computers, nuclear energy, telecommunications, detection of genetic

defects, and effective birth control, to list only a few – became a reality within only the past three decades, and their effects have already been profound. The implications for the United States of achieving zero population growth, for example, will be felt throughout the entire society. The United States population at present includes many more young than old people, the median age being only 28.9 years. Were zero population growth to be achieved today, relatively few children would be born to replace the present large population of young people when they reached middle and old age.

Throughout its history, the United States has been dominated by a youth culture simply because the young outnumbered the old. (The median age of all people in the United States in 1800 was only sixteen – 12.9 years fewer than now.) When there are two or three adults for every child, as is the situation now in Sweden and will eventually be in the United States if the birth rate continues to decline, major cultural changes are to be expected. One supposed opportunity in the United States has been that every youth has the potential to grow up to be president, if not of the country at least of a business or organization. In the past, when relatively few people survived to middle and old age, ambitious young people found few obstacles in the form of older people who had to be pushed aside. Under the conditions of a stable population, with at least as many people of fifty-five as of twenty-five, older people will not be so easily dislodged from full participation in society. And their claim to cultural respectability will no doubt be reinforced by medical contributions towards maintaining their vigour. The ambitious young person of the future will therefore have to struggle hard to become even a vice-president or a supervisor, since the pool from which mature managerial talent can be drawn will be so much larger. Whereas a college student could once hope to reach the top rung of the organizational ladder by the age of forty-five, for one belonging to the next generation the ladder will seem a lot higher and more people will be scrambling at the topmost rungs.

No one can safely predict at this point the response of young people to suddenly finding themselves in the minority. All institutions will unquestionably have to adapt to the reality of decreased opportunities for youth. Will an increase in generational conflict occur? Will social disorder among a more and more frustrated minority of young people become severe? Will the young conspire to seize power from the older majority? Probably none of these things will happen. Social stratification and differential access to wealth and power have always existed – and relative age has been the most prevalent basis for these differences. The present systems of stratification are more likely simply to adapt to new demographic patterns. In other areas as well, culture can be expected to change and to adapt to new conditions, as it has always done in the past.

\*

The continuing spread of modernization supports an optimistic view of the future of our species. Modernization has already improved major areas of life and it promises to do much more in the future. Often condemned for its emphasis on technology, modernization nevertheless offers the best opportunity for rediscovering values that are worth retrieving and that have been lost since the adaptation of the hunter–gatherers was abandoned. Modernization has been condemned for depleting the planet of the very raw materials that are essential to keep modern societies going. But the opposite is true. Available reserves of fuels and minerals, far from being reduced, have actually increased with the spread of modernization. Behind this paradox is the fact that the availability of reserves must depend directly upon the technology applied to finding them, the energy available for extracting them, and the capital required for exploiting them. All three of these are available only in modern societies. Whenever a modern society has needed a resource, and its members have been willing to invest in the technology to find it, that resource has been found. Aluminium cost $545 a pound in the 1920s; fifty years later it cost only about fifty cents a pound. The price dropped for the reason that once aluminium had proved one of industry's most versatile materials, the development of a technology for mining bauxite ore and converting it into the metal lowered the price to nearly the vanishing point.

Throughout the last half century, assertions have been made that the reserves of petroleum were running out, yet decade by decade those reserves have continued to increase. The explanation is that once older reserves run low, the tapping of vast new sources then becomes economically justified. Two decades ago it became economically feasible to drill for oil and natural gas offshore on the continental shelf; today it has become feasible to drill in the North Sea; as these reserves in turn begin to run out, it may become

In 1967 two 'futurists' at the Hudson Institute listed technological innovations they considered possible by the end of this century, ranging from the very likely to the remote. So rapid has been innovation that only a decade later some possibilities have been achieved. (Only a small number of their predictions are listed here.) ♂♀

## Very Likely Possibilities

1. The application of lasers for sensing, measuring, communication, cutting, welding, power transmission, defence, and other purposes (already partially achieved)
2. Worldwide use of high-altitude cameras for mapping, prospecting, census, land use, and geological investigations (achieved)
3. Major reductions in hereditary and congenital defects (partially achieved)
4. Three-dimensional photography, films, and television (partially achieved through holography)
5. Use of nuclear explosions for excavation and mining, for the generation of power, and as a source of neutrons (partially achieved)
6. New techniques for inexpensive, convenient, and reliable birth control (achieved)
7. Control of weather and climate
8. General and substantial increase in life expectancy, postponement of ageing, and limited rejuvenation
9. Chemical methods for improving memory and learning
10. Artificial moons for lighting large areas at night

## Less Likely Possibilities

1. Artificial intelligence (partially achieved with computers)
2. Artificial growth of new limbs and organs
3. Major use of rockets for commercial or private transportation
4. Effective chemical or biological treatment for most mental illnesses
5. Suspended animation for years or for centuries
6. Automated highways
7. Direct augmentation of human mental capacity by interconnection of the brain with a computer
8. Verification of some extrasensory phenomena
9. Practical laboratory conception and nurturing of human foetuses
10. Substantial manned lunar or planetary installations

## Remote Possibilities

1. Life expectancy extended to substantially more than 150 years
2. Almost complete genetic control
3. Interstellar travel
4. Practical and routine use of extrasensory phenomena
5. Laboratory creation of living plants and animals

feasible to tap the vast amounts of petroleum locked in the shale rocks of the planet. And, of course, the new energy sources of solar and nuclear power offer virtually unlimited supplies. At this writing, solar heating is nearly competitive in cost with electric heating. The world's energy supply is certainly sufficient to allow time to solve the technological problems associated with nuclear energy from both breeder and fusion reactors.

The present-day concern over the disposal of nuclear wastes is reminiscent of fears expressed at the beginning of this century that the vehicular traffic in London and Paris would bury those cities under mountains of horse dung. Then, of course, the automobile was invented and that problem was solved. The automobile in its turn has brought new forms of pollution, but that problem is also being attacked. London has so scrubbed its air that within two decades the winter sunshine of that city has increased by 50 per cent. It has likewise so cleansed the Thames of pollutants that for the first time in many decades the river abounds with fish. The sweep of hominid history provides a basis for believing that modernized humans will invent new techniques to meet new needs, as they always have in the past.

Modernization offers humankind an opportunity not available since the virtual disappearance of the hunting–gathering adaptation: the full development of the human potential. Modernization has already brought something closer to equality between the sexes, a greater intensity in the relations among family members, and a voice in important decisions for all members of the family. Perhaps the greatest contribution of modernization has been the wide range of freedoms it has produced. Although people around the world are still hampered by outmoded political and social systems, those in the modern nations are much less restricted than the rest. Many abuses still exist, of course, and modern societies of necessity have developed systems for regulating the complexities of behaviour that go with modernization. The authority they exercise is, however, far less repressive and brutal than in previous adaptations. Even in early industrial society, the physical beating of females and children was often part of the husband's role, and masters could beat and maim their serfs and servants with impunity. In western Europe only a century ago, well over a hundred crimes, most of which are considered minor today, were punishable by a lifetime of labour or by executions that were regarded as public entertainments. Even the seemingly egalitarian hunter–gatherers lived under powerful social constraints that made very plain the kinds of behaviour that were acceptable to the members of the society.

The governmental bureaucracy essential to modernization is often declared to have reduced freedom for the members of society. Many governmental restrictions, however, serve to increase freedom rather than to reduce it. The Pure Food and Drug Act in the United States, for example, restricts the freedom of a minority of business-men willing to sell tainted food and harmful drugs for profit, but it increases freedom from sickness for the rest of the population. Social Security limits somewhat the freedom of entrepreneurs to accumu-late profits, but it gives the mass of the population the freedom of an old age with at least a minimal income.

Human freedom is more than just the lessening of repressive social controls. It includes also freedom from back-breaking labour for child and adult alike, freedom from disease, from mental and physi-cal handicaps, and from the vagaries of the physical environment. For females, it includes freedom from a long succession of unwanted pregnancies. People are free when they can behave in ways inde-pendent of restrictions imposed by the natural and social environ-ments. Modern technology has made such choices possible. Techno-logical power is not in itself either good or bad. It is simply power that can be used ruthlessly – or with wisdom sufficient to avoid the frightening pitfalls of the next few decades. To this extent, the in-habitant of a modern society enjoys a range of choices that far sur-pass in richness and variety those that were available to the most tyrannical of emperors in the past.

And so, back to the question posed earlier in this chapter: Does our species have a future? I could not have undertaken this book without a personal opinion on this question. If we can survive a few great hazards that face us in the coming decades, then I forecast the ushering in of a new era expressive as never before of the human potential. One basis for qualified optimism is that our species has always been beset by problems. The uniquely human capacity to solve problems has always produced innovations – biological, cul-tural, and technological – which in turn have brought our species to new levels of adaptations. No reason whatever exists for doubting that such will continue to be the case in the future. I therefore have written this book not as an obituary for our species but as a cele-bration of it.

# Acknowledgments

This book received unusual care and attention from many people, from the very beginning of the project through the final production. My agent, Carl Brandt, has been an especially supportive advocate ever since I first broached the idea for such a book to him years ago. My editor, Robert Cowley, never flagged throughout his readings of the interminable drafts and never hesitated to show his concern that the book fully express what it set out to do; he has, in addition, been a loyal and enthusiastic friend. Once again, Amy Clampitt served admirably as the demanding copy editor and general worrier about the entire manuscript; once again too, Marjorie Weinstein showed intelligence and care in the reading of galleys and proofs; Sharon Fretwell was imperturbable during the last-minute rush of typing the manuscript. Janice Byer and Linda Glick of Houghton Mifflin Company lavished especial attention on the project and were conscientious throughout.

I could not have written this book without calling upon the resources, both physical and human, of the University of Massachusetts at Amherst. Numerous people at the University Libraries were invariably cheerful and helpful in obtaining research materials for me. Sections of the manuscript were read at various stages of completion by the following University faculty members, who offered numerous suggestions in their areas of specialization: George Armelagos (anthropology and biology), Charles Clifton (psychology), John P. Hewitt (sociology), and Wang Hui-ming (Asiatic culture and history). Since this book had to be of necessity a personal one that abstracted only several hundred pages from an immense archive of knowledge about human accomplishments, I could not always take their advice; none of the above, therefore, should be faulted for any lapses that might appear in these pages.

In addition to expressing my appreciation to all these, I must also express my indebtedness to others. A number of them have influenced my thinking in major ways over the years – and I happily acknowledged these intellectual debts in the Notes and Sources, at places that seemed most appropriate. My indebtedness to hundreds of other scholars, in many disciplines, should be clear from my listing of their works in the Bibliography. Even back and beyond all these, no inventory of indebtedness would be complete if I failed to mention my late brother-in-law Franklin Horch. During more than two decades, he was a generous and devoted friend; lacking his support, I could not have written the books that I felt needed doing.

PETER FARB
*Amherst, Massachusetts*

## Illustration Acknowledgments

*Page* 20–21, drawing by Eliza McFadden. Adapted from *Origins of Man* by John Buettner-Janusch, New York: John Wiley & Sons, 1966/27, drawing by Eliza McFadden. Adapted from *Human Ecology* edited by Norman Levine, North Scituate, Mass.: Duxbury Press, 1975/31, drawing by Eliza McFadden. Adapted from *The Natural History of Man* by J. S. Weiner, New York: Doubleday, 1973; and from *Monkeys and Apes* by Pru Napier, New York: Grosset, 1972/59, drawing by Eliza McFadden. Adapted from *The Human Species* by Frederick Hulse, New York: Random House, 1971, 2nd edition; and from *Man the Tool-Maker* by Kenneth P. Oakley, Chicago: University of Chicago Press, 1959/62, drawing by Eliza McFadden. Adapted from *Paleolithic Cave Art* by Peter J. Ucko and Andrée Rosenfeld, copyright © 1967 by Ucko and Rosenfeld. Used with permission of McGraw-Hill Book Company/66, drawing by Eliza McFadden. Adapted from *The Brain Changers* by Maya Pines, New York: Harcourt Brace Jovanovich, 1973/70, drawing by Eliza McFadden. Adapted from 'Tools and Human Evolution' by Sherwood L. Washburn, copyright © 1960 by *Scientific American*; all rights reserved/80, drawing by Eliza McFadden. Adapted from *The Roots of Mankind* by John Napier, New York: Harper & Row, 1970/94–95, drawing by Eliza McFadden. Adapted from *Man the Hunter* edited by Richard B. Lee and Irven DeVore, Chicago: Aldine Publishing Co., 1968/110, drawing by Eliza McFadden. Adapted from *Culture, People, Nature* by Marvin Harris, New York: Crowell, 1975/114–115, drawing by Eliza McFadden. Adapted from *Culture, People, Nature* by Marvin Harris, New

York: Crowell, 1975/134, drawing by Eliza McFadden. Adapted from *Peasants* by Eric Wolf, copyright © 1966 by Eric Wolf. Used with permission of Prentice-Hall, Inc., Englewood Cliffs, N.J./159, permission of Macmillan Publishing Co., from *The Human Adventure* by Gretel H. Pelto and Pertti J. Pelto, 1976/178, drawing by Eliza McFadden. Adapted from *Human Ecology* edited by Norman D. Levine, North Scituate, Mass.: Duxbury Press, 1975/244–245, drawing by Melanson Associates. Adapted from *Heredity, Evolution, and Society* by I. Michael Lerner and William J. Libby, San Francisco: Freeman, 1976, 2nd edition/248, drawing by Eliza McFadden. Adapted from *An Introduction to the Study of Man* by J. Z. Young, New York: Oxford University Press, 1971/256, courtesy of IBM Research Laboratory, San Jose, Ca./261, courtesy of The American Museum of Natural History/291, drawing by Eliza McFadden/298, permission of Random House, from *Psychology Today*, New York: CRM–Random House, 1972, 3rd edition.

# Notes and Sources

PAGE

vi    The quotation from Sophocles' *Antigone* is from the R. C. Jebb translation, reprinted in *The Complete Greek Drama* edited by Whitney J. Oates and Eugene O'Neill, Jr (New York: Random House, 1938), vol. 1, p. 432.

1. *Ape or Angel?*
Many points touched on only briefly in this introductory chapter can be found in great detail in Hockett (1973), Hulse (1971), and Buettner-Janusch (1966). And, of course, I will be expanding upon them in subsequent chapters.

11    Psalm 8, King James Version. From Disraeli's speech at the Oxford Diocesan Conference on 25 November, 1864.

14    Itard's influence has been very great. Contrary to the medical opinion of his time, he and his followers demonstrated that the mentally retarded could be educated. George Summer witnessed Itard's methods as they were practised in Paris and brought them back to the United States, where he began the first educational programme for the retarded on this continent. Maria Montessori later extended Itard's methods to the education of the normal pre-school child. A splendid book about Itard and the Wild Boy of Aveyron is Lane (1976). The quotation is from Lane (1976), p. 26.

15    The quotation is from *The Portable Medieval Reader* edited by James B. Ross and Mary M. McLaughlin (New York: Viking Press, 1949), p. 366.

15    The Baltimore example is in Gardner (1972). Spitz reported on this appalling statistic in his (1945).

18    The inventory of definitions was made by Kroeber and Kluckhohn (1952).

19    An excellent discussion of anthropocentrism is Murdy (1975).

## 2. The Importance of Being a Primate

This chapter is indebted for various facts and ideas to the following works in particular: Lancaster (1975), Eimerl and DeVore (1974), Dolhinow (1972), Jolly (1972), Weiner (1971), Kummer (1971), Young (1971), and Napier (1970). For wide-ranging studies of primates in the context of their adaptations, see Tuttle (1975). No listing of intellectual debts would be complete without personal acknowledgments to Phyllis Jay Dolhinow, who introduced me to primate behaviour at Columbia University, and to John Napier, with whom I had stimulating conversations while we were at the Smithsonian Institution; I am grateful to Napier also for freely making available to me some years ago his library of films of primate behaviour.

PAGE

24   I found this quotation in Lane (1976), p. 20.

33   Tool-making and other chimpanzee behaviours reported on in this chapter are discussed at much greater length in van Lawick-Goodall (1971).

33   The chimpanzees' reaction to the stuffed leopard is reported by Kortlandt and van Zon (1969).

34   The material on chimpanzee hunting and sharing is from Teleki (1973), and that on baboon hunting is from Strum (1975) and Harding (1975).

36   A recent summary of dominance in non-human primates, together with the implications for human societies, is Loy (1975).

37   Various reproductive strategies are discussed by Goss-Custard *et al.* (1972).

38   The last several pages rely heavily for information about primate social behaviour upon Lancaster (1975). A thought-provoking analysis of primate social structures from a different perspective is Eisenberg *et al.* (1972).

39   Information on protoculture in Japanese monkeys can be found in Kawai (1965) and Menzel (1966).

42   Some researchers have recently reported problem-solving and other mental skills in captive, but untrained, primates. See, for example, Beck (1973).

## 3. The Hominid Pattern

Several volumes were especially valuable in the research for this chapter: Campbell (1974), Fagan (1974), Howells (1973), Lasker (1973), Birdsell (1972), and Pilbeam (1972). All are textbooks, but they can be understood by anyone who has first read my chapter. More accessible to the general reader, and highly recommended, is Pfeiffer (1972).

PAGE

44     *Hamlet*, Act 1, Scene 5.

47     For the latest summary of information about the Ramapithecines, see Simons (1977).

50     A rather technical discussion of the Lake Turkana and Ethiopian excavations is Coppens *et al.* (1976).

51     A brief summary of the most recent hypotheses about the earliest hominids appears in *Science*, vol. 187 (1975), pp. 940–942.

53     At the time of the discovery of the first Neanderthal specimens, *Thal* was spelled with an *h*, even though it was silent in pronunciation. Early in this century, Germans altered their spelling style and the silent *h* in such words was dropped. That is why 'Neanderthal' has sometimes been spelled in recent decades without the *h*. I have retained the traditional spelling because it is deeply embedded in the scientific literature.

54     The Neanderthal adaptation is discussed in Campbell (1972), pp. 40–58.

56     For Neanderthal burials, see Solecki (1975) and (1972).

57     The idea of relating body build to weapons was first put forward by Brues (1959).

58     I learned about the Danish woodsmen from Hockett (1973), p. 495.

60     For the archer's body build, see Brues (1959).

62     A detailed analysis of the various theories that have been proposed to account for the uses of cave art can be found in Ucko and Rosenfeld (1967). The volume is heavily illustrated with examples.

*4. Becoming Human*

Many ideas in this chapter are derived from Lancaster (1975); although a brief work, it has an extremely high specific gravity and is full of fascinating insights. Campbell (1974), Pfeiffer (1972), and Napier (1970) have been listed as sources for previous chapters; ideas in them proved equally valuable for this chapter.

64     Statistics on brain size are from *Guinness Book of World Records* by Norris McWhirter and Ross McWhirter (New York: Bantam Books, revised edition, 1974), p. 36.

65     For these facts, and many others in this chapter about the human brain, I am indebted to Rose (1973). Both this book and Pines (1973) are highly recommended for the non-specialist.

PAGE

68   Very recent research at the California Institute of Technology indicates that the brain is not quite so non-symmetrical in regard to language as had been believed. That is, the right hemisphere is not completely silent. Some adults have been shown to possess in this hemisphere the grammatical ability of a five-year-old child, which is very advanced indeed for a supposedly non-verbal area.

71   This chapter could touch only briefly on brain function. Some papers that enlarge upon points I have made are Geschwind (1972), Luria (1970), and Gazzaniga (1967). More technical is Dimond and Beaumont (1974).

71   The New Testament quotation is from Matthew 10:30. Hair as a symbol is discussed in detail in Firth (1973), pp. 262–298.

73   Two excellent papers which uphold a position different from the one I have taken concerning the language of non-human primates are Fouts (1975) and Rumbaugh *et al.* (1975). Both maintain that the communication abilities of apes differ only in degree, not in kind, from human language, and that therefore human language is not unique (except for its use of a vocal channel). But, as I have tried to emphasize, the vocal channel is crucial to language. A fascinating collection of papers about the attempts to teach a chimpanzee named 'Lana' to communicate via a computer programme is Rumbaugh (1977).

76   For the features of language, see Hockett and Altmann (1968) and Hockett and Ascher (1964). For a fuller discussion of these ideas and others about language, see Farb (1974).

77   An excellent discussion of the brain and language from an evolutionary perspective can be found in Jerison (1976) and (1973).

77   An argument for the gestural origins of language, with the vocal channel developing relatively late, is offered by Hewes (1973).

78   A case for the Neanderthals' possible inability to speak can be found in Lieberman and Crelin (1971). For a fuller exposition of Lieberman's hypothesis about the evolution of speech, see his (1975). Among those who have contested his arguments is Le May (1975).

81   Many of my ideas about walking are from Napier (1970).

81   The scars of evolution are discussed by Krogman (1951).

83   I am indebted for the observation about art preceding utility, and also for documentary examples, to Cyril S. Smith, Institute Professor Emeritus at MIT.

86   That humans need crowds of other humans is the thesis put forth by
     Freedman (1975). I discuss the subject further in Chapter 8. The state-
     ment about the Bushmen is from Draper (1973).

86   That the debate continues is shown by McHenry (1975).

### 5. The Hunting-Gathering Adaptation

Basic sources for this chapter were Ucko *et al.* (1972), Bicchieri (1972),
Sahlins (1972), and Lee and DeVore (1968). The last is an especially important volume for understanding the hunting adaptation. Particularly
valuable for the Bushman were Lee and DeVore (1976) and Marshall (1976).
I also profited greatly from personal conversations with Irven DeVore, and
here express my gratitude. A basic source on the Pygmies is Turnbull (1962).
Several American Indian hunting–gathering societies are described in detail
in Farb (1978). A valuable short paper is Washburn and Lancaster (1968).

93    An excellent discussion of 'hunter's appetite' as well as many other
      aspects of the hunter–gatherer life is in Weiner (1971), Chapter 4.

96    For amino acids and human nutrition, see Scrimshaw and Young
      (1976).

97    *Leviathan*, Part I, Chapter 13.

97    *Roughing It*, Harper & Brothers Edition, 1871, pp. 131–132.

98    Sahlins (1972), Chapter 1.

99    The quotation from Father Biard appears in *The Jesuit Relations and
      Allied Documents*, edited by R. G. Thwaites (Cleveland, Ohio: Bur-
      rows, 1897), vol. 3, pp. 84–85.

100   *The Gentle Tasaday* by John Nance (New York: Harcourt Brace
      Jovanovich, 1975).

100   Sahlins (1972), p. 33.

101   My discussion of the Bushmen is based primarily on various publica-
      tions by Lee, especially (1972A), (1972B), (1969), and (1968). Of
      major importance are the papers collected in Lee and DeVore (1976).
      See also Marshall (1976).

103   Truswell and Hansen in Lee and DeVore (1976), pp. 166–194, provide
      additional details about the health of the Bushmen.

104   Lee (1972B), p. 359.

105   For the Arnhem Land studies, see McCarthy and McArthur (1960).
      The classic study of the Great Basin Shoshone is Steward (1938).

## 6. Food Production and Its Consequences

Excellent general sources for more details about food production than this chapter could possibly cover are: Braidwood (1975), Chard (1975), Fagan (1974), Lamberg-Karlovsky and Sabloff (1974), and Ucko and Dimbleby (1969). For specific discussions of origins and consequences, Flannery (1973) and (1969) and Smith (1976) are particularly important. Let me belatedly in these Notes discharge a pleasurable debt to Marvin Harris. His influence upon my thinking, both through his writings and through personal contact when I sat in his class in graduate school, can be seen in many chapters in this book, even though I have not always called specific attention to thoughts of his I have appropriated. More clear and original insights about our species can be found in his (1975) than in a bookshelf of anthropological works.

PAGE

109   The aurochs was the wild ancestor of domesticated cattle. It is probably the animal that in many versions of the Bible has been mistranslated as 'unicorn' (for example, Number 24:8). Caesar commented upon the aurochs' size and power when he saw it in Gaul, but he exaggerated when he stated that it was as large as an elephant. The aurochs was widespread in the ancient Near East, Europe, and North Africa, and the last known specimen survived until 1627 in Poland. In 1921 a German scientist set about to 'reconstruct' this extinct species, so far as possible, by cross-breeding several kinds of domesticated cattle that still had many of its characteristics. These animals very much resemble illustrations and descriptions of the ancient animals; several dozen of them are now in European zoos.

111   The use of microliths to harvest wheat is described by Harlan (1967).

113   The brief quotation is from Childe (1942), p. 49.

116   For a fuller discussion of pastoral nomadism, see Salzman (1971).

116   The quotation is from Childe's *The Dawn of European Civilization* (London: Routledge & Kegan Paul, 1925) – which is not listed in the Bibliography because it is seriously out of date and can be recommended only as a curiosity. A summary of the various hypotheses about the origins of food production in the Near East can be found in Wright (1971).

118   See Flannery (1969) for the most compelling statement of the ecological hypothesis. The subject of trade has assumed increasing importance in recent theorizing about the rise of complex civilizations, as, for example, in Sabloff and Lamberg-Karlovsky (1975).

119   Bushman fertility is discussed by Lee (1972A).

121   An excellent paper on the influence of population on the origins of agriculture, with particular attention to Peru, is Cohen (1975).

Population increase as both a cause and a consequence of early food production is discussed in detail by Bronson (1975).

123   Details about the origins of the most important domesticated plants and animals of the world can be found in Heiser (1973).

124   This observation on the growth habits of teosinte–beans–squash was made by Flannery (1973), p. 291.

125   Detailed information about Tehuacan can be found in MacNeish (1972).

125   For more about diseases, see Armelagos and McArdle (1976), Armelagos and Dewey (1973), and Cockburn (1971).

126   See Brues (1959) for a discussion of the body build of agriculturists.

127   Space did not permit a more extensive discussion of specific technologies. But such a discussion can be found, for both foraging and food-producing societies, in Spier (1970).

127   The brief quotation is from *Where Winter Never Comes* by Marston Bates (New York: Scribner's, 1952), p. 53. I profited greatly over a period of years from conversations with my friend Marston about the transition to complex civilization – which he, whimsical and civilized gentleman that he was, felt in his very bones had somehow been a wrong turn for humankind. The wisdom in his many books is as valuable today as when the books were written.

## 7. The Perennial Peasants

No chapter about peasants could be written without relying heavily upon Foster (1967) and Wolf (1966), as I have done. An excellent collection of readings about peasantry and the implications of this way of life is Shanin (1971). The position of peasants in modern societies could only be touched upon in my chapter, but it is discussed at greater length in Gamst (1974) and Mangin (1970).

130   Marx made his statement in *The 18th Brumaire of Louis Buonaparte*, and was referring to French peasants. His other writings, though, indicate that he took the same view of peasants in other parts of the world.

131   For a strong statement about the diversity of peasants, see Dalton (1972). For a discussion of similar religious observances regardless of the particular faith, see Michaelson and Goldschmidt (1976).

132   The quotation is from R. H. Tawney and is cited by Ward (1976), p. 65.

135   I learned about the Mecklenberg example from Wolf (1966), pp. 5–9.

136   The discussion of peasant diet relies largely on Stini (1971).

137 Observations on the lack of organizations in peasant communities, along with much else about peasant attitudes, can be found in Banfield (1958). For a literary approach to peasant attitudes, see *Fontamara* by Ignazio Silone (New York: Atheneum, 1960).

138 See Foster (1967), Chapter 6. The concept of 'limited good' has been widely adopted by social scientists, but several object to it. Some alternate explanations for peasant behaviour have been offered, most recently by Gregory (1975); but note the critical comments by other social scientists in the pages following his paper.

140 Much of this information about peasant attitudes towards family size comes from a paper presented at the 1975 annual meeting of the American Anthropological Association by Karen L. Michaelson.

141 The study of the Javanese is by White (1975).

141 The anecdote about sheep in Ecuador is from Harris (1964).

145 This quotation and much of my material about Chinese peasants is based on Skinner (1971) – whose claim for their uniqueness, however, I find somewhat extreme.

147 For my discussion of peasant rebellions, I am indebted to Landsberger (1973), Thrupp (1970), and in particular Wolf (1969). The original title of the novel translated by Buck is more accurately rendered into English as *Water Margin*; it was compiled by Shih Nai-an in the fourteenth-century Ming dynasty from earlier oral narratives. The affinity between Mao's revolution and earlier peasant rebellions is seen in the fact that Mao carried *Water Margin* with him during the Long March. Those North Americans and Europeans who have played the game of mahjong, which is a Westernized version of an ancient Chinese game, probably do not realize that the pieces originally represented the bandit-heroes in Shih's novel.

147 The statistics in nineteenth-century Russian peasant uprisings are from *History of the National Economy of Russia to the 1917 Revolution* by P. I. Lyashchenko (New York: Macmillan, 1949).

150 An excellent description, more detailed than is possible here, of peasants in the modernizing world can be found in the last chapter of Gamst (1974).

*8. Urban Influences*

For the basic outlines of the first half of this chapter I am indebted in particular to Ward (1976) and Chard (1975), but also to Fagan (1974), Lamberg-Karlovsky and Sabloff (1974), and Hauser (1965). An extensive collection of papers about almost all topics relating to urbanism is Ucko *et al.*

(1972). No one can write about cities without relying heavily for ideas upon the works of Lewis Mumford; I have listed a particular favourite, his (1961), in the Bibliography, even though some of his conclusions will have to be revised in light of more recent discoveries. A very spirited defence of the city is Freedman (1975). Two excellent collections of readings are Helmer and Eddington (1973) and Southall (1973). I discuss the evolution of complex societies further in Chapter 16, but readers interested in the subject at this point should read, in particular, Service (1975) and also Adams (1966). For overviews of the population problems of cities, see Davis (1974) and several papers in Worsley (1972).

PAGE

152   The early construction of the European megaliths is claimed by Renfrew (1973). For information about the writing found in Rumania, see 'The Tartaria Tablets' by M. F. Hood, *Scientific American*, vol. 216 (May 1968).

153   Jacobs (1969) has forcefully argued for the primacy of the city over agriculture. She has called attention to the important innovations made in cities which later caused revolutions in agricultural techniques; she has also directed attention to the development of cities independent of agriculture. Although many archaeologists and sociologists regard her thesis as overdrawn, her basic line of inquiry remains valid and provides fascinating reading.

153   I owe these observations about the necropolis to Mumford (1961).

154   The importance of trade to the early civilizations is discussed from many points of view in Sabloff and Lamberg-Karlovsky (1975). A paper on metallurgy and the trade in metals is Wertime (1973).

156   Book I of *The Laws* is entirely concerned with arguments for and against this point of view. I still consider the translation by Jowett the most pleasing. It can be found in *The Dialogues of Plato* by B. Jowett (New York: Random House, 1937), vol. 2. An excellent source dealing with warfare in the ancient Near East is Roper (1975). In fact, the entire volume in which it appears, Nettleship *et al.* (1975), is notable for its thoroughness in having brought together specialists in warfare from many disciples.

160   For the evolution of writing, see Jensen (1963), Gelb (1963), and Diringer (1962).

162   Ward (1976), p. 37.

163   For many of the thoughts as well as the statistics in the past several pages, I am indebted to Ward (1976).

164   The study of walking speed is by Bornstein and Bornstein (1976).

PAGE

165 The analogy of a dense city with an overloaded system is from Milgram (1970). The entire paper is a major discussion of the psychology of living in cities.

166 The quotation is from Freedman (1975), p. 8, and so is most of the information in the paragraph that follows.

167 The most informative study of bystander apathy, with particular reference to the Genovese case, is Latané and Darley (1970).

170 Most of the information on urban diseases in this chapter has been garnered from Levine (1975, Chapter 14), Cockburn (1971), Boyden (1970), and Brothwell and Sandison (1967). For a history of the Black Death, see Ziegler (1970).

172 An important survey of age–sex distribution and other demographic facts about cities is Cook (1960).

173 Jefferson is quoted in *The American City: A Documentary History* by Charles N. Glaab (Homewood, Ill.: Dorsey Press, 1963), p. 6. The Wright quotation is from his *The Living City* (New York: Horizon Press, 1959), p. 21.

173 As this book is being written, the revolutionary government of Cambodia is making an attempt to return to the food-producing adaptation. It has forcibly depopulated its cities, leaving them eerily silent. No one can predict with assurance whether or not a successful new society will be forged by a return to food production. If the attempt is successful, it will be the first time in history that a large society has intentionally undone several thousand years of urbanization.

## 9. Modernization: Towards the World City

No one can write about modernization without having been influenced by Bell, particularly his (1973). Other works to which I am indebted in this chapter are Lenski and Lenski (1974), Toffler (1970), Inkeles (1969), Weiner (1966), and Ellul (1964). A wide-ranging selection of readings, most of them pertinent to this chapter, is Worsley (1972). An excellent article on modernization by Gino Germani appears in the fifteenth edition (1974) of the *Encyclopedia Britannica*, vol. 9 of the *Macropaedia* section, pp. 520–527. And, once again, let me point out that I have profited greatly from reading the relevant sections in Harris (1975).

174 *The Education of Henry Adams* by Henry Adams (New York: Modern Library, 1931), p. 501 (originally published 1906).

175 These statistics are from Toffler (1970), p. 26.

177 A special issue of *Scientific American* for September 1971 (vol. 224) was devoted to energy, its role in various adaptations, and its social consequences.

179  Figures on caloric input are from Pimentel *et al.* (1973).

179  Information in this caption is from Levine (1975), pp. 329–332.

181  For much of this comparison between China and Europe I am indebted to Harris (1975), pp. 433–438. The classic study of the influence of water-control works in China upon political, social, and economic systems is Wittfogel (1957); the hydraulic hypothesis that forms the underpinnings of this work is supported by some investigators but has been challenged by numerous others as simplistic. Scholars in the past have often overlooked the fact that numerous technological innovations in Europe did not originate at the beginning of the Industrial Revolution; rather the innovations were made during the tenth to fourteenth centuries, long considered a stagnant era. Wind power and water power were harnessed, an iron industry developed, new architectural techniques were invented, and agricultural productivity increased markedly. For documentation, see Gimpel (1977).

182  Williams (1966) discusses the triangular trade in detail.

185  The consequences of modernization are discussed by Lenski and Lenski (1974), Part III.

188  The five components outlined here are adapted from Bell (1973).

189  Toffler (1970), p. 11.


*10. Male and Female*

A vast literature has grown up, particularly in the past decade, about sex differences and the behaviour expected of each sex in various societies. A most valuable brief summary of the general literature is Oakley (1972); I have consulted it often in writing this chapter and recommend it highly. Highly recommended also is Martin and Voorhies (1975); much of interest can be found in Kessler (1976). Recent scientific literature specifically about biological and psychological differences between the sexes is extensive. The most comprehensive study to date, one which evaluates almost all important previous research, is Maccoby and Jacklin (1974); also of interest is Sherman (1971). An excellent collection of papers on sex roles is Rosaldo and Lamphere (1974). A rather technical but important study of hormonal influences on sex differentiation is Money and Ehrhardt (1972). Increasing awareness of the subservient female role in society has resulted in numerous volumes; among those that proved most valuable were Huber (1973), Dreitzel (1972), and Seward and Williamson (1970). An excellent collection of papers on human sexual behaviour is Marshall and Suggs (1971). Various perspectives on sex roles, particularly that of females, are presented in Raphael (1975).

194 Mead's study was published in 1935. Some social scientists have objected to it on the basis of incomplete data and oversimplification. Nevertheless, Mead's general conclusions about the influence of a society on the behaviour of the sexes has been supported by more recent field-work; see, for example, Meggitt (1964).

197 Lerner and Libby (1976), p. 153.

199 The Pliny quotation is from his *Natural History*, translated by H. Rackham (Cambridge, Mass.: Harvard University Press, 1961), p. 549.

199 An excellent discussion of attitudes towards menstruation is Delaney *et al.* (1976).

200 The study of oestruslike behaviour in human females is by Udry and Morris (1968).

201 For the information in this paragraph, as well as in many other paragraphs throughout the chapter, I am indebted to Oakley (1972).

201 The two psychologists present their findings in Maccoby and Jacklin (1974).

203 These studies have been reported in Waber (1976).

205 An attempt to explain the universality of patriarchy is Goldberg (1973). See his pp. 238–245 for comments on the societies that are supposed exceptions to the rule of male dominance.

205 The Mbuti Pygmies are sometimes singled out as a society in which male dominance is absent. That is not so; see the definitive study of the Mbuti by Turnbull (1965).

207 A survey of division of labour by sex in 224 societies was undertaken by Murdock (1937).

207 The quotation is from *Male and Female* by Margaret Mead (New York: Morrow, 1949), p. 168.

209 A discussion of aggression can be found in Maccoby and and Jacklin (1974), particularly pp. 360–370 but elsewhere throughout the book as well.

209 It is impossible to be fair to these explanations in a brief space. For a well-reasoned presentation of the sexual-conflict hypothesis (with which I nevertheless disagree), see Collins (1972). The Marxist explanation was actually put forth by Friedrich Engels in *The Origin of the Family, Private Property, and the State* (1891). Numerous psychoanalytic explanations have been offered; that of the envious male was proposed by Bruno Bettelheim in *Symbolic Wounds: Puberty Rites and the Envious Male* (New York: Collier Books, 1962).

PAGE

210 The only exceptions known to the statement that females do not fight in hand-to-hand combat are guerrilla forces and some Germanic tribes of more than 2000 years ago. Burials of both male and female warriors have recently been discovered in Germany. That the females were truly fighters and not camp followers is indicated by several facts: They were given soldiers' burials; they wore male clothing; and all had died of wounds. In modern Germany, on the other hand, no females served in the armed forces until 1976, and then only as medical officers.

212 For my summary of the combat hypothesis, I am greatly indebted to Harris, particularly his (1974), pp. 61–107. The quotation is from p. 87 of that work. A fuller development of the hypothesis is Divale and Harris (1976); I am grateful to Harris for sending it to me in advance of publication. On the Yanomamo, see Chagnon (1974) and (1968).

213 An excellent paper on the way sex roles are perceived is Broverman *et al.* (1972).

213 The survey of sexual behaviour in numerous societies was by Ford and Beach (1951). Some have regarded it as incomplete and biased, yet it still represents the most thorough cross-cultural study of sexual attitudes ever attempted. A more recent but considerably less ambitious attempt to survey attitudes towards sex in many societies is Broude and Greene (1976). The institutionalization of homosexuality among the Mohave Indians is reported in Devereux (1937). A brief history of homosexuality in ancient Greece is contained in *The Natural History of Love* by Morton M. Hunt (New York: Knopf, 1959), Chapter 6. Also, see West (1968) on homosexuality.

214 The studies mentioned in this paragraph are summarized by Block (1973).

215 A description of Mangaian sexual behaviour appears in Marshall (1971).

216 On sexuality in India, see Nag (1972).

218 The situation in the Soviet Union was reported in *The New York Times*, 17 June 1975.

219 The studies of a generation ago were published in Kinsey, Pomeroy, and Martin (1953) and (1948). The 1972 data were published in Hunt (1974).

220 The quotation is from Shorter (1975), p. 254.

### 11. A Diverse Species

A wide-ranging introduction to material covered in this chapter and in the two that follow is Smith (1975). More scholarly treatments, but eminently readable ones nevertheless, are those by Lerner and Libby (1976) and Lasker (1973). Undoubtedly the most controversial subject discussed in this chapter is intelligence; fortunately a large literature on the subject exists. Probably the best selection of readings on the IQ controversy, together with a thorough analysis by the editors, is Block and Dworkin (1976). An excellent summary of the inherited and environmental components in intelligence is Cancro (1971). More controversial positions on IQ are taken by Jensen (1973, 1969) – whose position I totally reject – and by Kamin (1974), whose views I find much more congenial.

PAGE

222 The fascinating story of the debate about the humanity of the American Indian is told in *Aristotle and the American Indian* by Lewis Hanke (Bloomington, Indiana: Indiana University Press, 1959).

223 The quotation is from *Behaviorism* by John B. Watson (New York: Norton, 1925).

224 Father Cobo's quotation is found in Monge and Monge (1966), pp. 73–74. This slim volume is a classic study by two pioneers in high-altitude research. See also Frisancho (1975) and Clegg *et al.* (1970).

226 Information about responses to cold are in Steegman (1975) and Little *et al.* (1971). The Steegman paper is a particularly informative summary of findings on this subject. Other summaries of research are Roberts (1973) and Little and Hochner (1973).

226 *Julius Caesar*, Act 1, Scene 2.

226 I learned about the so-called born criminal from Molnar (1975), p. 10.

227 The basic source on body types (technically known as 'somatotypes') is Sheldon and Stevens (1942).

227 I am indebted for this illustration to Smith (1975).

229 Much of the material in the last few paragraphs is from Gould (1974) and Young (1971).

233 An excellent survey of twin studies is Mittler (1971).

234 The psychologist who opts for eight abilities is L. L. Thurstone; see *Psychometric Monograph 2* (Chicago: University of Chicago Press, 1941). The claim for 120 variables is made by J. P. Guilford in *The Nature of Human Intelligence* (New York: McGraw-Hill, 1967).

235 As this book is being completed, yet another attempt has been made to devise an IQ test free from cultural bias. In this one, developed at the University of California (Riverside), rather than score a child by com-

parison with a fixed nationwide standard, a comparison is made with the scores of other children from similar social, economic, and cultural backgrounds. In other words, the new test, known as SOMPA (System of Multicultural Pluralistic Assessment), gives a score that has been corrected for cultural differences. A Mexican–American child might score 100 (that is, 'average intelligence') on a traditional IQ test. But in comparison with other children from Spanish-speaking families at the lowest end of the economic scale in rural California, the corrected score might be 140 (which would indicate a 'gifted' child).

236    For details of the study of Dutch firstborns, see Belmont and Marolla (1973). One presentation of the dethroned-king hypothesis, in accounting for the disproportionate accomplishments of firstborns, is that by Richard Zweigenhaft in *Journal of Individual Psychology*, vol. 31 (1976), pp. 205–210.

236    See Bodmer and Cavalli-Sforza (1976), p. 508.

237    The Israeli kibbutz study is discussed by Ginsburg and Laughlin(1971).

238    One such study was made of two groups of children in an Iowa orphanage in the 1930s. Thirteen of them scored below 70 on IQ tests and were moved to a home for the mentally retarded which was less crowded, staffed by solicitous attendants, and where they were provided with stimulating toys and books. Three decades later all of these supposedly retarded children had finished high school and were employed as teachers, nurses, vocational counsellors, and office workers. In contrast, another group of twelve orphans who originally tested 'average' or above remained at the overcrowded, unstimulating orphanage. Within less than two years, their IQ scores had fallen to 61, lower even than that of the supposedly retarded group. And three decades later a third of them were still institutionalized and almost all of the remainder worked at menial jobs. The full study is reported in Skeels (1966).

## 12. *The Inheritance of Variation*

In writing this chapter, I found particularly valuable Bodmer and Cavalli-Sforza (1976), Lerner and Libby (1976), Molnar (1975), and Smith (1975). I wish to express my indebtedness to these authors for numerous ideas in this chapter that are not individually cited. A definitive volume, which demands close reading by the non-specialist, is Cavalli-Sforza and Bodmer (1971). An excellent brief article is Cavalli-Sforza (1974).

240    I was led to the story of Piero da Vinci by Smith (1975). The quotation and the account of Piero's life can be found in *Lives of the Most Eminent Painters, Sculptors, and Architects* by Giorgio Vasari, translated by Gaston De Vere (London: The Medici Society, 1912–1914), vol. 7.

PAGE

242 A much more detailed account of recessive genes than is possible in this brief summary can be found in Bodmer and Cavalli-Sforza (1976).

247 The material on interfaith marriage and geographical influences in gene flow is from Molnar (1975), p. 101, and Goode (1964), pp. 34–35.

247 'In Memoriam', Part 56, Stanza 4.

248 The Oxfordshire study was by Kuchemann *et al.* (1967).

250 Most of the books listed at the beginning of the notes for this chapter discuss sickle-cell anaemia in detail; see in particular Bodmer and Cavalli-Sforza (1976). A classic paper on the subject is Livingstone (1958).

252 Hopi albinism is discussed by Woolf and Dukepo (1969).

253 Information on the Xavantes can be found in Salzano *et al.* (1967).

254 I obtained these facts on dwarfism among the Amish from Lerner and Libby (1976), p. 343.

255 For Old Testament mention of Samaritans, see II Kings, Chapter 17; for Jesus' parable, see Luke, Chapter 10. Modern studies of the Samaritans are Talmon (1977) and Bonné (1966).

258 The statistics on blood group frequencies are from Boyd (1963). Correlations between blood type and fertility, mortality, and disease are discussed in Molnar (1975), pp. 133–140.

259 I am indebted to Davis (1974) for much of the information in the last few paragraphs on human migrations.

*13. The Chimera of Race*
Some of the basic works about race that served as sources for this chapter were Molnar (1975), Osborne (1971), Alland (1971), Garn (1971), and Simpson and Yinger (1965). The chapters on race in Harris (1975) are excellent and are highly recommended. Regarding the controversy about race and intelligence, the following were helpful: Kamin (1974), Montagu (1974), Cancro (1971), and Brace *et al.* (1971). A recent and very objective (but perhaps too cautious) study of the data available on this controversy is Loehlin *et al.* (1975); an excellent selection of readings on the subject is Block and Dworkin (1976).

262 For the complex Brazilian system of racial classification, see Harris (1970) and *An Introduction to Brazil* by Charles Wagley (New York: Columbia University Press, 1963), pp. 132–147.

263 Racial diversification in the house sparrow is described in 'House Sparrows: Rapid Evolution of Races in North America' by R. F. Johnston and R. K. Selander, *Science*, vol. 144 (1964), pp. 548–550.

PAGE

265 For the discussion of electrophoresis, I am indebted to Cavalli-Sforza (1974).

266 Information in this paragraph on classification systems is based on Loehlin *et al.* (1975), Dobzhansky (1972), and Garn (1971).

267 For a more complete discussion of nose form, see Wolpoff (1968).

269 Numerous sources have been relied on for this discussion of skin colour. In particular, see Harris (1975), pp. 96–115, Molnar (1975), pp. 117–127, Weiner (1971), pp. 165–169, and Hulse (1971), pp. 329–333. Loomis (1970) discusses rickets and skin colour.

270 I came upon this quotation in Harris (1975), p. 492; he in turn had found it in an article by Herbert Birch in Mead *et al.* (1968), pp. 49–58.

271 I learned about Ch'ien-lung from Harris (1975), pp. 433–434. The quotation is from *The China Reader*, edited by H. F. Schurmann and O. Schell (New York: Random House, 1967), p. 113.

274 A recent study of prejudice and race by nearly two dozen specialists from various disciplines is Watson (1974).

275 Jensen's point of view is presented in his (1973) and (1969).

275 See Block and Dworkin (1976), p. 332.

276 This is known as 'the Pygmalion effect'. It has been fully documented in *Pygmalion in the Classroom* by Robert Rosenthal and Lenore Jacobson (New York: Holt, Rinehart and Winston, 1968).

278 For this view of Black English, see *Black English* by J. L. Dillard (New York: Random House, 1972) and my own (1974).

278 *Genetics*, vol. 83 supplement (1976), p. 99.

## 14. The Intelligent Senses

This chapter and the next one cover a wide range of subdisciplines in psychology (primarily sensation, perception, and consciousness in this chapter; memory, learning, and cognition in the next). Consequently, it is difficult to recommend any two or three books on these many subjects to the general reader. The best place for a reader to start is with the psychology textbooks that are accessible even to those untrained in these disciplines. The choice is wide, but I particularly recommend Kagan and Havemann (1976), Brown and Herrnstein (1975), Munn *et al.* (1974), Mussen and Rosenzweig (1973), and Buss (1973). I have found all of them valuable in one way or another in writing these chapters. Excellent introductions to perception are Chase (1973), Gibson (1969), and Hochberg (1964); a wide-ranging collection of readings on the subject is Pribram (1969). A valuable and entertaining book on sleep, written by a pioneer researcher in the field, is Dement (1974). A collection of readings on altered states of consciousness is Tart (1969); a volume devoted primarily to drugs and various trance states is Harner (1973).

PAGE

286   An excellent volume on illusions is Gregory and Gombrich (1973).

288   A valuable brief summary of the field of perception, written by W. N. Dember, can be found in the *Encyclopedia Britannica Macropaedia*, 1974 edition, vol. 14; I am indebted to Dember for numerous points and for his bibliographical references.

291   The literature on ESP is huge, and not all of it is reliable. For a collection of papers generally favourable to the results claimed by ESP researchers, see Rhine (1971); a highly critical review is Hansel (1966). See also Schmeidler (1969).

292   Herskovits *et al.* (1969) present cross-cultural studies of perception.

292   The Sapir quotation is from his (1929), p. 209. Whorf's writings have been collected in his (1956).

293   The Navajo experiment is reported in Carroll and Casagrande (1958).

295   An extremely thought-provoking, though iconoclastic and even eccentric, examination of the origins of consciousness is Jaynes (1976).

296   Randy Gardner's record of wakefulness is described in Dement (1974), pp. 8–12.

296   The quotation is from Allan Rechtschaffen, 'The Control of Sleep', in *Human Behavior and Its Control*, edited by William A. Hunt (Cambridge, Mass.: Schenkman, 1971). I encountered it in Dement (1974).

299   The phrase is from *Macbeth*, Act 2, Scene 3.

300   A compelling theory of why we sleep, which I have only briefly summarized, has been proposed by Hartmann (1973).

301   Several recent books discuss biological rhythms in much more detail than I have done here: Ward (1971) on a popular level, Palmer (1976) and Conroy and Mills (1971) on a more technical one. An interesting discussion is in Chapters 2 and 3 of Chapple (1970).

302   The quotation from the Jesuit Father Fremin is from *The Death and Rebirth of the Senecas* by Anthony F. C. Wallace (New York: Knopf, 1970), pp. 59–60. One of Freud's earliest writings, published in 1900, is *The Interpretation of Dreams* (New York: Modern Library, 1950); *An Outline of Psychoanalysis* (New York: Norton, 1949), one of his last, contains much about dreams.

302   Schneider and Sharp (1969) discuss Yir Yoront dreams. For material in this section on dreams, and in the subsequent one on altered states of

consciousness, I am indebted to Bourguignon (1974), (1973), and (1972).

305   Wallace and Benson (1972) observed metabolic changes during trans-cendental meditation but Michaels *et al.* (1976) did not.

### 15. A World in the Mind

Some of the sources listed for the previous chapter are also important for this one, particularly the textbooks (which provide extensive bibliographies for specific topics). Excellent brief summaries of knowledge about memory are Norman (1976) and Howe (1970); also recommended are Tulving and Donaldson (1974), and Shiffrin and Atkinson (1969). One of the most thorough examinations of learning is Hilgard and Bower (1974); a brief introduction to this subject is Borger and Seaborne (1966). A wide-ranging collection of readings on creativity is Vernon (1970).

307   I learned about the William James experiment from Munn *et al.* (1974), pp. 264–265. See James (1890).

309   The story of the man with the phenomenal memory is told in detail in Luria (1968). Photographic and other remarkable memories are discussed by Norman (1976).

312   I discuss encoding and categorization in greater detail in my (1974), Chapter 9.

313   This material is based largely on a brief article by Roland Fischer in *Psychology Today*, vol. 10 (August 1976), pp. 68–72. See also his (1972).

313   The original experiment is reported in Haber (1970), the one with the 10,000 pictures in Standing (1973).

315   Experiments by Reitman (1974) support, to a limited extent, the decay explanation.

318   Pavlov has reported these experiments in his (1927) and Skinner has described his earlier work in his (1938). Skinner has explained his views on human behaviour and society in several works written for a general audience, among them (1948).

318   The Locke quotation is from his *Essay Concerning Human Understanding*, Book 2, Chapter 33, Section 15.

319   In this connection, let me recommend Gagné (1965), which makes a persuasive argument for a multipurpose theory that involves eight kinds of learning.

320   Skinner has attempted to explain language learning in behaviourist terms in his (1957). It was put through a devastating analysis by Noam Chomsky (1959), who asserted that the behaviourists' array of statistics

and terminology camouflaged their inability to explain language as the set of habits they had postulated. For a recent summary of the view of language learning accepted by many psychologists and linguists today, see Chomsky (1972).

322  For categorization, see Rosch *et al.* (1976).

323  Piaget's theory is backed by such voluminous detail that the general reader may find it difficult at first to understand his books without guidance. Two excellent summaries of Piaget's work, which should be read before tackling the work itself, are Phillips (1975) and Ginsburg and Opper (1969). Piaget's publications are too numerous to be listed in my Bibliography; Philips (1975) gives a quite complete list.

326  My discussion of thinking in infants was based on Kagan (1972). For more detailed information, see Kagan (1971).

329  This information is from Lehman (1953).

## 16. The Social Bond

Books that were particularly valuable in writing this chapter are Lenski and Lenski (1974), Williams (1970), and Nisbet (1970). I also found Chinoy and Hewitt (1975) filled with many good ideas, some of which I have freely appropriated. Although I can point to no particular paragraph of my own as an instance, the influence of Parsons (1971) and (1966) has been pervasive. For a more extended discussion of social change than I have been able to give, I suggest Allen (1971).

338  Numerous examples of cultural behaviours that differ from one society to another can be found in Hall (1976).

339  Darwin's observations on the Fuegians are in Chapter 10 of *The Voyage of the Beagle* (originally published in 1840). Additional detail was obtained from Oswalt (1970).

342  Stokes and Hewitt (1976) discuss the theoretical implications of behaviour in a modern world in which most actions are not covered by norms.

343  The Durkheim quotation is from *The Rules of Sociological Method* (New York: The Free Press, 1950), pp. 68–69.

345  For my entire discussion of deviance I am indebted to Hewitt (1976), Chapter 6, and to personal communication with him. A cross-cultural study of deviance is Edgerton (1976); a fascinating account of mental illness as deviance is Foucault (1965); an excellent collection of readings is Rubington and Weinberg (1973).

350  This book is not the forum to discuss in detail societal evolution and the development of different levels of socio-cultural integration; anyway, I

have already done so in Farb (1978). Over the years I have profited greatly from discussions on this subject with Elman R. Service. Two of his books on social evolution, both highly recommended, are (1975) and (1971).

351    The classic study is Ogburn (1950).

## 17. The Lowly and the Mighty

Two excellent brief introductions to social stratification are Gould (1971) and Tumin (1967). Chapter 7 in DeFleur *et al.* provides a good summary of the subject. Valuable collections of readings are Thielbar and Feldman (1972) and Béteille (1969). In writing this chapter, as with the one before, I found Lenski and Lenski (1974) most helpful. Two volumes specifically on the problems of United States society, both emphasizing that of inequality, are Jencks *et al.* (1972) and Turner (1972). The subject of wealth and stratification is covered well in Samuelson (1973).

355    *The Cheyenne Indians* by George B. Grinnell (New Haven, Conn.: Yale University Press, 1923), vol. 1, p. 129. This work is based on knowledge about the Plains Indians that Grinnell first began acquiring in 1870.

356    The statistics about wealth are from *The Concentration of Personal Wealth in America* by James D. Smith (Washington, D.C.: The Urban Institute, 1973).

358    The ranking of occupations was published in Hodge *et al.* (1964).

359    An excellent article on the Harijans is Srinivas and Béteille (1965).

362    I have drawn on many sources for this discussion of the caste system, among them Mencher (1974), Gould (1971), Nisbet (1970), Tumin (1965), Srinivas and Béteille (1965), and Shibutani and Kwan (1965).

364    The quotation is from *The City of God* (New York: Modern Library, 1950), p. 690.

365    Perhaps the best-known brief paper drawing a parallel between castes in India and the United States is Berreman (1959). The classic study is Dollard (1949).

366    On religion and social class in the United States, see Demerath (1965).

368    The Hawthorne quotation is from *The Heart of Hawthorne's Journals*, edited by Newton Arvin (Boston: Houghton Mifflin, 1929), p. 74.

370    Marrying up and marrying down are discussed by Scott (1969).

## 18. The Family as an Institution

The volume of sociological literature on marriage and the family is tremendous. Several works were particularly helpful, both in providing fact and as a spur to my own thinking. I could not have written this chapter without constant recourse to Clayton (1975), Kephart (1972), and Goode (1964). Although the Goode volume was written well over a decade ago, its perceptiveness concerning the family is undiminished. Of numerous other excellent studies, I wish especially to recommend Nye and Berardo (1973), in particular with reference to the family in the United States. A number of valuable collections of readings have made readily available a cross-section of the literature on marriage and the family. I found the following particularly useful: Sussman (1974), Winch and Spanier (1974), Dreitzel (1972), Anderson (1971), and Bohannan and Middleton (1968). A wealth of provocative thoughts about marriage and kinship systems greater than can possibly be included in a single chapter is to be found in Fox (1967). I also regret that I could not include more material from Shorter (1975), an extraordinarily enlightening history of the family in modern Western societies. A special issue of the *Journal of Marriage and the Family* (vol. 35, August 1973) is devoted to the history of the family.

PAGE

373 The antelope gift is discussed in Turnbull (1962).

377 One of the first interpretations of the modern family as a 'companionship unit' was Burgess and Locke (1960). For my discussion of the changing United States family I am indebted to an excellent summary in DeFleur *et al.* (1971), pp. 516–531.

378 Legitimacy is treated in much more detail in Goode (1964), pp. 20–30.

380 Payments by the groom's or the bride's family in societies around the world are tabulated in Coult and Habenstein (1965). On bridewealth and dowry, see Goody and Tambiah (1973).

382 For many of my points about divorce, I am indebted to Goode (1966). Statistics on marital dissolution are based on those gathered and interpreted by Davis (1973).

383 The quotation appears in Kephart (1972), pp. 352–353. His Chapter 12 is an excellent summary of the studies that have been made on romantic love. Because his copious footnotes cite the major references, I will not repeat them here. My discussion obviously owes a debt to his chapter and to his bibliography. I am also indebted to Goode for various thoughts in his publications, particularly (1964) and (1959).

385 The true–false quiz is adapted from Clayton (1975), pp. 366–374, who presents documentation, sources for the studies on which the questions are based – and also some caveats about the methodology used.

388 My discussion of nuclear and extended families was greatly aided by ideas put forward by Goode (1964).

392 Clayton (1975) gave me the idea of using the Oneida Community as an example of group marriage. I also found valuable the material in

Kephart (1972). The best extended description of the experiment is Carden (1970); Robertson (1972) recounts the causes for the break-up. A contemporaneous account by a gynaecologist of the intriguing sexual aspects of the experiment was published in the *American Journal of Obstetrics*, vol. 17 (1884), pp. 785–793; the article is reprinted in Hardin (1969), pp. 320–326. An excellent brief discussion of Oneida and several other communes is Hostetler (1974).

393 Fuller accounts of polyandry, as practised in the Himalayan region, are given by Berreman (1975) and Goldstein (in press).

393 The sample of polygynous marriages was by Murdock (1957), who also turned up only four polyandrous societies.

394 Kephart (1972), p. 56, presents the list of benefits afforded by mono-gamy. For a summary of marriage forms I am greatly indebted both to this work and to Clayton (1975).

396 The material on Bechuanaland, as well as that on marriage between close relatives at the beginning of this subsection, is from Lerner and Libby (1976), pp. 365–366.

397 Adams and Neel (1967) examined the offspring of incestuous unions.

397 The information about incest in the Ptolemaic dynasty comes from Caspari (1972), pp. 340–341. See also Adams and Neel (1967).

397 The study of Japanese inbreeding is by Schull and Neel (1965).

399 The Tylor quotation is from his 'On a Method of Investigating the Development of Institutions', *Journal of the Royal Anthropological Institute*, vol. 18 (1888), p. 267.

400 The Belcher Island Eskimo example is from Guemple (1971).

402 Fox (1967) has offered this demographic explanation. His (1972) is a full presentation of an incest theory that unfortunately is too complex and too detailed to be done justice to in my brief chapter. My section on incest could not have been written without appropriating nu-merous thoughts from his (1967), for which I wish to express my indebtedness.

403 The estimate was made by Cogswell and Sussman (1972).

403 For a discussion of the family in the kibbutz, see Talmon (1972). A collection of readings that emphasizes alternatives to traditional marriage is Kammeyer (1975).

## 19. The Human Ages

This book has so far discussed a number of things about being human that social scientists often call 'socialization': learning, the acquisition of language, sex roles, social stratification, the position of children in the various adaptations, and the family. Other aspects of the growth of the individual within society are discussed in this chapter. Williams (1972), Danziger (1971), and Clausen (1968) present wide-ranging studies of socialization. Many topics concerned with socialization, personality, and national character for which I did not have space here are treated at length in Barnouw (1973), Hsu (1972), and Wallace (1970). Particularly valuable studies of childhood are Dreitzel (1973) and Elkin and Handel (1972). An important history of society's changing images of the child is Bromley (1974). The classic volume on the biology of ageing is Comfort (1964); the chapters in Young (1971) are excellent.

PAGE

406 Tanner (1973) describes the biology of childhood growth.

407 For menstruation, see Frisch (1975) and Zacharias (1976).

408 These experiments in mothering were begun in the late 1950s by Harry F. Harlow and his associates at the University of Wisconsin, and they have continued for two decades. See especially Harlow (1974) and Mitchell (1968).

409 For this quotation and all my examples of the absence of mother love in pre-modern Europe, I am indebted to the pioneering study by Shorter (1975), particularly pp. 168–204.

409 For this quotation and all my examples of the absence of mother love in pre-modern Europe, I am indebted to the pioneering study by Shorter (1975), particularly pp. 168–204.

410 Ariès (1962) describes changes in the European family since the Middle Ages.

414 Turner has written extensively on the liminal phase in his (1974) and (1967). My discussion of the rites of passage is based largely on his work, plus that of Chapple (1970) and, of course, van Gennep (1960). The example of the paratrooper initiation is from Weiss (1967).

415 A view of the student-protest movement that differs from the one commonly held is Peterson (1970).

418 A number of social scientists have been intrigued by the significance of Santa Claus in United States society. Although the explanation I put forward differs from these, I find myself closest to Wolf (1964). Sereno (1951) has offered an excellent psychoanalytic explanation, with which I nevertheless disagree. An historical analysis of Santa Claus as part of the Christmas celebration is given by Barnett (1954). Oswalt (1970), pp. 6–11, presents a brief summary of the myth as a kind of pattern in United States culture.

419 The Tolstoy quotation is from Book 9, p. 709 of *War and Peace*, in the translation by Louise and Aylmer Maude (New York: Simon and

Schuster, 1942). I was led to it by Chinoy and Hewitt (1975), to whom I am indebted for many of my comments on socialization in this chapter. I wish also to express my indebtedness for many of the ideas of Hewitt (1976).

420 The study of national stereotypes is by Karlins *et al.* (1969).

422 My interest in national character was revived by Barnouw and in my discussion I am greatly indebted to his (1973). Excellent studies of Japanese national character are Norbeck and DeVos (1972), Norbeck and Parman (1970), Nakane (1970), Caudill and Plath (1966), Hall and Beardsley (1965), Silberman (1962), and Beardsley *et al.* (1959). Probably the leading proponent of national-character studies today is Hsu; see in particular his (1972) and (1971), which provide not only case studies but theoretical underpinnings as well. The Soviet Union has been second only to Japan as a subject of national-character studies. An excellent comparison of children in the Soviet Union and in the United States is Brofenbrenner (1970).

424 A study of the familial component in longevity is Abbot *et al.* (1974).

*Epilogue: The Future of the Species*
Primary sources for this chapter were Bodley (1976), Levine (1975), Mesarovic and Pestel (1974), Lenski and Lenski (1974), and Handler (1970). Numerous ideas came from reading Bell (1973) and Toffler (1970).

433 Much of the information about the consequences of the Aswan High Dam is from Farvar and Milton (1972) and from an article by Claire Sterling in *National Parks and Conservation Magazine*, August 1971, pp. 10–13; also helpful was a paper presented by Susan Meswick at the 1975 annual meeting of the American Anthropological Association.

434 An excellent discussion of pollution may be found in Chapter 15 of Levine (1975).

436 The statistics in the last several paragraphs are from Lerner and Libby (1976), Smith (1975), and Mesarovic and Pestel (1974).

439 Excellent summaries of the problems of population growth and food supply are to be found in Lerner and Libby (1976), Chapter 15; Levine (1975), Chapters 11 and 13; Revelle (1974); and Handler (1970).

441 Modern approaches to the treatment and prevention of genetic diseases are discussed by Motulsky (1974).

444 Much of the material in the last several pages about the possibilities of genetic engineering is derived from Lerner and Libby (1976), Chapter 22.

447 The predictions are adapted from Kahn and Wiener (1967), pp. 51–57.

# Bibliography

Abbott, M., *et al.* 1974. 'The Familial Component in Longevity, A Study of Offspring of Nonagenarians.' *Johns Hopkins Medical Journal*, vol. 134, pp. 1–16.

Adams, M. S., and Neel, J. V. 1967. 'Children of Incest.' *Paediatrics*, vol. 40, pp. 55–62.

Adams, Robert McC. 1966. *The Evolution of Urban Society*. Chicago: Aldine.

Alland, Alexander, Jr. 1971. *Human Diversity*. New York: Columbia University Press.

Allen, Francis R. 1971. *Socio-Cultural Dynamics: An Introduction to Social Change*. New York: Macmillan. (1971) London: Collier-Macmillan.

Anderson, Michael, editor. 1971. *Sociology of the Family*. Baltimore, Md.: Penguin. (1971) London: Penguin.

Argyle, Michael. 1972 (2nd edition). *The Psychology of Interpersonal Behavior*. Baltimore, Md.: Penguin. (1970) London: Penguin.

Ariès, Philippe. 1962. *Centuries of Childhood*. New York: Vintage.

Armelagos, George J., and McArdle, Alan. 1976. 'The Role of Culture in the Control of Infectious Diseases.' *Ecologist*, vol. 6, pp. 179–182.

—— and Dewey, John R. 1973. 'Evolutionary Response to Human Infectious Diseases.' In *The Ecology of Man: An Ecosystems Approach*, edited by Robert L. Smith (New York: Harper and Row, 1973), pp. 222–227. London: Harper and Row, 1973.

Banfield, Edward C. 1958. *The Moral Basis of a Backward Society*. Glencoe, Ill.: The Free Press.

Bardwick, Judith M. 1971. *Psychology of Women*. New York: Harper and Row.

Barnett, James H. 1954. *The American Christmas*. New York: Macmillan.

Barnouw, Victor. 1973 (2nd edition). *Culture and Personality*. Homewood, Ill.: Dorsey Press.

Beardsley, Richard K., *et al.* 1959. *Village Japan*. Chicago and London: University of Chicago Press.

Beck, Benjamin B. 1973. 'Cooperative Tool Use by Captive Hamadryas Baboons.' *Science*, vol. 182, pp. 594–597.

Becker, Ernest. 1973. *The Denial of Death*. New York: Free Press. (1976) London: Collier-Macmillan.

Bell, Daniel, 1973. *The Coming of Post-Industrial Society*. New York: Basic Books. London (1974) Heinemann Educational. (1976) Penguin.

Belmont, Lillian, and Marolla, Francis A. 1973. 'Birth Order, Family Size, and Intelligence.' *Science*, vol. 182, pp. 1096–1101.

Berelson, Bernard, and Steiner, Gary A. 1964. *Human Behavior: An Inventory of Scientific Findings*. New York: Harcourt Brace and Jovanich.

Berreman, Gerald D. 1975. 'Himalayan Polyandry and the Domestic Cycle.' *American Ethnologist*, vol. 2, pp. 127–138.

——. 1959. 'Caste in India and the United States.' *American Journal of Sociology*, vol. 66, pp. 120–127.

Béteille, André, editor. 1969. *Social Inequality*. Baltimore, Md.: Penguin. (1969) London: Penguin.

Bicchieri, M. G., editor, 1972. *Hunters and Gatherers Today*. New York: Holt, Rinehart and Winston.

Birdsell, J. B. 1972. *Human Evolution*. Chicago: Rand McNally. (1975) London: Rand McNally.

Block, Jeanne H. 1973. 'Conceptions of Sex Role.' *American Psychologist*, vol. 28, pp. 512–526.

Block, N. J., and Dworkin, Gerald. 1976. *The IQ Controversy*. New York: Pantheon. (1977) London: Quarter Books.

Bodley, John H. 1976. *Anthropology and Contemporary Human Problems*. Menlo Park, Calif.: Cummings. (1976) Cummings (distr. Book Centre).

Bodmer, W. F., and Cavalli-Sforza, L. L. 1976. *Genetics, Evolution, and Man*. San Francisco: Freeman. (1976) Reading: W. H. Freeman.

Bohannan, Paul, and Middleton, John, editors. 1968. *Marriage, Family, and Residence*. Garden City, N.Y.: Natural History Press.

Bonné, Batsheva. 1966. 'Are There Hebrews Left?' *American Journal of Physical Anthropology*, vol. 24, pp. 135–145.

Borger, Robert, and Seaborne, A. E. M. 1966. *The Psychology of Learning*. Baltimore, Md.: Penguin. (1970) London: Penguin.

Bornstein, Marc H., and Bornstein, Helen G. 1976. 'The Pace of Life.' *Nature*, vol. 259, pp. 557–558.

Bottomore, T. B. 1972. *Sociology, A Guide to Problems and Literature*. New York: Vintage. (1971) London: George Allen and Unwin.

Bourguignon, Erika. 1974. *Culture and the Varities of Consciousness*. Reading, Mass.: Addison-Wesley Module No. 47.

——. 1972. 'Dreams and Altered States of Consciousness in Anthropological Research.' In Hsu (1972), pp. 403–434.

——, editor. 1973. *Religion, Altered States of Consciousness and Social Change*. Columbus, Ohio: Ohio State University Press.

Boyd, William C. 1963. 'Genetics and the Human Race.' *Science*, vol. 140, pp. 1057–1064.

Boyden, S. V., editor. 1970. *The Impact of Civilization on the Biology of Man*. Toronto: University of Toronto Press.

Brace, C. Loring, *et al.* editors. 1971. *Race and Intelligence*. Washington, D.C.:

American Anthropological Association Anthropological Studies Number 8.

Braidwood, Robert J. 1975 (8th edition). *Prehistoric Men*. Glenview, Ill.: Scott, Foresman.

Bromley, D. B. 1974 (2nd edition). *The Psychology of Human Ageing*. Baltimore, Md.: Penguin. (1966) London: Penguin.

Bronfenbrenner, Urie. 1970. *Two Worlds of Childhood: U.S. and U.S.S.R.* New York: Basic Books.

Bronson, Bennett, 1975. 'The Earliest Farming: Demography as Cause and Consequence.' In Polgar (1975), pp. 53–78.

Brothwell, D. and Sandison, A. T., editors. 1967. *Diseases in Antiquity*. Springfield, Ill.: Charles C. Thomas.

Broude, Gwen J., and Greene, Sarah J. 1976. 'Cross-Cultural Codes on Twenty Sexual Attitudes and Practices.' *Ethnology*, vol. 15, pp. 409–429.

Broverman, Inge K., *et al.* 1972. 'Sex-Role Stereotypes: A Current Appraisal.' *Journal of Social Issues*, vol. 28, pp. 59–78.

Brown, Roger and Herrnstein, Richard J. 1975. *Psychology*. Boston: Little, Brown. (1975) London: Methuen & Co. Ltd.

Brues, Alice. 1959. 'The Spearman and the Archer – An Essay on Selection in Body Build.' *American Anthropologist*, vol. 61, pp. 457–469.

Buettner-Janusch, John. 1966. *Origins of Man*. New York: Wiley.

Burgess, Ernest W., and Locke, Harvey J. 1960. *The Family: From Institution to Companionship*. New York: American Book Company.

Buss, Arnold. 1973. *Psychology, Man in Perspective*. New York and Chichester: Wiley.


Campbell, Bernard G. 1974 (2nd edition). *Human Evolution*. Chicago: Aldine. (1967) London: Heinemann Educational.

——, editor. 1972. *Sexual Selection and the Descent of Man*. Chicago: Aldine. (1973) London: Heinemann Educational.

Cancro, Robert, editor. 1971. *Intelligence: Genetic and Environmental Influences*. New York: Grune and Stratton (distr. Wm Heinemann Medical Books Ltd).

Carden, Maren L. 1970. *Oneida: Utopian Community to Modern Corporation*. Baltimore, Md.: Johns Hopkins University Press (distr. IBEG Ltd).

Carroll, J. B., and Casagrande, J. B. 1958. 'The Function of Language Classifications in Behavior.' In *Readings in Social Psychology*, edited by Eleanor E. Maccoby *et al.* (New York: Holt, Rinehart and Winston, 1958; 3rd edition), pp. 18–31.

Caspari, Ernst. 1972. 'Sexual Selection in Human Evolution.' In Campbell (1972), pp. 332–356.

Caudill, William, and Plath, David W. 1966. 'Who Sleeps By Whom? Parent–Child Involvement in Urban Japanese Families.' *Psychiatry*, vol. 29 (1966), pp. 344–366.

Cavalli-Sforza, L. L. 1974. 'The Genetics of Human Populations.' *Scientific American*, vol. 231 (September), pp. 80–89.

—— and Bodmer, W. F. 1971. *The Genetics of Human Populations*. San Francisco: Freeman.

Chagnon, Napoleon A. 1974. *Studying the Yanomamo*. New York: Holt, Rinehart and Winston.

——. 1968. *Yanomamo: The Fierce People*. New York: Holt, Rinehart and Winston. (1977) London: Holt, Rinehart and Winston.

Chapple, Eliot D. 1970. *Culture and Biological Man*. New York: Holt, Rinehart and Winston.

Chard, Chester S. 1975 (2nd edition). *Man in Prehistory*. New York and Maidenhead: McGraw-Hill.

Chase, W. G. 1973. *Visual Information Processing*. New York: Acàdemic Press. (1973) London: Academic Press.

Childe, V. Gordon. 1942. *What Happened in History*. Baltimore, Md.: Penguin. (1969) London: Penguin.

Chinoy, Ely, and Hewitt, John P. 1975 (3rd edition). *Sociological Perspective*. New York: Random House.

Chomsky, Noam. 1972 (2nd edition). *Language and Mind*. New York and London: Harcourt Brace and Jovanovich.

——. 1959. 'A Review of B. F. Skinner's *Verbal Behavior*.' *Language*, vol. 35, pp. 26–58.

Clausen, John A., editor. 1968. *Socialization and Society*. Boston: Little, Brown.

Clayton, Richard R. 1975. *The Family, Marriage, and Social Change*. Lexington, Mass.: Heath.

Clegg, E. J., *et al.* 1970. 'The Impact of High Altitudes on Human Populations.' *Human Biology*, vol. 42, pp. 486–518.

Coale, Ansley J. 1974. 'The History of the Human Population.' *Scientific American*, vol. 231 (September), pp. 40–51.

Cockburn, T. Aidan. 1971. 'Infectious Diseases in Ancient Populations.' *Current Anthropology*, vol. 12, pp. 45–62.

Cogswell, Betty E., and Sussman, Marvin B. 1972. 'Changing Family and Marriage Forms: Complications for Human Service Systems.' *The Family Coordinator*, vol. 21, pp. 505–516.

Cohen, Mark N. 1975. 'Population Pressure and the Origins of Agriculture: An Archaeological Example from the Coast of Peru.' In Polgar (1975), pp. 79–121.

Collins, Randall. 1972. 'A Conflict Theory of Sexual Stratification.' In Dreitzel (1972), pp. 53–79.

Comfort, Alex. 1964. *Aging: The Biology of Senescence*. New York: Holt, Rinehart and Wiński. (1964) London: Routledge and Kegan Paul.

Conroy, R., and Mills, J. M. 1971. *Human Circadian Rhythms*. Baltimore, Md.: Williams and Wilkins. (1970) Edinburgh: Churchill Livingstone.

Cook, Robert C. 1960. 'The World's Great Cities: Evolution or Devolution?' *Population Bulletin*, vol. 16, pp. 109–130.

Coppens, Yves, *et al.*, editors. 1976. *Earliest Man and Environments in the Lake Rudolf Basin.* Chicago and London: University of Chicago Press.

Coult, Allan D., and Habenstein, Robert W. 1965. *Cross Tabulations of Murdock's 'World Ethnographic Sample.'* Columbia, Mo.: University of Missouri Press.

Dalton, George. 1972. 'Peasantries in Anthropology and History.' *Current Anthropology*, vol. 13, pp. 385–415.

Damon, Albert. 1975. *Physiological Anthropology.* New York: Oxford University Press.

D'Andrade, Roy. 1961. 'Anthropological Studies of Dreams.' In *Psychological Anthropology*, edited by Francis L. K. Hsu (Homewood, Ill.: Dorsey Press, 1961; 1st edition).

Danziger, Kurt. 1971. *Socialization.* Baltimore, Md.: Penguin. (1971) London: Penguin.

Davis, Kingsley. 1974. 'The Migrations of Human Populations.' *Scientific American*, vol. 231 (September), pp. 92–105.

——. 1973. 'The American Family in Relation to Demographic Change.' Berkeley, Calif.: International Population and Urban Research Institute, University of California.

Davis, Wayne H., editor. 1971. *Readings in Human Population Ecology.* Englewood Cliffs, N.J.: Prentice-Hall.

DeFleur, Melvin L. *et al.* 1971. *Sociology: Man in Society.* Glenview, Ill.: Scott, Foresman.

Delaney, Janice, *et al.* 1976. *The Curse: A Cultural History of Menstruation.* New York: Dutton.

Dement, William C. 1974. *Some Must Watch While Some Must Sleep.* San Francisco: Freeman. (1974) Reading: W. H. Freeman.

Demerath, N. J., III. 1965. *Social Class in American Protestantism.* New York: Rand McNally.

Deutsch, Karl W. 1974 (2nd edition). *Politics and Government.* Boston: Houghton Mifflin (distr. Eurospan).

Devereux, George. 1937. 'Institutionalized Homosexuality of the Mohave Indians.' *Human Biology*, vol. 9, pp. 498–527.

Dimond, S. J., and Beaumont, J. G., editors. 1974. *Hemisphere Function in the Human Brain.* New York: Wiley. (1974) London: Paul Elek Scientific.

Diringer, David. 1962. *Writing.* New York: Praeger.

Divale, William T., and Harris, Marvin. 1976. 'Population, Warfare, and the Male Supremacist Complex.' *American Anthropologist*, vol. 78, pp. 521–538.

Dobzhansky, Theodosius. 1972. 'Genetics and the Races of Man.' In Campbell (1972), pp. 59–86.

Dolhinow, Phyllis, editor. 1972. *Primate Patterns.* New York: Holt, Rinehart and Winston.

—— and Sarich, Vincent M., editors. 1971. *Background for Man.* Boston: Little, Brown.

Dollard, John. 1949 (2nd edition). *Caste and Class in a Southern Town*. New York: Harper.

Draper, Patricia. 1973. 'Crowding among Hunter-Gatherers: The Kung Bushmen.' *Science*, vol. 182, pp. 301–303.

Dreitzel, Hans P., editor. 1973. *Childhood and Socialization*. New York: Macmillan. (1973) London: Collier-Macmillan.

——. 1972. *Family, Marriage, and the Struggle of the Sexes*. New York: Macmillan.

Dumond, Don E. 1975. 'The Limitation of Human Population: A Natural History.' *Science*, vol. 187, pp. 713–721.

Eaton, G. Gray. 1976. 'The Social Order of Japanese Macaques.' *Scientific American*, vol. 235 (October), pp. 96–106.

Edgerton, Robert B. 1976. *Deviance: A Cross-Cultural Perspective*. Menlo Park, Calif.: Cummings.

Eimerl, Sarel, and DeVore, Irven. 1974 (2nd edition). *The Primates*. New York: Time, Inc. (1967) London: Time-Life International.

Eisenberg, J. F., *et al.* 1972. 'The Relation between Ecology and Social Structure in Primates.' *Science*, vol. 176, pp. 863–874.

Elkin, Frederick, and Handel, Gerald. 1972 (2nd edition). *The Child and Society*. New York: Random House.

Ellul, Jacques. 1964. *The Technological Society*. New York: Vintage. (1973) London: Vintage Books (c/o Lyon Grant and Green. Trade counter – European Book Service).

Erikson, Kai. 1966. *Wayward Puritans: A Study in the Sociology of Deviance*. New York: Wiley. (1969) Chichester: Wiley.

Fagan, Brian M. 1974. *Men of the Earth: An Introduction to World Prehistory*. Boston: Little, Brown.

Farb, Peter. 1978 (2nd edition). *Man's Rise to Civilization: The Cultural Ascent of the Indians of North America*. New York: Dutton. (1969) London: Secker and Warburg.

——. 1974. *Word Play: What Happens When People Talk*. New York: Knopf. (1974) London: Cape. (1977) London: Coronet.

Farvar, M. T. and Milton, J. P., editors. 1972. *The Careless Technology*. Garden City, N.Y.: Natural History Press.

Ferkiss, Victor C. 1969. *Technological Man: The Myth and the Reality*. New York: Braziller.

Firth, Raymond. 1973. *Symbols, Public and Private*. Ithaca, N.Y.: Cornell University Press. (1976) London: George Allen and Unwin.

Fischer, Roland. 1972. 'On the Arousal State–Dependent Recall of "Subconscious" Experience.' *British Journal of Psychiatry*, vol. 120, pp. 159–172.

Flannery, Kent V. 1973. 'The Origins of Agriculture.' *Annual Review of Anthropology*, vol. 2, pp. 271–310.

——. 1969. 'Origins and Ecological Effects of Early Domestication in Iran and the Near East.' In Ucko and Dimbleby (1969), pp. 73–100.

Ford, Clellan S., and Beach, Frank A. 1951. *Patterns of Sexual Behavior*. New York: Harper.

Foster, George M. 1967. *Tzintzuntzan: Mexican Peasants in a Changing World*. Boston: Little, Brown.

Foucault, Michael. 1965. *Madness and Civilization*. New York: Random House. (1971) London: Tavistock.

Fouts, Roger S. 1975. 'Capacities for Language in Great Apes.' In Tuttle (1975), pp. 371–390.

Fox, Robin. 1972. 'Alliance and Constraint: Sexual Selection and the Evolution of Human Kinship Systems.' In Campbell (1972), pp. 282–331.

——. 1967. *Kinship and Marriage*. Baltimore, Md.: Penguin. (1970) London: Penguin.

Freedman, Jonathan. 1975. *Crowding and Behavior*. New York: Viking. (1975) Reading: W. H. Freeman.

Freedman, Ronald, and Berelson, Bernard. 1974. 'The Human Population.' *Scientific American*, vol. 231 (September), pp. 30–39.

Frisancho, A. Roberto. 1975. 'Functional Adaptation to High Altitude Hypoxia.' *Science*, vol. 187, pp. 313–319.

Frisch, Rose. 1975. 'Critical Weights, Critical Body Composition, Menarche, and the Maintenance of Menstrual Cycles.' In *Biosocial Interrelations in Population Adaptation*, edited by Elizabeth Watts *et al.* (The Hague, Netherlands: Mouton, 1975), pp. 309–318.

Gagné, R. M. 1965. *The Conditions of Learning*. New York: Holt, Rinehart and Winston.

Gamst, Frederick C. 1974. *Peasants in Complex Societies*. New York: Holt, Rinehart and Winston.

Gardner, Lytt I. 1972. 'Deprivation Dwarfism.' *Scientific American*, vol. 227 (July), pp. 76–82.

Garn, Stanley M. 1971 (3rd edition). *Human Races*. Springfield, Ill.: Charles C. Thomas.

Gazzaniga, Michael S. 1967. 'The Split Brain in Man.' *Scientific American*, vol. 217 (August), pp. 24–29.

Gelb, I. J. 1963 (2nd edition). *A Study of Writing*. Chicago. University of Chicago Press. (1952) London: University of Chicago Press.

Geschwind, Norman. 1972. 'Language and the Brain.' *Scientific American*, vol. 226 (April), pp. 76–83.

Gibson, E. J. 1969. *Principles of Perceptual Learning and Development*. New York: Appleton–Century–Crofts.

Gimpel, Jean. 1977. *The Medieval Machine: The Industrial Revolution of the Middle Ages*. New York: Holt, Rinehart and Winston. (1977) London: Gollancz.

Ginsburg, Benson E., and Laughlin, William S. 1971. 'Race and Intelligence: What Do We Really Know?' in Cancro (1971), pp. 77–87.

Ginsburg, Herbert, and Opper, Sylvia. 1969. *Piaget's Theory of Intellectual*

*Development*. Englewood Cliffs, N.J.: Prentice-Hall. (1969) Hemel Hempstead: Prentice-Hall.

Glucksberg, Sam. 1966. *Symbolic Processes*. Dubuque, Iowa: William C. Brown.

Goldberg, Steven. 1973. *The Inevitability of Patriarchy*. New York: Morrow. (1977) London: Maurice Temple Smith.

Goldenson, Robert M. 1970. *The Encyclopedia of Human Behavior*. Garden City, N.Y.: Doubleday.

Goldstein, Melvyn C. In press. 'Fraternal Polyandry and Fertility in a High Himalayan Valley in Northwest Nepal.' *Human Ecology*.

Goodall, Jane. *See* van Lawick-Goodall, Jane.

Goode, William J. 1966. 'Family Disorganization.' In Merton and Nisbet (1966), pp. 493–522.

——. 1964. *The Family*. Englewood Cliffs, N.J.: Prentice-Hall. (1964) Hemel Hempstead: Prentice-Hall.

——. 1959. 'The Theoretical Importance of Love.' *American Sociological Review*, vol. 24, pp. 38–47.

Goodman, Morris. 1974. 'Biochemical Evidence on Hominid Phylogeny.' *Annual Review of Anthropology*, vol. 3, pp. 203–228.

Goody, Jack, and Tambiah, S. J. 1973. *Bridewealth and Dowry*. New York: Cambridge University Press. (1973) London: Cambridge University Press.

Goss-Custard. J. D., *et al.* 1972. 'Survival, Mating and Rearing Strategies in the Evolution of Primate Social Structure.' *Folia Primatologica*, vol. 17, pp. 1–19.

Gould, Harould A. 1971. 'Caste and Class: A Comparative View.' Reading, Mass: Addison-Wesley Module 11.

Gould, Stephen Jay. 1974. 'Sizing Up Human Intelligence.' *Natural History*, vol. 73, pp. 10–14.

Gregory, James R. 1975. 'Image of Limited Good, or Expectation of Reciprocity?' *Current Anthropology*, vol. 16, pp. 73–92.

Gregory, R. L., and Gombrich, E. H., editors. 1973. *Illusion in Nature and Art*. New York: Scribner. (1973) London: Duckworth.

Guemple, Lee. 1971. 'Kinship and Alliance in Belcher Island Eskimo Society.' In *Alliance in Eskimo Society*, edited by Lee Guemple (Seattle, Wash.: American Ethnological Society Proceedings Supplement), pp. 56–78 (1973) London: University of Washington Press (c/o American University Publishers Group).


Haber, Ralph N. 1970. 'How We Remember What We See.' *Scientific American*, vol. 222 (May), pp. 104–112.

Hall, Edward T. 1976. *Beyond Culture*. Garden City, N.Y.: Doubleday.

Hall, John W., and Beardsley, Richard K. 1965. *Twelve Doors to Japan*. New York and Maidenhead: McGraw-Hill.

Handler, Philip, editor. 1970. *Biology and the Future of Man*. New York: Oxford University Press.

Hansel, C. E. M. 1966. *ESP: A Scientific Evaluation*. New York: Scribner.

Hardin, Garrett. 1972. *Exploring New Ethics for Survival*. New York: Viking.

——, editor. 1969 (2nd edition). *Population, Evolution, and Birth Control*. San Francisco: Freeman. (1969) Reading: W. H. Freeman.

Harding, Robert S. 1975. 'Meat Eating and Hunting in Baboons.' In Tuttle (1975), pp. 245–257.

Harlan, Jack R. 1967. 'A Wild Wheat Harvest in Turkey.' *Archeology*, vol. 20, pp. 197–201.

Harlow, Harry F. 1974. *Learning to Love*. New York: Jason Aronson.

Harner, M. J., editor. 1973. *Hallucinogens and Shamanism*. New York: Oxford University Press.

Harris, Marvin. 1975 (2nd edition). *Culture, People, Nature*. New York: Crowell.

——. 1974. *Cows, Pigs, Wars, and Witches: The Riddles of Culture*. New York: Random House. (1975) London: Hutchinson. (1977) London: Fontana.

——. 1970. 'Referential Ambiguity in the Calculus of Brazilian Racial Identity.' *South-western Journal of Anthropology*, vol. 26, pp. 1–14.

——. 1964. *Patterns of Race in the Americas*. New York: Walker.

Harrison G. A. *et al.* 1977 (2nd edition). *Human Biology*. New York and London: Oxford University Press.

Harrison, Robert. 1973. *Warfare*. Minneapolis, Minn.: Burgess.

Hartmann, Ernest L. 1973. *The Functions of Sleep*. New Haven, Conn.: Yale University Press.

Hauser, Philip M., and Schnore, Leo F., editors. 1965. *The Study of Urbanization*. New York: Wiley. (1965) Chichester: Wiley.

Heer, David M. 1975 (2nd edition). *Society and Population*. Englewood Cliffs, N.J.: Prentice-Hall. (1975) Hemel Hempstead: Prentice-Hall.

Heiser, Charles B., Jr. 1973. *Seed to Civilization*. San Francisco: Freeman. (1973) Reading: W. H. Freeman.

Helmer, John, and Eddington, Neil A. 1973. *Urbanman: The Psychology of Urban Survival*. New York: The Free Press.

Herskovits, Melville J., *et al.* 1969. *A Cross-Cultural Study of Perception*. Indianapolis, Ind.: Bobbs-Merrill.

Hewes, Gordon. 1973. 'Primate Communication and the Gestural Origin of Language.' *Current Anthropology*, vol. 14, pp. 5–24.

Hewitt, John P. 1976. *Self and Society*. Boston: Allyn and Bacon.

Hilgard, E. R., and Bower, G. H. 1974 (4th edition). *Theories of Learning*. New York: Appleton–Century–Crofts. (1975) Hemel Hempstead: Prentice-Hall.

Hinton, John. 1972 (2nd edition). *Dying*. Baltimore, Md.: Penguin. (1971) London: Penguin.

Hochberg, Julian E. 1964. *Perception*. Englewood Cliffs, N.J.: Prentice-Hall. (1978) Hemel Hempstead: Prentice-Hall.

Hockett, Charles F. 1973. *Man's Place in Nature*. New York and Maidenhead 1973: McGraw-Hill.

—— and Altmann, Stuart A. 1968. 'A Note on Design Features.' In *Animal Communication*, edited by Thomas A. Sebeok (Bloomington, Ind.: Indiana

University Press, 1968), pp. 61–72 (c/o American University Publishers Group, London).

—— and Ascher, R. 1964. 'The Human Revolution.' *Current Anthropology*, vol. 5, pp. 135–168.

Hodge, Robert W., *et al.* 1964. 'Occupational Prestige in the United States: 1925–1963.' *American Journal of Sociology*, vol. 70, pp. 286–302.

Hoselitz, Bert F., editor. 1970 (2nd edition). *A Reader's Guide to the Social Sciences*. New York: The Free Press.

Hostetler, John A. 1974. *Communitarian Societies*. New York: Holt, Rinehart and Winston.

Howe, Michael J. 1970. *Introduction to Human Memory*. New York and London: Harper and Row.

Howells, William W. 1973. *Evolution of the Genus Homo*. Reading, Mass.: Addison-Wesley.

Hsu, Francis L. K. 1972 (2nd edition). *Psychological Anthropology*. Cambridge, Mass.: Schenkman.

——, editor. 1971. *Kinship and Culture*. Chicago: Aldine.

Huber, Joan, editor. 1973. *Changing Women in a Changing Society*. Chicago and London: University of Chicago Press.

Hulse, Frederick S. 1971 (2nd edition). *The Human Species*. New York: Random House.

Hunt, Morton. 1974. *Sexual Behavior in the 1970s*. Chicago: Playboy Press.

Inkeles, Alex. 1969. 'Making Men Modern.' *American Journal of Sociology*, vol. 75, pp. 208–225.

——, and Levinson, Daniel J. 1969. 'National Character: the Study of Modal Personality and Sociocultural Systems.' In *The Handbook of Social Psychology* edited by Gardner Lindzey and Elliot Aronson (Reading, Mass.: Addison-Wesley, 1969; 2nd edition), vol. 4, pp. 418–505. (1969) London: Addison-Wesley.

Jacobs, Jane. 1969. *The Economy of Cities*. New York: Random House. (1972) London: Penguin.

James, William. 1890. *The Principles of Psychology*. New York: Holt. (1957) Dover Publications Inc. (distr. Tiptree Book Services Ltd).

Jaynes, Julian. 1976. *The Origins of Consciousness in the Breakdown of the Bicameral Mind*. Boston: Houghton Mifflin.

Jencks, Christopher, *et al.* 1972. *Inequality: A Reassessment of the Effect of Family and Schooling in America*. New York: Basic Books. (1975) London: Penguin.

Jensen, Arthur R. 1973. *Educability and Group Differences*. New York: Harper and Row.

——. 1969. 'How Much Can We Boost I.Q. and Scholastic Achievement?' *Harvard Educational Review*, vol. 39, pp. 1–123.

Jensen, Hans. 1963 (3rd edition). *Sign, Symbol and Script*. New York: Putnam.

Jerison, Harry J. 1976. 'Paleoneurology and the Evolution of Mind.' *Scientific American*, vol. 234 (January), pp. 90–101.

———. 1973. *Evolution of the Brain and Intelligence*. New York: Academic Press. (1974) London: Academic Press.

Johnson, Roger N. 1972. *Aggression in Man and Animals*. Philadelphia: Saunders. (1972) London: W. B. Saunders.

Jolly, Alison. 1972. *The Evolution of Primate Behavior*. New York: Macmillan. (1972) London: Collier-Macmillan.

Kagan, Jerome. 1972. 'Do Infants Think?' *Scientific American*, vol. 226 (March), pp. 74–82.

———. 1971. *Change and Continuity in Infancy*. New York: Wiley.

———, and Havemann, Ernest. 1976 (3rd edition). *Psychology: An Introduction*. New York and London: Harcourt Brace and Jovanovich.

Kahn, Herman, and Wiener, Anthony. 1967. *The Year 2000*. New York: Macmillan.

Kamin, Leon J. 1974. *The Science and Politics of I.Q.* New York: Wiley. (1977) London: Penguin.

Kammeyer, Kenneth C., editor. 1975. *Confronting the Issues: Sex Roles, Marriage, and the Family*. Boston: Allyn and Bacon.

Karlins, M., *et al.* 1969. 'On the Fading of Social Stereotypes: Studies in Three Generations of College Students.' *Journal of Personal and Social Psychology*, vol. 13, pp. 1–16.

Kawai, M. 1965. 'Newly Acquired Precultural Behavior of the Natural Troop of Japanese Monkeys on Koshima Inlet.' *Primates*, vol. 6, pp. 1–30.

Kelso, A. J. 1970. *Physical Anthropology*. Philadelphia: Lippincott.

Kephart, William M. 1972 (3rd edition). *The Family, Society, and the Individual*. Boston: Houghton Mifflin.

Kessler, Evelyn S. 1976. *Women: An Anthropological View*. New York and London: Holt, Rinehart and Winston.

King, Mary-Claire, and Wilson, A. C. 1975. 'Evolution at Two Levels in Humans and Chimpanzees.' *Science*, vol. 188, pp. 107–116.

Kinsey, Alfred, *et al.* 1953. *Sexual Behavior in the Human Female*. Philadelphia: Saunders. (1953) London: W. B. Saunders.

———. 1948. *Sexual Behavior in the Human Male*. Philadelphia and London: Saunders.

Korten, F. F., *et al.*, editors. 1970. *Psychology and the Problems of Society*. Washington, D.C.: American Psychological Assn.

Kortlandt, A., and van Zon, J. C. 1969. 'The Present State of Research on the Dehumanization Hypothesis of African Ape Evolution.' *Proceedings of the Second International Congress of Primatology, Basel*, pp. 14–16.

Kottak, Conrad P. 1974. *Anthropology, The Exploration of Human Diversity*. New York: Random House.

Kroeber, Alfred L., and Kluckhohn, Clyde. 1952. 'Culture: A Critical Review of Concepts and Definitions.' *Papers of the Peabody Museum of*

*American Archaeology and Ethnology, Harvard University*, vol. 47, no. 1 (Vintage edition, 1963).

Krogman, Wilton M. 1951. 'The Scars of Human Evolution.' *Scientific American*, vol. 185 (December), pp. 54–57.

Kuchemann, C. F., *et al.* 1967. 'A Demographic and Genetic Study of a Group of Oxfordshire Villages.' *Human Biology*, vol. 39, pp. 251–276.

Kummer, Hans. 1971. *Primate Societies*. Chicago: Aldine-Atherton.

Lamberg-Karlovsky, C. C., and Sabloff, Jeremy, editors. 1974. *The Rise and Fall of Civilizations*. Menlo Park, Calif.: Cummings.

Lancaster, Jane B. 1975. *Primate Behavior and the Emergence of Human Culture*. New York and London: Holt, Rinehart and Winston.

Landsberger, Henry A., editor. 1973. *Rural Protest: Peasant Movements and Social Change*. New York: Barnes and Noble. (1975) London: Macmillan.

Lane, Harlan. 1976. *The Wild Boy of Aveyron*. Cambridge, Mass.: Harvard University Press. (1977) London: George Allen and Unwin. (1978) London: Paladin Books.

Lasker, Gabriel W. 1973. *Physical Anthropology*. New York and London: Holt, Rinehart and Winston.

——. 1969. 'Human Biological Adaptability.' *Science*, vol. 166, pp. 1480–1486.

Latané, Bibb, and Darley, John M. 1970. *The Unresponsive Bystander: Why Doesn't He Help?* New York: Meredith.

Le May, Marjorie. 1975. 'The Language Capability of Neanderthal Man.' *American Journal of Physical Anthropology*, vol. 42, pp. 9–14.

Lee, Richard B. 1972A. 'Population Growth and the Beginnings of Sedentary Life among the Kung Bushmen.' In *Population Growth: Anthropological Implications*, edited by Brian Spooner (Cambridge, Mass.: The MIT Press, 1972), pp. 329–342.

——. 1972B. 'The Kung Bushmen of Botswana.' In Bicchieri (1972), pp. 327–368.

——. 1969. 'Kung Bushmen Subsistence: An Input–Output Analysis.' In *Environment and Cultural Behavior* edited by Andrew P. Vayda (New York: Doubleday, 1969), pp. 47–79. (1976) University of Texas Press, c/o American University Publishers Group.

——. 1968. 'What Hunters Do for a Living; or, How to Make Out on Scarce Resources.' In Lee and DeVore (1968), pp. 30–48.

——, and DeVore, Irven, editors. 1976. *Kalahari Hunter–Gatherers*. Cambridge, Mass.: Harvard University Press. (1976) Harvard University Press (distr. Oxford University Press).

——. 1968. *Man the Hunter*. Chicago: Aldine.

Lehman, H. C. 1953. *Age and Achievement*. Princetown, N.J.: Princeton University Press.

Lenski, Gerhard, and Lenski, Jean. 1974 (2nd edition). *Human Societies*. New York: McGraw-Hill. (1978) Maidenhead: McGraw-Hill.

Lerner, I. Michael, and Libby, William J. 1976 (2nd edition). *Heredity, Evolution, and Society*. San Francisco and Reading: Freeman.

Levine, Norman D., editor. 1975. *Human Ecology*. North Scituate, Mass.: Duxbury Press.

Lieberman, Philip. 1975. *On the Origins of Language*. New York: Macmillan.

———, and Crelin, E. S. 1971. 'On the Speech of Neanderthal Man.' *Linguistic Inquiry*, vol. 2, pp. 203–222.

Little, Michael A., *et al.* 1971. 'Population Differences and Developmental Changes in Extremity Temperature Responses to Cold among Andean Indians.' *Human Biology*, vol. 43, pp. 70–91.

———, and Hochner, David H. 1973. 'Human Thermoregulation, Growth, and Mortality.' Reading, Mass.: Addison-Wesley Module 36.

Livingstone, Frank B. 1958. 'Anthropological Implications of Sickle Cell Gene Distribution in West Africa.' *American Anthropologist*, vol. 60, pp. 533–562.

Loehlin, John C., *et al.* 1975. *Race Differences in Intelligence*. San Francisco and Reading: Freeman.

Loomis, F. W. 1970. 'Rickets.' *Scientific American*, vol. 223 (June), pp. 77–91.

Loy, James. 1975. 'The Descent of Dominance in *Macaca*: Insights into the Structure of Human Societies.' In Tuttle (1975), pp. 153–180.

Luria, A. R. 1970. 'The Functional Organization of the Brain.' *Scientific American*, vol. 222 (March), pp. 66–78.

———. 1968. *The Mind of a Mnemonist*. New York: Basic Books. (1969) London: Cape.


MacNeish, Richard S. 1972. 'The Evolution of Community Patterns in the Tehuacán Valley of Mexico and Speculation About the Cultural Process.' In Ucko *et al.* (1972), pp. 67–93.

Maccoby, Eleanor E., and Jacklin, Carol N. 1974. *The Psychology of Sex Differences*. Stanford, Calif.: Stanford University Press.

Mangin, William, editor. 1970. *Peasants in Cities*. Boston: Houghton Mifflin. (1971) H. M. distr. Eurospan, London.

Marshack, Alexander. 1972. *The Roots of Civilization*. New York: McGraw-Hill.

Marshall, Donald S. 1971. 'Sexual Behavior on Mangaia.' In Marshall and Suggs (1971), pp. 103–162.

———, and Suggs, Robert C., editors. 1971. *Human Sexual Behavior*. New York: Basic Books.

Marshall, Lorna. 1976. *The Kung of Nyae Nyae*. Cambridge, Mass.: Harvard University Press (distr. Oxford University Press).

Martin, M. Kay, and Voorhies, Barbara. 1975. *Female of the Species*. New York and London: Columbia University Press.

Masters, W. H., and Johnson, Virginia E. 1966. *Human Sexual Response*. Boston: Little, Brown.

McCarthy, Frederick D., and McArthur, Margaret. 1960. 'The Food Quest and the Time Factor in Aboriginal Economic Life.' In *Records of the Australian–American Scientific Expedition to Arnhem Land, Vol. 2: Anthropology and Nutrition*, edited by C. P. Mountford (Melbourne, Australia: Melbourne University Press).

McClintic, J. Robert. 1975. *Basic Anatomy and Physiology of the Human Body*. New York and Chichester: Wiley.

McHenry, Henry M. 1975. 'Fossils and the Mosaic Nature of Human Evolution.' *Science*, vol. 190, pp. 425–431.

Mead, Margaret. 1935. *Sex and Temperament in Three Primitive Societies*. New York: Morrow. (1977) London: Routledge and Kegan Paul.

——, *et al.*, editors. 1968. *Science and the Concept of Race*. New York: Columbia University Press. (1969) London: Columbia University Press.

Meggitt, Mervyn J. 1964. 'Male–Female Relationships in the Highlands of Australian New Guinea.' *American Anthropologist*, vol. 66, pp. 204–224.

Mencher, Joan. 1974. 'The Caste System Upside Down: Or, the Not So Mysterious East.' *Current Anthropology*, vol. 15, pp. 469–478.

Menzel, E. W. 1966. 'Responsiveness to Objects in Free-Ranging Japanese Monkeys.' *Behavior*, vol. 26, pp. 130–149.

Merton, Robert K., and Nisbet, Robert A., editors. 1966 (2nd edition). *Contemporary Social Problems*. New York: Harcourt Brace and Jovanovich. (1976) London: Harcourt Brace and Jovanovich.

Mesarovic, Mihajlo, and Pestel, Eduard. 1974. *Mankind at the Turning Point*. New York: Dutton.

Michaels, R. R., *et al.* 1976. 'Evaluation of Transcendental Meditation as a Method of Reducing Stress.' *Science*, vol. 192, pp. 1242–1244.

Michaelson, Evalyn J., and Goldschmidt, Walter. 1976. 'Family and Land in Peasant Ritual.' *American Ethnologist*, vol. 3, pp. 87–95.

Milgram, Stanley. 1970. 'The Experiences of Living in Cities: A Psychological Analysis.' *Science*, vol. 167, pp. 1461–1468.

Mitchell, G. D. 1968. 'Persistent Behavior Pathology in Rhesus Monkeys Following Early Social Isolation.' *Folia Primatologica*, vol. 8, pp. 132–147.

Mittler, Peter. 1971. *The Study of Twins*. Baltimore, Md.: Penguin.

Molnar, Stephen. 1975. *Races, Types, and Ethnic Groups*. Englewood Cliffs, N.J. and Hemel Hempstead: Prentice-Hall.

Money, John, and Ehrhardt, Anke A. 1972. *Man and Woman, Boy and Girl*. Baltimore, Md.: Johns Hopkins University Press. (1973) Johns Hopkins Press (distr. IBEG).

Monge, Carlos M., and Monge, Carlos C. 1966. *High Altitude Diseases*. Springfield, Ill.: Charles C. Thomas.

Montagu, Ashley. 1974 (5th edition). *Man's Most Dangerous Myth: The Fallacy of Race*. New York: Oxford University Press.

Motulsky, Arno G. 1974. 'Brave New World?' *Science*, vol. 185, pp. 653–663.

Mumford, Lewis. 1961. *The City in History*. New York: Harcourt Brace and Jovanovich. (1961) London: Secker and Warburg. (1973) London: Penguin.

Munn, Norman L., *et al.* 1974 (3rd edition). *The Growth of Human Behavior.* Boston: Houghton Mifflin (distr. Eurospan, London).

——. 1974 (3rd edition). *Introduction to Psychology.* Boston: Houghton Mifflin. (1972) London: George Harrap.

Murdock, George P. 1957. 'World Ethnographic Sample.' *American Anthropologist*, vol. 59, pp. 664–687.

——. 1949. *Social Structure.* New York: Macmillan. (1965) Free Press (US) distr. Collier-Macmillan.

——. 1937. 'Comparative Data on the Division of Labor by Sex.' *Social Forces*, vol. 15, no. 4.

Murdy, W. H. 1975. 'Anthropocentrism: A Modern Version.' *Science*, vol. 187, pp. 1168–1172.

Mussen, Paul, and Rosenzweig, Mark R. 1973. *Psychology, An Introduction.* Lexington, Mass.: Heath.

Nag, Moni. 1972. 'Sex, Culture, and Human Fertility: India and the United States.' *Current Anthropology*, vol. 13, pp. 231–238.

——, editor. 1975. *Population and Social Organization.* Chicago: Aldine.

Nakane, Chie. 1970. *Japanese Society.* Berkeley, Calif.: University of California Press. (1970) London: Weidenfeld and Nicolson. (1973) London: Penguin.

Napier, John. 1970. *The Roots of Mankind.* New York: Harper and Row. (1971) London: George Allen and Unwin.

Nettleship, Martin A., *et al.*, editors. 1975. *War, Its Causes and Correlates.* Chicago: Aldine.

Nisbet, Robert A. 1970. *The Social Bond.* New York: Knopf.

Norbeck, Edward, and DeVos, George. 1972. 'Culture and Personality: The Japanese.' In Hsu (1972), pp. 21–70.

——, and Parman, Susan, editors. 1970. *The Study of Japan in the Behavioral Sciences.* Houston, Texas: Rice University Press.

Norman, Donald A. 1976 (2nd edition). *Memory and Attention.* New York and Chichester: Wiley.

Nye, F. I., and Berardo, Felix M. 1973. *The Family: Its Structure and Interaction.* New York: Macmillan.

Nye, Robert D. 1973. *Conflict Among Humans.* New York: Springer.

Oakley, Ann. 1972. *Sex, Gender, and Society.* New York: Harper and Row. (1972) London: Maurice Temple Smith.

Ogburn, William F. 1950. *Social Change.* New York: Viking.

Osborne, Richard H., editor. 1971. *The Biological and Social Meaning of Race.* San Francisco: Freeman. (1972) Reading: W. H. Freeman.

Oswalt, Wendell H. 1970. *Understanding Our Culture.* New York: Holt, Rinehart and Winston.

Palmer, John D., *et al.* 1976. *An Introduction to Biological Rhythms.* New York and London: Academic Press.

Parsons, Talcott. 1971. *The System of Modern Societies*. Englewood Cliffs, N.J. and London: Prentice-Hall.

——. 1966. *Societies: Evolutionary and Comparative Perspectives*. Englewood Cliffs, N.J.: Prentice-Hall.

Pavlov, Ivan P. 1927. *Conditioned Reflexes*. New York: Oxford University Press and Dover Publications (distr. Tiptree Book Services Ltd).

Peterson, R. E. 1970. 'The Student Protest Movement.' In Korten *et al.* (1970), pp. 388–394.

Pfeiffer, John E. 1972 (2nd edition). *The Emergence of Man*. New York and London: Harper and Row.

Phillips, John L., Jr. 1975 (2nd edition). *The Origins of Intellect: Piaget's Theory*. San Francisco and Reading: Freeman.

Piaget, Jean. *See* Phillips (1975).

Pilbeam, David. 1972. *The Ascent of Man: An Introduction to Human Evolution*. New York: Macmillan. (1972) London: Collier-Macmillan.

Pimentel, David, *et al.* 1973. 'Food Production and the Energy Crisis.' *Science*, vol. 182, pp. 443–449.

Pines, Maya. 1973. *The Brain Changers*. New York: Harcourt Brace and Jovanovich. (1974) London: Allen Lane.

Polgar, Steven, editor. 1975. *Population, Ecology, and Social Evolution*. Chicago: Aldine.

Pribram, K. H., editor. 1969. *Perception and Action*. Baltimore, Md. and London: Penguin.

Raphael, Dana. 1975. *Being Female*. Chicago: Aldine.

Renfrew, Colin. 1973. *Before Civilization: The Radiocarbon Revolution and Prehistoric Europe*. New York: Knopf. (1973) London: Cape. (1976) London: Penguin.

Reitman, Judith S. 1974. 'Without Surreptitious Rehearsal, Information in Short Term Memory Decays.' *Journal of Verbal Learning and Verbal Behavior*, vol. 13, pp. 365–377.

Revelle, Roger. 1974. 'Food and Population.' *Scientific American*, vol. 231 (September), pp. 161–170.

Rheingold, Harriet L., and Eckerman, Carol O. 1970. 'The Infant Separates Himself from His Mother.' *Science*, vol. 168, pp. 78–90.

Rhine, Jospeh B., editor. 1971. *Progress in Parapsychology*. Durham, N.C.: Parapsychology Press.

Roberts, D. F. 1973. 'Climate and Human Variability.' Reading, Mass.: Addison-Wesley Module 34.

Robertson, Constance N. 1972. *Oneida Community: The Breakup*. Syracuse, N.Y.: Syracuse University Press.

Roper, Marilyn K. 1975. 'Evidence of Warfare in the Near East from 10,000–4,300 B.C.' In Nettleship *et al.* (1975), pp. 299–343.

Rosaldo, Michelle Z., and Lamphere, Louise, editors. 1974. *Woman, Culture, and Society*. Stanford, Calif.: Stanford University Press.

Rosch, Eleanor, *et al.* 1976. 'Basic Objects in Natural Categories.' *Cognitive Psychology*, vol. 8, pp. 382–439.

Rose, Steven. 1973. *The Conscious Brain*. New York: Knopf. (1973) London: Weidenfeld and Nicolson. (1976) London: Penguin.

Rosenzweig, Mark R., *et al.* 1972. 'Brain Changes in Response to Experience.' *Scientific American*, vol. 226 (February), pp. 22–29.

Rubington, Earl, and Weinberg, Martin S., editors. 1973 (2nd edition). *Deviance: The Interactional Perspective*. New York: Macmillan. (1973) London: Collier-Macmillan.

Rumbaugh, Duane M., editor. 1977. *Language Learning by a Chimpanzee*. New York and London: Academic Press.

Rumbaugh, Duane M., *et al.* 1975. 'The Language Skills of a Young Chimpanzee in a Computer-Controlled Training Situation.' In Tuttle (1975), pp. 391–401.

Sabloff, Jeremy A., and Lamberg-Karlovsky, C. C. 1975. *Ancient Civilization and Trade*. Albuquerque, N.M.: University of New Mexico Press.

Sahlins, Marshall. 1972. *Stone Age Economics*. Chicago: Aldine-Atherton. (1974) London: Tavistock.

Salzano, F. M., *et al.* 1967. 'Further Studies on the Xavante Indians.' *American Journal of Human Genetics*, vol. 19, pp. 463–489.

Salzman, Philip. 1971. 'Comparative Studies of Nomadism and Pastoralism.' *Anthropological Quarterly*, vol. 44, pp. 104–210.

Samuelson, Paul A. 1973 (9th edition). *Economics*. New York: McGraw-Hill. (1976) Maidenhead: McGraw-Hill.

Sapir, Edward. 1929. 'The Status of Linguistics as a Science.' *Language*, vol. 5, pp. 207–214.

Schmeidler, Gertrude F., editor. 1969. *Extra-Sensory Perception*. New York: Atherton.

Schneider, David, and Sharp, Lauriston. 1969. *The Dream Life of a Primitive People*. Washington, D.C.: American Anthropological Assn. Studies, No. 1.

Schull, W. J., and Neel, J. V. 1965. *The Effects of Inbreeding on Japanese Children*. New York: Harper and Row.

Scott, John F. 1969. 'A Comment on "Do American Women Marry Up?"' *American Sociological Review*, vol. 34, pp. 725–727.

Scrimshaw, Nevin S., and Young, Vernon R. 1976. 'The Requirements of Human Nutrition.' *Scientific American*, vol. 235 (September), pp. 50–64.

Sereno, Renzo. 1951. 'Some Observations on the Santa Claus Custom.' *Psychiatry*, vol. 14, pp. 387–396.

Service, Elman R. 1975. *Origins of the State and Civilization: The Process of Cultural Evolution*. New York: Norton.

——. 1971 (2nd edition). *Primitive Social Organization: An Evolutionary Perspective*. New York: Random House.

Seward, Georgene H., and Williamson, Robert C., editors. 1970. *Sex Roles in Changing Society*. New York: Random House.

Shanin, Teodor, editor. 1971. *Peasants and Peasant Societies*. Baltimore, Md. and London: Penguin.

Sheldon, W. H., and Stevens, S. S. 1942. *The Varieties of Temperament*. New York: Harper.

Sherman, Julia A. 1971. *On the Psychology of Women*. Springfield, Ill.: Charles C. Thomas.

Shibutani, Tamotsu, and Kwan, Kian M. 1965. *Ethnic Stratification: A Comparative Approach*. New York: Macmillan.

Shiffrin, R. M., and Atkinson, R. C. 1969. 'Storage and Retrieval Processes in Long-Term Memory.' *Psychological Review*, vol. 76, pp. 179–193.

Shorter, Edward. 1975. *The Making of the Modern Family*. New York: Basic Books. (1976) London: Collins. (1977) London: Fontana.

Silberman, Bernard S., editor. 1962. *Japanese Character and Culture*. Tuscon, Ariz.: University of Arizona Press.

Simons, Elwyn L. 1977. 'Ramapithecus.' *Scientific American*, vol. 236 (May), pp. 28–35.

Simpson, George E., and Yinger, J. Milton, 1965 (3rd edition). *Racial and Cultural Minorities*. New York: Harper and Row. (1972) London: Harper and Row.

Skeels, H. M. 1966. 'Adult Status of Children with Contrasting Early Life Experiences: A Follow-up Study.' *Monographs of the Society for Research in Child Development*, vol. 31.

Skinner, B. F. 1957. *Verbal Behavior*. New York: Appleton-Century-Crofts.

——. 1948. *Walden Two*. New York: Macmillan. (1976) London: Collier-Macmillan.

——. 1938. *The Behavior of Organisms*. New York: Appleton-Century-Crofts.

Skinner, William G. 1971. 'Chinese Peasants and the Closed Community: An Open and Shut Case.' *Comparative Studies in Society and History*, vol. 13, pp. 270–281.

Smith, Anthony. 1975. *The Human Pedigree*. Philadelphia: Lippincott. (1975) London: George Allen and Unwin.

Smith, Philip E. L. 1976. *Food Production and Its Consequences*. Menlo Park, Calif.: Cummings.

Solecki, Ralph S. 1975. 'Shanidar IV, a Neanderthal Flower Burial in Northern Iraq.' *Science*, vol. 190, pp. 880–881.

——. 1972. *Shanidar: The Humanity of Neanderthal Man*. Baltimore, Md.: Penguin. (1973) London: Allen Lane.

Southall, Aidan, editor. 1973. *Urban Anthropology*. New York: Oxford University Press.

Spier, Robert F. G. 1970. *From the Hands of Man: Primitive and Preindustrial Technologies*. Boston: Houghton Mifflin. (1971) H. M. distr. Eurospan, London.

Spitz, René. 1945. 'Hospitalism: An Inquiry into the Genesis of Psychiatric Conditions in Early Childhood.' *Psychoanalytic Study of the Child*, vol. 1, pp. 53–74.

Srinivas, M. N., and Béteille, André. 1965. 'The "Untouchables" of India.' *Scientific American*, vol. 216 (December), pp. 13–17.

Standing, Lionel. 1973. 'Learning 10,000 Pictures.' *Quarterly Journal of Experimental Psychology*, vol. 25, pp. 207–222.

Steegman, A. T., Jr. 1975. 'Human Adaptation to Cold.' In Damon (1975), pp. 130–166.

Steward, Julian H. 1938. *Basin–Plateau Aboriginal Socio-Political Groups*. Washington, D.C.: Bureau of American Ethnology Bulletin 120.

Stini, William A. 1971. 'Evolutionary Implications of Changing Nutritional Patterns in Human Populations.' *American Anthropologist*, vol. 73, pp. 1019–1030.

Stokes, Randall, and Hewitt, John P. 1976. 'Aligning Actions.' *American Sociological Review*, vol. 41, pp. 838–849.

Strum, S. C. 1975. 'Primate Predation: Interim Report on the Development of a Tradition in a Troop of Olive Baboons.' *Science*, vol. 187, pp. 255–257.

Sussman, Marvin B., editor. 1974 (4th edition). *Sourcebook in Marriage and the Family*. Boston: Houghton Mifflin.


Talmon, Shemaryahu. 1977. 'The Samaritans.' *Scientific American*, vol. 236 (January), pp. 100–108.

Talmon, Yonina. 1972. *Family and Community in the Kibbutz*. Cambridge, Mass.: Harvard University Press. (1974) Harvard University Press (distr. Oxford University Press).

——. 1964. 'Mate Selection in Collective Settlements.' *American Sociological Review*, vol. 29, pp. 491–508.

Tanner, J. M. 1973. 'Growing Up.' *Scientific American*, vol. 229 (September), pp. 35–43.

Tart, C. T., editor. 1969. *Altered States of Consciousness*. New York and Chichester: Wiley.

Teleki, Geza. 1973. *Predatory Behavior of Wild Chimpanzees*. Harrisburg, Pa.: Bucknell University Press. (1975) Bucknell University Press.

Teyler, Timothy J. 1975. *A Primer of Psychobiology*. San Francisco and Reading: Freeman.

Thielbar, Gerald W., and Feldman, Saul D., editors. 1972. *Issues in Social Inequality*. Boston: Little, Brown.

Thomas, Elizabeth M. 1959. *The Harmless People*. New York: Vintage.

Thrupp, Sylvia L., editor. 1970. *Millennial Dreams in Action*. New York: Schocken.

Tiger, Lionel, and Fox, Robin. 1971. *The Imperial Animal*. New York: Holt, Rinehart and Winston. (1972) London: Secker and Warburg. (1974) London: Paladin Books.

Toffler, Alvin. 1970. *Future Shock*. New York: Random House. (1970) London: Bodley Head. (1973) London: Pan Books.

Tulving, E., and Donaldson, W., editors. 1974. *Organization of Memory*. New York: Academic Press. (1972) London: Academic Press.

Tumin, Melvin M. 1967. *Social Stratification*. Englewood Cliffs, N.J. and Hemel Hempstead: Prentice-Hall.

Turnbull, Colin M. 1965. *The Mbuti Pygmies: An Ethnographic Survey*. New York: The American Museum of Natural History Ethnographic Papers, vol. 50, part 3.

——. 1962. *The Forest People: A Study of the Pygmies of the Congo*. Garden City, N.Y.: Doubleday. (1974) London: Cape. (1976) London: Pan Books.

Turner, Jonathan H. 1972. *American Society: Problems of Structure*. New York: Harper and Row.

Turner, Victor. 1974. *Dramas, Fields, and Metaphors*. Ithaca, N.Y.: Cornell University Press. (1975) Cornell University Press, distr. by IBEG Ltd.

——. 1967. *The Forest of Symbols*. Ithaca, N.Y.: Cornell University Press. (1969) Cornell University Press, (distr. IBEG Ltd.)

Tuttle, Russell H., editor. 1975. *Socioecology and Psychology of Primates*. Chicago: Aldine.

Ucko, Peter J., *et al.*, editors. 1972. *Man, Settlement, and Urbanism*. Cambridge, Mass.: Schenkman. (1972) London: Duckworth.

—— and Dimbleby, G. W., editors. 1969. *The Domestication and Exploitation of Plants and Animals*. Chicago: Aldine. (1969) London: Duckworth.

—— and Rosenfeld, Andrée. 1967. *Paleolithic Cave Art*. New York: McGraw-Hill.

Udry, J. Richard, and Morris, Naomi M. 1968. 'Distribution of Coitus in the Menstrual Cycle.' *Nature*, vol. 220, pp. 593–596.

van Gennep, Arnold. 1960 (originally published 1908). *The Rites of Passage*. Chicago: University of Chicago Press. (1977) London: Routledge and Kegan Paul.

van Lawick-Goodall, Jane. 1971. *In the Shadow of Man*. Boston: Houghton Mifflin.

Vernon, P. E., editor. 1970. *Creativity*. Baltimore, Md. and London: Penguin.

Waber, Deborah P. 1976. 'Sex Differences in Cognition: A Function of Maturation Rate?' *Science*, vol. 192, pp. 572–573.

Wallace, Anthony F. C. 1970 (2nd edition). *Culture and Personality*. New York: Random House.

Wallace, Robert K., and Benson, Herbert. 1972. 'The Physiology of Meditation.' *Scientific American*, vol. 226 (February), pp. 84–90.

Wallach, M. A. and Wing, C. W. 1969. *The Talented Student: A Validation of the Creativity–Intelligence Distinction*. New York: Holt, Rinehart and Winston.

Ward, Barbara. 1976. *The Home of Man*. New York: Norton. (1976) London: Deutsch. (1976) London: Penguin.

Ward, R. R. 1971. *The Living Clocks*. New York: Knopf.

Washburn, Sherwood L., and Lancaster, C. S. 1968. 'The Evolution of Hunting.' In Lee and DeVore (1968), pp. 239–303.

Watson, Peter, editor. 1974. *Psychology and Race*. Chicago: Aldine.

Weiner, J. S. 1971. *The Natural History of Man*. New York: Universe. (1971) London: Weidenfeld and Nicolson.

Weiner, Myron, editor. 1966. *Modernization: The Dynamics of Growth*. New York: Basic Books. (1966) Basic Books (distr. Pages Ltd, London).

Weiss, Melford S. 1967. 'Rebirth in the Airborne.' *Trans-action*, vol. 4 (May), pp. 23–26.

Wertime, Theodore A. 1973. 'The Beginnings of Metallurgy: A New Look.' *Science*, vol. 182, pp. 875–888.

West, D. J. 1968. *Homosexuality*. Baltimore, Md.: Penguin. (1969) London: Penguin.

White, Benjamin. 1975. 'The Economic Importance of Children in a Javanese Village.' In Nag (1975), pp. 128–146.

Whiting, Beatrice B., and Whiting, John W. M. 1975. *Children of Six Cultures: A Psycho-Cultural Analysis*. Cambridge, Mass.: Harvard University Press (distr. Oxford University Press).

——, editor. 1963. *Six Cultures: Studies of Child Rearing*. New York: Wiley.

Whort, Benjamin L. 1956. *Language, Thought, and Reality*. Cambridge, Mass.: MIT Press.

Williams, Eric. 1966. *Capitalism and Slavery*. New York: Capricorn Books. (1964) London: Deutsch.

Williams, Robin M., Jr. 1970. *American Society, A Sociological Interpretation*. New York: Knopf.

Williams, Thomas R. 1972. *Introduction to Socialization*. St Louis, Mo.: Mosby.

Wilson, Edward O. 1975. *Sociobiology*. Cambridge, Mass.: Harvard University Press (distr. Oxford University Press).

Winch, Robert E., and Spanier, Graham B., editors. 1974 (4th edition). *Selected Studies in Marriage and the Family*. New York: Holt, Rinehart and Winston.

Wittfogel, Karl A. 1957. *Oriental Despotism: A Comparative Study of Total Power*. New Haven, Conn. and London: Yale University Press.

Wolf, Eric R. 1969. *Peasant Wars of the Twentieth Century*. New York: Harper and Row. (1971) London: Faber and Faber.

——. 1966. *Peasants*. Englewood Cliffs, N.J. and Hemel Hempstead: Prentice-Hall.

——. 1964. 'Santa Claus: Notes on a Collective Representation.' In *Process and Pattern in Culture*, edited by Robert A. Manners (Chicago: Aldine, 1964), pp. 147–155.

Wolman, Benjamin B., editor. 1973. *Handbook of General Psychology*. Englewood Cliffs, N.J. and Hemel Hempstead: Prentice-Hall.

Wolpoff, M. 1968. 'Climatic Influence on the Skeletal Nasal Aperture.' *American Journal of Physical Anthropology*, vol. 29, 405–424.

Woodburn, James. 1972. 'Ecology, Nomadic Movement and the Composition of the Local Group among Hunters and Gatherers: An East African Example and Its Implications.' In Ucko *et al.* (1972), pp. 193–206.

Woolf, Charles M., and Dukepo, Frank C. 1969. 'Hopi Indians, Inbreeding, and Albinism.' *Science*, vol. 164, pp. 30–37.

Worsley, Peter, editor. 1972. *Problems of Modern Society*. Baltimore, Md.: Penguin.

Wright, Gary A. 1971. 'Origins of Food Production in Southwestern Asia: A Survey of Ideas.' *Current Anthropology*, vol. 12, pp. 447–477.

Young, J. Z. 1971. *An Introduction to the Study of Man*. New York: Oxford University Press. (1974) London: Oxford University Press.

Zacharias, Leona, *et al.* 1976. 'A Prospective Study of Sexual Development and Growth in American Girls.' *Obstetrical and Gynecological Survey*, vol. 31, pp. 323–337.

Ziegler, P. 1970. *The Black Death*. Baltimore, Md.: Penguin. (1969) London: Collins and (1970) London: Penguin.

# Index